POPULAR MODERNISMS

ART, CARTOONS, COMICS, AND CULTURAL IN/SUBORDINATION

First published in 2024
as part of the Arts in Society Book Imprint
doi:10.18848/978-1-86335-217-8/CGP (Full Book)

Common Ground Research Networks
60 Hazelwood Drive
Champaign, IL 61820 USA
Ph: +1-217-328-0405

Copyright © Bruce Barber, 2024

All rights reserved. Apart from fair dealing for the purposes of study, research, criticism or review as permitted under the applicable copyright legislation, no part of this book may be reproduced by any process without written permission from the publisher.

Library of Congress Cataloging-in-Publication Data

Names: Barber, Bruce, author.
Title: Popular Modernisms: Art, Cartoons, Comics, and Cultural
   In/Subordination / Bruce A. Barber.
Description: Champaign, IL: Common Ground Research Networks, 2023. |
   Includes bibliographical references. | Summary: "Popular Modernisms
   examines a process that has occurred throughout the history of art; one
   that accelerated with the social effects of the industrial revolution,
   the development of capitalism and the inception of modern social
   relations. It argues that the shocks of modernist art encouraged the
   production of visual satires, parodies, ironies and pastiches; and that,
   in the company of other forms of text or performance based criticism,
   these were the means by which those in marginal, or subordinate social
   positions could exercise their displeasure and opposition to the ruling
   ideas and dominant classes of the day. Expressing feelings ranging from
   mild discomfort to pure rage, this criticism enabled social subordinates
   to contest or resist the dominance of high culture over low; in terms
   eloquently described by Antonio Gramsci, as the hegemony of the dominant
   centre culture over its margins. The focus upon graphic satires (cartoons
   and comics) of modern art attempts to provide some practical explication
   of the symbolic contest of power as this process represents the struggle
   to achieve and maintain, cultural hegemony. A further aim in this book
   is to investigate the symbolic contestation of cultural meanings in
   social terms and thereby enrich our understanding of classed society.
   There are, I believe, many social and political confluences that
   intersect within the symbolic construction and interpretation of
   culture. This contest of power can be read as ideological conflict
   between various dominant, and subordinate groups, classes and class
   fractions"-- Provided by publisher.
Identifiers: LCCN 2020019018 (print) | LCCN 2020019019 (ebook) | ISBN
   9780949313768 (hardback) | ISBN 9781863352161 (paperback) | ISBN
   9781863352178 (pdf)
Subjects: LCSH: Art, Modern--Caricatures, cartoons, etc. | Social classes
   in art. | Comic books, strips, etc.--Themes, motives.
Classification: LCC NC1763.A66 B37 2023 (print) | LCC NC1763.A66 (ebook)
   | DDC 741.5/9--dc23
LC record available at https://lccn.loc.gov/2020019018
LC ebook record available at https://lccn.loc.gov/2020019019

Cover Photo Credit: Sprod, Punch July 18, 1951. © Punch Cartoon Library, Top Foto.

POPULAR MODERNISMS

ART, CARTOONS, COMICS, AND CULTURAL IN/SUBORDINATION
_____

BRUCE BARBER

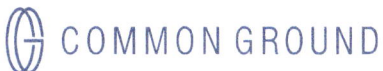

It is too easy to forget the importance and often radical content of cartoons published in magazines like Mad, National Lampoon and the New Yorker . Well, Bruce Barber manages, with intelligence, humour and strict analysis to shake up a topic we thought not particularly important, or superficial. In fact, thanks to this book, we learn, not only about the complexity of the history of humour, irony, parody and satire but also how vital cartoons were in the understanding of debates surrounding the concept of modern art and culture after the Second World War. The author, by digging up many caricatures from popular magazines, manages to show us that cartoons are indeed no joke but rather part of an important and fierce series of debates surrounding issues shaking the new modern world.

This study clearly reframes the conditions in which Cartoons were produced in order to resist hegemony and ideological control. Thanks to them, democracy was able to keep debates alive and class differences central to the understanding of ideological struggles. With his traditional in/subordination, professor Bruce Barber, through his precise, serious and in depth research, adds to the understanding of our multifaceted world thanks to wit, fun and irony.

Serge Guilbaut

Popular Modernisms: Art, Cartoons, Comics and Cultural In/Subordination shows us how relationships between modernist art and popular culture might be better understood through the politics of humor presented in cartoons and comics, and in particular, the extraordinary capacity of some popular modernisms to implicitly critique class and power relations. Although some artists successfully straddled both realms, cartoons and comic art somehow never acquired proportionate currency in the so-called "high cultural" realms of the "serious" artworld. This forensically researched and beautifully written book goes a long way to addressing this historical incommensurability.

Sean Lowry

A delightful, intellectually provocative and original volume. Modernist art encourages and deserves such an acute overview of graphic satire, a juicy combination of humor and serious social analysis. Nobody is better prepared for the task than artist and scholar Bruce Barber. This book opens a whole new chapter in cultural criticism.

Lucy R. Lippard

TABLE OF CONTENTS

Acknowledgments ....*IX*

Preface..*XI*

Introduction 1

1. Revisiting Ideology, Class and Hegemony 17

2. Cartoons and Cultural In/Subordination 27

3. Humour, Pleasure, Pain, and Power 45

4. Visual Irony, Parody and Satire 63

5. Modern Art's Nemesis 79

    Art *90*

    Finally *90*

    Dynamic Art *92*

    The Armory Show *101*

    The New Yorker *105*

6. The Pile of Junk 119

7. The Rock with the Hole 143

8. Even A Monkey Could Do It! 165

9. The Art Comics of Ad Reinhardt 203

10. Walt Disney's Avant-Garde 239

11. MAD'S Mad Art World and The Art News of National Lampoon............ 251

12. Thalia Meets Melpomene 271

Summary 291

Bibliography *295*

ACKNOWLEDGMENTS

Popular Modernisms owes its existence to several key individuals. I am specially indebted to research assistant Rosemary Donegan who several years ago helped compile a listing of cartoons from Punch and The New Yorker that referenced art, artists and art history; to editors Phillip Kisubika and Kerry Dixon Managing Editor/ Books Common Ground Research Networks, Patricia Alonso, Assistant Editor and External Reviewers.

Art historians who have offered constructive criticism to papers that I have presented at the UAAC (Universities Art Association of Canada) conferences over the years include: Serge Guilbaut, John O'Brian, Thierry de Duve, Mark Cheetham, David Howard, Jayne Wark, Joyce Zemans, and in the U.S. at the CAA (College Art Association) and Popular Culture Association meetings; Leonard Diepeveen of Dalhousie University English Department who was a first reader of this manuscript and artist colleagues: Alan Sekula, Adrian Piper, Alan Sondheim, and Richard Bolton for their supportive comments after reading individual chapters. I would also like to acknowledge NSCAD assistant Jane Mothersell for word processing several sections of the manuscript; My dear partner Pauline, for reading chapters of the manuscript and putting up with my complaints about work load and research time. I also gained much insight into the archival status of cartoons and comics with the assistance of Lucy Caudwell, Chief Librarian and Curator of the Pop Cult library at the Wexner Centre at Ohio State University, Punch Librarian Amanda Jane Doran, and New Yorker Cartoon Editor Lee Lorenz.

I owe a special debt to several New Yorker cartoonists for responding to my detailed questions: Special thanks go to Anatol Kovarsky and wife Lucille, to Lee Lorenz, Cartoon Editor of the New Yorker 1973-1994, Ed Koren, Dana Fradon, Frank Modell, Whitney Darrow Jr. and Harry Bliss. I'm also very indebted to cartoonist Dan Piraro and Christy Higgins Piraro of Bizarro H.Q., and to Pop Cult collectors, Mark Cohen, Jurg Spahr and Martin Heller.

I would also like to acknowledge a large number of friends, teachers, colleagues and former students. Teachers who stimulated my interest in the relationships between art history, popular culture and class politics include, at the University of Auckland, members of the Art History Department: Professors Tony Green, Michael Dunn, Robin Scholes, Leonard Bell, Wystan Curnow (Department of English) and at NSCAD University, Eric Cameron, Dennis Young, Vivian Cameron, and William Clark (Queens, City University of New York). Thanks also to Terry Smith, Ian Burn, Nigel Lendon and other members of the Australian Media Action Group who introduced me to *How to Read Donald Duck: Imperialist Ideology in the Disney Comic* authored by Ariel Dorfman and Armand Mattelart, translated by David Kunzle whom I also wish to acknowledge for his excellent work on the early history of comic strips and cartoons. Members of the American Popular Culture Association Pierre Horn, Donald Palumbo and the Universities Art Association of Canada, colleagues and students at the NSCAD University and University Kings College. Former students and friends, over the years, who have sent me examples of cartoons and comics include: Tim Bider, Paul Artz, Micah Lexier, Andre Jodoin the (Gallery Director at Western) Dave Merritt, Tsia Carson, Doug Lloyd, Bill Conrad, Alan Griffiths and Ihor Holubizky.

I am especially grateful to the Canada Council for the receipt of a critics grant 1984-5 and NSCAD internal SSHRC (Social Science and Humanities Research Council of Canada) Awards during the years 1984, 86, 87, 89 that enabled me to travel to undertake research in New York, Ohio, and present my book chapters in the form of papers at various conferences in Canada and the United States. Last but not least, my family members, partner Pauline, daughter Claire, son Lachlan, and of course, the golden retriever family members we have enjoyed for over two decades: Abby, Bella and now Chloe, without whom my leisure time would have less beneficial for subsequent work anxieties beyond teaching and administrative duties. I would also like to acknowledge the extraordinary endorsements published on the book's rear cover which were received from Sean Lowry of Melbourne, Australia, Serge Guilbaut of Vancouver, Canada and Lucy R. Lippard, New Mexico, USA.

PREFACE

Like Janus, the Roman guardian of doorways and gateways, it is common for a book preface to exhibit two faces. The first introduces the subject and scope of the study and speaks to its origin, and the second provides an opportunity for the author to self-efface; that is, to expose any regrets or inadequacies, and to speak of what could not be accommodated, of what lay beyond his/her, or their efforts to contain in one book, thus indirectly providing the impetus for another. Such is the condition of this preface. The origin for *Popular Modernisms: Art, Cartoons, Comics and Cultural In/Subordination* can be found in my chance encounter several years ago, at a rural Nova Scotia flea market, with two Walt Disney comic satires of late modernist art. This fortuitous experience brought together—I could say crashing together, but it seems this only upon reflection—several previously separate parts of my life: my early childhood fascination with cartoons, comics and humor magazines (British and American), a progressive fine arts education, and the reading, sometime in 1976, of *How to Read Donald Duck*, Ariel Dorfman and Armand Mattelart's classic study of imperialist ideology in the Disney comic. Although my interest in popular graphic art and the politics of visual humor had been stimulated earlier through a study of seventeenth century caricature and the grotesque that I had undertaken as a graduate student at the University of Auckland, New Zealand, I was not able to fully match these experiences with my childhood induction into the pleasures of popular culture until my flea market 'epiphany' several years later. Over the course of the next few years I began to collect reproductions of cartoon satires and parodies of modernist art. My collecting slowly gained momentum and in late 1984, I obtained a leave of absence from my place of employment at the Nova Scotia College of Art and Design (NSCAD University) and obtained a Canada Council grant to assist the development of the research project that evolved from the material I was gathering. The idea of writing a book length text presented itself to me at this time, but it was not until the late 1990s that the book's present form began to take shape. During the ensuing years the research and writing of *Popular Modernisms* has been challenged often by my production and exhibition activities as an artist, six other book publication projects, one *Trans/actions: Art, Film and Death* (2009) the result of my Doctoral study in Media and Communications at the

European Graduate School (2001-2005), as well as my continuing responsibilities as a teacher and program administrator at NSCAD University. At times it must have seemed to my family, friends and colleagues that the pilot light was out on the back burner for this book, but I confess that it was always a source of much anxiety and a prominent item on my New Year's resolution lists. I can now say with some degree of satisfaction that it has benefited from this long curing process. Certainly, my understanding of the theoretical complexities and potential relevance of this work has matured over time.

During the course of my research, I became increasingly aware of the number of artists, academics, dentists, doctors, business people, and others who use cartoons and comic strips culled from the pages of the mass media as vehicles for social communication, either by placing them on their office doors (fig. 1) and bulletin boards, using them in lectures or circulating them to friends and colleagues via email or on social media which is an increasingly popular pastime. At my place of employment, a university college of art, craft and design, art related single panel cartoons and comic strips appear frequently on faculty office doors, library and departmental bulletin boards. In my home important cartoons with art, family, or pet content—Dan Piraro's syndicated daily *Bizarro* is a personal favorite—are regularly attached by magnets to the refrigerator door and home office bulletin boards, sharing limited space with family photos, clipped recipes, advertisements, school newsletters, broadsheets, gallery announcements and other paraphernalia of domestic interest.

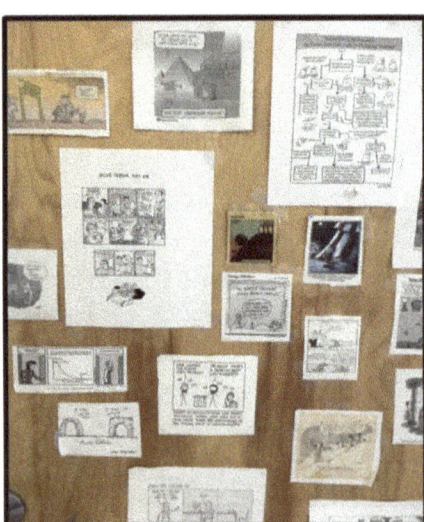

Figure 1: Dalhousie University Faculty Office Door, 2019. Photo taken by Bruce Barber.

Cartoons and comic strips appear everywhere in university and college contexts, but they are usually isolated from the academic curriculum itself.

Few art schools, universities and college art departments offer degrees in cartooning and comic art. Where such programs do exist, they are usually subordinated to the real business of Fine Arts Education and marginalized to departments of continuing education and other ancillary or community interface programs.[1] During the past two decades this situation began to change, with more colleges augmenting their core program offerings with courses in this area, partly as a result of the museum acceptance of comic art references in the work of 1960's Pop artists Richard Hamilton, Roy Lichtenstein, Andy Warhol and Claes Oldenburg, as well as the more recent references to street graffiti and underground comics in the work of Banksy, Michael Basquiat, Keith Haring, Sue Coe and Art Spiegelman.[2] Major museum retrospectives of the work of Winsor McCay (*Little Nemo in Slumberland*), George Herriman (*Krazy Kat*), Charles Schultz (*Peanuts*), Carl Barks (*Donald Duck*), Robert Crumb (*Fritz the Cat*), Art Spiegelman (*Maus*), among other major cartoon and comic artists, have also provided legitimation in the high culture domain for these popular art forms. A growing number of institutions now offer degree certificates and diplomas in cartooning, comic art, graphic novels, animation, gaming…and there are many developing popular culture, cultural and visual studies programs, including some very well established, at Bowling Green University, the University of Ohio and the Birmingham University Centre for Contemporary Cultural Studies,[3] where it has been possible, for many years, to undertake advanced-level research toward graduate degrees in graphic humor. These programs are the exception rather than the rule however, and as far as university level education is concerned, cartoons, comic art and scholarly research in this field, still occupy a relatively low position on the academic register.[4] During the past decade threats

---

1. "Few universities are offering sequential graphic art as a stand-alone or interdisciplinary subject at present, although there are some exceptions at undergraduate and postgraduate levels in the UK and the US. For example, in the UK, Staffordshire University's BA in Cartoon and Comic Arts has been running for some years now. In the US, the University of Oregon offers an interdisciplinary Comics and Cartoon Studies minor, and Minneapolis College of Art and Design offers a Comic Arts major option on their Bachelor of Fine Arts degree. Savannah College of Art and Design offers undergraduate and postgraduate degrees in sequential art, which are also available in Hong Kong and online. California College of the Arts offers a Master of Fine Arts degree in comics, as does the Center for Cartoon Studies in Vermont. No doubt there are others too, though I haven't found any outside the US/UK. For example, there are no such courses in Australia at present, though the Sydney Comics Guild suggests keeping an eye on MIT in Melbourne, presumably because they may establish a future program. Although the UK has few courses, it does have other initiatives. For example, the Journal of Graphic Novels and Comics is based in the UK. This journal focuses on the production and consumption of comics in their cultural, institutional, and creative contexts. An international Research, Outreach and Pedagogy Network (ReOPeN) for graphic novels and comics is based at Lancaster University." Reference from https://helenkara.com/2017/11/23/cartoons-comics-and-graphic-novels-in-research-and-academia/ Accessed January, 2018

2. At a presentation at the Nova Scotia College of Art and Design (NSCAD University) in October 1997, artist Sue Coe suggested that her edgy cartoon-like paintings and drawings were being subordinated to the "real artwork" of others when it was shown in major group exhibitions in New York museums and galleries.

3. In June 2002, the enormously successful Birmingham University Graduate program in Culture studies was closed.

4. In 1998 the journal Inks: Cartoon and Comic Art Studies, one of the few venues for the publication of academic research associated with cartoon and comic art scholarship, had to cease publication for lack of economic support

against and killings of cartoonists in European cities, such as Copenhagen[5] and the 2015 Charlie Hebdo terror attack in Paris,[6] have increased the urgency in the sociological study of political satire and several recent publications have resulted in renewed interest in the social and political power of cartoons and comics.[7]

> As a cartoonist, if there's someone I haven't alienated, it's just a matter of time. Cartoons are one of the most universally accessible forms of journalism. They can make people angry, amused or ideally represented. It only takes seconds for a well-crafted cartoon to incite laughter or rage, and in an imperfect world... change.[8]

During the course of my research, several important questions troubled me. It seemed somewhat incongruous that cartoons and comics could be used so extensively as a vehicle for communication throughout society, functioning like one model of humor itself—as a form of social grease—yet this important function did not permit cartoons, comics and their creators to win the prestige that society has the capacity to bestow upon its high culture artists, even if, as I recognized, it does not always do so. It is true that a parallel hierarchy exists within the popular world of comic and cartoon art that evidences many of the traits of its model in the world of high art. Indeed, some artists, Saul Steinberg, Art Spiegelman, Ed Koren, Dan Piraro and Harry Bliss, for example, successfully straddle both worlds and are respected for doing so. Generally, however, cartoons and comic art do not acquire the same cultural (ideological) power as the so-called fine arts of painting, printmaking or sculpture. Comic artists do not usually receive the cultural accolades commensurate with the use of their products within society. Still, they are often better off economically from the fruits of their labors than most of their high-culture cousins. I surmised that

---

from the University of Ohio. See Caswell, Lucy Shelton & Gardner Jared (eds.) *Drawing the Line: Comics Studies and INKS,* 1994–1997 University of Ohio Press (2017)

5. https://www.theguardian.com/world/2015/feb/14/copenhagen-blasphemy-lars-vilks-prophet-muhammad-krudttonden-cafe accessed March, 2019.

6. https://www.theguardian.com/media/charlie-hebdo acccessed April, 2019.

7. See Klausen, Jytte. *The Cartoons That Shook the World.* Yale University Press. 2009.
Klausen's book documented the dozen cartoons published in Denmark that initiated the anger of Muslims around the world for the graphically satiric depictions of Mohammed. https://www.nytimes.com/2009/08/13/books/13book.html accessed November, 2018.
The recent beheading of a French teacher who showed his students satirical cartoons of Mohammed has only served to inflamed the French public over Islamic Immigration. https://www.bbc.com/news/world-europe-54598546 Accessed October, 2020.

8. Bruce McKinnon, Cartoonist for the Chronicle Herald, Halifax, Page D7 November 1st, 2018.

high culture was ideologically dominant, but that popular culture was achieving economic dominance. These thoughts merely had the status of conjectures and certainly required further articulation, but from my perspective as a working artist and cultural historian, it seemed obvious that there was a very strong power differential at work, one worthy of closer investigation.

As my research continued, I was amazed and continue to be so, by the sheer quantity of cartoons, comics, novels, magazine articles, films and television programs that parody, satirize, ironize, lampoon, burlesque, and in other ways— humorously and not so humorously—critique the institutions of high culture. Not a week goes by without my becoming aware of, being sent, or collecting another example. My collection of modernist (and postmodern) art related cartoon reproductions and comics now consists of approximately 4000 examples —many also posted on Pinterest—[9] and while this book concentrates upon graphic work, cartoons and comics in the print media, my PhD research concentrated on the ironies, parodies and satires of modernist and postmodernist art within the rich domains of cinema and television. My work in these domains adds support to the claims made in this book about the relationships between visual humor, culture, class, ideology and power. In this sense, these two books are companion texts, and I have begun researching for another publication that explores art, artists and art history themed short stories and novels.

---

9. https://za.pinterest.com/barber3825/art-cartoons/

INTRODUCTION

Class is defined by men and women as they live their own history, and, in the end, this is its only definition (E.P. Thompson 1963:11)

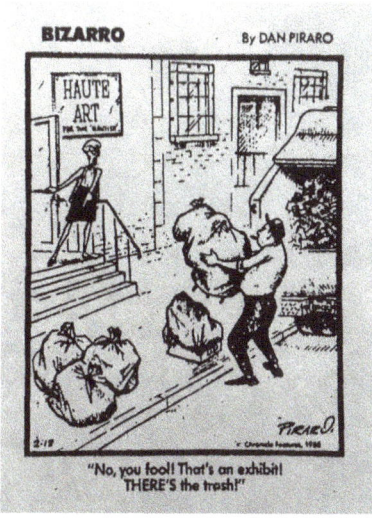

Figure 2: Dan Piraro, *Art Trash* 1986 © Bizarro Comics

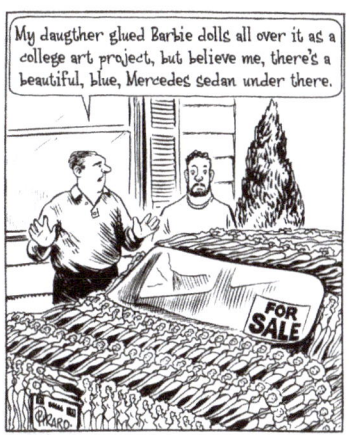

Figure 3: Dan Piraro, *Barbie Art* 1986 © Bizarro Comics

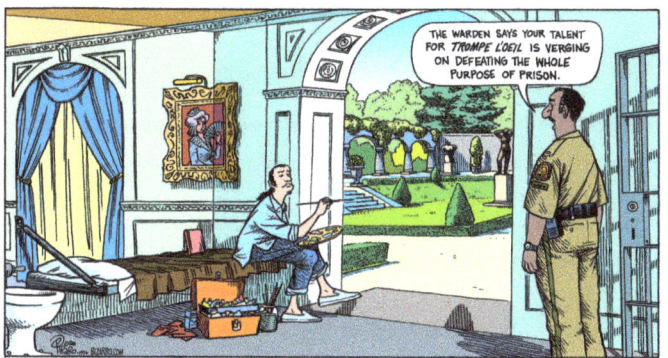

Figure 4: Dan Piraro (Bizarro), *Trompe L'Oeil* 2018 © Bizarro Comics

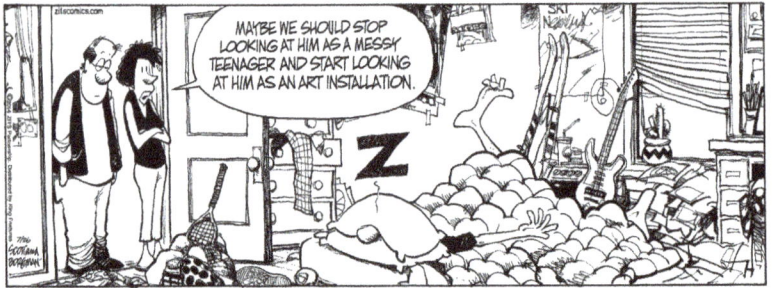

Figure 5: ZITS, *Installation Art* 2007

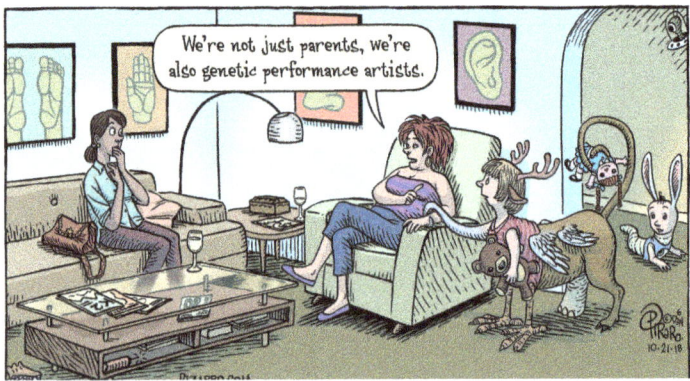

Figure 6: Dan Piraro (Bizarro), *Performance Artists* 2018 © Bizarro Comics

How are cartoons illustrated spanning three decades (figs. 2-6), by Dan Piraro (Bizarro)[1] and ZITS (Jerry Scott and Jim Borgman), received by the general public? How did the average person—if there is such a being—read the images *Art Trash* and *Barbie Art* from the thousands—perhaps millions—who may have come across them in the comic pages of the dozens of newspapers in which they appeared throughout North America in 1986? Did readers understand the humor in these images? Did they recognize the images as graphic satires of contemporary art? Did Piraro's cartoons reinforce or undermine their understanding of the value of contemporary art, or indeed, of culture in general? Can we read these as representations of the cartoonist's personal feelings

---

1. "In 1976, Dan Piraro earned himself a four-year fine arts scholarship to Washington University in St. Louis. But he quickly became 'utterly disillusioned:' "It was all about non-representational art, and performance art. Anything recognizable got you a 'C'; to get an 'A', you had to come up with some unrecognizable, conceptual bullshit—like a pile of broken glass—then write four paragraphs of bullshit justifying why it was special." Zachary Crockett. http://priceonomics.com/the-bizarro-life-of-cartoonist-dan-piraro/, accessed July, 2015.

about the value of high culture, or is he merely representing and ironically commenting upon the general public's (mis)understanding of the projects of contemporary art? Are the cartoons a politically nuanced index of public reception, or a simple example of aesthetic irony, good for a quick laugh or a smile and nothing more?

Like some of the avant-garde art and artists his work satirizes, Dan Piraro's cartoons could become sites for discussing many critical issues about the status and value of art in society. As a relatively complex ensemble of signs differently oriented and accented, the cartoons engage us on a number of levels, both general and specific, with questions relating to the value of art and culture in society, particularly when we place them in the context of the thousands of other art related graphic satires that have appeared in the popular media throughout the last century. These cartoon images are actually more complex than they first appear. In the first cartoon (fig.2), a garbage collector is shown in the process of picking up what appears to be a bag full of trash from the curbside of an art gallery. A sign on the wall adjacent to the gallery door reads "HAUTE ART for the Hautish," a humorous reference to *haute couture* (high culture or fashion), that in this context can be very loosely translated as "high art for the (fashionably) highest." A tall, thin woman standing at the top of the stairs vigorously points to three other garbage bags and exclaims loudly to the garbage collector: "No, you fool! That's an exhibit! THERE'S the trash!" The reader's immediate recognition is that the cartoon presents a case of mistaken identity. The garbage collector has mistaken the bundled work of art (à la Christo) on the sidewalk for garbage![2] Piraro's cartoon signals that Art = Trash. In semiotic terms, art becomes the signifier and trash the signified. The cartoonist's image has rendered high art the equivalent of garbage. The cartoon also reinforces some general stereotypes about people, social differentiation, education, and the value of menial labour—in a word—*class*. The garbage collector is pot-bellied, smoking, and is presumed to be under-educated and unintelligent because he mistakes the

---

2. A web message I received in January, 2005 informed me that a German museum was offering art appreciation lessons to Frankfurt's sanitation workers, after garbage collectors had lugged away a public art sculpture and sent it to the incinerator. "Peter Postleb head of the city's Clean Frankfurt initiative claimed responsibility Monday for the case of mistaken identity, after garbage collectors picked up and disposed of what they thought to be construction rubbish. Though indeed made from yellow plastic sheeting used to encase cement, the item was actually a sculpture by Berlin artist Michael Beutler. It was part of a series of 10 sculptures commissioned by the municipal art society and exhibited around the city. Postleb pointed out that in the past, his quick-moving, garbage-collection teams have avoided trashing outdoor sculptures made from everyday objects, including a car filled with sand and a bathtub tied to a tree with a leash. Starting Sunday, the Städel Museum, at which Beutler studied, will begin monthly Check Your Art Sense! classes, at which the city's garbage collectors can learn about understanding and appreciating art. Beutler has taken the situation in stride, saying that the trashed piece was a temporary work only to be displayed until Sunday and that the series was to be recycled after that anyway."

art for the trash, although the similarity perhaps renders this an honest mistake for anyone to make. The woman is represented as a stereotypical agent of *haute couture*. Tall, slim, well dressed and coiffed, sporting high heels, earrings and spectacles, she is every inch the elegant representative of high culture power and privilege, probably the curator or owner of this gallery of Haute Art.

The *Installation* cartoon by the cartoonist duo ZITS (fig. 5) refers to recent art installations by Tracy Emin and others, collapsing the difference between the disgusting mess in a teenager's bedroom to a similar looking 'disgusting mess' in a high culture museum funded by public money. Dan Piraro has produced dozens of cartoons about art, including most recently in 2019 his collaborative work with Wayno, a fellow cartoonist. As a professed self-educated artist,[3] Dan Piraro is familiar with the power of avant-garde art and the manner in which it can foment public controversies and promote the formation of common epithets of (mis)understanding such as: "that's trash," "garbage!" "crap!" "wtf?" or… "that's shit!" Although Piraro may not be totally familiar with the theoretical intricacies of modernist and postmodern discourse, his art cartoons reveal that he also understands the concept of "The Readymade" (1913) introduced to art history by Marcel Duchamp. Duchamp's "happy idea" to upturn a bicycle wheel and attach it to the seat of a kitchen stool and watch it turn shook the aesthetic beliefs of the art world and cemented the foundations of one edifice of critical modernism. In his *Trash* cartoon, Piraro may also be acknowledging art exhibitions by contemporary artists such as Mierle Laderman Ukeles, Tony Cragg, Mike Kelly, Tracy Emin, Banksy and many others, who have mined Duchamp's readymade concept for their own use by recycling garbage as elements in their art installations. The cartoonist may be familiar also with some of the more rarefied and critical avant-garde conflations of art and crap; for instance, the punning equation between art and shit written in 1914 by Marcel Duchamp: "arrhe over art=Arhre = merdre over merde" a note referring to the readymade (and assisted readymade) that he included in his notes and projects for *The Large Glass* (1915-1923), or Italian avant-gardist Piero Manzoni's special edition of signed and numbered cans of *Artist's Shit* (1961). It may be somewhat presumptuous to assume that the average reader has knowledge of these historical reference points for the cartoon. But even without this specialized art historical knowledge on the part of the viewers, Piraro's cartoon remains a representative example of symbolic conflict over the meaning and value of contemporary art.

---

3. Piraro's website http://www.ucomics.com/bizarro/bio.htm describes him as "an avid artist since childhood (who) worked as a commercial illustrator before becoming a cartoonist." His "Bizarro" single panel cartoon was syndicated in 1985. In 1999, he was awarded the 1999 "Reuben Award for Best Newspaper Panel Cartoon."

The features of modernist art, specifically the products and behavior of the artistic avant-gardes, initiate what many years ago Ian Dunlap termed appropriately "the shock of the new" (Dunlap, 1972: i). In the late nineteenth century and throughout the twentieth century the shocking qualities of modernist art can be identified in the thousands of cartoon and comic satires published in the popular media. These provide a rich record of popular responses—*popular modernisms*—to the powerful representations and challenging aesthetic strategies of the historical avant-garde(s). In the same category as Piraro's garbage/ art example discussed above, there are literally hundreds, possibly thousands of cartoon satires of Picasso's early cubist portrait paintings that show ugly flat faces bearing unnaturally distorted eyes, ears and noses. Other cartoons satirize Piet Mondrian's meaningless colored rectangles; Jackson Pollock's (Jack the Dripper's), expressionistic drips and splatters; Alexander Calder's piles of junk, and Henry Moore's sexualized rocks with holes. For many members of the general public, these cartoon images confirmed their understanding of what constituted unconventional, unnatural and therefore questionable or illegitimate art practice.

In my earlier book *Trans/actions: Art, Film and Death*, I argued that beyond the popular cultural critiques of high culture represented in films such as *Bucket of Blood* (1960) directed by Roger Corman, Martin Scorsese's *After Hours* (1985) and Graeme Campbell's *Still Life* (1992), there are a large number of graphic works, produced within the ideologically dominant (high) cultural domain that parody, satirize and, in other ways, humorously critique the activities and products of the dominant culture. Similar in form to those produced outside of the cultural institutions "which are concerned in part with the ascription and renewal of symbolic value" (Thompson, 1990: 161), these critiques have different audiences, consumers, status groups, or what Gans (1974) termed, somewhat problematically, "taste cultures." To some degree, these social groups share a commitment and understanding of the projects produced within high culture, a result simply of shared ideologies, ethos or worldview. Also, the sub-cultural avant-gardes have consistently used and developed ironic strategies with which to confront and resist the more conservative modernist values held by the elites of the dominant culture while maintaining, on the most fundamental level, its material (socio-economic) ties with the dominant classes, attached, as Clement Greenberg famously identified, "by an umbilical cord of gold" (Greenberg, 1939:37).

In *Popular Modernisms*, I examine a process that has occurred throughout the history of art, one that accelerated with the social effects of the Industrial

Revolution, the development of capitalism and the inception of modern social relations. I argue that the prototypical 'shocks' of modernist art encouraged the production of visual satires, parodies, ironies and pastiches. And that, in the company of other forms of text or performance-based criticism, these were the means by which those in marginal or subordinate social positions could exercise their displeasure and opposition to the ruling ideas and dominant classes of the day. Expressing feelings ranging from mild discomfort to pure rage, this criticism enabled social subordinates to contest or resist the dominance of high culture over low, in terms eloquently described by Antonio Gramsci as the hegemony of the dominant center culture over its margins.

Postmodern critiques of post-enlightenment originary concepts and foundational categories question the singularity and legitimacy of the terms: culture, class and ideology. Many scholars have also criticized the binary oppositions high/low and center/periphery. Art Historian Serge Guilbaut, for example, writes:

> The hegemony of centres has in fact vanished, since art is propagated at lightning speed simultaneously all over the Western world through gallery franchises like Castelli, Boone, Maeght etc. and through magazines published in different languages, catering to different publics with different emphases (Guilbaut, S., 1990:xi).

The most appropriate model of the contestation of cultural power may now be described as heterogeneous, multi-inflexionary, polyvalent, or to use Mikhail Bahktin's powerful yet still somewhat problematic terms, "dialogic" and "heteroglossic," which he used to underline the social character of discourse, (Hirschkop and Shepherd, 1989). But these fluid categories may implicitly relativize a socio-cultural and political process that I believe has a high degree of clarity, particularly when one registers it strategically as the symbolic articulation/representation of relations of power between various social groups and classes. Post-structuralists consider class to be an over-determined concept, however, the work of a number of researchers[4] maintain its legitimacy as a useful category distinction for the examination of social relations within capitalism. As English social historian E.P. Thompson suggested,class difference is not merely a product of political economy with one's place in the labour process determined by one's location in the social and cultural register. It is also a symbolic process of individuation or identity

---
4. Bourdieu (1977, 1984, 1987); McNall, et al. (1989); Pahl (1990), and Aronowitz (1992).

construction. Thompson calls this personal history, which may provide class with its only workable definition.

The formation of ironies, parodies and satires of the products and ideas of high culture by various groups who are technically outside of the principal production/reception sites of cultural dominance may be described generally as one critical tendency within Western modernism. But as many writers have argued, satire, irony and parody (including pastiches, rebus forms, burlesques and grotesques) are not peculiar to modernism (or postmodernism) but rather appear throughout history.

Forms of graphic criticism have occurred with greater frequency since the separation of art from its early primitive, sacral and courtly functions into a realm of relative autonomy (Burger, 1987) that we have come to recognize as the province of modernism. I argue that graphic parodies, ironies and satires of art are one of the means through which those in subordinate or marginal social positions can contest, disavow, and even subvert the hegemony of what Frederic Jameson termed a "cultural dominant" (Jameson, 1991:4). They are also a means by which subordinates who communicate their ironic apprehension and/or appreciation can accommodate and thereby reproduce the hegemonic interests of the dominant classes.

Only a small number of modernist (and postmodern) artists have received extraordinary critical attention in the form of graphic satires of their work in the mainstream press. The art of Courbet, Manet, Picasso, Munch, Matisse, Van Gogh, Duchamp, Magritte, Mondrian, Calder, Moore, Pollock and Warhol, and, more recently, artists such as Cindy Sherman, Tracy Emin, Jeff Koons, Ai Weiwei and Banksy have occasioned cartoon and satirical responses far beyond that normally received by artists within their respective generations. This is now, ironically, considered a prime indicator of their successful careers. The relative placement of modern artists within the Western art historical canon(s) can even be measured in proportion to the number of satires, parodies, and other popular critical responses that their work received during their career and even continued after their death. Only a small number of the most famous modernist artists became the targets of popular and mass cultural criticism, but all of the officially recognized modernist avant-garde movements (i.e. Futurism, Dada, Surrealism) came to the attention of popular cultural critics working within various classes and class fractions. I will demonstrate that each of the so-called modernist art styles and movements—the plethora of 'isms' within modernism[5]—have been targeted for the duration of their national or international prominence and, for a few of these movements, even later in some contexts. The reasons for this are complex and provide one important impetus for this study. On a simple level, this process, which in privileging some political value for humor I have termed critical, appears to be related to the distinctive characteristics of modernity, the specific character of forms of modernist art, and the place of modern artists within institutionalized avant-garde sub-cultures (Hall et al., 1976). The general character of such cultural criticism is influenced by the theoretical and critical discourses of modernist and postmodern art that emerge from the institutions of the dominant culture: the art colleges, universities, public museums, dealer galleries, journals, magazines, newspapers, as well as specific radio and television programs, blog sites and social media.

A major determining influence on the proliferation of cartoons and other critical representations of an art movement, style or artist appears to be the public formation and cementing of various stereotypes for modern and postmodern artists and their work. These stereotypes that may be recognized as one index of public reception, are self-perpetuating and *generative*. Graphic satires of art can occur in contexts both outside and inside the dominant culture's producer and consumer groups. I have found it useful, therefore, to differentiate between these forms of cultural criticism through the use of two primary categories. The *endogenous* category includes those critical representations that occur within the same producer group, subculture or class fraction; for example, Ad Reinhardt's art world comic, cartoon parodies, and satires (see Chapter 9). The *exogenous* category I have reserved for those cultural critiques that are directed from outside toward a specific vanguard producer group, for instance, Walt Disney's satires of neo-avant-garde kinetic, performance and body art of the 1960s, 70s and 80s (see Chapter 10); MAD magazine's satire of the role of the artist and the institution of art history, and National Lampoon's burlesque of Art News (Chapter 11). Boundary articulation is also an issue of great importance with respect to the location and interpretation of the symbolic contest of meaning between various social groups. It should be understood, therefore, that these two primary categories occasionally overlap and can be further differentiated as intra-class, inter-class, and infra-class, respectively.

Cultural criticism can take many forms. As I argued in my earlier study *Trans/actions: Art, Film and Death*, in/subordination is always the basis of

---

5. Realism, Naturalism, Symbolism, Impressionism (its Neo and Post-varieties), Expressionism, Fauvism, Cubism, Expressionism, Orphism, Vorticism, Futurism, Dadaism, Constructivism, Productivism, Suprematism, Surrealism, Abstract Expressionism, Op and Pop Art, Minimalism, Process Art, Conceptual Art (Conceptualism), Performance Art as well as several genres within Postmodernist Art.

popular criticism; that the critical act, whatever that may be—an ironic aside, performed parody, graphic satire, subversive or transgressive broadside—engages both the subject's will to resist, and the will to overcome its (dominating) object. This is the critical character of *in/subordination*, that is distinguished somewhat from the more restrictive familial and military definitions of disobedience and rebelliousness. In/subordination represents an urge to disavow or refuse an extant cultural law or legitimation in progress. I am well aware that in using the term in/subordination I am invoking a comparison with the use of the term subaltern in postcolonial discourse.[6] My use of the term in/subordination, however, should not be confused with the use of subalternity, which I take to have greater currency in the debates around identity and subject politics, rather than class. Homi Bhabha argues:

> The move away from the singularities of 'class' or 'gender' as primary conceptual and organizational categories, has resulted in an awareness of the subject positions of race, gender, generation, institutional location, geopolitical locale, sexual orientation that inhabit any claim to identity in the modern world. What is theoretically innovative, and politically crucial, is the need to think beyond narratives of originary and initial subjectivities and to focus on those moments or processes that are produced in the articulation of cultural differences. These 'in-between' spaces provide the terrain for elaborating strategies of self-hood singular or communal that initiate new signs of identity, and innovative sites of collaboration and contestation, in the act of defining the idea of society itself. (Bhabha, 1994:1-2)[7]

Homi Bhabha argues that the social processes associated with subalternity "may emerge in displaced, even decentered strategies of signification." And importantly, this "does not prevent these positions from being effective in a political sense, although it does suggest that positions of authority may themselves be part of a process of ambivalent identification" (145). I would suggest also that the littoral spaces between class and identity must be negotiated before any "innovative sites for collaboration and/or contestation" can occur. Thompson's view of class as a lived experience evidencing political agency finds acceptance in the work of many contemporary writers on class and identity politics. To this end, Stanley Aronowitz suggests:

---

6. See Said, (1978, 1984); Spivak, (1988); Guha, (1989) and Bhabha, (1994).

7. The problems of political agency in the colonial subject are discussed at length in the volumes 1-6 (1983-1990) of *Subaltern Studies*, New Dehli: Oxford University Press edited by Ranajiit Ruha. See also Ashcroft, Griffiths, G. and Tiffin, H. *The Post-Colonial Reader*, London, New York: Routledge, 1995.

> What has occurred in the last quarter century is that, on the assumption that the working class shares in the general level of material culture, class has been removed ideologically and politically from the politics of subalternity, at least in late capital societies, and has been replaced by new identities or by conceptions according to which the "new" middle classes—hardly oppressed social categories—have emerged as political agents, but on their own behalf. (Aronowitz, 1992: ix)

My focus on graphic satires (cartoons and comics) of modern art attempts to provide some practical explication of the symbolic contest of power as this process represents the struggle to achieve and maintain cultural hegemony. A further aim of this book is to investigate the symbolic contestation of cultural meanings in social terms and thereby enrich our understanding of classed society. There are, I believe, many social and political confluences that intersect within the symbolic construction and interpretation of culture. This contest of power can be read as an ideological conflict between various dominant and subordinate groups, classes and class fractions. The French sociologist Pierre Bourdieu has written persuasively on this process:

> Different classes (and social fractions) are engaged in a specifically symbolic struggle to impose the definition of the social world most in conformity with their interests. The field of ideological positions reproduces in transfigured form the field of social positions.

And further, in the same passage he emphatically states:

> The field of symbolic production is a microcosm of the struggle between the classes. (Bourdieu, 1977:112)

Cultural criticism begins within the dominant classes and later, during periods of acquiescence and affirmation, permeates through to other levels at the margins of high culture. For this reason, I examine the various modes of cultural criticism, the specific registers at which it occurs, its timing, its forms and also how such criticism was received, responded to and reproduced within the various producer groups. This necessitates a close reading of the taste-making, canon-building elements in accordance with the critical/interrogative aspects of the symbolic visualization and discourse accompanying ideological conflict. These can perhaps best be described as the 'modes and manners' of cultural in/subordination.

These discursive problematics enrich yet also complicate the business of examining and categorizing types of class-specific, class-directed representations, oscillating as they do between the poles of reception and critique. Throughout *Popular Modernisms*, therefore, I investigate the various sources of this form of criticism, of where and at what times it occurs. I considered the more sociologically extreme option, statistical evidence of the frequency of occurrence within the so-called discursive field, but in the course of my research, it also became apparent that quantitative analyses would begin to over-determine the kind of interpretations that could be constructed from a close reading of the cartoons and comics themselves, as distinct, initially, from the social contexts within which they reside. This has been a particular problem with many so-called empirical studies of popular culture. While initially of some importance as an index of reception, I found the frequency of occurrence of these cartoons and comics less useful ultimately for understanding the actualities of power relations than were specific representations of in/subordination, resistance and accommodation to cultural dominance within the total interpretative field. Moreover, I realized that the function of ideology in the process of cultural subordination, as well as forms of in/subordination could not be reduced simply to the number of cartoons attaching to the work of a specific artist or cultural event nor to a surface reading of content. Neither, it became apparent upon closer investigation, of these representations of cultural conflict could be related specifically to the internationalities or the class of origin of the producers of criticism themselves, although, to be sure, these became very important considerations throughout my inquiry and served more than once to affirm my quasi-ethnographic participant/observer status. My discussions and communication with a number of the producers of these cartoons and comics of modernist art, as well as many of their readers, have often confirmed my reading of the cartoons and provided evidence for some of my prior suppositions.

The frequency of graphic satires and parodies of modernist art can sustain preliminary generalizations such as those with which I began. Although we would have to strain to locate graphic examples in the charcoal, ochre and blood wall drawings of thousands of years ago, I suggest that this critical phenomenon has occurred throughout the history of art, that it accelerated with the development of visual satire and caricature in the late Renaissance, and was further entrenched with the class formation processes associated with the early development of European capitalism and those ideologies we now associate with the early nineteenth century construction of modernity and modernist culture. It is less useful here to make any finer judgements relating to class/culture, particularly the production and reproduction of ideological conflict. Indeed, for these questions to develop any legitimacy, I found early on that my research had to become historical, contextual, and yet, in a crucial sense, non-denominational or discipline-bound. While the subject I, as reader/interpreter of this research, could not pre-dominate, neither could the assumed roles of popular culture researcher, sociologist or art historian. While at times it seemed, extravagantly, that each role was assumed in order to test this or that assumption, criticism and conjecture, I adopted my positions as much as this was possible with the perspicuity of a skeptic. At times, it felt as if I was assuming one role or stance in order to question, or refute, the judgments pronounced by another. At times, vulgar and weak judgments on my part were accorded more weight, simply in order to elicit greater interpretative and explanatory use value. In these senses, this book conforms somewhat to the interdisciplinary projects of cultural studies as these were articulated in the early years of the Birmingham School.[8] With this consideration it is appropriate to briefly outline the wider context and scope of this study here.

In the 1960s and throughout the 1970s, a burgeoning academic interest in popular culture became evident in the proliferation of university courses covering various topics within communication and culture/media studies. Book and journal publishing began to take on a new urgency and, with the publication of several key texts in the fifties and early sixties (Rosenberg, and White, 1957, 1971; Lowenthal, 1961; Denney, 1963; White and Abel, 1963), it seemed that the research and historiography of popular culture had secured a kind of legitimacy, both within academic contexts and further afield, within culture generally. During the past three decades, the examination of popular culture has assumed a new identity. Armed with the theoretical and methodological approaches developed by the Birmingham School, European post-structuralism, feminism, Anglo-European and American neo-Marxism; post-colonial studies, as well as the theoretical, empirical and historical work of various academic associations (the Popular Culture Association, the American Studies Association, and their sister organizations in the United States, Canada, Europe and Australasia), greater confidence became evident in the work of researchers who had previously been the victims of various forms of intellectual and academic marginalization. As a consequence, the histories of indigenous, popular, folk, and other marginal cultures are now being given the academic attention that is their due. The theoretical approaches have also expanded since the work of the

---

8. The Birmingham University Centre for Contemporary Cultural Studies.

Frankfurt School. Nevertheless, few researchers have taken the academic risks demanded early on in cultural studies by Stuart Hall and his colleagues of the Birmingham Centre for Contemporary Cultural Studies, who recognized the inter-relatedness of various theoretical and methodological approaches to popular culture yet insisted upon the absolute political character of their project. This book attempts to underwrite and reinforce the political character of the cultural studies project. Accordingly, throughout *Popular Modernisms,* I discuss questions pertaining to the differentiations between elite and popular culture, culture/class, issues pertaining to the categories of dominance and subordination, the binary oppositions 'high/low,' center/periphery,[9] cultural conflict, and relations of power, this last, writ' large as the *conditio sine qua non* of my research.

Throughout the book, I discuss the forms, methods, and meanings of cultural criticism, the politics of satire, parody, pastiche, caricature, and the grotesque, as well as the distinguishing characteristics of cultural in/subordination; privileging, throughout, the social and political meanings, not what has so often been the case, the social/psychology of humor. The twelve chapters follow a format that initially permits the articulation of theory, followed by specific historical and contemporary examples that extend and explicate the theoretical frameworks established in the introductory chapters.

Chapter One revisits the theoretical negotiation and interpretation of class and discusses various approaches to culture, power and social conflict. For example, the various theories of Gramsci, Volosinov, Althusser, Bourdieu, Williams, and Žižek, with some of their interpreters and critics, are examined in relation to culture, class, language, ideology, and relations of power. The discussion affirms the continuing relevance of Gramsci's concept of hegemony for the development of theoretical models of dominance, subordination, resistance, accommodation, and in/subordination.

---

9. This opposition is acknowledged as a metaphorical construction; one which, however, is used practically, if somewhat *dialogically,* to discuss, as simply as possible, the contestation of power, which is much more complex than the metaphors themselves can present. It should become obvious that what is high/low, or inside/outside, is dependent upon a broad range of ideological positions from which to *articulate* differentiation. The consciousness of such power relations is dependent upon both the experience of power and powerlessness, as well as the language used to describe it. The one is recognised in the presence, or absence, of the other. Power is not necessarily self-evident. As Bourdieu suggests in the conclusion to his *Distinction: A Social Critique of the Judgement of Taste* (1984), "The reality of representation" [may become] indistinguishable from "the representation of reality."—"Those who classify themselves or others, by appropriating or classifying practices or properties that are classified and classifying, cannot be unaware that, through distinctive objects or practices in which their 'powers' are expressed and which, being appropriated by and appropriate to classes, classify those who appropriate them, they classify themselves in the eyes of other classifying (but also classifiable) subjects, endowed with classificatory schemes analogous to those which enable them more or less adequately to anticipate their own classification" (Bourdieu, 1984:482).

In Chapter Two, the discussion revolves around questions pertaining to the political dimensions of humour and the symbolic contest of meaning represented in various ironies, parodies, and satires of modern and postmodern art. This chapter begins with a paradigmatic reading of a New Yorker cartoon by the late Ed Koren, who is also a trained art historian, that satirizes the elevation of graffiti to the realm of high culture. Three museum exhibitions are then discussed. The first, an exhibition of art cartoons that took place in 1973 at the Tate Gallery in London, and two later exhibits at the Whitney Museum (1984) and at the Museum of Modern Art in New York (1990), which had as their theme the fraught relationships between modern art and popular culture.

Chapter Three continues to explore humour and power, focusing on the politics of graphic humor in caricature, parody, satire, burlesque, and the grotesque. I focus on the differences and various compatibilities between the humor theories of Bergson, Freud, Kris, and Bahktin, among others. I also discuss aspects of art historiography, popular culture and class conflict, the incidence and meanings of popular and mass culture critiques of avant-garde art, as well as the trafficking, co-optation and absorption dynamic—cultural appropriation—within elite and popular culture.

Chapter Four provides a more detailed discussion of the theory and politics of parody, irony, and satire in visual and scripto-visual (*ekphratic*) representations. I argue that humor can serve several social purposes. It cannot only register in/subordination and resistance, as in a situation where overt or covert conflict is present; it may also function as an ironic sign of accommodation and tacit acceptance of an alienating concept or cultural form. The chapter concludes with a discussion of a number of French cartoon examples from various sources, *circa* 1850-1860, that satirize early modernist art and the institutions of art. Some aspects of the discussion address the binary distinction high/low, dominant/subordinate as these pertain to the class background, "cultural competency" (Bourdieu, 1984:2), and institutional roles of caricaturists and artists.

Chapter Five discusses outsider critiques of the dominant culture's sub-cultural avant-garde. Pierre Bourdieu's concepts of symbolic and cultural capital are further discussed as these relate to the class background and ideological affiliations of the cartoonists, their views on contemporary art, and the editorial policies of the magazines for which they worked. Specific cartoon examples are discussed in terms of their chronological relationships to contemporary art movements, exhibitions, newspaper reviews, and public debates. The final section of this chapter focuses upon several prolific art satirists working for *The*

New Yorker and *Punch* magazines: *Punch* magazine's George Morrow, G.L Stampa, Fougasse and H.M. Bateman; with Anatol Kovarsky, Whitney Darrow, Barney Toby, Dana Fradon, Frank Modell, and Harry Bliss from *The New Yorker*.

Chapter Six discusses cultural stereotyping and the paradigmatic status of popular responses to the modernist sculptures of the famous American sculptor Alexander Calder, specifically as this is represented in the "pile of junk" cartoon satires of his so-called 'mobiles' and 'stabiles.' The discussion centers specifically upon arguments pertaining to popular resistance to the development of abstraction in modernist sculpture, both from American and English viewpoints, and reveals how these graphic satires are linked to several satirical sub-genres for modernist sculpture.

Chapter Seven continues themes developed in the preceding chapters with a discussion of several powerful cartoons of the art of U.K. artist Henry Moore, one of the 20th century's most distinguished sculptors. In this chapter, arguments are developed with respect to the erotic significance of the hole in Moore's sculpture, specifically as this is represented in the graphic satires of his art. Topics of relevance to this discussion include the expression and repression of sexuality in the sculptor's work, the inviolability of the body, public morality and censorship. This chapter also provides a critique of a certain hagiographic tendency within art history literature.

Chapter Eight examines three books that attack modern artists, modern art and modernist discourse: *Are you fed up with Modern Art?* (1952), by Clarence Canning Allen, and two other books from the 1970s: Kenneth Forbes's *Great Art to the Grotesque* (1972), and Tom Wolfe's famous art world satire *The Painted Word* (1975). The chapter concludes with a discussion of a wide range of popular cartoon responses to modernist strategies of abstraction, from Picasso and Mondrian to Pollock and Reinhardt; with art movements from Cubism to Minimalism and Conceptual art. Focusing upon the popular critiques of the work, behavior and institutionalization of the Abstract Expressionists, this chapter also touches on themes relating to primitivism, biologism, archeology, the sociology of poverty, the denial of God, existentialism, sexuality and questions of value and freedom in art.

Ad Reinhardt's 1940s *P.M.*, *Transform/ation* and *Art News* art comics and cartoons are the subjects of discussion in Chapter Nine. This chapter explores the insider's—endogenous—critique of the high culture art establishment and discusses the critical class consciousness of several artists: Honore Daumier, Lyonel Feininger and Ad Reinhardt. Their attachment to popular culture is discussed with respect to a common dilemma of socially committed artists of the avant-garde. The chapter advances some ideas about artists as cartoonists and the so-called status incongruity of the working class and/or politically committed artists operating within the absorptive institutional domains of the dominant culture.[10]

Chapter Ten provides a reading of outsider criticism through the exploration of two examples of Walt Disney's comics that satirize Kinetic, Performance, and Body Art of the 1960s and 1970s. The discussion develops arguments concerning the subordinate world of children and cultural propaganda for the underclasses. Two exogenous art critiques are discussed in Chapter Eleven: *MAD* magazine's art world satires of the 1950s and *National Lampoon*'s parody of *Art News* are viewed as reflections of the negative status of modernist art within popular culture. The discussion questions the significance of the representation of popular cultural critiques of the dominant high culture within classed society for juvenile and adult comic consumers.

"Thalia meets Melpomene" Chapter 12 explores the political meaning of the many cartoons that were inspired by the purchase of Barnett Newman's painting *Voice of Fire* by the National Gallery of Canada. A version of this chapter was previously published in the book *Voices of Fire: Art, Rage, Power and the State*, which the author co-edited.[11]

---

10. A version of this chapter was recently published in Buckley, Brad and Conomos, John (eds), *Erasure: The Spectre of Cultural Memory* U.K. Libri Publishing pp121-144 2015

11. Barber, Bruce, Guilbaut, Serge and O'Brian John (eds), *Voices of Fire: Art, Rage Power and the State*. Toronto: U of T Press, 1996.

CHAPTER 1

Revisiting Ideology, Class and Hegemony

> In considering such transformations a distinction should always be made between the material transformation of the economic conditions of production, which can be determined with the precision of a natural science, and the legal, political, religious, aesthetic or philosophic-short ideological forms in which men become conscious of this conflict and fight it out. (Marx, K., 1968:182)

> Consequently, to put it in old-fashioned Marxist terms, the central task of the ruling ideology in the present crisis is to impose a narrative which will place the blame for the meltdown not on the global capitalist system as such, but on secondary and contingent deviations (overly lax legal regulations, the corruption of financial institutions, and so on). (Žižek, S., 2009:19)

As I wrote in my earlier book *Trans/Actions: Art, Film and Death*, ideology has had an extraordinarily rich yet often problematic existence as a concept within social class and culture studies, primarily because it is both conflated with and used as a descriptive, or synonym for other key concepts, as in the famous passage from Marx cited above and the Žižek quote from his chapter "It's Ideology Stupid" in *First as Tragedy, Then as Farce* (2009). Ideology has been defined as everything from false consciousness—a distorted or upside-down view of reality—to a set of philosophical beliefs, positionings and political posturing. In my earlier study, I cited the German Marxist philosopher Wolfgang Fritz Haug, who wrote: "Ideology—one word and so many meanings," as he reflected upon the question, "are ideologies on ideologies our fate?" (1982:9). Haug, with other members of the Project Ideology Theory (PIT) group, struggled to separate the denotative ideology from the highly connotative ideological. Other writers, for example, Roland Barthes, Jacques Derrida, Judith Butler and Slavoj Zizek, have tended to privilege the connotative aspects of ideology at the expense of the denotative. The shifts in semiotic emphasis from the denotative to the connotative have caused as many problems as they have attempted to solve. At this time, it appears that the relativizing tendencies contained within the connotative approach to ideology and its effects/affects have center stage. As far as visual representation is concerned, this connotative approach has resulted methodologically in a postmodern emphasis upon processes of reading and interpretation as opposed to analysis.

Within the Marxist canon ideology has had a very contested existence. Perhaps, given its early origin in post-enlightenment discourse as "the science of ideas" (Kennedy 1978:215), this should be so. Ideology has been discussed generally as an instrumental component of culture and specifically as a principal agent in the individual formation of consciousness. Marxists discuss the ideological in various ways: in terms of its forms and powers on social life in general (Marx and Engels, 1885-6); as a network of struggles (Lenin, 1902); visual ideology (Hadjinicoloau, 1973); and as compromise formations (Haug, 1982). Althusser's concept of the "ideological subject effect" defines the human subject as the "animal ideologique," who in his/her daily life acts within a complex matrix of ideologies that bonds/binds (interpellates), her/him to the social order. He argued provocatively that the ideological apparatuses of the State: education, the legal system, the police, the military and, in some cases, the media, as well as the governing institutions themselves, are the powerful instruments of domination, subordination and control. Althusser shifted the emphasis away from Marx's model of a determining economic base, a compliant ideological superstructure and, with it, the dominance of the social economic over the cultural. He theorized not only that the ideological apparatuses of the State are as determining as the economic base but also that, as ideological agents, human subjects are themselves implicated in the reproduction of the State's structured agenda. Althusser was among the first to recognize the importance of the special dialectical relationships between institutional structures and human agency with respect to the role that ideology plays in the maintenance and, therefore, reproduction of the hegemony of the dominant culture. If *structure* was privileged by many of the early theorists of ideology, now under the influence of postmodern discourse(s), *agency* has acquired greater currency. The truth probably lies somewhere in between, that is in the liminal modalities of both structure and agency. In this study, I have employed a practical model of structure with respect to class working in tandem with individual agency. This model can provide some explanation as to why minority elite cultures can exercise their ideological hegemony over popular culture, which are often economically dominant, and moreover, why those in subordinate positions accept the naturalness of their fate.

Since Marx's evocation of ideology as false consciousness, the role of ideology in the formation of group psychology has waxed and waned. In the early work of the Birmingham cultural studies researchers, editors and writers for the film journal *Screen, Block and Cinetique*, the reconciliation of the separate discourses of Marxism and psychoanalysis in the work of Althusser and Lacan seemed complete. The conflation of social and psychological discourses permitted researchers to argue that while individuals may believe that they speak freely, ideology actually speaks through them. As I have acknowledged and written previously, for many writers, this helped explain why individual members of subordinate groups—classes and class fractions—often act less in their own best interest than in the interests of their class. This model provides an understanding of how an individual subject's consciousness of their subordination may change, yet in most external respects, their social position remains the same as other members of their class. For sociologist Paul Willis, this model explained how class consciousness is reproduced and "why working-class kids get working class jobs" (Willis, 1977:1).

The Italian Marxist Antonio Gramsci argued that there is a material or common-sense basis to ideology, a lived comprehension or understanding that further naturalizes the power relations subsumed under the mantle of hegemony. For Gramsci, ideology is not simply a set of ideas or beliefs but has a material and specific sense. Using one sense of ideology adopted from the early writings of Marx, he argued that consciousness itself is structured as ideological. If this is true, the question of how a subject articulates, acts out, or symbolically represents their common-sense lived relationships within ideology becomes a key to understanding its social and cultural affects. If common sense is, as Gramsci suggests, the "sub-stratum of ideology," then these lived ideas, many of which are unconsciously held yet consciously acted upon, become the key to understanding class consciousness and class relations. His articulation of hegemony explained why class divisions and class antagonisms are reproduced through time.

Pierre Bourdieu argued that ideologies are "legitimating discourses" which operate with a great deal of complexity and contrariness. He acknowledged moreover, that these discourses and the institutions from which they emanate provide the sites within which our understanding of ideological effects, influences, and power must be located.

> The most successful ideological effects are the ones that have no need of words, but only of laissez faire and complicitous silence (Bourdieu, 1990:133)

The difficulties of defining ideology and explaining both its effects and affects have not deterred the maintenance of its status as a keyword within cultural studies. If anything, it has encouraged its use. Under the influence of feminism, postmodernist and postcolonial discourse, the work of a number of recent writers demonstrates that there have been some shifts in the strategies and methods used to address the representation of ideology and its affects. These range from quasi-scientific forms of sociological analysis to forms of reading and textual interpretation within various interpretive communities (Nelson and Grossberg, 1988; Grossberg, Nelson, and Treichler, 1992). This shift in attention has occurred without lessening ideology's value as an explanatory concept but rather lending it greater use value by contextualizing it within discursive fields marked by their interdisciplinary and theoretical heterogeneity. This makes the business of class ascription a more difficult, if nonetheless, interesting proposition.

From a conventional Marxist perspective, social classes are defined in relation to other classes within a given system of production; their formation is the consequence of property ownership, labour and wealth accumulation. For many sociologists, class, like ideology, is one-dimensional: one's class is objectively located and established on the basis of certain discrete criteria and relatively autonomous categories such as education, occupation and income. For some within the cultural studies orbit (Frith, 1986), class is a relatively autonomous category. For others, however, class is contextual, dynamic, and "resonates with political meaning." (McNall, et al., 1991:3). Since E.P. Thompson's landmark study, *The Making of the English Working Class* (1963), much has been done to try and establish bases for understanding the dynamics of class structures, as well as the modes and manners by which class is expressed and reproduced. Bourdieu has discussed this typical class conundrum as an attempt to locate the objectivity of the subjective. He writes:

> The objectivist vision [of social class] is able to extract the 'objective' truth of class relations as power relations, only by destroying everything that helps to give domination the appearance of legitimacy. But it falls short of objectivity by failing to write into its theory of social classes the primary truth *against* which it is constructed, in particular the veil of symbolic relations without which, in many cases, class relations would not be able to function in their 'objective' truth as relations of exploitation (Bourdieu, 1990:136).

E.P. Thompson has critiqued the seeking of objective truth in autonomous class categories, arriving at the matter-of-fact explanation that a class may participate in its own making as much as it is made, a commonsense notion that has become (almost by default) the stock-and-trade of much of the best cultural studies and new sociological research. Thompson's position suggests that it is important to consider class as *relational* as distinct from oppositional, although the differences between the two are often difficult to locate. For the purposes of my research, I have taken class to be multi-dimensional and somewhat less homogeneous than many sociologists would admit. I have resisted the urge to homogenize social reality into a classless *lebenswelt* populated by apolitical agents and actors and either reduced to individualized identity politics or heterogeneous taste cultures. I wish to emphasize that the objective categorizations of class grounded in education, occupation, income, and what Bourdieu has termed "symbolic" or "cultural capital," must also be subjectively understood and confirmed by the classed subject. In these terms, class may be less objective or subjective than contingent, its boundaries shifting constantly, but not yet boundaryless (permeable)—or worse, invisible.

Ideology enters significantly into the formation of classes through the manner in which individuals' lived experiences are represented, reconstituted, and communicated. Communication occurs through various forms of discourse: speech, stories, visualizations, performances, dress codes, eating habits, and consumer preferences. As Eric Hobsbawm has argued, class "is ideology as well as structure." Class-consciousness is articulated "as a group's awareness and understanding of itself that grows out of opposition to other groups" (Hobsbawm, 1984:8). In other words, the individual classed subject comes to know and understand his/her class position *only* in terms of their opposition to others, and this is signified (represented) through various means as a relation of power. This dynamic provides the basis for understanding how dominant/subordinate relationships can develop in a wide variety of social circumstances that are not necessarily the result of institutional structures.

It should be apparent from this brief discussion of ideology and class that class divisions and class-consciousness are extremely difficult to isolate and identify. Sociological models do not always provide adequate criteria for the correct placement of individuals within social and/or cultural hierarchies and, in some cases, are too restrictive. A traditional class indicator such as education may be less useful than it at first appears, even when Bourdieu, whose models of symbolic and cultural capital accumulation have considerably enriched this important category for class ascription, employs it. No simple correlation or equation such as social class = cultural class can be made with any degree of certainty as to its general applicability to patterns of cultural consumption or production or even to the description, analysis, and determinations thereof. The phenomenon dubbed in the literature as "cultural straddling" by various class fractions (Gans, 1974:109)[1] is accompanied in the domains of production and consumption by another: borrowing and "trafficking" (Sekula, 1983:1).[2] The appropriation or expropriation of the products of one group by another, a process tied ultimately to market conditions, is one of the most salient characteristics of social relations at all levels within capitalist society. Class mobility and trans-cultural mobility—whether actual or perceived on the part of any group studied—are also important in any study which attempts to link cultural (ideological) distinctiveness to socio-economic (class) difference. More comprehensive sets of class indicators have to be employed for adequate sociological methodologies to be developed. And where these criteria are developed, they must be used with some caution; that is, with the realization that both the subjects of this process and the process of class ascription itself is complex, dynamic rather than static, and moreover, exists within complex discursive fields of interpretability that tend to undermine differentiation, one of the principal goals of sociological inquiry itself.

Hegemony has also had a somewhat contested existence as a keyword within cultural studies. In many ways, however, using the term hegemony obviates the necessity for providing reductive definitions for the other keywords, ideology and class, and is therefore useful in this respect. Since its emergence in the early writings of the Russian political strategists Plekhanov (1895) and Lenin (1902) and subsequent elaboration in the prison notebooks of Gramsci (1920)[3], the term hegemony has obtained currency in the work of many cultural research-

---

1. There are some problems with Gans's use of this term. The notions of *taste cultures* with which he underlines the concept of 'straddling' raise the problem of the determining power of 'false consciousness.' How is it that those whose taste is 'governed' by certain class interests and training consume the products of other (competing classes)? Bourdieu's concept of cultural capital does much to explain the straddling issue without resorting to the negativism within the term false consciousness. Bourdieu's work demonstrates that *class* cannot be reduced, simply, to *taste*.

2. This rich concept, itself the product of popular cultural discourse (traffic trade in commodity literally and figuratively), has recently become useful in the broader context of discussions attending the politics of representation. In the company of related terms in recent theoretical discourse, "appropriation" and "expropriation," "trafficking" lends some material and economic substance to the trans-valuative terms "representation" and "appropriation." See Sekula, A. "The Traffic in Photographs" in Buchloh, B., Guilbaut, S., and Solkind, D., *Modernism and Modernity: The Proceedings from the Vancouver Conference*. Halifax: NSCAD and NYU Press (1983).

3. Gramsci, A. *Selections From the Prison Notebooks of Antonio Gramsci* edited and trans. Q. Hoare and G. Nowell Smith, London, Lawrence and Wishart (1971). A selection from the original Italian Edition: A. Gramsci *Quaderni del Carere (1928-1935)* (ed) V. Gerratana, Turin, Einaudi, 1948-51; Gramsci, A. *Selections from Political Writings Vol I 1910-1920* and *1921-1926 Vol II,* edited and translations by Hoare, Q. and Mathews London: Lawrence and Wishart 1977, 1978.

ers. It has been especially relevant for those investigating the representation and contestation of cultural, as well as political and economic power. Most importantly, the keywords embraced, if not subsumed by hegemony—culture, ideology, and class—have been permitted to transcend the more mechanical, economistic, and 'fatal' aspects[4] of historical materialism,[5] becoming in the process much more useful tools with which to approach, interpret and analyze social/cultural relations within modernity.

According to many of his other interpreters, Gramsci viewed hegemony as both the process and the evidence of relations of power, particularly the power that the dominant classes exercise through various means—culture, education, law—over subordinate and marginal groups. The evidence is not only reflective of the imposition of power in a mechanical and authoritarian fashion, that is, through coercion or direct enforcement through the policing apparatuses of the State. But it is also presented in cultural terms that appear and, moreover, are acknowledged as being totally natural, legitimate and, in some crucial senses, inviolable. This naturalness is underscored by the distinction, first advanced by Lenin and elaborated by Gramsci, between political and civil society.[6] Where political society and its institutional forms of governance allow for and, in fact, encourage various forms of coercion in the maintenance of control, civil society is composed of those non-coercive and seemingly non-political (cultural) elements of society (Williams, G. 591). According to Gramsci, hegemony cannot be defined strictly in economic terms, hence its relevancy for those researchers interested in moving beyond economistic models that emphasize causality and determination without devolving into extreme forms of postmodern relativism.

Hegemony is not a *priori* and universal phenomenon. Rather, it is reproduced and sustained, according to Gramsci, as a "moving equilibrium," containing relations of forces favorable to this or that tendency (589). It is in the cracks and fissures that one recognizes the normalizing tendencies and, in stronger

---

4. For Gramsci, historical materialism is too deterministic and therefore capitulates to some form of teleological position with respect to history. He called this resignation to history a form of "fatalism." Aspects of Gramsci's critique of historical materialism occurs in *Selections from the Prison Notebooks* (eds. and translation) Hoare, Q. and Nowell Smith, G., London: Lawrence and Wishart (1978: 419-472).

5. For a useful study of developments in contemporary marxism see Anderson, Perry *Considerations on Western Marxism* London: NLR (1976) "Hegemony" (78-81, and passim). Also Gurevitch, M., Bennett, T., Curran J. and Woollacott, J., (eds) *Culture, Society and the Media* London: Methuen (1982), and Bennett, Woollacott et al. (eds) *Culture, Ideology and Social Process: A Reader* London: Open University Press (1981), particularly Section 4 "Class Culture and Hegemony" (185-251). See especially, Chantal Mouffe's contribution in this collection: "Hegemony and Ideology in Gramsci" (219-235).

6. See Williams, Gwyn A., "Gramsci's Concept of Egemonia" *Journal of the History of Ideas* 21:4 (586-99), republished in Hymes, Del, *Reinventing Anthropology*. See also Bocock (1986: 21-37).

terms, the institutionalization, or cementing, of hegemonic relations of power. This is where control is being contested and resisted. Just as the dominant class is recognized in the forms of its subordinates, so too is hegemony recognized for what it effects/affects, produces and reproduces, outside of its own domain. Gramsci's work demonstrates how ideology and culture generally can exert a powerful hegemonic influence on the production and reproduction of structural inequalities within a society. Within classed society, hegemonic conflict, or better, the struggle to achieve hegemony, can occur anywhere: within government, business, within various institutes of education, religious and other community groups, private and public sector unions, but especially the media, and as this book argues, in cartoons, comics and other forms of visual representation. These struggles may take place on a large scale: in institutions of government, at public meetings, in television debates, in the print media and on the Web. Alternately, they can exist at the micro-level, that is, at the level of the ideological signification of the sign, and within ensembles of signs. In the context of the research for this book, the macro level is the cartoon in its social and historical context. The micro level is present in the details of a graphic image, a single frame in a comic strip, a balloon caption, a phrase or word within a caption. Images, written texts, and speech are important vehicles for both the contestation and cementing of hegemony and are, therefore, useful sites for research.

It is important to recognize the compatibility of various theoretical approaches to the key concepts discussed above. Like Ludwig Wittgenstein and Raymond Williams, Gramsci had a deep appreciation for the philosophical character of ordinary language. He also argued that language, itself, is the site of power differentials, the potential ground for the contest of meaning to erupt, always signifying ideological if not class difference. His understanding of language is compatible with earlier theoretical positions on the importance of language in class ascription elaborated by the Russian formalists Volosinov and Bahktin.

For Volosinov:

> Class does not coincide with the sign community, i.e. with the community, which is the totality of users of the same set of signs of ideological communication. Thus, various different classes will use one and the same language. As a result, differently oriented accents intersect in every ideological sign. *Sign becomes the arena of class struggle*. (V. N. Volosinov, 1986: 23)

This study of the proliferation of cartoon, comic art satires, and parodies of the "-isms" of modernist art, and the artists associated with these styles and movements reveals the social and cultural significance of the struggle to resist hegemony. The study also encourages the recognition of this process as the struggle to achieve hegemony. In a somewhat more limited sense, the discussion of these popular critiques of art can promote an understanding of the contestation over the meaning of the sign(s) of modern art and, in the senses articulated by Bourdieu and Volosinov, the intersection of "differently oriented accents" of the sign(s). The discussion of these images also indicates how processes of reading and interpretation encourage comprehension and valuation to occur. In linguistic terms, it is not the structure of the units of language that is analyzed or the syntactical variations within this structure but the manner in which these units may be accented in a variety of ways by their users and, therefore, subjected to differing ideological inflections as they are read. This remains a principally symbolic contest of meaning. Another fundamental aspect of this study will be to reveal how these accents can be used to either reinforce a particular set of resistant social practices or encourage subjects to accommodate themselves to the social order.

> All processes of socialization and all social struggles or political articulations inevitably connect themselves with ideological powers. At the core of concrete historical studies must be placed (the dimension of) hegemony (Hanninen & Paldan 1982:13).

Cartoons and comics that ironize, parody or satirize art are important vehicles for negotiating and contesting the terms of value for modernist culture as a whole. Culture is the privileged terrain of investigation in this book, and yet my discussions are not limited to this. Throughout it, I stress the existence of power relations and social conflicts within modernist culture. I will attempt to show that the symbolic representations of these contests of power are not neutral in character but instead represent deeply entrenched antagonisms between various social groups and constituencies classes, and class fractions about the meaning and value of modernism itself.

Thus far, the discussion has merely revisited the difficulties and complexities attached to class and, moreover, of establishing its very legitimacy as a mode of sociological enquiry. However, one important means of perceiving and interpreting cultural and class difference is to examine the ways in which one constituency, class, or class fraction responds to, represents, and, through its cultural representations, criticizes another class or class fraction. My claim here is that the examination of these critical representations reveals hegemonic and counter-hegemonic tendencies that, if not determined *in extenso*, are certainly influenced in a dialogical fashion by those conflicts occurring at the social/economic level. The struggles, conflicts, and points of resistance within the domains of cultural production (and consumption) are as significant as those that occur elsewhere; far from being separate from class conflict as a whole, they are undoubtedly wedded to it. Within contemporary society, the contestation of ideological dominance occurs at all social and cultural levels, often representing patterns of accommodation to the prevailing order—subordination—but, more often, providing the evidence of contestation and resistance counter—hegemony, or what I prefer to call in/subordination. The task now is to elucidate these claims practically.

CHAPTER 2

Cartoons and Cultural In/Subordination

> I wonder if art history will know what to do with class conflict in art once it is properly described. (Baxandall, 1979:2)

The discipline of art history was subjected to many challenges in the 1970s and 1980s: from Marxist scholars who questioned the formalist asocial and apolitical characteristics of conventional art history methodologies and from feminist scholars who questioned the predominance of male artists in the historical canon. But in comparison to other academic disciplines such as film and literary studies, art historians, with a few notable exceptions, were late to respond to the critical interventions of postmodernist and post-colonial discourse in the areas of theory and methodology.[1] During the past three decades, this situation has changed somewhat, and art historians can no longer ignore the changes wrought on the discipline by these discourses. The signs of change were evident in the early 1980s when a small number of art historians, critics, and curators began to explore the complex inter-relationships between folk, popular, and ethnic cultures and the dominant (high) culture, in some ways confirming critic Harold Rosenberg's prediction of 1975:

> By a process seemingly irreversible, one-time cultural outsiders and undersiders are being lifted into visibility. This movement may well turn out to be one of the most radical art accomplishments of the twentieth century (Rosenberg, 1975:293).

Rosenberg was writing specifically about high culture's legitimation of folk art, using his ideologically loaded statement to preface his polemic against

---

1. This is obviously a much larger and intellectually richer issue than can be accommodated here. For more information about critical debates within the art history discipline see: Rees, A.L. and Borzello, F. (eds.) *The New Art History* London: Camden Press 1986; Preziosi, D. *Rethinking Art History: Meditations on a Coy Science* New Haven and London: Yale University Press (1989); Cheetham, M. Holly, M-A and Moxey, K. (eds.) *The Shape of Art History* Cambridge, New York: Cambridge University Press (1997).

members of Art & Language, the radical Anglo-American conceptual art group, who had questioned the primacy of the art object. Despite the truth of Rosenberg's claims, his inadequate understanding of the class-bound nature of art history imbued his prophecy with a more general encompassing emphasis, one predicated upon the omnipotence of high culture. The complicated trajectories of modernist art movements, particularly their peripatetic engagement of love/hate relationships with popular culture, also undermined his arguments about the importance of this radical intervention in the continuance of the cultural status quo. Like Rosenberg, many art historians writing about the relationships between high art, popular, folk, and ethnic cultures have appropriated and valorized the work of their outsider/undersider artists without recognizing the power relationships reproduced in the trafficking process. In their quest to enrich cultural history in general, these curators have often ignored the powerful ideologies they are reproducing in their texts. In this way, appropriation and trafficking confirm certain benefits for the dominant culture at the center at the expense, usually, of the subordinate culture(s) at the margins. Ignoring postmodern and postcolonial critiques of this process, these writers have tended to accommodate popular culture's relation to high art in ways that further legitimize the dominant culture's hegemony over its subordinates.

The chapters that follow discuss cartoon and comic examples that are formally, thematically, and historically consistent. They constitute a cultural type or genre, one that allows for and, in fact, presumes a high degree of differentiation. Without disturbing the cohesiveness of the primary genre, I argue that there are many sub-genres within this larger corpus. For example, art cartoons that satirize modern and postmodern paintings are somewhat different from those that satirize modernist sculpture or performance art, but, in most respects, they are consistent with the model. I show that examples within the genre contain forms of inter-culture criticism that contest, resist or encourage accommodation to the hegemonic processes of the dominant cultures.

Many writers within the orbit of the Frankfurt School argued that mass culture's appropriation of the forms of high culture results in the production of *ersatz* or *kitsch* cultures (Greenberg, 1939). Dwight Macdonald argued that popular culture was not really a culture at all, that instead, it functioned "as a parody of highcult" (MacDonald, 1963:3). Thomas Crow (1996) argued that the modernist avant-garde artists' appropriation of popular forms permits them to engage in a form of advanced research and development, allowing them to serve "as a kind of research and development arm of the culture industry." (Crow, 1996:35) Crow's arguments are provocative and richly articulated. But comparing his model in political-economic terms with the expropriation of Third World resources by First World capitalists does warrant pause for reflection and poses the question: how progressive is this reproduction of cultural hegemony?

The appropriative tendencies of the dominant culture have always been in evidence. The recognition of the politics involved in trans-cultural appropriations, however, is more recent, stemming from criticisms of cubism's appropriation of African sculpture, Pop Art's use of comic art, the quoting of African rhythms by Paul Simon, Steve Reich and other musicians in the late 1970s, and the elevation of subway art graffiti to the high cultural domain in the 1980s, through to the present. Popular culture researchers now acknowledge the trafficking between marginal, folk, indigenous, popular and elite cultures, the sub-cultures within each category, and borrowing or appropriating what it needs from the other. The ideological and economic benefits of such traffic—who wins and who loses in the transactions—are still open to debate, and some examples of cultural appropriation are entering courtrooms as lawsuits.

In this chapter, my discussion will focus upon three exhibitions that explored some of the transactions between high and low and the political questions associated with appropriation and inter-culture criticism. The first discussion will concern a 1973 exhibition revealingly titled *A Child of Six Could Do It,* curated for the Tate Gallery in London by George Melley and J.R. Glaves-Smith. This will be followed by a discussion of *The Comic Art Show*, curated in 1983 for the downtown Whitney Museum by Sheena Wagstaff and John Carlin, and the massive *High and Low: Modern Art and Popular Culture*, curated in 1990 by Kirk Varnadoe and Adam Gopnik for the Museum of Modern Art. I will follow this with a close reading of a cartoon by New Yorker cartoonist Ed Koren that satirizes the elevation of subway graffiti art into the high culture domain.

A Child of Six Could Do It was the first major gallery exhibition to show cartoon parodies and graphic satires of art. The exhibit contained over eighty cartoons representing an extensive range of parodies and graphic satires of modernist art. A catalogue accompanying the exhibit reproduced illustrations of many of the works, framed by two essays, an introduction and a post-script by the curators. "Jokes About Modern Art," George Melley's introductory essay reflected both the strengths and weaknesses of the exhibition as a whole.

This writer attempted to reveal the satirizing of art as a general phenomenon with roots in the public reaction to radical developments within modernist culture. Melley dismissed the political character of his subject, satisfying himself with a broad overview of cartoon responses to the various modernist movements. His essay neglected the biographies and possible intentions of his cartoonists to finally privilege the official culture of the museum and the sustaining ideologies of modernism. The final paragraph of his essay suggested to the viewer that after experiencing the cartoon exhibit, he/she should visit the Tate Gallery's modern collection to view the paintings which "aroused so much scorn and laughter" but to remember that it is "the painters, and not those who tried to make them seem such crooks or fools, who have the last laugh." (Melley, 1974:14)

Melley's discussion of the cartoons is framed by a reductive psychologistic paradigm derived from Sigmund Freud's theory of the comic. "These cartoonists," he suggests, "have left behind them a humorous graph of the impact of various phases of modern art." (9) They have revealed the general public response to avant-garde art and "by doing so they helped that same public economize on unconscious thought." Melley engaged Freud's theory of joke apperception to explain the public responses to the cartoons, but the abstract and generalizing character of Freud's theory has limited value as soon as one examines the cartoons themselves, which as Melley himself noted, are extraordinarily diverse both "in form and intention." However, as soon as one includes the context of both production and reception the limitations of Freud's "saving on psychic energy" hypothesis become apparent. Melley suggested, with little justification, that as the strategies of the avant-garde become more familiar and the 'shock of the new' is no longer a shock, nor new, the incidence of cartoon parodies and satires will subsequently diminish.

For both curators, the cartoons exist as apolitical representations of the shock value of modernism. Melley focuses upon the avant-garde artists perceived attack on basic standards of morality. He lists a number of important modernist works that elicited strong public responses: Edouard Manet's *Olympia* (1863), Henri Matisse's *La Danse* (1909), Marcel Duchamp's *Nude Descending a Staircase* (1912), Jacob Epstein's sculptures *The Rock Drill* (1913), Salvador Dali's *The Persistence of Memory* (1931), and Henry Moore's sculptures with holes from the 1950s. He concludes that the origin of the extraordinary cartoon production responding to these works is sexual. The artists whose work has become the subject of satirical response have somehow transgressed a moral code that aroused frustration and anxiety. Manet's famous representations of nudes in his paintings *Olympia* (1863) and *Dejeuner sur l'herbe* (1863) aroused anxiety because the context of a nude in a contemporary setting "prevented the spectator from distancing or concealing his feelings." (11) Similarly, Duchamp's *Nude Descending a Staircase* (1912) is said to have caused difficulty because it was "unrecognizable as a nude" and thus "failed to fulfill the promise of its provocative title." (12) He then proceeded to list a number of sexual metaphors in the work of Picasso, Dali, Epstein, and Moore, suggesting that he was "somewhat struck" by their confirmation of Freud's theories on the meaning of jokes; "that much of the tension they help release is of a sexual origin." (13)

Beyond the strictly instrumentalist recapitulation of the Freudian humour paradigm, Melley did offer a few important observations of the satirical material he was examining. He confessed surprise at the 'irrational violence' to which many modernist works were subjected by the hands and eyes of the cartoonists of the popular press and he was shocked by the correlation between works of modern art, social conflicts, and the ravages of war. He cites many examples of cartoons that illustrate formal similarities between the impressionistic techniques of Auguste Rodin's artful severing of limbs and body mutilations as a consequence of war. Cartoons in the exhibition clearly demonstrated the equation between the modeling of separate body parts and mutilation. Melley suggested that many of the cartoons (predominately from Punch) illustrating the relationship between modern art and war are assisted by title substitutions that provide a comic incongruity for the viewer/reader. In one cartoon framed abstract or quasi-abstract paintings resembling Cubist, Futurist or Vorticist paintings find no buyers in the gallery sale until an enterprising salesperson changes the conventional titles for those illustrative of the Great War, such as *In the Wake of the Huns* and *Ruin of a Window in Rheims Cathedral*. An excellent example of this substitution method is provided in Frank Reynolds's Punch cartoon (fig. 7), a cartoon that shows a portly mother and her army officer son (a double for English comedian John Cleese) at an exhibition of Nevinson's Vorticist paintings of *Life at the Front*. The mother asks the son, whom we are informed in the caption "has seen terrible things in battle," if the paintings are an adequate representation of life at the front. His reply: "Thank Heaven no, mother!" a protest suggesting that modernist art is much worse!

Melley's reading of the cartoons touches but does not elaborate upon two important features of the graphic satires, their diversity and stereotypicality. His

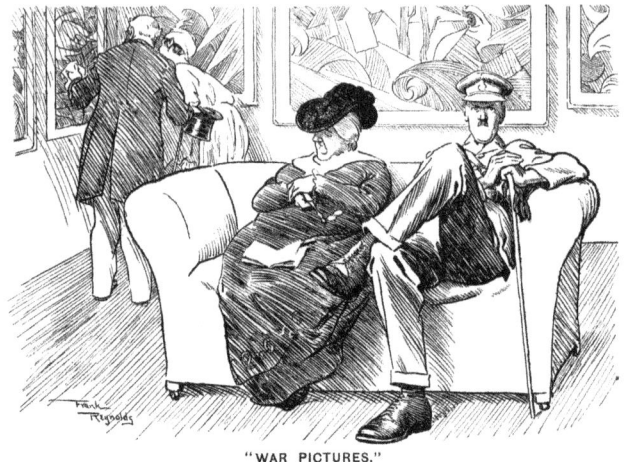

Figure 7: Frank Reynolds *War Pictures* Punch July 31st 1918 © Punch Cartoon Library, Top Foto

resigned statement, "inevitably we have felt forced to include some examples of the least inventive, most repetitive line of thought, that modern art must be the work of drunks, children, madmen or monkeys, that the pictures must be upside down, that primitives or cavemen must be responsible" does not do justice to the complex political meanings inscribed in these ubiquitous images. Had Melley asked himself the simple question of why these images exist in such conformity, in such numbers and as a continuing phenomenon, he would have been forced to admit a *political dimension* into his discussion and not simply assume that it was modernism's natural right to be pilloried by the disrespectful philistines in our midst. Ironically, he did ask these questions of communist and fascist societies, noting, "The totalitarian systems' dislike of modernism yielded comparatively little material." (13) He suggests that the few extant Russian examples emphasize that "bourgeois American formalists paint their pictures with their feet (are) scarcely devastating attacks." This seems a convincing argument if we consider the dominant social realist style in the USSR promoted officially by the culture minister Zhdanov in 1930. There are many cartoons in Soviet and other Eastern European magazines that incisively satirize the social realism of the nineteen thirties, forties, and fifties as well as subsequent styles of Soviet art since the late 1960s. Graphic satires, parodies, and pastiches of high (or official), art are not exclusive to western modernism.

Author Melley's lack of research into the early period of fascism in Germany and Italy of the 1930s does not substantiate the position that "Hitler's rabid loathing of modernism" produced few satirical attacks on modernist art. An examination of German and Italian cartoons from this period would perhaps corroborate Melley's presumption that the number of examples was small. This could be attributed as much to the fact that the Nazis already had at their disposal, and under new laws, very effective legal means of discriminating against and rejecting modernist art. The political ideology of fascism did not need confirmation of the moral degeneration of modernism from the artists of the popular press to reinforce its political and cultural agenda.[2]

"Cartoons and the Popular Image of Modern Art," Glaves-Smith's essay contribution to the catalogue, suffers from a similar myopia to political economy. In contrast to Melley, however, he does introduce some important issues with respect to negotiated meanings in the public responses to the cartoons. He suggests that the cartoonists are restricted in their satirical activities by the limits of what the public understands. "If the jokes have to be explained, their impact is lost." (97) This simple assertion allows him to reflect upon the context within which the cartoons are produced and consumed. As the cartoons respond to the known or familiar, they can become an index of the level of understanding of the forms of vanguard art among the readers of a particular newspaper, magazine or journal. The French sociologist Pierre Bourdieu describes this understanding quotient as 'cultural literacy' or competency. As competency markers, the cartoons are an index of cultural and social reception. Glaves-Smith argues "this need for instant recognition leads to the exploitation of stock situations." He suggests also that this familiarity allows cartoons to have an internal development that "need not bear much relation to what is going on in the world they purport to represent." As he says, this leads to the cartoon representations of "modern works unlike any created." (97) It is the very stereotypicality of the artworks that encourages these art cartoons to be interpreted both as forms of social criticism and as an index of resistance to the dominant culture. It is only from the position of the insider—the artist, art historian, curator or critic—that the art cartoons may appear to lack fidelity to the subject satirized. For a constituency of outsiders these cartoons evidence all or most of the attributes of the original. As will be noted in subsequent chapters, many of the cartoon art

---

2. See the following texts on fascist aesthetics: Hannah Arendt (ed) Walter Benjamin: *Illuminations: Essays and Reflections* (New York: 1968); Adorno, T., and Horkheimer, M., *Dialectic of the Enlightenment*, (1947); Adorno, T. "Wagner, Hitler and Nietzsche" Kenyon Review IX, I (1947); Sontag, S, *Under the Sign of Saturn* New York: (1980); Friedlander, S. *Reflections on Nazism, An Essay on Kitsch and Death* New York: (1982).

works are strikingly similar to the art works they satirize. Employing processes of dissimulation, reversal, textual substitution, and other forms of parodic/satiric meaning deformation and reformation, the cartoons reveal the features of the modernist avant-garde works that elicit public misunderstanding, estrangement, and alienation. Such features confirm the power and authority of the modernist work of art and its buttressing institutions. The significant difference is that they reproduce those attitudes for an audience that may have already confirmed what modern art means to them, not what it should or could mean. As a knowledgeable insider, Glaves-Smith can point to the inadequacies of the cartoon with respect to its model in the museum, but with less cultural capital at their disposal, the viewers can only recognize the difference between their understanding of art and that represented in the cartoon image. Glaves-Smith's arguments have a contrariness about them which evidence a modernist art historian's drive to come to terms with the existence of cartoon parodies and satires as forms of public criticism of the high flown pretensions of high art and his desire to place these in their proper place as images of contempt; symbolic examples of the ignorance of Philistines. This contrariness indicates a divergent class position with respect to avant-garde and modernist art represented in the cartoons themselves, as well as in the ideological beliefs held by the artists who produced them. To Glaves-Smith, the cartoons represent a certain provincialism or distance from the cultural center. In this respect, he is as guilty of othering as the cartoonists he criticizes. Their success as satirists is dependent upon the speed with which they respond to the avant-garde work of art, which, Glaves Smith suggests, is commensurate with the power of the image. He cites the best of The New Yorker's cartoons as being 'devastating satires.'

    The Whitney Museum's *Comic Art Show* also engaged some of the problems associated with the application of critical methodologies derived from art history and high culture to the examination of popular culture. The idea for this exhibition was extremely interesting, particularly when framed by the architecture of one of the major institutions of the dominant culture, the Whitney Museum, albeit the Downtown Branch. The exhibition's premise was to show the work of popular culture producers in the company of art works that influenced or were influenced by the work of high culture artists. For example, Pop artists Roy Lichtenstein and Andy Warhol were shown in the company of Chester Gould's *Dick Tracy* and E.C. comics' *Captain Marvel*. However, as several reviewers of the *Comic Art Show* noted, the discussion of the works in the catalogue tended to bypass cultural studies models, which could have provided both an ideological reading and discussion of the political significance of the works in the exhibition. Instead, the curators and essayists collapsed these differences to concentrate upon a formal discussion of the similarities between them. In his review of the exhibition David Deitcher argued:

> (The curators) have used a paradigm of excellence derived from a fine art tradition.

And further,

> (Their) tendency to see comics through the distorting lens of (modernist) aesthetics encouraged viewers to interpret the comic strips often-playful relation to visual codes, as a trace of modernist self-reflexivity. (1984:101)

Deitcher cited a number of examples of the problems such a mismatch can produce. For instance, the curator's discussion of the play on the mistaken identity of ink as coffee in Harvey Kurtzman's cartoon *Silver Lining* was said to resemble Magritte's painting *The Wind and the Song*. Not content with merely criticizing the *Comic Show*'s curators, Deitcher also took the *Village Voice* art critic Roberta Smith to task for following Wagstaff and Marshall's lead in aestheticizing the comic strips by reading them in purely formal terms, according to the Greenbergian modernist paradigm. In Smith's review of the exhibition, the characters in Frank King's comic strip *Gasoline Alley* (1931) are described as walking through Frank Stella's *Protractor* series of paintings. And Winsor McCay's *Little Sammy's Sneeze* (1905) constitutes an extraordinary "shattering of the picture plane." (103) Deitcher also cites an outrageous example of high cultural connoisseurship from Richard Marshall's catalogue essay. Of Cliff Sterrett's *Polly and her Pals* (1929) Marshall writes:

> The resultant rhythm (of this strip) gives 'Polly' an abstract harmony which perfectly syncopates the elements of the static comic strip into a masterly rendering of movement and music. (Sterrett's abstract comic strips bring him close to Kandinsky's Wagnerian "*gesamtkunstwerk*.")

The reviewer concluded his essay with the bold assertion that in the curators' desire to see comics as art they had actually 'transformed the comics into art.' Like Harold Rosenberg's description of the appropriation of folk art to the institutions of high culture and the elevation of subway art and graffiti to the galleries of Soho, the curators of *The Comic Art Show* have subsumed the history of comic strips into the history of art at the high cultural level. As a form of co-optation and absorption this erases or blurs the concrete ideological differences and antagonisms between the class cultures while at the same time reinforcing the dominant culture's hegemony over its subordinates. Deitcher sanguinely suggests that the urge "to transform comics into art and thereby isolate them from ideology is hardly limited to the work of these curators." (105)

In providing an exclusive rational for the appropriation of popular culture to the high culture domain that directly and indirectly privileges the institutions of the dominant culture, many curators, historians, researchers and collectors of popular culture have neglected the ideological reading(s) of the images and, by extension, the socio-political significance of satirical humour. In company with Harold Rosenberg's prophetic erasure of the cultural (and social) divisions between folk and high culture, these curators have provided further legitimation to the importance of high culture, its sustaining ideologies and justification for the construction of a parallel cultural paradigm that evidences all of the hierarchical, political-economic traits of its model. Beyond its stated egalitarian imperatives, this exhibition serves merely to reinforce the hegemony of the dominant culture. The powerful modernist ideologies sustained by the curatorial objectives of the Whitney Museum failed to erase the differences between high and low. They merely reinforced them.

Sponsored generously by AT&T, the glitzy exhibit *High and Low: Modern Art and Popular Culture* opened on October 6th, 1990 at New York's Museum of Modern Art. Curated by Kirk Varnadoe, curator of painting at MOMA, and Adam Gopnik, critic for the New Yorker, the exhibit remained on view until January 1991 and subsequently toured to the Art Institute of Chicago and the Museum of Contemporary Art in Los Angeles. *High and Low* contained over 250 drawings, studies, paintings, and sculptures produced by some 50 European and American artists spanning the modernist, late modernist, and postmodern periods with works by artists Jenny Holzer, Jeff Koons and Ashley Bikerton representing the most contemporary work in the exhibition.

The frontispiece for the massive (457-page) catalogue noted that the exhibition was conceived and produced collaboratively, with Varnadoe acting as the principle author of three sections of the exhibition: "Words," "Graffiti" and "Advertising" and Gopnik the sections: "Caricature," "Comics" and "Contemporary Reflections." While each section demonstrated that some extensive research had been undertaken in relating popular and mass culture imagery to high culture production, this exhibit, in company with the earlier ones at the Tate and Whitney, revealed that the curators had yet again privileged high culture's art at the expense of 'low,' reinforcing the simplistic thesis that mass culture, like so-called 'primitive art' before it, existed merely to satisfy the avariciousness of high culture's avant-gardes. In their introduction, Varnadoe and Gopnik casually dismissed dozens of authors and hundreds of texts that would have challenged their thesis and enriched understanding of the subjects:

> Although an enormous body of writing about 'mass culture', and the avant-garde already existed, this corpus seemed disproportionately weighted by the work of commissars and scholiasts. The pronouncements of theorists appeared all too frequently to be engaged, at best, in the skillful juggling of abstract concepts; and at worst, to imposing dogmatic narrow, and historically untenable (not to say untestable) categories on the complex realities of modern history. (Varnadoe and Gopnik 1990, 11).

The casual attitude of the curators toward their subjects encouraged a number of critical reviews. Douglas Crimp wrote: "Varnadoe and Gopnik summarily dismissed the entire range of serious thinking about their subject, from Frankfurt School mass culture and aesthetic theory and the cultural studies initiated during the 1960s at Birmingham, to disparate contemporary and postmodernist analyses." (Crimp 1995: 30) Throughout the catalogue very little emphasis was given to a reading of the mass culture sources of the examples of high art and the attention to the complex political economy involved in the business of cultural trafficking was negligible and as a result high culture invariably came out on top. As viewers of the exhibition we bear witness to the high culture appropriation of newspapers and magazines by the Cubists, the Dadaists and Surrealist montaging of the detritus of everyday life, newspaper advertisements, cheap mass produced commodities etc. a supremely unproblematized process similar to the appropriation of African, Melanesian and Asian art by Picasso, Braque and other early modernists. The show elevated Warhol's simulation of popular commodities, Oldenburg's hamburgers, Lichtenstein's enlarged and détourned comic strip exercises as exalted parodic exercises in commodity fetishism. Even the relative weighting of the popular works included in the exhibition, the size of their reproductions and placement in the overall scheme of the catalogue reproduced the inequity between high and low. Another reviewer noted: "In the layout of the exhibition, the certified geniuses of High Art (especially the Cubists and their heirs), are presented surrounded by their 'sources' like princelings attended by lackeys." (Bentley-Mays, 1990).

As comprehensive as the curators suggested the exhibit was, there were several notable absences among those artists who regularly used popular sources for political reasons, among them: the Russian Futurists and Productivists, the Berlin Dadaists, Raoul Hausmann, John Heartfield and closer to the present, political artists such as Barbara Kruger, Hans Haacke, Adrian Piper and Martha Rosler among others. Including these artists would have disturbed the curators' limited thesis, for most of these artists employ the same strategies as the popular media to get their messages across. Their work is not premised on the notion that art should transcend material reality but rather, that it should engage with social reality in an operative and politically efficacious fashion.

The Exhibition companion catalogue *Modern Art and Popular Culture: Readings in High and Low*, an anthology of art historical essays on topics relating to the exhibit, is a far richer document than the principal catalogue authored by Varnadoe and Gopnik. This book contains some informative essays that discuss some of the issues reflected in various sections of the exhibit, establishing the social historical links between modernism, popular culture influences, and at crucial times, drawing fine distinctions between the hierarchical and class-based nature of cultural production and reproduction. Even in this context however, the relationships between high art and popular culture are discussed, for the most part, according to the paradigms provided by conventional art history. The reductive formalist reading of the subjects at hand reproduced the flagrantly apolitical, atheoretical agendas of the exhibition's curators. One searches in vain throughout these pages for any discussion of the political characteristics of the trafficking between high and low, the relationships between ideology and modern culture, the politics of irony, parody or satire, capitalism, class and the subordinate cultures' resistance to the dominant culture.

Graffiti as High Art: A Clip from the Power Index:

Riff revolutionized graffiti with the first top-to-bottom. It was beautiful. It was a half-car wide, yellow 'Riff' with red, bloody drips coming down. And it had cracks painted on it. It took everybody out all over New York, everybody was talking about it. I first saw it when I was on my way to court with my mother; I was jumping up and down on the train. She didn't understand. (Castleman, 1982:57)

The cartoon illustrated (fig. 8), drawn in Ed Koren's familiar straw line style, shows an art guide or docent, possibly an art instructor or critic displaying his knowledge and critical talents to a polyglot group of students of contemporary

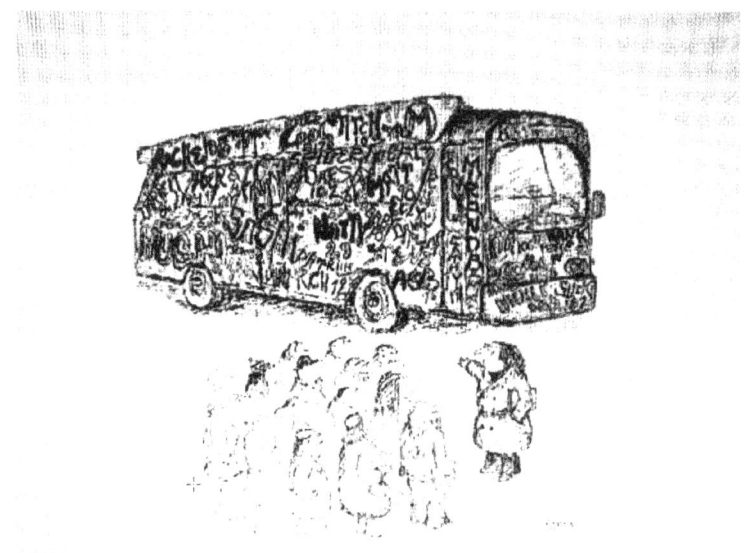

"Note the densely distributed, yet perfectly balanced, relationship between the expressive line and the organic whole—how unity of surface is achieved by overtly lyrical variations of scale, texture, and color, giving three-dimensional form a spontaneous, plastically graphic definition."

Figure 8: Ed Koren The New Yorker January 20, 1973 © Conde Nast

art. The object of instruction is a transit bus marked up (tagged), in a similar manner to New York City subway cars during the 1980s and 1990s. The names on the bus: Rachel 88, Slick 162, Rich 72, Julie Cool, and Titch 103, are graffiti artist tags, or as the artists themselves call them, writers' 'pen names.' The numbers are suggestive of residential districts and street numbers from Manhattan, the Bronx, Brooklyn and other greater New York City boroughs. The names speak of geography, community and place, reinforcing a specific sense of social and individual identity. They also provide a defensive, exclusive form of anonymity to the general public and importantly, the law.

There are several ways of navigating the meanings surrounding this cartoon, that is, several readings that we may undertake to engage our themes of culture, class, ideology and relations of power. Each reading represents conflicting interpretations and at times, extremely divergent ideological positions with respect to this cartoon, graphic satire in general, parody, the art institution—in all its complexity—and last but not least, crime. Koren's cartoon employs several ironies that engage the reader in thinking about the legitimacy of the competing claims of the art institution with respect to the public reception of a work of art. The first irony is invoked through the cartoon caption, a translation of the museum guide's speech to his students.

> Note the densely distributed, yet perfectly balanced relationship between the expressive line and the organic whole—how unity of surface is achieved by overtly lyrical variations of scale, texture and colour, giving three-dimensional form a spontaneous graphic definition.

The parodic language used to describe the bus—borrowed conceivably, from a lecture or essay[3] on Abstract Expressionist art—functions in this context as a parody of modernist discourse and would have been recognized as such by many New Yorker readers. The formalist reading of the "expressive line and the organic whole" provides a coded vehicle for the recognition of the second irony, the *objet trouvé* status of the bus. A third irony is evident in the conflation of art/crime and the institutional repercussions of this with respect to critical, and by extension, art historical discourse. Finally, the cartoon questions the open category of the work of art and the nominating power of the critic to assign it aesthetic value. Koren's cartoon provides a site for the recognition of high culture's appropriation of graffiti, and becomes therefore, a potential ground for its critique. The cartoonist is representing a process that was actually beginning to occur at this time, the valorization of the work of a few of the authors of graffiti and their subsequent elevation to the realm of high culture. Michael Basquiat, who produced his work under the pen name SAMO, is the prime example, as is more recently the British artist Banksy who chooses to remain anonymous.

What is the meaning of this high culture legitimation of the illegal, anti-social activities of youthful members of a sub-culture whose creative activities consist of merely vandalizing public transport vehicles with a spray can or felt tip pen? This is not an easy question to answer. From the position of the high culture insider or vanguard critic, one who enjoys the prospect of a constantly evolving, aesthetically inventive and politically progressive avant-garde, the tagging of a subway car may represent a tactical and strategic advance on the work of

---

3. It is interesting to put this in the context of Koren's position as a Professor of Art History at Brown University. A question addressed to the artist (correspondence, December, 1992) "is this text borrowed from a famous modernist critic, or is it your own?" elicited the following reply: "In making up the caption, I made liberal use of modernist critical language with which I was familiar and which afforded the requisite fatuity of the drawing" (reply, January 1993).

the historical avant-gardes, represented for example, in Dada and Surrealism, the neo-primitive work of Picasso and other early modernists, as well as the *détournements* of the neo-avant-gardes, the wall slogans, graffiti and détourned posters of the Nouveaux Realistes, Lettristes and International Situationists of the late 1950s and 1960s. These movements were actually discussed as formal, art historical prototypes for the work of the New York subway writers. Critics believing in the continued efficacy of a progressive avant-garde cultural practice viewed the work of the graffiti artist as a step toward praxis—the sublation of the institution art into life (Burger, P. 1984), and *vice versa*. This type of thinking characterized the positions of a number of writers on graffiti, including Greil Marcus (1989), who argued that graffiti, the music and behavior of Johnny Rotten and the Sex Pistols and other punk rock groups, was a direct continuation of the anti-bourgeois strategies of the Dadaists, the Lettristes and Situationists, providing a *topos* which finds its ultimate millennialist incarnation in the figure of the anti-Christ. Other writers argued that the graffiti writers were not following closely the nominating and behavioral strategies of the historical avant-gardes. They conceded that while in some instances, a case could be made for this; that is, in common with a few generally acknowledged strategies of the avant-garde, the graffiti artists were actively getting their name up and out, aggrandizing their persona, displaying their daring and commitment to the graffiti project to other members of their sub-culture group.

To other critics, the late Robert Hughes for example, the writers' class backgrounds, untrained and undisciplined work habits, their lifestyles, as well as their general anti-social and illegal behavior, mitigated against the conclusion that they were artists working within an authentic, historically conventional avant-garde sub-culture. Critics such as Hughes had difficulty accepting the arguments provided by avant-garde sympathizers: that the bus graffiti represents an attack on modernism, as well as the institutionality of art practice, and that, indeed, these attacks are actually closer to an authentic avant-garde project than those which pass for the contemporary avant-garde, or neo-avant-garde itself. Several features of graffiti militate against this conclusion. These include the often working class ethnic origins of the writers, coupled with their lack of education and professional training—low "cultural competency" in Bourdieu's use of this term—the fact that their work exists outside the museum and other institutional support structures and finally the framing of the graffiti artists' work as illegal and willfully destructive by the Metropolitan Transit Authority, the police and the general public.

The behavior of the graffiti artists is both like and unlike, that of the historical, and neo-avant-gardes. On one level, the critical language associated with the discourse of tagging is very different from the critical discourse of neo-expressionism. It can be made to *appear* the same in various ways by the writers/artists themselves, their critics, gallery dealers, art historians and other agents of cultural legitimation, as indeed it was during its period of co-optation by the postmodern museo-critical establishment. In the beginning stages of its legitimation, however, the essential differences between institutionalized modernist art and the conventional avant-garde projects, restricted the entry of graffiti into the mainstream art establishment, that is until the 1992 Whitney Museum retrospective of the work of the late Michael Basquiat.[4] For the first few years of the 1980s, the identity, the intentions and goals of the graffiti artists seemed to be far apart from those of artists working within high culture's sub-cultural (neo) avant-gardes.

In his book on the sub-culture of the subway writers, social anthropologist Craig Castleman gives a useful description of the in-group language of the graffiti artists. According to Castleman, tagging, unlike other forms of graffiti writing, does not receive the same in-group accolades as the painting of a whole subway car or train by a single artist or group of collaborators but rather, it is a proverbial 'step to the top.' Discussed in formal terms that reproduce the coded discourses of legitimate art history, the tag parallels within the art institution are the sketches, roughs, and other preliminary drawings by a developing master. They also represent the preliminary subordinate work of the master's apprentice. In contrast to these tag/sketch works, the painting of a whole car demands greater risk and is therefore only attempted by those who have in a real sense either made it, have mastered their art or wish to make it by producing a master work that "will take out all of New York!" In this way the hierarchy within the world of the graffiti writers seemed to resemble and even parody, that of the art world itself.

In his cartoon, Ed Koren has used the nominal tag form rather than the master works—the painting of whole trains—as the primary work of the graffiti artist's trade. In so doing he has reproduced its middle-class stereotype as anti-social or vandalistic act. This is not the quintessential abstract "all-over painting" proscribed by modernist critics Harold Rosenberg and Clement Greenberg, a 'top to bottom' riff with its drips, and splatters, *a la* neo-expressionism. The bus is received/perceived as a work of art only by virtue of

---

4. Basquiat died a sudden death at the age of 23 reportedly as a result of his excessive lifestyle.

the institutional context within which it is placed. In company with Marcel Duchamp's readymade Urinal (1917) signed/tagged R. Mutt, one of the key works from the historical avant-garde that confirmed the nominating power of the artist, the bus becomes an *objet d'art* worthy of critical veneration, although in this case it is the critic and of course Koren himself (as parodist/ satirist of the process), acting out the multiple roles of the various agents and agencies of cultural legitimation. The ironic and parodic elements within the cartoon provide the vehicle for the artist's satirical intentions. I will have more to offer later about this double coded form.

In Koren's cartoon, the writers/artists become targets of a colonizing process. They are anonymous but for their coded tags that act as signatures within the group. From without, the tags lack direct referents that could attach them definitively to the history, theory and practice of art. This attachment can only be constructed artificially by projecting the tagged bus into the sculpture court of any large, and we would assume, progressive museum such as the Museum of Modern Art and framing it as a typical object for aesthetic veneration. Captioned with a modernist text that parodies the critical discourse of high culture results in the ironic collision between high and low. The recognition of the incongruity/dissimulation of this collision provides the humor. It can also be argued, however, that the character of this incongruity is tendentious, reproducing the very conditions at which it is aimed.

Koren's act of ironic substitution is similar to many other art cartoons, for example, those which make the crypto-graphic language of cave men subjects of contemporary aesthetic discourse. Like these examples, Koren's graffiti cartoon can be read as a sign of historical, cultural and perhaps ethnic superiority. In the semiotic complexity of his cartoon, we can witness the struggle over the meanings of modern art. The claim can be strengthened. We witness the contestation over the power of the signs of modernism. This multi-inflected and conflicted sign ask the questions— "who gets to assign legitimacy to the work of art?"— "who names?" "who assigns meaning, legitimizes and valorizes meaning?" "How is it that this vandalized bus can be entered into the hallowed cultural realm of high art?" And if the bus is indeed a work of art, "what does this say about the professional role and training, of the artist, his/her work, the institutions of art, the museum, the journal, criticism…art history?"

To the culturally competent—high art literate, and informed—readership of The New Yorker, Koren's parody of the received (institutionalized) language of formalist criticism, reveals its inadequacy as a language to describe and interpret this example of spontaneous vandalism. In parodying the high culture text Koren is revealing his own ambivalence, if not his indignation and rejection of the appropriation of graffiti as art and its subsequent valorization at the high culture realm. The mid-culture cartoonist[5] is moved to satirize a process that was well under way by 1973, the erasing of the borders, the collapsing of relatively distinct cultures into one another, not because he wishes to acknowledge directly the political nature of this process, contestation of the hegemonic order, but because, to an artist sharing the liberal ideologies of the majority of his readers,[6] it seemed an absurdity, an offence, to permit examples of willful damage to become expensive objects of museological interpretation and veneration. In correspondence with the author, Ed Koren offered the following statement with regard to the elevation of graffiti to the high culture realm:

> Clearly, I was perplexed. And I was intrigued how easily it was given this status, and surrounded by the validation of those who were able to construct a critical importance for what I thought of as a rather facile skill, some of it, (he later qualified), quite good" (Correspondence, January 1993).

Koren's cartoon disavowal is a symbolic form of denial, a form of resistance aimed at debunking high-culture's willingness to subsume for profit anything into its domain. His graphic satire would probably have found a very sympathetic response from many readers of The New Yorker, who, as (mostly) righteous and law-abiding members of the *arte liberale*, would have been almost unanimous in their rejection of graffiti as a form of art, even less to the graffiti writers' claims and others of them, to be legitimate artists.

---

5. Koren's biography is very interesting. His training for the most part was similar to many fine artists (see chapter 3). Within the institutions of cartooning he worked at the highest level, receiving national and international awards for his work, exhibiting and publishing extensively.

6. Dwight Macdonald, a former contributor to The New Yorker has suggested that the magazine's readership was composed primarily of those from the middle class. In his terms, The New Yorker is a mid-culture (mid-cult) magazine, although this was not always the case and it cannot easily be descibed as such now.

CHAPTER 3

Humour, Pleasure, Pain, and Power

Humour: a bastard kind of pleasure.
(Thomas Wright, 1875)

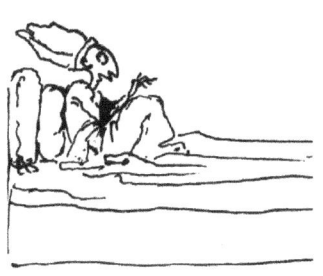

Figure 9: Bernini, G.L. *Caricature of Pope Innocent XI* 1676-80. Public Domain.

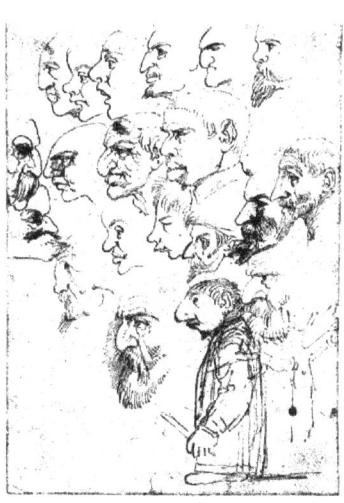

Figure 10: Carracci, A. *Sheet of Caricature Heads* 1594. Public Domain.

The pleasure and pain of caricatures and cartoons—the dual character of humour itself—has been tacitly acknowledged by many writers on the subject, from Aristotle, Baudelaire, Champfleury, Bergson and Freud, to those working in the present.[1] Until the 1960s however, there was very little research activity to verify any premises about the sociological character of humor. Most of the

---

[1]. See Powell, Chris, and Paton, George E.C. (1988). In their afterword, the editors note that their examination of two major sociological journals up to 1965 turned up a total of only five articles on the sociology of humor.

research activity occurred, somewhat predictably after Freud's seminal work, within the field of psychology. The result of this has been that the social conditions for the experience of humor and its understanding in terms of class politics have become somewhat shrouded in the discourses of psychology. And these subject centered discourses have reinforced various reductive paradigms that subordinate, or deny altogether, the socio-political agency and ideological complexity of various types of humor. Fortunately, during the past decade social scientists and cultural studies researchers have begun to recognize the importance of multi-disciplinary approaches to humor-based research that can accommodate its social relevance in political terms.

Most theories of humor drawn from the work of Sigmund Freud and other early researchers, tend to explicitly or implicitly endorse either of two models: one that describes humor as a product of conflict and the other as a form of social control. The first model posits humor as an individual or group reflex action aimed at a display of power; the second articulates humor as a mechanism for individual and social control. The conflict model is represented and performed by various means including satire, parody, irony, caricature, cartoons and burlesque. Discussing the social characteristics of these forms of humor, R. M. Stephenson, a researcher writing in the 1950s, suggested that humor may be viewed as either a way of concealing overtly aggressive behaviour, or as a means of accommodating differing points of view held by various individuals or groups. "The particular adaptability of humor as a conflict weapon lies in the fact that humor may conceal malice and allow expression of aggression without the consequences of other overt behavior."

"As a means of social control," he continued:

> humor may (also) function to express approval or disapproval of social form and action, express common group sentiments, *develop and perpetuate stereotypes, relieve awkward or tense situations and express collective, sub-rosa approbation of action not explicitly approved.* Humor as expressed in the controlled laugh or smile may serve as a means of communication, signaling the intent of the communicating parties. (Stephenson, 1951: 569-70), Emphasis added.

Stephenson's articulation of humor's complexity matches many contemporary views suggesting that humor can perform several social (and political) functions simultaneously. In their humor research, Dines, Levy and Smith (1988) Barker (1981) and Husband (1988), have reinforced the complex ideological and class correlations between humor, ethnicity and sexuality, without building an inflexible and unidimensional structure for their explication. In their work, humor can be recognized as a register of insubordination and resistance, as in a situation where overt or covert conflict between groups and individuals is present. It may also function, sometimes simultaneously, as a form of ironic complicity and a sign of accommodation to a display of power.

Various forms of graphic (scripto-visual) humor: caricatures, cartoons, comic strips, graffiti and latrinalia, participate in the complex processes associated with social conflict and control, although they may do this less directly than performative modes of address such as joke telling, stand-up comedy and burlesque. In this chapter I will explore relationships between visual humor, power and politics with a specific emphasis on the dialogical—pleasure/pain—aspects of caricature. This will be followed in the next chapter by a more detailed theoretical discussion of visual irony, parody and satire as these pertain to the production and reception of cartoon and comic critiques of high art. Together, these chapters provide the background for subsequent discussions of graphic satires of modern art and the work of specific modernist artists.

The birth of graphic art as a basis for political satire can be traced to the origin of caricature in the early Italian Renaissance. Thomas Wright, author of one of the earliest English language studies of visual and literary humor, *The History of Caricature and the Grotesque in Literature and Art* (1875), called caricature "a bastard kind of pleasure." Wright's trope is particularly interesting because in one short phrase it alludes to the complex characteristics of caricature: that it is somehow bastard—illegitimate—but it is this very illegitimacy which provides the caricaturist, his/her readers (and occasionally the caricatured subject), with pleasure. This complex and contradictory notion may underlie other forms of graphic art, and perhaps provide the genesis and meaning of humor itself. The "bastard pleasure" alludes to what many writers acknowledge to be the dialogical processes (Bahktin, 1981) involved in humorous communication; that is, the conflation of pleasure and pain into the painful/pleasure—of humor. The "bastard" in the phrase refers to caricature's existence as the illegitimate offspring of more conventional drawing practices that do not seek to pillory their subject. Wright's statement combines two contradictory notions that encourage us to consider humor as a sado-masochistic operation which has moral and political consequences. The trope also provides some insight into the nefarious intentions of the producers of graphic humor and implies the anti-social consequences of an overly zealous use of their art. Wright's bold statement secures a useful platform from which to articulate the power relations sustained or enacted through the uses and abuses of humor; social transactions where power is exercised, control contested, subverted and/or accommodated.

Wright's statement on humor's ambiguous pleasure shares company with many others. In his famous essay on the essence of laughter published in 1855, Baudelaire wrote, "The wise man laughs only with fear and trembling" (Baudelaire, 1972:141). And writing a century later, Ernst Kris provides an illuminating anecdote about caricature that underscores the psycho-social complexity of visual humor. He quotes the German painter Max Liebermann who purportedly said of one of his contemporaries: "A face like his I can piss into snow" (Kris, 1952:192). Kris discusses how Liebermann's statement marries a basic scatological motif, the so-called "material bodily principle" from the grotesque tradition to the reductive and exaggerated process of drawing a portrait caricature. By emphasizing this scatological motif however, Kris has shifted caricature from other genres of political protest (slurs, oaths, insults, scurrilous attacks, indignities and broadsides), thereby incarcerating caricature in the reductive discourse of Freudian psychology. Throughout his *Psychoanalytic Explorations into Art* (1952), Kris consistently removes the humorous visual insult from its social and political context—as a representation of both the condition for and relations of power—thereby reinforcing the mechanistic paradigms for humor established by his intellectual mentors Henri Bergson and Sigmund Freud.

The English social anthropologist Mary Douglas has done much to elucidate the intellectual parallelism between Bergson and Freud's writings on humor.[2] She does not however, discuss their theories in the context of class politics, a task which has been undertaken, in this chapter and the book as a whole. Douglas argues that Freud and Bergson's respective texts on humor (1911, 1922) can be said to represent the end of an intellectual tradition—post-enlightenment romanticism—and the beginning of a new era dominated by the sustaining ideologies of techno/scientific rationalism and progressive modernity. For Bergson and before him, Champfleury and Baudelaire, the essence of human nature was recognized in spontaneity and freedom. Bergson argued that laughter reinforces these human essences every time individuals act or behave rigidly and against their true nature. In other words, he understood humor as a symbolic denial of the increasing mechanization of modern society and the alienation of humankind from nature. From this premise, Bergson argued, humor demonstrates the superiority of nature to culture, intuition to logic, and by implication, the organ-

---

[2]. See Douglas. M. "The Social Control of Cognition: Some Factors in Joke Perception" Man 3:3: 361-376 (1968).

ic life force (élan vital) to the mechanistic motors of modernity. Bergson likens humor to a vital and spontaneous force that attacks a rigid mechanical entity: "Humor consists in perceiving something mechanical encrusted on something living" (Bergson, 1911:37). This position is implicitly romantic; a moralistic (Rousseauian) soft-primitivism common to many of his contemporaries, who were beginning to criticize what they perceived to be the anti-human characteristics of industrial development and capitalist exploitation. According to Douglas, Bergson's metaphoric binarism encouraged him to articulate humor in ethical, moral and theological terms, but it also opened the door for investigating, albeit in a somewhat limited fashion, humor's politics. But the social effects of humor are viewed simply, as good overcoming evil. Something bad, evil, mechanistic, "encrusted"—the result of scientific rationalism—is attacked by something pure, spontaneous, instinctive and vital.[3] Douglas argues that there is no sense in Bergson of a "transacted or negotiated meaning" (Douglas, 1968:364), which can be taken to mean, any meaning that is socially constructed, open to elaboration, question and denial; one that can either evidence, or elicit, social and political consequences. Humor may not always be perceived as a consequence of morality and there may not always be an ethical or moral issue at stake in the humor transaction. And if there is, as Douglas insists, it may not always operate in this way (364). Bergson's approach to humor does not encourage the wide variety investigation of social transactions that occur in humorous communication and the complex opportunities for interpretation this may occasion. His humor theory does not encourage an understanding of other complex forms of humor such as wit, parody or irony where "two forms of life are confronted without any moral judgment being passed in either." Bergson's thesis, Douglas continues, does not allow for a neutral, detached, impassive and apolitical humor. She concludes that the recognition of "something encrusted on something living" (364), may not be a situation which necessarily lends itself to a humorous response. Bergson's description of the processes of humor may reveal more about his antipathy toward the processes of modernization and his subsequent romanticized nostalgia for a lost utopia, than his understanding of either the sociology or psychopathology of humor.

The value of Bergson's thesis, however, one that Douglas downplays in her quest to promote the intellectual parallelism between his work and Freud's, is that Bergson located humor firmly within a context in which political judg-

---

3. This could be compared to the reductive sociology of criminality developed by Scipio Sighele (1891), and the theories of mob psychology developed by Gustave Le Bon (1895). See Park (1972) and Nye (1975).

ments and power relations were being transacted, negotiated and transcribed. Whatever shortcomings his theories had in psychological terms; Bergson defined a space within which the political function of humor can be recognized for what it is—an index of power. And although his investigation of the social meanings of humor anticipated many of Freud's, there is one essential difference. Where Bergson attempted to place humor within a social context, Freud tended to subordinate the social to the primacy of the individual subject, thereby inaugurating a psycho-social and subjective bias in the research of humor that has continued to the present day.

Many writers have acknowledged that the basis of Freud's theory of humor is a form of psychic economism. This conceptual framework encouraged him to hypothesize a form of time management that constituted a form of "psychical economy of mind." In Freud's theory we recognize his famous triumvirate of the id, ego and super-ego struggling against one another to impose meaning on the world and maintain some form of psychological equilibrium for the subject. Humor acts as a kind of grease or lubricant for the efficient working of the mind; "a joke causes a response which inhibits the control system (alter ego) or places it in a kind of suspension thus giving the monitoring system (the ego) a holiday" (Douglas, 1968:364). As the ego expends considerable energy in a constant effort to maintain homeostatic equilibrium, there is "a saving in psychic (energy) expenditure" (365). With the suspension, or transcendence of the ego, the libido or primary process gains control which enables pleasure to be experienced. For Freud this assumed the status of a formula.

> The pleasure of wit originates from an economy of expenditure in thought and that of humor in an economy of expenditure in emotion. (Kris, 1952: 204).

If Bergson located his theory of humor within a model of society; Freud found his within a model of the individual subject. Both employed similar tropes relating to the exercise of power in order to describe the humor transaction. The essence of humor is that something organized and stable, a rational system, is overtaken for a time by something which is spontaneous and vital—in Bergson's case, the élan vital and for Freud, the energetic (libidinous) *id*. As Douglas observes in her essay, the "common denominator seems to be that humor is an attack on control" (1968:365). This emphasis on control is an attractive conclusion that presumes and allows the political dimension of humor to be understood as a complex and dynamic psycho-social process. As I suggested earlier however, Freud and Bergson stopped short of examining the social agency of humor or its politics *per se*. As intellectual heirs to The Enlightenment, they sought to construct a coherent and organic theory that exercised great explanatory power. Subsequently many questions are left unposed and hence, unresolved. Both men for instance infer the existence of a normative set of human behaviors with the result that examples of excessive uses of humor and humorlessness could therefore be taken as signs of abnormality. Their writings suggest also, that while humor may be understood as a process which exerts a powerful influence on control, there may not be any perceivable change from the original condition of the subject, the "I" for Freud, and "the social subject" for Bergson. Their theories are products of essentialist thinking that subordinates the role of culture, ideology, class, gender, ethnicity in facilitating the interpretation of humor. They are unable therefore, to fully acknowledge the importance of a context for reading and interpretation which can elicit radically different meanings from a single humorous subject or event. Given the physiological restrictions of the body, there is a limit also to the number of ways one can experience, represent and perform humor. Laughter, like yawning, is infectious, and therefore physiology—mimesis—comes into play. According to recent neurological research, laughter is not only a response to a humorous object or performance but rather a social response to people and the context within which the humorous experience is had. Consequently, laughter is also an index of how we feel about the people with whom we are together. We laugh more when we like and emotionally identify with people. [4] Thus depending upon the subject's identity as well as the content and direction of the humorous situation, there may be innumerable ways to interpret and negotiate the meanings of humor. This is as true of speech and written language as it is of graphic humor.

Freud did not advance a cohesive thesis on graphic humour, but two subsequent writers, art historian Ernst Gombrich and psychologist Ernst Kris (1940, 1952), have elaborated upon his "attack on control" model with respect to caricatures and cartoons. Kris makes a distinction between simple and complex forms of graphic humor. The simple forms he suggests, affect us like the circus clown and our pleasure derives from a comparison between the image and the reality from which it arises. Employing Freud's model of psychic economism he argues that the pleasures of humor originate in the pre-conscious mind and that this therefore results in the saving of an expenditure of thought. He concedes that this model is not entirely satisfactory and that these types of images

---
4. Provine RR (2016) "Laughter as a scientific problem: an adventure in sidewalk neuroscience." Journal of Comparative Neurology, 524:1532-1539

are extremely rare. The more complex cartoons and caricatures are of a more tendentious kind and are often 'politically' motivated.

> The (caricatures) are aimed at an individual or a type whom they portray with single features exaggerated; the natural harmony of an appearance is destroyed, and this has the result in many cases of revealing a contrast between looks and character (Kris, 1952:204).

For Kris, caricature is a graphic form of wit. He supports this judgment through a comparison of individual examples of wit with caricature. Moderating Freud's examples discussed in *Wit and its Relation to the Unconscious* (1905), Kris proceeds from the negative of wit, the riddle. "The riddle conceals what wit reveals. In wit the matter is known, and the manner is secret; in riddles the manner is known and the matter to be discovered (176). Arguing that certain features common to both the riddle and wit have their origins in mythic and totemic cognitive behaviour, Kris compares the two forms by using a psychiatric patient's behaviour as an illustration. This particular individual, he relates, "was incapable of deriving pleasure from a joke, but was under the compulsion to read the first line only, and then guess the point. He converted a joke into a riddle" (176). He argues therefore that an analogous form of reaction could be tested empirically by anyone engaged in a scientific study of caricature. Many early caricatures, he suggests, have undergone a transformational process that parallel his example and this, therefore, changes their meaning. They have become a rebus form which compels us "to resolve connections and allusions by guesswork" (176). In other words, some knowledge of the subject represented is necessary for a full disclosure (or constitution) of meaning to occur in the viewer's mind. With early caricatures (Figs. 8 and 9), the allusions and connections remain obscure precisely because the viewer/reader may have no immediate knowledge of the individual caricatured upon which to base his/her comparison. For the parody to be understood, the original object of comparison must be available for it to be legitimately sustained. A viewer requires the existence of the original subject, a simulacrum, or at the very least, partial knowledge of the original to ensure the legitimacy (and value) of any parody or satire. This recognition has immediate relevance with respect to the study of cartoon satires of art. Is it possible to make a comparison between caricature, a graphic form of wit, its (human) subjects, and a cartoon satire with its (often inanimate) subject? I would argue yes, that in a crucial sense both forms, the caricature and the cartoon, presume the reader's knowledge of the subject represented. In the case of the human subject, this knowledge is of the cartoon figure's individual physiognomy, and in the case of the graphic satire, the reader requires some prior knowledge of the form(s) represented. For the cartoons to be effective they must anticipate the viewers' knowledge, their intimacy, or at the very least, partial familiarity with the subject ironized, parodied or satirized, whether this be an individual, an artist, his or her work, an art style, movement or institution.[5] The effective graphic satire requires prior knowledge and interpretive participation on the part of the reader for the humor to be experienced and understood. In this transaction the matter is to be known, while the manner may be kept secret. Context and familiarity become the determining elements for reader comprehension.

Parody is at the basis of both caricature and the satirical cartoon. Visual parody may be considered an *accented ensemble* of signs, a graphic, or symbolic representation of ideology. As such, the graphic form of wit may be invested with criticism and hence, as I argue, *political* meaning. Irony, parody, satire and their relationship to the ideological interpellation of the human subject is properly the topic of the next chapter. I raise it now to associate the visual representation of these forms of humour with their origin in caricature, for throughout this book I have argued that visual ironies, parodies and satires of modernist art operate structurally, strategically and politically in a similar fashion to caricatures of people. To understand this last comparison, I will now discuss in detail the genesis, discourse and forms of caricature in the Renaissance, following this with an introduction to Bahktin's dialogical processes as these pertain to relations of power and class politics.

Although the word caricature was not coined until the late C17th, drawings very close in form to caricatures were being produced long before this time. According to many art and comic historians the exact genesis of the word caricature is uncertain, although most sources seem to prefer to nominate the C17th Italian painter Annibale Carracci (1560-1609) as its inventor (Gombrich and Kris, 1940, 1952; Lavin 1981). It is possible that the very first appearance of the word 'caricature' (*caricare*) appears in an introduction to Simon Guillains' (1646) edition of etchings after the Carracci academy and those of several other Bolognese artists. The folio introduction (1846) was written by the Italian critic and historian Mosini. According to art historian Denis Mahon, who interpreted the comments in Mosini's introduction, the caricaturists of the C17th were following, albeit in reverse, the basic philosophical tenets of the neo-classicists

---

5. This recognition process was discussed in conection with Ed Koren's graffiti art satire in Chapter 2.

(Mahon, 1947:37), specifically those beliefs contained in the famous Zeuxis anecdote, which contains the argument, that as perfection does not exist in reality, ideal beauty can only be obtained through the selection of perfect fragments or details from imperfect models. For these artists, nature's deformities and disproportions, evident in such physiognomic 'abnormalities' as thick noses, over-large mouths, long necks etc., were "playful caprices of nature." And in imitating subjects such as these, the artists were really just confirming the capriciousness of nature herself. The reader of the caricature would be all the more amused if the artists were to exaggerate nature's deformities and incongruence while maintaining a veracity to the essential ingredients. According to Mosini, Annibale Carracci and his contemporaries were striving in their work to achieve a conflated ideal of deformity or ugliness (*perfetta deformita*) to which the French refer, with somewhat different connotations to the conflation of the beautiful/ugly in the phrase *une belle laid*.

> Is not the caricaturist's task exactly the same as that of the classical artist? Both seeing the lasting truth beneath the surface of mere outward appearance. Both try to help nature accomplish its plan. The one may strive to realize it in his work, the other to grasp their perfect deformity, and thus reveal the very essence of a personality (Shikes and Heller, 1984:11).

Theoretical discussions by Agucci (1646) and Bellori (1672), who described Annibale's caricatures as "*rittrati burleschi overo caricati*" (Mahon: 46), followed by elaborate interventions from Baldinucci, the biographer of the Renaissance sculptor Lorenzo Bernini, finally determined the nature of caricature. They defined '*rittrati carichi*' as literally *loaded* portraits (Lavin: 1980, 1990). The similar term *portrait charge*, coined by French diplomat Chantelou, appeared in print eleven years after the Mosini introduction and similarly describes the significance of caricature in its "loaded" aspect. Both the Italian and the French terms for caricature have additional semantic values in the association with the verbs *caricare* and *charger* which describe the loading or charging of firearms. This semantic relationship underlines succinctly the overtly conflict qualities, the sublimated aggression that many subsequent theorists, Freud being the most notable, have suggested is inherent in the caricaturing and cartooning process.

The development of the discourses associated with the grotesque and caricature up until the 19th Century illustrates some of the theoretical problems equated with the appearance/reality dialectic. Bergson's essay *On Laughter* contains one of the most elaborate descriptions of caricature in modern literature:

> However regular we may imagine a face to be, however fine its lines and supple its movements, their adjustment is never altogether perfect: there will always be discoverable the sign of some impending bias, the vague suggestion of a possible grimace, in short, some favourite distortion toward which nature seems inclined. The art of the caricaturist consists in detecting this at times imperceptible tendency and in rendering it visible to all eyes by magnifying it. He makes his models grimace as they would do themselves if they went to the end of their tether. Beneath the skin-deep harmony of form, he divines the deep-seated recalcitrance of matter. He realizes disproportions and deformations which must have existed in nature as mere inclinations, but which have not succeeded in coming to a head, being held in check by a higher force. This art which has the touch of the diabolical raises up the demon who has been overthrown by the angel. Certainly it is an art which exaggerates and yet the definition would be far from complete were exaggeration alone alleged to be its aim and object, for their exist caricatures that are more lifelike than portraits, caricatures in which the exaggeration is scarcely noticeable whilst inversely it is quite possible to exaggerate without obtaining a real caricature (Bergson, 1911:26).

Employing the metaphysical and idealistic language characteristic of his work as a whole, Bergson discusses how a true caricature may be distinguished from one that is not. For him, exaggeration is not enough; the true caricature must exhibit certain spiritual or soul-like tendencies. Moreover, it is only the representation of an individual with this kind of intrinsic physiognomic, psychological, ultimately metaphysical veracity, that permits Bergson to proclaim it as an example of the highest (diabolical), and therefore most politically efficacious form of caricature. He alludes to the Platonic claim so succinctly expressed by Max Liebermann in answer to the dissatisfied criticisms of his sitter during a portrait session. "This painting my dear sir, resembles you more than you do yourself" (Gombrich, Hochberg and Black, 1972:36). Bergson's "diabolical" representation of a subject's physiognomy is an expression of the unique individualism that Petrarch argued constituted an essence, a distinct aria, evincing the particular shadings and nuances of character (36). Portrait caricatures became a means of representing extreme individual subjectivity and of providing a symbol of the person's character in every aspect of its psychological veracity. In other words, the image was truer than reality itself! In a very postmodern psychoanalytic sense, the image of the subject, speaks the subject.

In common with other theorists of caricature and the grotesque in art and nature, including his near contemporary Jules Champfleury (1865), Baudelaire's study (1855) led him into an extended philosophical inquiry into the genesis of laughter and the comic. He distinguished two types: the first confirmed the philosophical position of man's innate superiority to nature, a belief underlying many conceptions of the comic noted by scholars from Aristotle onwards, whose famous dictum "of all living creatures, only man is endowed with laughter" provided the basic premise for differentiation. His second type was labelled "satanic," which he associated with the demonic, the mysterious and the terrifying. He also distinguished between the "significative comic" dependent wholly upon allusions and references to specific human subjects (caricatures) and the "absolute comic" (the grotesque) that originates in the imagination of the artist and is thus associated with the modernist aesthetic principles associated with *l'art pour l'art*. For Baudelaire, this made it far superior to the "mere imitation of nature." Both types have specific relationships to reality, with one privileging the imagination of the artist, and the other the reader for its meanings.

Writing two decades later, Wright discerned a number of characteristics that belong equally to the grotesque and caricature. He suggested that the "monstrous" is closely allied to the grotesque and both come within the province of caricature when this form is taken in its widest possible sense (1875:8). In his introduction to this early treatise on the history of caricature, Barasch indicated that Wright's use of the terms caricature and grotesque are not synonymous. He suggests that for Wright caricature employs a "sense of ridicule," while the primary sense he accords the term grotesque is the "fantastic or excessively ugly or comic" (57). Wright emphasized the aggressive elements of both but suggested that the grotesque was a subgenre of caricature.

Throughout the history of the discourses associated with the comic and its affects, the theoretical emphases have changed dramatically. At times they have emphasized the social character of the comic, and at other times the biological/physiological, followed somewhat later by psychology. At the basis of each commentator's discussion on the nature of the comic is the question of individual power and social control, which I suggest moves from a position of privileging the group—the community—in the pre-Renaissance periods, to a concentration upon the individual subject, from the late C17th to the present.

I will now explore the origin of theories of the grotesque, and their relation to theories and definitions of satire and parody, which will bring us to a discussion of the politics of humour and graphic criticism, that are the final subjects of this chapter. In his famous book on Rabelais, Bahktin (1965) quotes Pinsky (1962), a Russian Renaissance scholar who suggests that:

> In the grotesque life passes through all the degrees from the lowest inert and primitive to the highest, most mobile and spiritualized; this garland of various forms bears witness to their oneness, brings that which is removed, combines elements which exclude one another, contradicts all current conceptions. Grotesque in art is related to the paradox in logic (Bahktin, 1965).

Classical scholars have noted that Western grotesque imagery has its origin in the mythology and archaic art of the Greeks and Romans of the pre-classic period. Humorous vase decorations from this period show grotesque scenes depicting fertility symbols and comic rituals. During the classic period it seems that the grotesque was subordinated to the ideological tenets of officially sanctioned art. It did survive however, in certain isolated areas that were essentially untouched by the dominant classicizing influences. Ancient carnival and folk festivals assisted in sustaining a growing grotesque tradition that was to reach a high point with an injection of new images from the East. The dominant aesthetic ideology, however, developed along classical lines but without a consistent definition or theory, the grotesque became in some respects a kind of materialist sub-culture counter balance to the predominant hegemony of the ideal classic tradition.

Under the influences of medieval culture, particularly folk humour, realism, an indispensable element essential to the grotesque, was gradually shaped during this early period. The word grotesque first appeared in the C15th to describe a curious type of ornament brought to light during the excavation of the Titus baths. these ornaments were called *grotesca* from the Italian grotta meaning cave or den. As Vasari relates in his influential *Lives of the Most Eminent Painters, Sculptors, and Architects* (1550), these grotesques were received favorably by many Renaissance painters and their patrons.

> Filipino Lippi was the first to bring to light grotesques in imitation of the antique and he executed them with more design and grace than the men before him; wherefore it was a marvelous thing to see strange fancies that he expressed in his paintings. (Vasari: 274)

These ornaments impressed the Renaissance members of the artistic community by their extremely free, fanciful treatment of plant, animal and human forms. Through Vasari we find that many artists: Perino del Vagi, Giovanni da Udine, Taddeo Zucchi, Michelangelo and Raphael adopted some of the peculiarities of the genre for their own work. For Vasari the connotations of the word grotesque were numerous; from "divine" through to "bizarre fancies," "beautiful and imaginative," or "strange fancies." He wrote the following statement in response to Michelangelo's "composite" style in the Medici tombs:

> an ornamentation in composite order, in more varied and more original manner than any other masters of any time…for in the novelty of the beautiful cornices, capitals, bases, doors, tabernacles and tombs he departed not a little from the work regulated by measure, order and rule, which other men did according to common use after Vitruvius and the antiquities to which he did not conform. That license had done much to give courage to those who had seen his methods and new fancies have since been seen which have more of the grotesque than of reason or rule in their ornamentation. (p. 274)

Judging by these remarks it is uncertain whether Vasari approved of the new style. His comments on Michelangelo's use of grotesque elements were positive. In relating the grotesque to Vitruvian canons, he had aligned himself with both Vitruvius and Alberti, his C15th commentator who condemned the grotesque from a classical standpoint as a gross violation of the classical ideal that provided more natural forms and proportions. To many classicists the implicit mannerism of Michelangelo's new style was outside of their frame of reference and had entered the aberrant realm of the human imagination, beyond the timeless God-ordained order of rule and reason. To the classicists, the grotesque became synonymous with irregular, irrational, licentious, amoral and demonic. To the neo-Vitruvians the ancient grotesques exhibited in the Baths of Titus were no more than the products of a decadent culture, a sign of a waning and academic phase in Roman art, one that was to be avoided if a true resurrection of proper antique canons was to be effected.

Vasari's ambivalent attitude toward the grotesque is typical of many of his contemporaries. However, the humanist ideology of the high renaissance was founded upon a number of ancient sources that were constantly being reinterpreted, and revised, according to the developing ethos. At the root of some of this ambivalence was man's relationship to God and nature. An influential essay *Ut Pictura Poesis, The Humanistic Theory of Painting* argues that this Renaissance ambivalence arose because the C16th theorists "applied to painting a doctrine which the ancients had developed chiefly as it concerned the art of literature" (Lee, 1940:204). As Lee suggests, in basing their theories on Aristotle, the Renaissance theorists had argued that painting, like poetry, was an imitation of nature "by which they meant human nature not as it is but as it ought to be raised" (204). This doctrine has been encountered before, albeit dressed in new clothes. This is the transcendental basis of Bergson's comic thesis and the

German notion of *seele karikature*, a representation of subjects, not necessarily as they exist in reality but as they may appear in certain exceptional circumstances. As Lee proposes, the doctrine of ideal imitation had not yet entirely supplanted the older notion of art as a mimetic or literal imitation of nature. It was not unusual to find both co-existing during this period.

Vasari was certainly heir to this intellectual dilemma. We can witness this in his praising of Raphael whom he suggests may be considered the purest exponent of the High Renaissance style for his "unsurpassed naturalism." Naturalism under these circumstances is allied to Pliny's account of "those ancient painters (Apelles) who created so convincing an illusion of life that animals and men, nay artists themselves mistook their art for reality" (204). It is not hard to understand why the introduction of grotesque elements at this time would become subject to both acceptance and prohibition. In an era where rule, reason and good government was gaining respect, the grotesque offered nothing but ambiguity, paradox and dissimulation.

In a now famous introduction to his book *Rabelais and His World* (1965), Bakhtin discussed many aspects of the early C16th attitudes to the grotesque, particularly as it was manifested in pre-Renaissance folk carnival humour. He suggested that folk humour was opposed to the official and serious tone of medieval ecclesiastical and feudal culture and he distinguished a number of popular forms: ritual spectacles, carnival pageants, comic shows of the market place, comic verbal compositions, parodies (oral, written, drawn or painted) and lastly various types of billingsgate curses, oaths, burlesques and so on. Bakhtin then proceeds to describe each of these forms at length, suggesting that the carnivals with their long and complex pageants and processions, the so-called *festa stultorum* (feast of fools), the feast of the ass, and the carnivals proper, were ceremonies and rituals with extremely complex social and political meanings,

> which in the early stages of pre-class and pre-political social (pre-renaissance and baroque) order were equally sacred and equally official." (Bahktin, 1965:6)

During carnival time, civil and social ceremonies took on a festive aspect as fools, clowns and other comic agents mimicked serious rituals, and ceremonies, such as the transfer of feudal rights, the initiation of knights, and the tributes paid to victors of tournaments. Even the election of a king and queen to preside at a banquet for "laughters sake" (*un roi pour rire*) showed the lengths to which medieval society was prepared to take the indoctrination of a form of parodic "comic protocol," one that was no less important than the official one.

During carnival time, according to Bakhtin, all systems of rank and hierarchy were suspended. An analogy can be presented here in Bergson and Freud's reflections upon humour as an "attack on control" that have become the basis of the so-called conflict and control models for humour. Bakhtin's observations, however, underscore the importance of issues of control and social conformity.

To Bakhtin, the dialogic or parodic character of the grotesque becomes a primary distinguishing feature of medieval comic traditions and the social meanings for humour as distinct from those operating in the C16th and C17th. The very fact that in the middle age's documentary sources reveal that up to three months a year, or more, could be devoted to such reversal behaviour illustrates the difference in attitudes between the periods. He suggests that rank, which was especially evident during official feasts where everyone was expected to appear in their full regalia to show his/her position in society, was a sign of "consecrated inequality" (1965:10). During carnival time everyone was considered equal, and a kind of *faux* democracy reigned among people, who under normal circumstances, were strictly divided by barriers of property, profession, gender and age. The socio-political implications of this phenomenon for a class-based discussion are interesting. Bakhtin suggests that while the common people actually assumed a measure of control and power at these times, this maintained and actually reinforced the existing power differentials.

Interpreting the evidence from contemporary sources as well as from his study of Rabelais' novel *Gargantua and Pantagruel*, Bakhtin interprets the symbols and agents of the folk carnival as being filled with a "pathos of change and renewal, with the sense of gay relativity of prevailing truths and authorities" (11). He accords to medieval folk and carnival humour the characteristic reversal logic of the inside out, or turnabout, a parodistic shifting of emphases through the suspension of control.

> A continual shifting from top to bottom, front to rear and of numerous parodies and travesties, humiliations, profanations, crownings and uncrownings" (Bahktin, 1965:11).

Although folk humour denies, and negates (the established hegemonic order), it revives and renews (this hegemony), at the same time. Bahktin's discussion of the dialogic character of medieval humor could be described in very contemporary terms, as a form of resistance and accommodation, or in/subordination. Reversals and turnabouts reveal that counter-hegemonic tendencies exist within the carnival space, but these serve merely to reproduce and reinforce the existing hegemonic order. The absolutely nihilistic and aggressive characteristics of many C17th forms of parody, grotesques, caricatures, through to the present day, are completely foreign to folk culture. Furthermore, as Bakhtin suggests, the images associated with food, wine, sex and defecation, and generally the organs of the body that play such a large part in Rabelais' writing, as well as in the work of Cervantes, Bosch, Callot, and Breughel, had a strongly universalizing tendency, which under the growing power of the idealist philosophies and individualism, began to disintegrate.

Bahktin argues that with the domination of classical ideologies in all areas of cultural activity in the late C16th, C17th and early C18th, the materialist impulses of the grotesque were supplanted by an ethical, moralist and individual humanistic orientation which altered irrevocably the collective and materialist concerns of the middle ages. The positive aspects of this medieval materialism, with its images of flux and renewal, slowly began to serve the purposes of literary and graphic satire. In terms of visual representation as well as theatre, satire became a negative form, which through the process of abstraction, weakened the positive naturalism explicit within the grotesque, to result in caricature. Bakhtin describes this problem of distinction, or better, difference, in these terms:

> The grotesque as it is related to the culture of folk humour was excluded from great literature; it descended to the low comic level or was subject to the epithet "gross naturalism" (p. 11).

This reinscription is both the ideological heart of the matter of difference and the justification for the Bakhtinian dialogic. At stake here are the distinguishing characteristics of irony, satire and parody, underscored in the semiotic complexity of the tropes with which I began this section—Wright's sense of humour as a "bastard pleasure" and Alexander Liebermann's "a face like his I could piss in the snow." In a sense, the snow has melted.

Bakhtin suggested that humour can serve several socio-political functions: it can represent attempts by subordinate groups to contest the power of a dominant group, usually, in the medieval period, a monarchy; and it can also serve to lubricate and ensure the efficient workings of the prevailing status quo, the hegemony of the dominant class(es). The theory he articulated in *The Dialogic Imagination*, Bahktin argued that these two operations can occur simultaneously—dialogically—humour can say one thing and mean another. A sign can be *doubly-coded*, or, as he asserts in an important tract regarding the semiotic coding of language, "within a single utterance there may occur two intentions, two voices" (Matejka, 1971:180). The dialogistic or "double-voiced" character of most types of humour is an attractive conclusion to arrive at, for genre types are often difficult to differentiate and distinctions between irony, parody and satire are not always readily apparent. There are always exceptions to any models that one may feel inclined to build for the way humour functions in social terms. For example, one reading of an ironic statement may correctly identify the intentionality *of* the author, while another reading may identify the critic's intentions *for* the author and his/her/their text. Since the 1970s and the inception of the postmodern distrust of definitions, and foundational concepts, this has been a hot topic in certain circles. Accordingly, contemporary definitions, or rather, interpretations of irony, parody, and satire, tend to differ. Some researchers place emphasis on the forms themselves; others, the author's intentions, or the power of the reader to interpret and control meaning, irrespective of the immediate authority of the author, the text, or the context within which the reading occurs. With this final acknowledgement, we may now be in a better position to negotiate in the following chapter, the related concepts of irony, satire and parody, after which we shall return to the problems associated with the interpretation of the symbolic contestation of power in selected examples of mid C19th graphic imagery.

CHAPTER 4

Visual Irony, Parody and Satire

> Irony may be a weapon in a satirical attack, or a smokescreen concealing a retreat, or a device for turning the world or oneself inside out; irony may be found in words and attitudes, in events and situations; or we may find nothing on earth and quite certainly nothing in heaven that is not ironic. (Muecke, 1969:3)

The previous discussion of the political economy of Ed Koren cartoon in Chapter 2 revealed how the art of graffiti was interpreted through the social purview of a given time period - the 1970s - specific social groups, including the graffiti writers' sub-culture, the art world, the cartoonist and the readers of The New Yorker. I used this image also to begin to articulate some of differences between visual irony, parody and satire. In this chapter I will move back in time to the beginning of modernism to discuss a small number of French graphic satires of art from the 1850s, using these images to explore further the visual representation of political ideologies. I will conclude the chapter with some theoretical discussion on the differences between textual and visual irony, parody and satire before interpreting some more popular criticisms of modernism in chapter five.

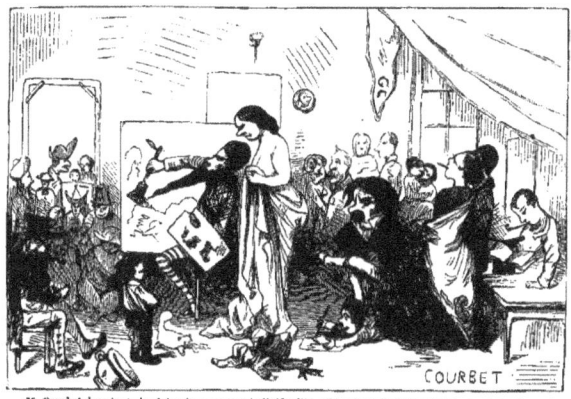

Figure 11: Quillenbois, *The Studio* L'Illustration July 21, 1855 Public Domain.

The first cartoon example I will discuss is a satire of a famous painting from the mid 19th century, Gustave Courbet's *The Studio: A real allegory determining a seven-year phase of my artistic life* (*L'Atelier du peintre: Allegorie reelle determinant une phase de sept annees de ma vie artistique*, 1855). Drawn by Quillenbois (Charles-Marie de Sarcus), the cartoon (fig.11) was published in the journal L'Illustration in the summer of 1855, one of a number of graphic satires of Courbet (1819-1877) and his paintings that appeared in the French press over a ten-year period. Quillenbois' cartoon is a biting satirical response to Courbet's famous Realist Exhibition of 1855 held simultaneously and in competition to The Exposition Universelle, a large exhibition profiling the works of the major academic artists of the day, including the two salon giants, Ingres and Delacroix. From a contemporary viewpoint the issues at stake in this image may seem slight, but projected back into its own context, the cartoon provides us with an understanding of why Courbet's political and aesthetic beliefs should become the object of this kind of satire.

Courbet's life and work and this painting in particular, have been the subject of extensive discussions by a number of writers: Riat (1906), Schapiro (1941), Nochlin (1967), Clark (1973), Nicholson (1973), and Rubin (1980). I do not wish to paraphrase their writings here, except to acknowledge the coincidence of their belief that Courbet's *Studio* is one of the earliest and most important art works in the history of modernism, representing the artist's strong identification with the working class and the politics of revolutionary socialism. Linda Nochlin, for example, has impressively argued that the painting allegorically represents the utopian socialism of Charles Fourier and his circle. T. J. Clark discusses the "quixotic revolutionary" materialist ideas articulated in this painting as an index of Courbet's struggle to accommodate his bourgeois aspirations while simultaneously practicing anti-bourgeois and proto-revolutionary behaviour in his life. Rubin articulates the relationship between the bohemian Courbet and the socialist ideas of one of his key intellectual mentors, the philosopher Pierre-Joseph Proudhon (1809-1865), pointing out the importance of the intellectual context within which both men worked and the influential socialist writings of the period. He underlines the important influences upon the social thinking of major writers of the 1830s and 1840s, among them: Louis Blanc, Auguste Compte, Charles Fourier, Theophile Thoreau, and Henri de Saint-Simon, suggesting that the impetuous young Courbet was attempting to use his avant-garde realist art to establish a new platform for progressive socialist ideas and to promote a new school of art.

In a famous letter to Champfleury written in the winter of 1854-55, Courbet described some of his intentions and identified many of the figures in the painting. He wrote: "There are those who live on life and those who live on death. It is a society at its top, bottom and middle. In a word, it is my way of seeing society in its interests and passions" (Rubin, 1980:39). The artist identified the figures on the left of the painting as the exploiters and the exploited—the "people who live on death"—a London Jew clutching a money box, whom the painter suggested is saying "It is I who am on the right track"; a ruddy-faced Catholic priest, a veteran of 1793, holding his ammunition bag ("possibly for begging"), a hunter with dogs, a reaper, a strong man, a buffoon, a textile peddler, a workman's wife, a worker, an undertaker, a death's head on a newspaper, an Irishwoman suckling a baby and an artist's dummy. In the middle of the painting is the artist himself at his easel, painting a landscape representing that of his native region and watched intently by a nude model, a white cat—a symbol of fidelity in this case, promiscuity, if black—an act of racial discrimination—and an impressionable young country boy. To the right of the artist are his "*les actionnaires*" (39), members of his artistic circle, friends and supporters. To the rear of the space stand Promayet with his violin, Bruyas, an art collector and early Courbet supporter, Cuneot, Buchon, Proudhon, Champfleury (seated), an unidentified upper class woman of the world promenading with her husband, a couple in a private discussion, and to the far right in a solitary mode, reading, Charles Baudelaire, soon to become chief modernist theorist and critic.

Quillenbois' cartoon takes many liberties with Courbet's painting. For a start, Courbet's narcissistically arrogant pose (showing his good "Assyrian" side), is highly exaggerated. His long thin beard is pointed toward the painting, in what could be a kind of perspective, providing an ironic allusion to its potential use as a painting tool. The brush that the artist is actually using to paint the landscape resembles one used by a building painter, which makes this cartoon an early member of the dauber sub-genre, a type of cartoon image representing technical ineptitude, that became the popular basis, subsequently, for literally thousands of cartoon satires of modernist art. Quillenbois' parodic caption (he parodies the title of the painting), and satiric (he subverts it), provides the suitable invective and underlines the technical criticism conveyed in his cartoon.

> M. Courbet in all the glory of his own individuality, a real allegory determining a phase of his artistic life. (see the programme, where it proves victoriously that he was never able to master perspective!)[1]

Many of the figures in the cartoon are disposed in a manner similar to those within the painting itself. A few however, have changed remarkably. Quillenbois has caricatured the Jew and the veteran. He has given the undertaker a monstrous visage and turned the hunter figure on the left, who in the actual painting is accompanied by two hunting dogs, into a human figure resembling a dog. The sweet child's face in the Courbet painting has been rendered as a toad-like parody in the cartoon. Champfleury has been turned into a monstrous figure with a huge head and spindly legs, his moustache grossly exaggerated and displaying a deep frown as he gazes upon the narcissistic pose and perceived technical ineptitude of his friend Courbet. Similarly, the model is turned into an ugly whore-like, perhaps even masculinized parody of the figure in Courbet's painting. And in the left foreground, a chamberpot tips dangerously close to shedding its contents on the whole scene, a strong insight into the cartoonist's view of Courbet's place within the art world of his time. The couple conversing in the shadowed, right background area of the painting are now locked in a lovers' embrace and the *haut bourgeois* couple are looking disdainfully upon the scene before them. The well-dressed woman is now identifiable as a courtesan with a fag hanging out of her mouth, less woman of the world, than streetwalker. To the far left an uncharacteristically adolescent Charles Baudelaire neutrally smokes his pipe while reading a book. Clearly, Quillenbois' cartoon has turned Courbet's painting from a "real allegory" into a grotesque masquerade.

The cartoonist's political perspective is clear. His cartoon savagely mocks the pretension of Courbet's enterprise, turning the young master's high-flown mission, which is no less than to found upon his example, a politically and aesthetically progressive new school of art, into a cheap untutored and narcissistic exercise of camp debauchery. His political satire would have probably found a very receptive audience among many members of the Parisian cultural elite who would have been incensed at Courbet's stylish egotism, not to mention his well-documented faux rustic penchant for booze and women; furthermore, they would have perceived his fellow traveler politics and theoretical theatrics as a form of hypocrisy.

---

1. *M. Courbet danse toute la gloire de sa propre individualite, allegorie reelle determinant une phase de sa vie artistique. (Voire programme, ou il prouve victorieusement qu'il n'a jamais eu de maitre...de perspective).*

Visual Irony, Parody and Satire 67

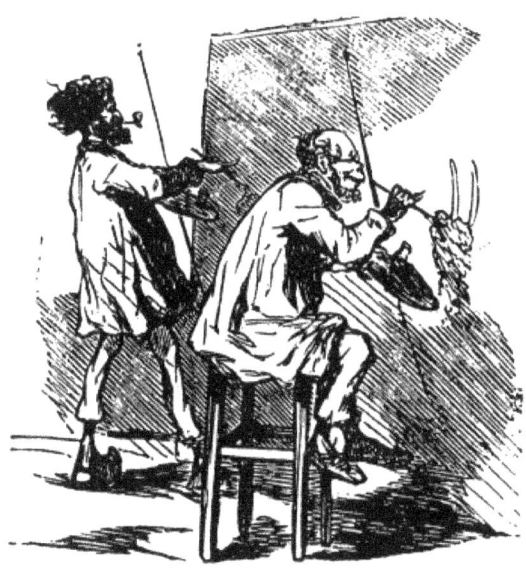

Figure 12: Cham *Courbet and Proudhon Painting* 1855 Public Domain

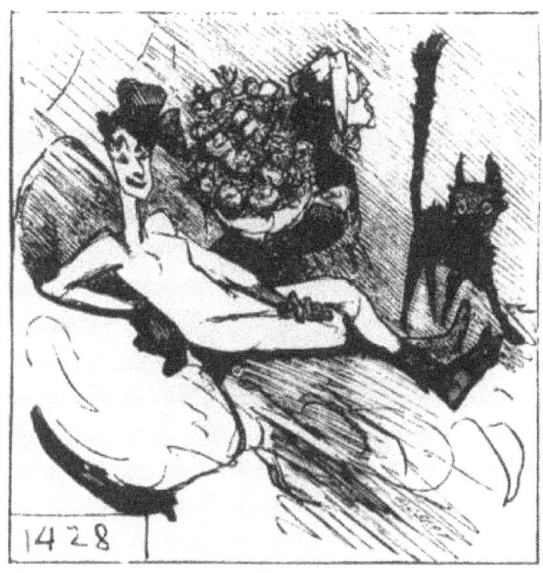

MANET.
La Naissance du petit ébéniste.
M. Manet a pris la chose trop à la lettre :
Que c'était comme un bouquet de fleurs !
Les lettres de faire-part sont au nom de la mère Michel
et de son chat.

Figure 13: Cham *Olympia* 1865 Public Domain

It is important to view Quillenbois' cartoon in the context of another (fig. 12) by Cham (Charles Amédée de Noé), that shows a bohemian and spindly looking Courbet in the company of a very simian looking Proudhon, mahlsticks victoriously in hand as they work diligently on the same socially loaded, (we may presume), canvas. Both these cartoons are severe denunciations of the progressive politics of these members of the avant-garde, direct attacks on the chief ideologues of social and cultural modernity and their bequests.

The following examples are perhaps better known now than those discussed above, even though in his own time, Honore Daumier (1808-1879), the artist who produced them, was neglected in favour of his contemporaries: Cham, Meissonier, Garvani and Decamps. During his life Daumier produced over 4000 lithographs and 1000 woodcuts, many of them acknowledged masterpieces of their respective media. An artist from a working-class background, Daumier produced many cartoons reflecting his sympathy for the poor and disenfranchised as well as hundreds of cartoons satirizing the institutions of his day including the government, judiciary, the theatre and the art world. The cartoons representing art and artists are less direct than his political subjects, but they are nevertheless insightful as ironic statements on the questionable morals of the rich and powerful and dissertations on the foibles of humanity. They compare favorably to his other famous *News Item* subject series: the weather, transport, the legal profession, the theatre and local politics. The *News Items* were published after repressive measures were placed in the press by the Government in 1851, an action satirized in an extraordinarily powerful Daumier cartoon, *Patricide* (16 April 1850), which showed Adolphe Thiers, former journalist and defender of free speech, as newly installed government minister, hypocritically wielding a club against the press which he now wanted to become mouthpiece of the state and servant of law and order.

The first Daumier art cartoon (fig. 14), I wish to discuss is from his *Les Bons Bourgeois* (*Worthy Bourgeois*) series. This cartoon gently reveals the hazards of plein air painting. An artist painting a landscape winces as a young girl and her parents' peek over his shoulder at his work in progress. In answer to a naive question from the young girl about the form of the image being painted, the father answers paternalistically with a statement laced with heavy irony "But of course my dear, I assure you, Monsieur is painting a landscape…is that not so, Monsieur?" He questions again in a mock innocent fashion, "Aren't you painting a landscape?"

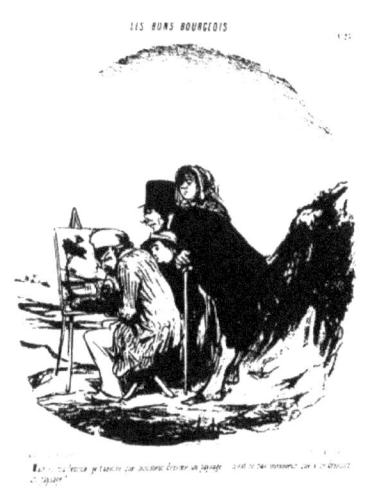 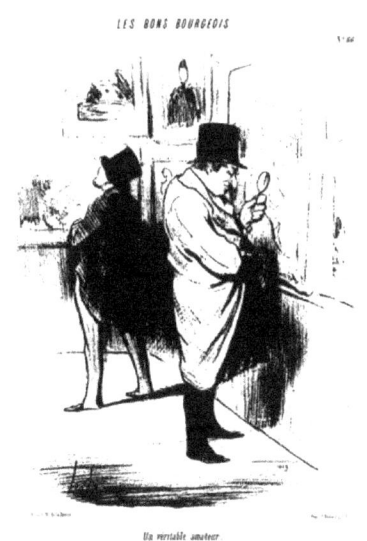

Figure 14: Daumier, H., *Les Bon Bourgeois* 13 November 1846, British Museum.

Figure 15: Daumier, H., *The Real Connoisseur* 16 May 1847, British Museum.

Another *Bons Bourgeois* cartoon image bears the caption *Un Veritable Amateur* (fig. 15), that Passeron translates as *The Real Connoisseur*, but which could also be translated as *Real Amateur*, thus conveying the meanings of lover, enthusiast, devotee or fan. The cartoon shows a hook-nosed bourgeois viewer examining the lower register of a painting with a magnifying glass. The picture he is examining so closely is an unidentifiable figurative painting but perhaps the posture and gaze of the figure could also be read as somewhat suggestive of a male engaging in some kind of auto-erotic activity, employing the image as a fetish stimulus. This type of clever allusion is not foreign to some of Daumier's work or to cartoon art satires as a whole. The complexity of the signs in a seemingly straightforward image such as this can lead to many contradictory readings.

A Daumier cartoon bearing the innocuous title *The Public at the Salon* is captioned with "Classical art lovers who are more and more convinced that the cause of art in France is lost." This image may provide evidence of Daumier's approval of some of the most progressive modernist art of his time, but I believe that he was equally interested in its ironic condemnation. A contemporary reader, then as now, could view this as vindication of their progressive views just as an irate conservative could identify with these two anti-modernists.

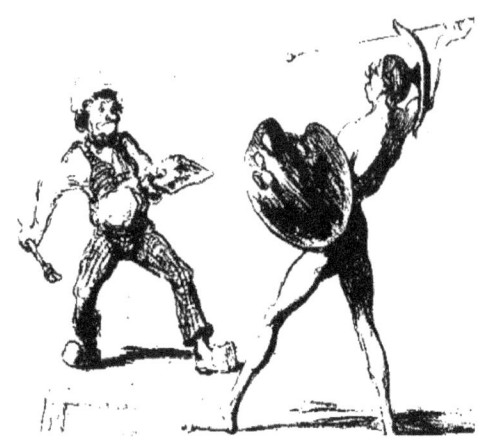

Figure 16: Daumier, H. *Combat des Ecoles: L'Idealisme et le realism*
Charivari April 24, 1855 Public Domain

The competition between the various schools of art in mid-century France is expressed with greater clarity by Daumier in another cartoon titled *Combat des Ecoles: L'Idealisme et le realism* (fig. 16) which shows a caricatured figure of a squat realist painter in peasant clothes squaring off against a skinny nude and bespectacled academician. The cartoon is consciously modelled after *The Battle of the Romans and the Sabines* (1799), a famous neo-classical painting by J. L. David that would have been instantly recognized by the readers of Charivari. Daumier's academician is posed after Romulus, the heroic figure throwing a javelin at Titus Tatius his opponent in the David painting. The weapons of choice in the cartoon signal a difference between the aesthetic ideologies of the two schools; the realist painter grasps a tradesman-like thick brush and square palette shield contrasted with the academician's professional palette shield and mahlstick.

Daumier was eager to satirize members of the academy, the aristocracy and the old guard, but his energies in these works were also directed at the pretensions of the bourgeois public, (the culture vultures), who in their desire to acquire cultural capital, feigned interest in the art of their day. A good example of this false commitment to high art is displayed in a cartoon titled *The Salon* which represents a bourgeois or petit bourgeois couple viewing a "devotional painting" while a very aristocratic yet bohemian artist looks on. His thoughts provide the caption which plays on the adjective devotional and the verb devoted, to allude ironically to both religious art and art as religion. It reads: "These cretins! You paint a devotional painting for them, and they laugh…they are not even devoted to art."

The *Auction Room* shows a half-length portrait of an auctioneer from an oblique angle confronting his top-hatted bourgeois clients who squint and peer intently at the object of desire, a framed print held aloft by the auctioneer calling out for bids. Each of the faces is carefully drawn and provides us with a summary of the world of auctions, the social types who buy and those who attend to enjoy the spectacle of others bidding. Another, gentler cartoon satire of the exhibition viewing public, titled *Exhibition of 1859* (fig. 17) shows a *petit bourgeois* couple moving around a jam-packed exhibition at the Salon. The husband says to his wife.

> My dear, as a whole day would not be long enough to see everything, look at the pictures on the right…I shall look at those on the left, and when we get home, we shall tell one another what we have seen.

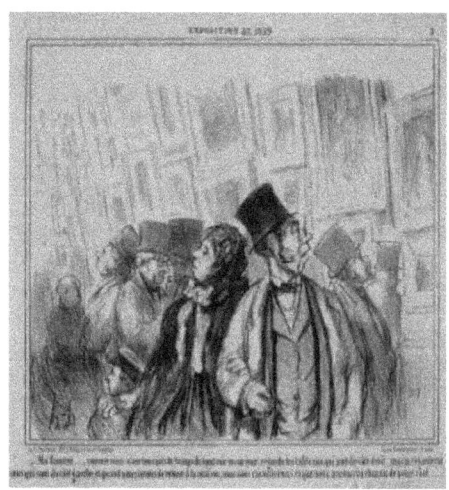

Figure 17: Daumier, H. *Exhibition of 1859* Charivari, British Museum

While he achieved fame and notoriety early on as an artist working for the popular press, Daumier's fortunes as a (high) artist were tied to his role as a caricaturist. In his time, as is generally the case today, cartooning and caricature were not accorded the same high art status as painting or sculpture. Mass produced newspaper and journal cartoons did not have the same status as unique art works which even existing as ideas in the heads of their creators, were destined for the salon. Daumier's contemporaries in the world of high art rented or owned their own studios, employed assistants, regularly exhibited their work in the salon, sold it to members of the establishment and received commissions from wealthy patrons, church and state. In contrast, Daumier's movements for many years were restricted to the daily grind of producing graphic work for the press. While he produced approximately 300 paintings in his lifetime, few of them received much attention from either his peers or the public. He was very reluctant to conform to the exhibition and commission conventions typical of exhibiting high culture artists of his day and did not promote or regularly send his work to the salons. And although he received much attention in his final years (an offer of the Legion d'Honneur, which he refused), had it not been for a subvention from the State he would have died heavily in debt. During his lifetime he had but one solo exhibition of his work, and this in the final year of his life. It took several months of determined negotiations by his friend Geoffroy-Dechaune to arrange the exhibition which opened on the 17th April and ran to June 15, 1878, a mere eight months before Daumier suffered a stroke. He died on the 10th February leaving an enormous legacy for the world to learn from and admire and some powerful insights that he provided into the contest of meanings over the signs of modernist art.

As I noted in *Trans/Actions: Art, Film and Death,* definitions of irony, parody and satire currently in use relate primarily to texts as distinguished from images. The privileging of the text problematizes the use of these categories with respect to cartoons and graphic parodies and satires such as those of Koren, Quillenbois and Daumier previously discussed. But what are the differences between textual and visual irony, parody and satire? Thus far it may have seemed that I have been somewhat indiscriminate in my use of the terms; that I have either blurred the distinctions between the three or rendered them interchangeable. This is not my intention. But what does distinguish them?

With its expressly critical and political dimensions, satire has remained a somewhat problematic genre for historians of literary and visual humour. In his study of satire Feinberg (1967), suggested that "dissimulation is the richest source of satire," a human response to hypocrisy and pretense" ample evidence of a "double standard in the structure of our society" (Feinberg 1967:23). He attributes this further to a sociological mismatch between what we desire and the actuality to which we address our desires. The satirist, he argues, is stimulated to attack by his/her perception of a "violation of social norms" (33). He suggests that parody may also serve the purposes of critique through dissimilation such as "emphasizing the affectations and excesses of style, and the superficiality and absurdity of content" (185). The Quillenbois cartoon discussed earlier is a brilliant example of this. The Charlie Hebdo killings have foregrounded the importance of studying visual satire as it pertains to alterity, morality and ethics. [2]

---

2. https://www.nybooks.com/daily/2015/01/09/charlie-hebdo-laughter-terror/

Johnson's introduction to his early anthology of great works of satire from Aesop and Juvenal to Thurber and Thomas Wolfe, provides some indication of why satire is such a problematic genre for literary historians and lay people alike. "Everybody recognizes satire," he writes, "(but) nobody knows what it is" (Johnson, 1945:3). Accordingly, he settles for a wide range of satirical types ranging from "high spirited mockery to torment" (5), colorfully castigating those who have argued that there must always be an element of humour in satire.

> No description of satire can hold water unless it takes all the aspects of satire into account. Sometimes the satirist tumbles in giggling, thumbing his nose, wielding slapsticks and bladders, smacking people on their fannies, and administering electric shocks. Sometimes he bawls abuse or hisses denunciations, flays his victim and then pours oil or acid in the wounds. Sometimes austere as Dante stalking through the murk of Hell, he grimly describes evil fallen into its proper torments, plunged in flame or locked in thick-ribbed ice (7).

Johnson distinguishes two types of satire, the direct and indirect. The direct is a form of invective that he relates to melodrama, further characterized as "violent emotional satire" (67). His model here—the altering or magnifying of parts of a subject to startling proportions—is similar to types of visual humour such as the Cham caricatures of Courbet and Proudhon. Melodrama, he relates to the burlesque, but unlike melodrama, "burlesque knows what it is up to." "When burlesque inflates things to grotesqueness just for fun, it is one of the forms of humour: when it inflates them in order to deflate them, it is satire" (67). In this sense, Johnson likens the satire to pictorial caricature. He also distinguishes between a satiric and a grotesque form of burlesque. The Quillenbois cartoon is a satiric form of burlesque, simultaneously inflating Courbet's aesthetic project in order to denounce it. Johnson is a proto postmodernist in that he focuses upon description and interpretation, rather than definition and analysis, privileging one word common to all of those cognitive processes—criticism—to satisfy his desire for categorization. It is the urge to criticize, he suggests that stimulates the producer of satire (and parody) to attack. Criticism precipitates a "kind of unmasking" (9), and in this sense may be compared to forms of disavowal, dissimulation and/or dissembling. These, I believe, can be read concurrently as signs of resistance and in/subordination.

A number of recent discussions articulating the similarities and differences between irony, parody and satire, responding to studies from the 1960s by Macdonald (1960), Blackmur (1964), Feinberg (1967), and Paulson (1967) have continued to argue their cases by employing various theoretical models derived from literary criticism. I will now suggest the appropriateness of developing an understanding of the semiotic interrelationships between the genres that will, I hope, encourage an understanding of the polyvalent conditions for reading and interpreting visual humour, thus giving us further entry into debates concerning the politics of humour, and the symbolic representation of class conflict. Lehman (1963), offered an open definition of parody but confined it to literature:

> I understand here under parody only such literary products that formally imitate in toto or in part a known text, or secondary appearances, manners and customs, events and persons. This imitation is seemingly accurate, but in fact distorted, with conscious and recognizable humour (Lehman, 1963:3).

By way of contrast, Joseph Dane argues that like beauty, parody is in the mind of the beholder. "The reader" he writes, "has the power to read any text as a parody" (Dane, 1989: 11-12). He stresses also, "there should be constraints on such power" to ensure that authors, critics and other literary specialists, have more control over their work and its meaning. Of course, this is comforting for postmodern readers, who assume that they have license to negotiate and articulate, meaning irrespective of the author's intention. We can acknowledge, however, that as many differences exist between irony, parody, satire, as there are between beauty, ugliness and the grotesque. We should acknowledge also that these concepts are too contingent upon a wide range of situations to assume either conditionality or commonality as a virtue.

Parody, Dane argues, has been "conflated with the plastic arts," its parasitical nature and its history too strongly constituted with its sister genres, the grotesque, caricature and pastiche. An examination of the literature, however, confirms that the discussion of parody, if not satire, has been focused very much upon the literary, and not the visual or performing arts. And although many writers have taken great pains to show the differences between the two genres, it is often the similarities that they privilege when discussing specific examples. As Linda Hutcheon suggests, parody has been explicitly and implicitly, conflated with satire by many theorists and yet, she writes, "calling parody satire seems a little too simple as an instant way to give parody a social function" (1985:43). Some writers have bypassed the identity problem altogether and used the terms interchangeably. Hutcheon concludes that the major reason for the confusion of satire and parody is they are often used together. This is particularly true of caricatures and, as I argue throughout this book, cartoons and comics which take modernist art as their subject. Hutcheon also questions those who attempt to differentiate between the two on the basis of binary oppositions, arguing instead that parody and satire may operate both positively and negatively—simultaneously. Just as I noted in the previous chapter how the French have the term *une belle laid* for the virtually untranslatable concept in English of the beautiful/ugly, so too we must admit the possibility of androglossic concepts such as parodical/satire and the satirical/parody, without denying that the two can quite happily and regularly do assume separate identities when the context or the occasion demands.

From Socrates to Schlegel, Mann, Richards, Frye, and Paul De Man, the literary critics and theorists of irony have each, in their various ways, raised the impossibility of defining irony, since the practice of ironizing—disassembling—from its generic Greek root *eironeia*, meaning simulated ignorance (*eiron*, dissembler), invariably engages the notion of saying one thing and meaning another. Many theorists consider irony to be vehicle within which parody, satire and their various interrelated forms, function. Defining irony has presented many problems. Muecke suggests that the art of irony, is the art of saying something without really saying it. It is an art that gets its effects from below the surface, and this gives it a quality that resembles the depth and resonance of great art triumphantly saying much more than it seems to be saying. (Muecke, 1969:7)

Several theorists of irony: Muecke (1969), Enright, (1986), Dane (1991), and Hutcheon (1994), acknowledge both directly and indirectly, the heteroglossic character of irony and warn of the limitations of reductive and formalist definitions. Dane for instance, distinguishes between rhetorical irony, romantic irony and critical irony, arguing that "the history of irony and the novel involves the disparity between the language of the novel and that of the critic" (187). Linda Hutcheon provides a definition of parody that encompasses both the literary and visual 'text'. She argues that parody is a form of imitation, "but imitation characterized by ironic inversion, not always at the expense of the parodied text" (Hutcheon, 1985:55). She suggests that we must examine parody, satire and irony, in both their literary and visual forms, as processes of reading and interpretation. We must negotiate "the enunciation of the contextualized production and reception of texts, if we are to understand what constitutes [them]" (55). Accordingly, she developed an overlapping Venn diagram consisting of three circles: Satiric Ethos, Ironic Ethos and Parodic Ethos, in order to better explain the interrelationships between each form. She argued that while each ethos can harbour or invoke criticism, the satiric ethos has a slightly stronger proprietary interest in social critique and is therefore (potentially) more politically efficacious. Irony is inscribed in most forms of parody and satire and serves the interests of both humour and criticism.

Some humour researchers have used semiotic theory to undercover the coded relationships between the forms and functions of various humour genres. Ziva Ben Porat's study of MAD T.V. satires for example, examines the close semiotic relationship between parody and satire without making them synonymous. In her essay parody becomes the coded vehicle within which satirical intentions are mediated. She describes parody as,

> an alleged representation, usually comic, of a literary text or other artistic object—i.e. a representation of a 'modeled reality', which is itself already a particular representation of an original 'reality'. The parodic representations expose the model's conventions and lay bare its devices through the co-existence of the two codes in the same message.

and follows with a compatible description of satire as:

> a critical representation, always comic and often caricatural, of "non-modeled reality," i.e. of the real objects (their reality may be mythical or hypothetical) which the receiver reconstructs as the referents of the message. The satirized original "reality" may include mores, attitudes, types, social structures, prejudices and the like.[3]

Ben-Porat's reductive and binary construction of a "modeled" and "unmodeled reality" presents some problems, but her reference to the importance of the reader and the instrumentality of the genres, challenges many earlier models and legitimizes the non-conventionality of her approach. A few other contemporary theorists have tended to differentiate between irony, parody and satire on the basis of instrumentality or utility, demonstrating, in so doing, that the social and political use value for humour may be one defining attribute, even when the forms are coded together. For the purposes of this study satire tends to be more strategic than parody in its relation to its 'target' and more predisposed towards the negative. Its intention(s) are often to subvert the power and authority of its object, without necessarily introducing, implicitly or explicitly, a replacement. In this study a comparison between examples of graphic and literary

---

3. Ben-Porat, Z. "Method in Madness: Notes on the Structure of Parody, Based on MAD TV Satires," Poetics Today 1 245-72 requoted in Hutcheon (1985: 49).

satire, reveal a strong disposition towards negative and pejorative criticism in satire, while irony and parody are more affirming, seeking often to induce in the reader an ironic and complicit distancing, without this becoming overtly rejective. To Hutcheon "irony's double-voicing both allows the distance and makes inevitable the implication. It therefore allows a questioning from within" (Hutcheon, 1991:142). I would stress that if there are close formal relationships between irony, parody and satire, and related genre ascriptions such as travesty, grotesque and burlesque, we can often distinguish the form(s) through their effect(s), in the same manner that we might judge the performance of a stand-up comic in the social arena. When the three work together, as Bahktin and others have suggested, the burden of interpretability is ultimately the readers. Like all readers' interpretations however, these may be reinterpreted when subjected to the machinations of various new contexts and discursive communities. The distinguishing attributes of irony, parody and satire are often contested on the grounds of the intentionality of the author versus those of the viewer/reader. An intended parody may be read as a satire and *vice versa*, one as complementary, the other perhaps as derisive or antagonistic. The reader's efforts may not after all, coincide with the producers', and commonsensically, this is what happens all the time in social transactions—the phrase "I don't get it!" says as much.

It is possible to understand visual and textual humour transactions in social terms, as the articulation of ideologically accented signs whose meaning is dependent upon the complex interaction of an interpretive or discursive community.[4] As Voloshinov argues:

> Every sign, as we know, is a construct between socially organized persons in the process of their interaction. Therefore, *the forms of the signs are conditioned above all by the social organization of the participants involved and also by the immediate conditions of their interaction.* When these forms change so does the sign. And it should be the tasks of the study of ideologies to trace the social life of this sign. (Voloshinov, 1929, 1973:21) (emphasis in the original).

This theoretical model allows us to infer that every ideological sign and ensemble of signs—for instance a work of art, a graphic image or cartoon—is shaped by *social interaction*, which comes "about through the process of social intercourse" and is interpreted by the "social purview of the given time period

---

4. The discussion of discursive communities by Michel Foucault (1972, 1977) is the obvious reference point here. A number of other studies Radway J., (1984), and Lutz C.A and Collins, J. L., (1993), have illustrated the fecundity of this approach.

and a given social group" (21). In this and earlier chapters, I have attempted to demonstrate this process in my reading of cartoon satires and to reveal how it is possible to assign a political dimension to this communication. The next chapter will engage with aspects of this process as these were moderated by the introduction of abstraction into 20th century art and critical discourse.

CHAPTER 5

Modern Art's Nemesis

> Realism is a complete failure, and the two things that artists should avoid are modernity of form and modernity of subject matter. (Oscar Wilde, 1891)[1]

One of my concerns in writing this book has been to examine the history of modernist art *inter alia*; that is, to look at the outside, the underside and occasionally, the dark side. In the two previous chapters, I discussed the pleasure/pain and politics of humour and attempted to articulate the differences between visual forms of irony, parody and satire. In this chapter, I will discuss the public reception of modern art in England and the United States, by focusing upon art world related graphic satires produced by cartoonists working for Punch magazine from the late 1850s through to 1950s, and The New Yorker from 1930 to 1975. This discussion provides the background to subsequent chapters where I will interpret graphic satires of the work of two prominent modern artists, Alexander Calder and Henry Moore, which appeared in both magazines. In addition, I will continue my exploration of Pierre Bourdieu's concept of cultural capital, how it relates to the class background of the cartoonists discussed, their views on contemporary art, and the editorial policies of the magazines for which they worked. Finally, I will turn my attention to the art of a few artists from each journal: George Morrow, George Loraine Stampa, Robert Bateman from Punch; with Anatol Kovarsky, Whitney Darrow and Barney Toby from The New Yorker. Over the years studied, these artists, with the exception of Bateman, published the largest number of art related cartoons for their respective magazines.

During the past twenty years, historical periodization has become a subject for discussion within several academic fields among them: archeology, history, art history and literary studies. In some instances, art historical research initia-

---

1. Wilde, Oscar. "Intentions: The Decay of Lying" in *The Artist as Critic: Critical Writings of Oscar Wilde*, edited by Richard Ellmann, New York: Vintage Books, Random House (1968:319)

tives originating from these discussions has resulted in the revision of dates for an art movement or the establishment of certain styles, as well as the questioning of the relative importance of specific artists within the historical canon. For example, the legitimacy of the modernist telos that placed Charles Baudelaire's *The Painter of Modern Life* (1863) and Edouard Manet, (not Constantin Guys), at the base and Clement Greenberg and Jackson Pollock at the apex, has been questioned by art historians who lay claim to an earlier beginning for modernism, suggesting instead origin points such as the Revolution of February 1848, the bohemian cenacles of Victor Hugo's Paris of the 1830s, or even the first French Revolution of 1789. In their research activities, practitioners of the so-called "new art history," have attempted to reveal the complex socio-historical relationships between the development of modernity and modernist ideologies through an analysis of various "spatio-temporal settings," "fields of interaction," and "social institutions" (Thompson, 1990:282), In so doing, they have revised our understanding of the usefulness of conventional concepts of individual genius, style, periodization, as well as the construction of a unidimensional (diachronic), *telos* based upon notions of *progress* and *innovation* for the development of western art history. Under the power of certain postmodern ideologies that eschew specific origins and autonomous identities, art historical discourse is now more likely to accommodate modernism as a provisional conflation of several competing ideologies, in contrast to the earlier reified edifice. The singular modernism no longer appears without some relativizing plurality and the artists and signal events that attended modernism's birth and assisted the subsequent construction of the canon, are now identified with greater provisionality than previous scholarship had permitted.[2]

We can understand much about the determinations of modernist ideologies by examining the broader social, economic and cultural contexts of modernity. In the late 1970s, the English art historian T.J. Clark argued that elements of popular culture were often used by 19th century artists to challenge the received models of neoclassical art, which was, at this time, the dominant cultural mode of artistic expression. These elements of popular culture encouraged artists like Courbet and Manet to inject their work with the realistic immediacy of their own social milieu. In an essay published in Screen magazine, Clark suggested that satirical reviews and cartoons of Edouard Manet's canonical painting *Olympia* (1863), provide an index of the symbolic struggle over the meaning of woman

---

2. See Guilbaut, S., (ed.) *Reconstructing Modernism: Art in New York, Paris and Montreal*, Cambridge Mass., London, MIT Press, 1990.

in mid-century French society. His discussion of three cartoon satires of *Olympia* which appeared in the French press shortly after the painting was exhibited in the salon of 1865 underwrite his claim that Manet's painting is situated within two discourses:

> in which the relations and disjunctions of the terms Woman/Nude/Prostitute were obsessively rehearsed (which I shall call, clumsily the discourse on Woman in the 1860s), and the complex but deeply repetitive discourse of aesthetic judgement in the Second Empire" (Clark 1978:23).

It is appropriate to add other discourses to the discussion of modernist art, beyond those identified by Clark in his discussion of Manet's painting. These would include the editorial policies of the media, the politics of humour, race, class and gender, as well as the institutionalized roles of the artist, critic and art historian. Mass produced graphic work of the type that was being produced for La Caricature and Charivari in France, Simplissimus in Germany, Punch in England and Puck, in the United States, provided the vehicles for the advanced art of the day to be examined critically by those working within and outside the centres of high art discourse. In the late C19th the academies, salons, museums, galleries, arts clubs and journals, became sites where the past was being re-interpreted and re-evaluated. In these sites also, artists' reputations were becoming established while the consignment of cultural value was being contested and legitimated. The humour journals were not innocent players in the business of aesthetic judgement. In these sites however, aesthetic evaluation assignments were often less about myth making, canonization and the overall buttressing of the dominant culture, than with its subversion and degradation. It is somewhat ironic that the popular sites where cultural controversies were fomented are now used to reinforce the power of the modernist avant-gardes.

Punch: The London Charivari

There are many books documenting the extraordinary success of Punch,[3] a journal that over the course of its existence became enormously popular and a leading model for many other humour publications. Even before it's unfortunate demise,[4] Punch cartoons would appear at times uncited and with new or altered captions in many magazines, papers and journals around the world. Punch: The Doctors' Humour Magazine, for example, regularly appropriates many Punch cartoons to complement its other major sources for medical cartoons, The New Yorker, Playboy, and Hustler. R.G. Price, a regular Punch contributor during the 1950s, wrote one of the most informative histories of Punch. Published in 1957, Price's book documents the relationships between the writers, cartoonists and editors for each period of the magazine up to the early 1950s. This was quite a task, given that the journal was already 110 years old when he began writing, and more so, when questions relating to its exact origins were still in dispute. During this time, Punch had only seven managing editors, a situation which provided for extraordinary stability in the overall management of the journal, as well as formal continuity from year to year. From 1841-1966 the editors were: Mark Lemon (1841-1870) Shirley Brooks, a.k.a. Epicurus Rotundus (1870-1874), Tom Taylor (1874-80), Sir Francis Cowley Burnand (1880-1906), Sir Owen Seaman (1906-32), E.V. Knox, a.k.a Evoe (1932-1949), and Sir Malcolm Muggeridge (1953-1966). The art editors included: Russell Brockbank, George Morrow, F.H. Townsend, Frank Reynolds, 1920-1930, and Kenneth Bird (1949-52).[5] Price suggests that while each editor imprinted his own style on the magazine's form and management they did little to alter the general tone of the magazine which remained a coherent if somewhat eclectic mix of humorous essays, reviews, poems, witty anecdotes and cartoons.

---

3. An excellent bibliography is contained in Price R.G.G. *A History of Punch* London: Collins (1957). For other sources: see Spielmann, M.H. *The History of 'Punch'*, New York: Cassell Publishing Co. (1895). Many books on individual editors and artists also contain excellent bibliographies, for example: Adrian, Arthur, A. *Mark Lemon, First Editor of Punch*. London: Oxford University Press (1966).

4. At the time of writing, Punch was in the process of being resuscitated.

5. Principal sources for information on Punch include: The Punch reprint of first 50 years by The Times (two years per volume, 1900), Spielmann, M.H. *The History of Punch* (1895); Williams, R.E. *A Century of Punch, Anthology of Pictorial Humour*, Encyclopedia Britannica; Gaunt, William T*he Pre-Raphaelite Tragedy* (1942), *The Aesthetic Adventure* (1945), and *Victorian Olympus* (1952). Other useful sources of information include Ruskin, J., *The Art of England*. (1883), Reitlinger, H. *From Hogarth to Keene* (1938), and Hannay, James, *Satire and Satirists* (1854).

Price and M.H. Spielmann, the historian of Punch's first half century, provide conflicting evidence about the origin and early history of the journal. They acknowledge that depending upon whose family opinion one endorsed, the title of founder of Punch could go to Henry Mayhew, Joseph Last, Ebenezer Landells, or Douglas Jerrold. If financial backing was to become the sole consideration, then the title would have been bestowed upon Ebenezer Landells. If the establishment of the meetings between key players was to become the sole criterion, then journalist and dramatist Henry Mayhew, or printer Joseph Last, would have been accorded the honor, for it was Last who introduced Lemon and Mayhew to Landells, owner of a successful engraving firm, who promised to back the weekly comic journal with the substantial sum of 2000 pounds in seed capital. If editorship dictated the founding of the journal then the title would go to Jerrold, the founding editor, who with Mark Lemon developed the policies, design and overall look of the magazine.

In the 1830s and 1840s, London was the stamping ground of many other comic newspapers, including some with unappealing masthead names like: The Satirist, The Ass, The Wasp, The Scorpion, and The Town. Much of the graphic humour contained in these newspapers and journals derived from models of the Georgian period and before this, the important 18th century satirical drawings and caricature of James Gillray and the social commentary of Rowlandson and Cruikshank, with the major difference being, that these artists drew usually for etchers and metal engravers, while those working in the late C19th drew primarily for wood engravers. Other early influences on Punch's visual material were the topical pamphlets, broadsheets of the day with their powerful wood block drawings.[6] It was clear from the early discussions between the founders however, that images from the C18th should not become the models for their new journal. The major influences on Punch's design were contemporary and French; the beautifully produced, politically very progressive yet short lived La Caricature, morale, religeuse, literaire, et scientifique (1830-1835), and the Paris-based Le Charivari, both of which contained the extraordinary lithographs of Daumier, Philipon, Cham and other important French cartoonists of the period. Given these models it was not surprising that the first Punch appeared on the 17th July 1841 bearing the subtitle The London Charivari, together with an Arthur Henning's cover of grotesques watching a Punch and Judy show. At the time other humour jour-

---

6. See Price (1957), and the appendix therein by art editor Kenneth Bird which documents the change in reproduction methods used by artists working for Punch.

nals were appearing with various names derived from the *comedia del'arte*, the popular Italian improvisatory theatre, or the opera, such as Punchinello, Figaro in London, and the Cambridge Punch, which was modelled loosely upon the earlier Pickwick Papers.

Mark Lemon, as one of three original contributing editors with Jerrold and Mayhew, undertook the task of preparing the press release announcing the forthcoming issues of the new weekly. His brief established what was to become, for many years, the somewhat organic *raison d'etre* of the magazine.

> This guffawgraph is intended to form a refuge for destitute wit—an asylum for the millions of orphan jokes the superannuated Joe Millers—the millions of perishing puns, which are now wandering about without so much as a shelf to rest upon! (Price, 1957:30)

Between them, the editors decided that the journal would contain special departments covering broadly the cultural life of the day: the arts, social events, politics, music, fine arts (painting and sculpture), theatre, book, poetry reviews, fashion, the law and sports. After some difficulties, the first issue appeared on the 17th July 1841 with an editorial titled "The Moral of Punch," written by Lemon, when Douglas Jerrold, who was in Europe at the time, failed to deliver to deadline. This editorial stated another important aim of Punch, that its "higher object" should be "pleasant instruction" (31). There followed several difficult months during which the weekly had to be further bankrolled to save it from folding. With these pressures, Lemon and company decided they needed to find another financial backer and approached the printing firm of William Bradley and Fred Evans who, after some serious negotiation, took over the financial management of the fledgling journal. In 1842, Bradley and Evans became the sole owners of Punch and signed on Lemon as chief editor.

The journal moved shop several times in the early days, and while Lemon directed most of the practical matters pertaining to its production, it was Douglas Jerrold with his working-class background (the son of a printer and self-educated), perhaps more than any other individual, who became responsible for the left liberalism of the paper during the first two years of its existence. With Jerrold's valuable assistance, Lemon also did much to shape the original form of the journal, including during its early years, its progressive left/liberal bias. Lemon became very much a champion of the poor and dispossessed. The editors' progressive support of various social causes, many of which were very unpopular with the English aristocratic and ruling classes, was demonstrated regularly in early issues of the magazine. Lemon was a journalist first, and a dramatist second, but he believed that graphic art was to be an important and politically progressive complement to the literary aspects of the journal. Accordingly, he engaged some very talented artists to work upon the visual content of the journal, including John Leech, one of the first, and in the opinion of many, one of the finest artists to ever work for Punch. He began contributing in 1842 and continued working in an extraordinarily prolific manner for more than twenty years, during which time he executed some 3000 drawings, over 600 of them cartoons. Leech was a former medical student (a few other early contributors were former medical students, which gives some indication of the kind of class background they came from), and a friend of the very talented, upper class, William Makepeace Thackeray, who became one of the most popular of the early Punch contributors. Richard (Dickie) Doyle another of the Punch cartoonists from the first decade produced the cover design that was finally adopted for the magazine's masthead.

During the first ten years, there was much evidence of the contesting of the editorial terrain in ideological and class terms, which is not surprising given the heterogeneous class backgrounds and political beliefs of some of the chief players. Jerrold's working class left liberalism clashed with the conservative values of the class-conscious Thackeray and Leech, who wanted to shift the tone and content of Punch toward the culture of the upper classes, aristocrats and landed gentry. Lemon, a great liberal himself, let each pursue their own ideological positions with little direct editorializing of their work, valuing each for their individual contributions, but never allowing any one of them to foreground their own class and ideological positions in the journal. John Tenniel, another early Punch cartoonist, was won over to the popular domain from the world of high culture. He contributed cartoons and drawings from 1850 and was particularly popular among the readership for his political cartoons. Other early cartoonists included, Charles Keene, a former student colleague of Tenniel, and somewhat later, the French born George du Maurier (Kiki), who began to work consistently for the journal from 1852. Throughout the first three decades of the journal these artists, in the company of the inimitable Phil May, produced a large number of art world related cartoons, some gently ironical representations of the foibles and pretensions of academicians, and many direct satires of every aspect of the art system as it was then constituted, not all of them identified as by their hand. As was common practice in many humour journals of this time, writers would either promote certain visual ideas which the artists would illustrate, or the more likely scenario, they would attach captions to an artist's image after it was completed. Often a text would be interspersed with visuals that would illustrate the regular diet of linguistic puns served up by the writers. The Punch staff called these the "small cuts." In the first decades the journal was text heavy with images subordinated to the witty ironical and satirical texts that accompanied them. Drawings were made directly on to wood blocks that were then sent to the engravers who would prepare them for the press. This was a highly skilled and labour intensive activity on the part of all those involved. It is unfortunate, that as a result of these production methods, for the first forty years of the journal many of the original drawings, with the exception of some preparatory studies, have been lost.

The full-page drawings in the first volume of Punch were often headed under the title "Mr. Punch's Penciling." The second volume changed this to "Penciling" and for a short time "Social Miseries." Price suggests that these were the ancestors of the individual joke drawing dominating the cartoon genre today. In 1843 a public competition for the decoration of the new Houses of Parliament led Punch to parody the process. The Punch editors developed their own entries, using the term cartoon, which for several hundred years had been reserved as a technical description for large scale preparatory work for the interior decoration of architecture commissioned by the church, Europe's royal families and landed gentry. By 15th July 1843, cartoon parodies appeared in the place of the "Penciling." The term cartoon was dropped for a time but soon returned, making Punch responsible for the conjoining of distinct forms of pictorial and textual humour into one form, the cartoon as we know it today. As editor, Lemon was primarily responsible for the elevation of the artists' work to a position equal to the writers for the journal. In the early days he would drive to his artists' studios and according to Price, the short journeys were always in a Hansom Cab using the same cabman (48).

In his *Art of England* (1883) lectures, John Ruskin devoted some space to the discussion of the Punch artists,[7] showing by this time how the artists had been incorporated, albeit at a subordinate level, into the domains of high art and subsequently, the cultural historiography of an era. This did not prohibit the cartoonists, during the first three decades of the journal, from producing large numbers of cartoons and drawings ironizing and satirizing the predomi-

---

7. Ruskin's lectures were presented at the Slade. Price suggest that Ruskin's "aesthetic theories and his politics were at odds," which lead him to praise the technical drawing skills of Leech, du Maurier, and Tenniel, (comparing du Maurier to Holbein, and Tenniel to Tintoretto), but that they were altogether "too middle class." "John Bull was always shown as a farmer, never as a manufacturer or shopkeeper" (Price: 119).

nant features of the London art world. Many of the best were collected together into an anthology edited by J.A. Hammerton under the title *The Punch Library of Humour: Stage, Study and Studio*.[8] This volume included the work of many of Punch's early graphic artists including: Fred Barnard, W.S. Bruncton, George Du Maurier, Ernest Griset, Charles Keene, John Leech, Phil May, Gordon Thompson, H.M. Bateman, J.L.C. Booth, W.K. Haselden, Philip Baynes, Thomas Maybank, and Charles Pears. Many of the cartoons included in this volume satirize various aspects of the high art institutions of the day, including: aesthetics, creativity, art criticism, the Royal Academy, the role of the artist, artist's models, commerce, talent, genius, and the modes and manners of English class relations. Class difference was always a favourite early topic of the Punch satirists, whether working with pen or pencil.

In the first years of the magazine, full page drawings, so much a feature of the Paris based Charivari, were limited in number. The Punch staff dubbed the large scale cartoon the "big cut" (44), a possible reference to its potential for carrying invective as much as for its control over the space of each page. The small cuts remained as humorous and usually subordinate additions to linguistic puns and anecdotes. Price provides us with some important insights into how the editors related to the art world of their day. Burnand, he suggested, had none of the intellectual interests of editor Shirley Brooks, who followed Mark Lemon as managing editor. According to Price, this period of Punch's coverage of the arts "lacked sharpness":

> Art was treated primarily as a commodity; in the 1870s and 1880s nearly every number had a joke about a painter or his patrons. There was a stereotype of a modern artist or poet and that remained as fixed as Keene's drunken cabbies or Tenniel's national bestiary. Punch attacked the Aesthetic Movement without much clear idea of how the aesthetic movement was developing.

And subsequently,

> In the sixties [1860s], Punch had recognized Meredith and Whistler well ahead of the general public, but now more and more it reacted to vitality with philistine guffaws. There was far too much about Wilde's poses, far too little precise satire of the Movement he publicized. Generally speaking, Punch under Burnand, as under Seaman, was interested in art only for its eccentricities. For years at a time the subject was virtually ignored (131).

---

8. Hammerton, J.A., *Punch Library of Humour, Stage and Studio* London: Educational Book Co.

Price is somewhat correct in his observations regarding Seaman and Burnand, yet a closer examination of both the content and the volume of satires during this period, do not really confirm his observation that the art world was "virtually ignored." Hundreds of art world cartoons reveal that the Punch artists were vigorously attacking the very basis of the developing art market, as well as class privilege and patronage. In the last decades of the nineteenth century, Punch cartoonists directed much critical attention to the art world and the shocking developments of contemporary art. This corresponded to the topical attention accorded the development of modernism by this journal's sister publications, Simplicissimus, and Charivari, in Germany and France. The Punch cartoonists' satirical critiques of the forms of modernist art coincided not only with their attention to the early development of the art market in Britain, but also with their engagement with topical debates in the Nation's parliament, struggles in the colonies, the further stratification of the classes under the pressures of capitalist development, as well as the armed conflicts in South Africa, and Europe culminating in the outbreak of World War I. Then, as now, cartoonists demonstrated that they were "up with the play."

From the 1840s onward, class was often foregrounded in witty essays, poems and cartoons. Many of the art cartoons represent stereotypical characters with captions revealing that they are speaking with regional or class-based accents. The dialogue in these captions typically contrasts the received pronunciation of the educated upper-and middle-class members of the Academy—the King's English—with the heavily inflected speech of the urban working classes or the provincial dialects of rural peasants. For example, a Phil May cartoon from the 1850s shows a painter receiving the following question from his Irish model: "Would you mand telling me, sorr, who was the greatist arrrtist iver been—av' course prisent company always excepted!" A similar Booth cartoon shows a pipe smoking artist, who suggests to his rustic model "You'd better "rest" a bit. Sitting still seems very tiring to you," to which the model replies, "(mindful of instructions of local photographer), It ain't the sitting still mister. It's the 'olding me breath!" The caption writers parody and contrast of regional dialects and class accents is a common device to provide some levity to what might otherwise be a rather conventional studio portrait.

Systems of patronage as well as the developing institutionalization of the art world kept Punch cartoonists busy with ironic caption/image combinations during the first decades of the journal. From 1910 to 1940, however, the art and behaviour of the historical avant-gardes increasingly engaged their satirical attention. Many of the cartoons during these decades carry lengthy captions identifying Cubists, Vorticists and Futurists, occasionally conflating very different avant-garde art styles for satirical affect. The first Post-Impressionist exhibition held in London in 1910 produced a crop of cartoons satirizing the avant-garde art forms of the day. Of these artists' relationship towards modernist art, Price suggested:

> The Punch artists had less and less curiosity about what their colleagues in other fields were doing, and this isolation was paralleled by the curious jokes in the paper about "Modern Art," which changed very little until the end of World War II. One difficulty that must in fairness be mentioned, was that from the nineties of the last century to the forties of this, contemporary art was far less representational than before or since. The illustrators were left high and dry. It was not until after 1937 that the humorous possibilities of early twentieth century art were seized and then they were seized nearly a generation late (158).

Again, some aspects of Price's description ring true until one examines more closely the evidence provided in the cartoons themselves. Many of those published from the 1890s to the late 1930s are clearly topical and reveal that the artists had a keen understanding of both the development of modernism and the cultural strategies of the historical avant-gardes, more so perhaps, than their writer colleagues. I believe that Price's statement represents his own distance from what Punch artists were doing during his tenure with the journal. Perhaps the fact that these artists were not as visible in their relationship with the magazine than some of the writers lead him to assume that they were working in isolation and were somewhat out of touch with what their artist colleagues were doing in the Academy. Punch's artists, several of whom were subsequently admitted to the Royal Academy, demonstrated a keen interest in deflating the egos of many of their exhibiting R.A. colleagues. This parallels the position some thirty years later of New Yorker cartoonists with respect to the successes enjoyed by some of their avant-garde colleagues.

For many years, George Morrow's pastiches of the annual Royal Academy exhibits were published under the headline "Academy Depressions." The "Glossary for the Opening of the Royal Academy" (1908), by R.J. Richardson, contains a list of aphorisms bearing similar ironic content to some of the "Depressions" cartoons and has a very contemporary relevance, even today.

Art

An Artist is a person who paints what he sees.

An Amateur is a person who thinks he paints what he sees.

An Impressionist is a person who paints what other people thinks he sees.

A Popular Artist is a person who paints what other people think they say.

A Successful Artist is a person who paints what he thinks other people see.

A Great Artist is a person who paints what other people see they think.

A Failure is a person who sees what other people think they see.

A Portraitist is a person who paints what other people don't think he sees.

A Realist is a person who sees what other people don't paint.

An Idealist is a person who paints what other people don't see.

The Hanging Committee are people who don't see that other people think they paint.

A Royal Academician is a person who doesn't think and paints what other people see.

A Genius is a person who doesn't see and paints what other people don't think.

A Critic is a person who doesn't paint and thinks what other people don't see.

The Public are people who don't see or think what other people don't paint.

A Dealer is a person that sees that people who paint don't think, and who thinks that people who don't paint don't see. He sees people who don't see people who paint; he thinks that people who don't see people who see; and he sees what people who don't paint think.

Finally

A Reader is a person whose head swims (189-90).

Early Punch parodies of the Academy and art world discourse are extremely witty and irreverent, but they do not match the incisive quality of many of the satires from the post-World War II period which concentrated upon modern arts shocking shift from naturalist and realist representation toward greater abstraction and theoretical complexity. Prior to 1920, however, there are a few cartoons that stand out for their close understanding of contemporary art.

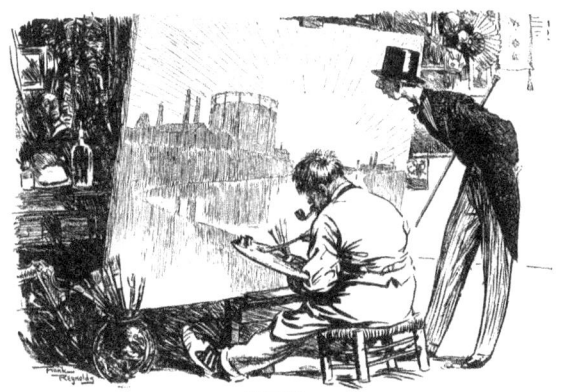

Figure 18: Frank Reynolds *Realism*, Punch Sept 24, 1913
© Punch Cartoon Library, Top Foto

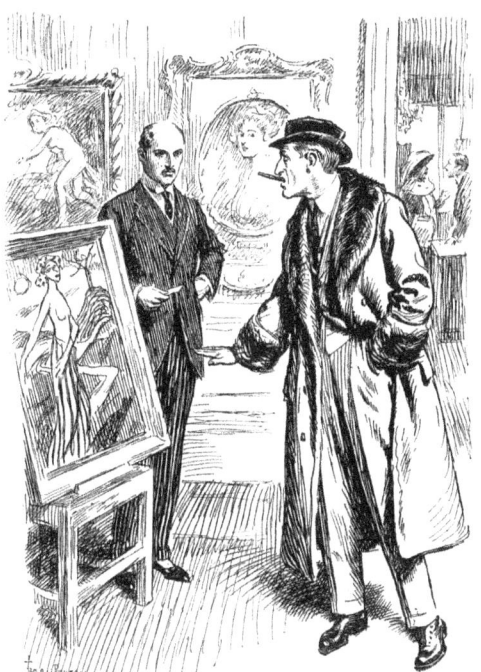

Figure 19: Fred Pegrail *The Tapestry Mode* Punch December 13, 1913
© Punch Cartoon Library.

Frank Reynolds' cartoon (fig. 18), for example, shows an upper-class twit, top hat and tail, described in the caption as an "Impressionable Visitor" (a simple pun on Impressionism), looking at a stereotypical bearded artist who is painting a large canvas of a gasworks by a river. As he scrutinizes the painting he exclaims "By Jove! The Gas Works! Now that really is top hole! Do you know, I'll swear I smelt gas as I came in!" The caption title "Realism" indicating the painting of the gas works is contrasted with the reality that the "impressionable" visitor smells when he enters the studio. The subtle allusion to farting would not have been lost on the alert Punch readership; neither for some, would the subtle reference to art world debates about the social relevance of impressionistic versus realist representations of socialist subject matter.

According to its wordy caption, Fred Pegrail's cartoon (fig.19) shows "A (cockney) nouveau riche millionaire" (declining to purchase the Post-Impressionist creation), offered by a stereotypical bourgeois art dealer. The cockney says: "Noth'n Doin! Why my maiden a'nt cud darrn a better picture 'n that." Together this cartoon image and caption challenges the conventional aesthetic codes of high and popular art, underlining the difference between the unique character of academic painting and the popular hooking and crocheting methods of image production (from mass produced patterns), practiced and enjoyed by the lower and lower middle classes.

The first introduction of the Futurist avant-garde to London in 1912 provided very fertile ground for many graphic satires and many punning reviews, including the following witty example:

Dynamic Art

It is very gratifying to learn that the Italian Futurists who are now flabbergasting London with the exhibition of their works at the Sackville Gallery will be succeeded during the coming Summer by some even more wildly sensational Schools of Painting. These consist of three groups (or speeds), the Present, The Imperfect, and the Pluperfect Subjunctivists, all hailing from the banditti-infested regions of Sicily, and they will give their performance at Olympia just after the horse show. They have thrown over the obsolete and archaic traditions of the Futurists, who "stand upon the summit of the world and cast their challenge to the stars." The Subjunctivists "sit upon the stars and bite their thumbs at the moon."[9]

---

9. Punch March 20, 1912.

Modern Art's Nemesis

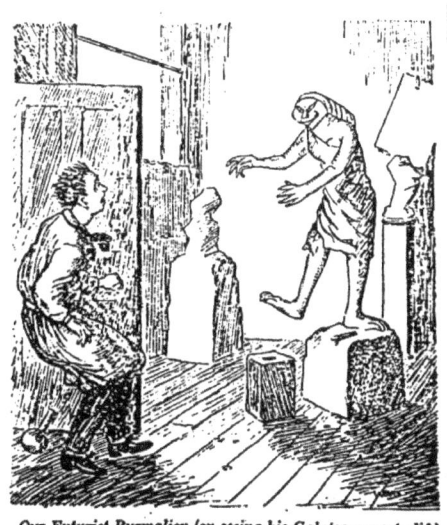

Figure 20: Ward, Punch April 1, 1914 © Punch Cartoon Library.

A Punch cartoon by Ward from 1914 (fig. 20), recapitulates the idealist/ materialist split. Positioned in the midst of the Punch Charivaria section, this image ironizes the Pygmalion and Galatea myth with the caption "Our Futurist Pygmalion on seeing his very ugly Galatea come to life— "Oh, why didn't I remain an idealist."

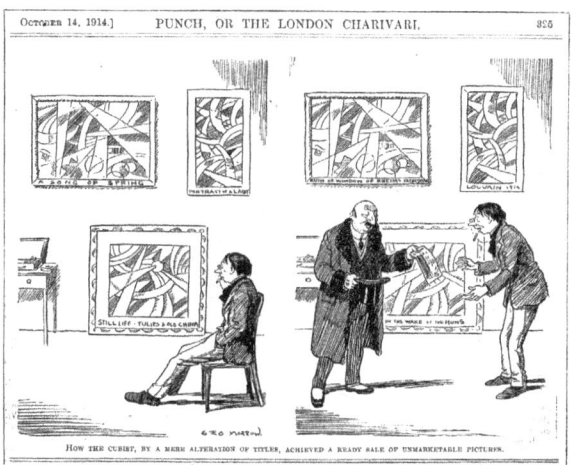

Figure 21: Geo Morrow, Punch October 14th 1914,
Punch Cartoon Library Top Foto

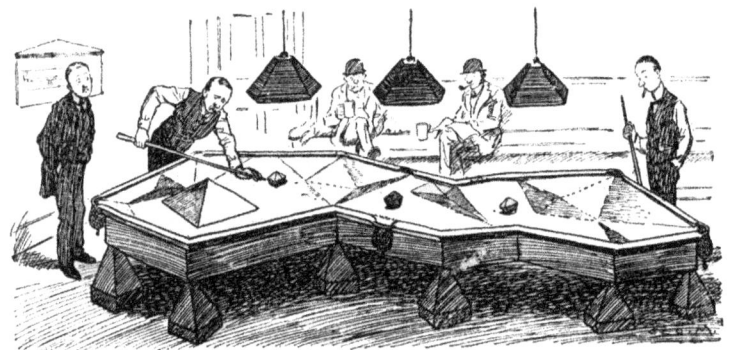

Figure 22: Geo Morrow, *Spread of Cubism*, Punch 29 April 1914.
Punch Cartoon Library Top Foto.

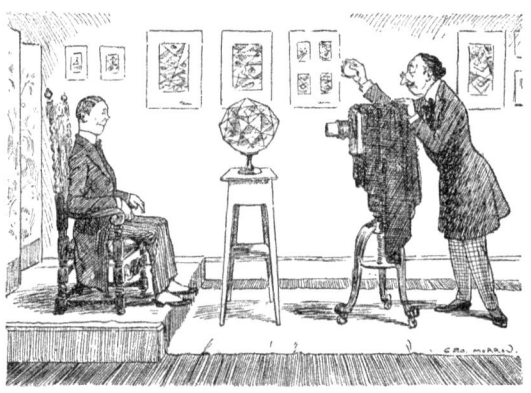

Figure 23: Geo Morrow, *Cubist Photographer*, Punch 17 June 1914.
Punch Cartoon Library Top Foto.

By the late 1920s, graphic satires of Cubism and Futurism were appearing in many newspapers and journals throughout Europe and North America. Punch contained some hilarious cartoons in response to the showing of Cubist art in the Post-Impressionist shows prior to the outbreak of World War I. Two brilliant examples were provided by the prolific art satirist George Morrow. *The Spread of Cubism* (fig. 22), represents a functioning—on paper at least—cubist billiard table with polygonal table, pyramid legs and cubist balls. Morrow produced a similar cartoon *The Cubist Photographer* (fig. 23) which shows an artist photographing his young male subject through a large polygonal cut glass lens that wildly anticipates the invention of the mosaic lens and other devices used for creative fractionizing of images today.

As Melley and Glaves-Smith noted in their exhibition catalogue (see Chapter 2), the destruction of World War I became a subtext in many of the art cartoons from this period. In a two-panel work, George Morrow satirizes the spread of Cubism through a superbly ironic association with the contemporary conflict in Europe. Here, in order to secure approval and/or a sale from his patron, the artist simply changes the titles of some of his parodies of Cubo-Futurist paintings. A substitute for *Song of Spring* is provided in the title *Ruin of Window at Rheims Cathedral*; *Portrait of a Lady* becomes *Louvain*—site of one of the first disastrous battles of WWI—and the ultra-conventional painting *Still Life, Tulips, and Old China* assumes a new identity armed with the provocative new title *In the Wake of the Huns*. Morrow's cartoon reveals the political naivety of any artist attempting to imbue his work with 'political correctness' through the inappropriate use of titles, and the hypocrisy of the patron who likely could demonstrate his recent purchases to his friends as his contribution to the war effort. For satirical affect, many of the captions of Punch cartoons from this period conflate the distinct periods and strategies of the historical avant-gardes by providing the artists with impossible titles such as "Post-Cubist-Impressionist Sculptor" and "Post-Realist-Cubist-Vorticist Painter." In another extraordinary cartoon of the period Morrow reveals the widespread antipathy toward Cubism demonstrated by those in high art circles principally South Kensington art educators and members of the Royal Academy—by showing "an aged academician compelled to sit for his portrait by a Cubist." This cartoon was paired with another, showing a group of upset Scotsmen, Robert Burns Club members, "Constrained to assist at an Englishman's reading of a selection from the works of the poet in the vernacular." Above both cartoons the revealing caption reads, "Compulsion all round as a means of hardening the national character," an ironic reference to war time propaganda in the media which promoted Nationalist agendas throughout this period of conflict. From 1914-1918, Futurist abstraction continued to be the subject of many satires. This provided a particular irony, since Marinetti's famous Le Figaro manifesto (1909), in company with other Futurist texts propagated the anarchistic belief that war—"The Health

Giver of the World"—was an acceptable *tabula rasa* upon which to build a technological utopia.

Another Morrow cartoon cleverly satirizes the elitist boundaries of high art's sub-cultural avant-garde. It shows a *plein air* painter, cigarette coolly dangling from his lower lip being addressed by a rustic farmer. Forestalling rustic criticism directed at his progressive abstraction the artist says, "Yes, I know this isn't like a sheep, and the house isn't like that house and the trees are the wrong shape and colour. I'm sorry!" But the farmer, identified as a national service man from Chelsea (possibly a conscientious objector undertaking essential rural labour), replies in perfect King's English: "My dear fellow, you don't do yourself justice. Your work interests me extremely. I should describe it as neo-cubistic Vorticism, I think."

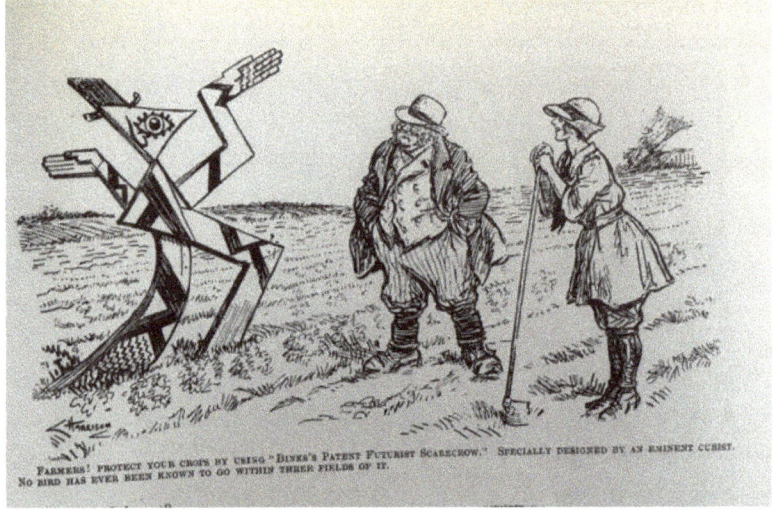

Figure 24: Harrison, Punch July 17, 1918. Punch Cartoon Library Top Foto.

A cartoon by Harrison (fig. 24), published just four months before the armistice, alludes indirectly to the employment of avant-garde artists to produce camouflage for ships, tanks, planes and other war materiel of this period. The camouflage, in the form of a modernist scarecrow—"Binks patented Futurist Scarecrow," designed by an eminent Cubist—is so aggressive that it protects the crops from all voracious birds. The "sweet young thing" promoting its use to the portly gentleman farmer tells him that "no bird has ever been known to

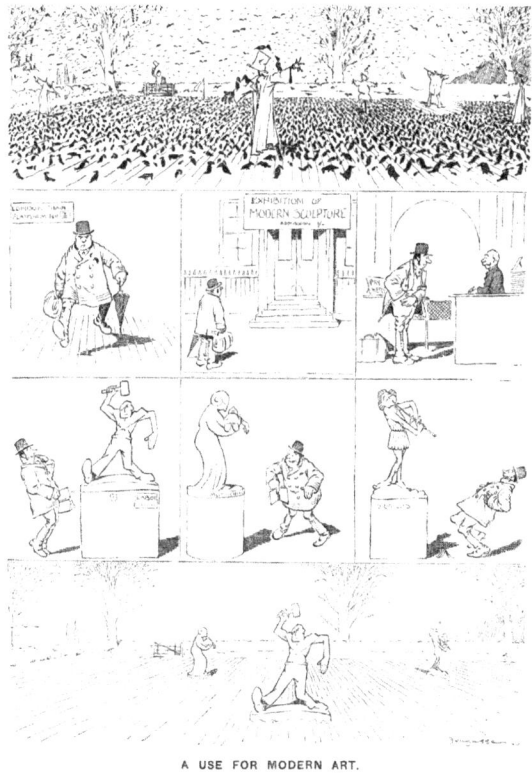

Figure 25: Fougasse, *A Use for Modern Art Punch*. May 5, 1920. Punch Cartoon Library Top Foto.

go within three fields of it." In Fougasse's "A Use for Modern Art" (fig. 25), a multi-frame cartoon panel of the same year, a non-functional modernist sculpture[10] is employed as a scarecrow, thus cementing for some fifty years a solid satirical relationship between modern art and crop protection.

Throughout the war years, George Morrow continued his satirical attacks on modern art, succeeding in becoming the most prolific satirist of modernist art who ever worked for Punch. During the 48 years, he contributed to the journal, he published nearly a hundred cartoons satirizing modern art, artists and art world foibles. The reason for this prolific activity is evident when we examine what little is known about his class origins and his own attitudes towards modernism.[11]

---

10. This sculpture bears a resemblance to some social realist work of the period.

11. Dictionary of British Book Illustrators and Caricaturists.

George Morrow (1869-1955), his brothers Albert (1863-1927), and Edwin (1903-1914), also Punch contributors, were born in Belfast, Northern Ireland. As sons of a working-class house decorator they would have acquired little cultural capital in the form of education. But typical of some progressive working and lower middle-class class families, at least one of the sons may have been encouraged to seek cultural capital in the form of an education, thus achieving some measure of class transcendence, although university level education would have been unusual. George Morrow demonstrated an early aptitude towards art and managed to travel to Paris in the 1890s, where he was greatly influenced by the work of the socialist artist Alexandre Steinlen, whose pseudonym Caran D'Ache (pencil) graced the pages of the left wing and anarchist magazines *Gil Blas Illustre* and *L'assiette au beuree*. In 1924, at the age of 54, Morrow began to contribute his work to Punch and eight years later, he became art editor, serving in this capacity for five years. He continued to draw for the magazine until one month before his death in 1955. In the last years of his life, he was finally admitted to the Royal Academy and exhibited there and with the Royal Society for British Artists. But from all accounts he remained a bohemian throughout his life. For many years he produced the Academy "Depressions" which represent a range of satirical responses to those official artists exhibiting their work in the bastions of high culture. His entry into the academy in later life may have been a source of some amusement to himself and consternation to his old working-class friends. But perhaps, after fifty years of pillorying modernist art, the Academy, which by the late 1940s had become a bastion of cultural conservatism, was the right place for Morrow and some of his anti-modernist colleagues.

George Loraine Stampa, another prolific art cartoonist for Punch[12] was born in London on the 29th November 1875. The son of an architect, Stampa was educated at the Bedford Modern School. Unlike Morrow, he received an extensive and quite traditional fine arts education, which at this time, would have necessitated much technical study of the figure, drawing from plaster casts of the antique, and very little or no academic work in the form of art history study and language arts.

---

12. Punch cartoonists who produced large numbers of art cartoons from 1909-1950), include: "Anton" (H. Underwood Thompson and Mrs Antonia Yeoman) (1950-60, 17 cartoons), Russell Brockbank, (1950-60, 9 cartoons), H.M Bateman (* 9 cartoons), Beauchamp (12 cartoons), Eric Burgin, 1950-60 (11 cartoons), Louis Baumer (15 cartoons), W. Bird (Jack B. Yeats). (20 cartoons), Kenneth Bird (Fougasse), (21 cartoons), Robert Cruikshank, George du Maurier F. Rowland Emett (20 cartoons), Michael ffolkes (1950-60 33 cartoons), William Hewison, H.J., Hod (Bernard Hollowood), Ionicus (J.C. Armitage), Charles Keene, Kenneth Mahood (1950-60, 18 cartoons), Edwin Morrow, George Morrow* (75 art cartoons), W Mills (17 cartoons) E.T. Reed, Frank Reynolds (* 26), William Scully (20 cartoons) , Ronald Searle, L.H. Siggs (1950-60, 11 cartoons), W.A. Sillince (1950-60 7 cartoons), Smilby (F.W. Smith), (1950-60 21 cartoons), George Sprod (1950-60 14), G.L. Stampa, L.H. Starke, J.W. Taylor (1950-60 7 cartoons), John Tenniel (7 cartoons).

He studied art at Heatherly's School (circa, 1892), and this was followed by a period of five years at the Royal Academy Schools 1895-1900. Stampa was described as a "raffish bohemian" and as a "spiritual successor to Charles Keene and Phil May, preferring the London streets for his drawings than the salons of Mayfair"[13] He contributed to Punch for fifty-five years from 1895-1950, as well as to the Moonshine (1898), and The Graphic (1910). For Punch, during this time, he produced over thirty-four art world related cartoons, including, in my view, some of the most extraordinary examples from the early years of the 20th century. He produced as well large numbers of very naturalistic low life drawings for Punch and other humour magazines.

Frank Reynolds (1876-1953), the next highest on the ladder of prolific art satirists for Punch produced twenty-six cartoon satires over the period studied. He was born 13 February 1876 in London and like Stampa studied at Heatherleys before taking up work as an illustrator for the Illustrated London News and The Sketch. Reynolds subsequently joined the Punch staff in 1919 and became art editor for twelve years during the editorship of Owen Seaman. Cyril Kenneth Bird (Fougasse), another active art satirist working for Punch had an unusual dot and dash style of drawing. By the 1930s, he had become one of the most widely recognized cartoonists in the world. Fougasse did not originally study art but obtained a BSc degree and had for the time a rather unconventional introduction to art and cartooning through correspondence with the Percy V. Bradshaw Press Art School. His education was interrupted by the war, where a wound in the spine that he received at Gallipoli in 1914, left him crippled for life. His pen name, Fougasse, was borrowed from the small French landmine that was responsible for his injuries. In 1917 he submitted his first Punch cartoon and by 1937 he became the art editor, and twelve years later, a full editor of the journal. In later years he began work on a survey of British and American cartoon art under the title *The Good-Tempered Pencil* (1956). Fougasse was an early proselyte for the art of cartooning, using the radio as his chief broadcast instrument. He believed "(cartoon) humour to be more important than (high) art" and stated often that "it's really better to have a good idea with a bad drawing than a bad idea with a good drawing."[14]

---

13. Biographical Entry, British Dictionary of Book Illustrators and Caricaturists.
Digital images of Punch Art Cartoons are available at https://punch.photoshelter.com/gallery-image/Art-Cartoons/

14. In 1948 Fougasse produced a beautiful cartoon in his mature dot and dash style with radio as his theme. "The Disturber of the Peace" shows a cut away view of life in an apartment building with a radio blaring away in every room, the sound represented by lines exploding in all directions.

Henry Mayo Bateman (1887-1970) immortalized as "The man who drew the twentieth century" (Anderson, 1982: i) is a good example of the antipathetic relationship towards modern art held by many of the Punch artists of the time. Bateman was born in Sutton Forest, New South Wales, Australia and after first receiving some education at Forest Hill House School, he returned with his parents to England, subsequently enrolling in classes at Westminster and New Cross Art Schools. His apprenticeship included a period in the studio of Charles von Avermaet from whom he would have received an introduction to fine art, but he began drawing for comic journals in 1906. Bateman received some important early encouragement from Phil May and his work was soon being compared to Caran D'Ache and to the styles of artists working for Simplicissimus. He contributed to nearly all of the leading journals of the day and like his colleague Fougasse, he was not afraid to strongly voice his concerns and opinions about art—"art ain't all paint," he suggested frequently. In his excellent biography of Bateman, Anthony Anderson underlines the artist's deeply conservative attitudes toward art, modernist avant-garde art in particular.

> Despite the fact that in his own way he was an innovator, a creative artist of originality, he, like many of his contemporaries, distrusted the trends in modern art which led away from the figurative towards abstraction. (Anderson, 1982:145-46)

Anderson reveals that Bateman had a profound disliking of modernist art, that he "detested Matisse' and "thought Picasso a trickster—that in its search for freedom art had lost its way" (146). Bateman argued that the subject in art was the most important thing for an artist to consider and that abstract art had evacuated the reason for art as a system of representation.

> A couple of beer bottles, a chamber pot, an ashcan...the move is towards the abstract when the object ceases to matter at all. What does count is an expression of the painter's mind...the public is invited to solve a riddle. If there is any sign of delusion, tension or other mental disturbance so much the better. (146)

Bateman satirized Roger Fry's Grafton Street exhibition Post-Impressionism and the subsequent 1914 Exhibition of Futurist art. He often worked with a comic story in several panels without frames. His "Brother Brushes" cartoon follows the desperation of a figurative painter who is introduced to modern art by a fashionable young contemporary. After puzzling over this new work, he undergoes a conversion. In the top right panel, he is shown performing some contortionist acts, painting on his knees, through his legs, bending over backwards, standing upside down, to produce a variety of Cubo-Futurist inventions bearing the titles: "A Man," "Peace," "Storm," "The Arrival," all clearly related to the Italian Futurist Boccioni's paintings of 1911-12, with the addition of the clearly satirical "Mugwumps" style painting for comparison. The final frames reveal the artist being courted by a wealthy collector. The artist's avant-gardism has enabled him to achieve success and notoriety, and he is pictured being driven off in a chauffeur driven limousine. As he and his wife drive by, their noses held high in self-esteem, crowds of admirers line the roadway cheering and doffing their top hats. It is tempting to attribute Bateman's scorn toward intellectuals and members of the Imperial ruling classes to his working-class colonialist background.

Punch magazine was a very responsive vehicle to the public appreciation and lack thereof, of modern art. Its writers and artists acted as a kind of barometer of opinion, registering in symbolic form, the shock of the new in modernist art. They also represented the difficulty that many individuals had in accommodating major challenges to their beliefs and assumptions about the value and meaning of art in society. The arrival of European modernism to America provides further insight into this dynamic and how the media can become a site for registering the temperature of public opinion.

The Armory Show

An event of near legendary status, the Armory Show has been credited with establishing European modernist values firmly within the American context. Its importance as an early example of the shock of modernism, and the resulting public disaffection for modern art should not be underestimated. While it has been the subject of several books and articles[15] and is mentioned in nearly every art history text on modernist art, I would like to examine this event in passing before we proceed to discuss The New Yorker and its principal art satirists.

The Armory Show represents a bridge between Europe and North America. Many of the art works appearing in exhibitions organized by Roger Fry for the Grafton Gallery which had previously ignited the public in London, turned up in New York a few weeks later at the Armory Show. In fact, Fry was an-

---

15. See Brown, M.W. *The Story of The Armory Show* New York: The Joseph H Hirshorn Foundation, (1963); *The Armory Show International Exhibition of Modern Art 1913* Vols I, II, III, New York: Arno Press (1972).

noyed that one of his shows had to be cut short to meet the commitments to the American organizers of the exhibition. The International Exhibition of Modern Art, its proper title, was organized by executive members of the Association of American Painters and Sculptors: Arthur Davies, Elmer MacRae, Walt Kuhn, and Walter Pach, for the 69th Infantry Armory at Lexington Ave and 25th Street, New York City, February 15th March 15th, 1913. The exhibition toured subsequently to Chicago and Boston.[16] The Armory, deemed the only space large enough to accommodate the show provided the necessary space for over 1300 works[17], two thirds by contemporary American artists: Hopper, Davies, McRae, Bellows, Sloan, Kuhn, and others, and the other third consisting of work by many leading European artists tracing the development of modernism: Delacroix, Ingres, Coot, Cezanne, Degas, Rodin, Brancusi, Redon, Van Gogh, Gauguin, Matisse, Picasso, Braque, Duchamp, and Picabia. The organizers printed some 120.000 pamphlets, postcards and catalogues, and sent press releases to every major paper in New York, a process that was followed to a somewhat lesser extent in the later venues, Chicago and Boston. This mass advertising of the event stimulated the desired result, encouraging thousands of people to attend the exhibit, over 85,000 visitors— 75,000 paying—in New York alone. Thousands more saw the exhibition when it travelled to the other venues.[18] Some members of the progressive New York cultural scene were previously familiar with the European avant-garde through books, catalogues, and journals, from England and France, as well as through the pioneering exhibitions mounted by Alfred Stieglitz at the Photo-Secession Gallery, 291 Fifth Avenue, but the American public as a whole, and indeed, many of the exhibiting artists were unprepared for the type of work sent by the Europeans. They were appalled. The avant-garde works in the exhibition from Europe stimulated many savage denunciations from members of the public, and a veritable feeding frenzy of media attention from critics, editorial writers and cartoonists. It is no understatement to suggest that the battle for the hearts and minds of the public was played out in the pages of the newspapers of Hearst and Pulitzer. The headlines described the avant-garde art as rebellious, subversive, revolutionary, extremist, and lawless, the product of deficient minds. As one contemporary commentator wrote, the mob had become the art critic.[19]

---

16. The Chicago Art Institute March 24-April 16, 1913, and the Copley Society April 28 May 19, 1913.

17. An exact figure is not available because some uncatalogued works were added to the show at the last minute.

18. Approximately 13,000 visitors in Boston, and 20,000 in Chicago.

19. "Mob as Art Critic," Literary Digest XLVI (March 29, 1913:708-9).

The New York Times Magazine headline said it all: CUBISTS AND FUTURISTS MAKING INSANITY PAY. Although none of the Futurists were able to participate because of prior exhibition commitments in Europe, their fame had preceded them. The New York World (February 17, 1913) published several graphic satires under the revealing caption "NOBODY WHO HAS BEEN DRINKING IS LET IN TO SEE THIS SHOW." In all three cities the newspaper cartoonists went to town, producing some very incisive cartoon satires of modernist art. One of the best of these was published in the New York Evening Sun, under the lead line SEEING NEW YORK WITH A CUBIST, by J Griswold. His cartoon *The Rude Descending a Staircase (Rush Hour at the Subway)*, satirized Marcel Duchamp's *Nude Descending a Staircase* (1912), the work singled out as the most outrageous in the show. Duchamp's *Nude* became the focus for much of the public's derision and was subjected to many visual and textual pastiches, parodies, lampoons, and satires. The American Art News offered a $10 prize for the best solution to the whereabouts of the nude which was won with a poem titled "it's only a man."

> You've tried to find her
> And you've looked in vane
> Up the picture and down again,
> You've tried to fashion her of broken bits,
> And you've worked yourself into seventeen fits;
> The reason you've failed to tell you I can,
> It isn't a lady but only a man.

M.W. Brown recounts how the Duchamp work was labeled in the press with many colourful descriptives such as: "A lot of disused golf clubs and bags"; "an assortment of half-made leather saddles"; an "elevated railroad stairway in ruins after an earthquake"; "a dynamited suit of Japanese armor"; a "pack of brown cards in a nightmare"; an "orderly heap of broken violins"; "an academic painting in an artichoke," and the one that eventually stuck "an explosion in a shingle factory," attributed to Julian Street, or Joel Spingarn (Brown, 1963:110). As is common to most art controversies, the Armory show stimulated a number of parodists to get in on the act. Mock modernist exhibitions of Cubist and Futurist art—burlesques containing pastiches of the offending works, were orchestrated, some by the most offended members of the National Academy of Design, and others by hastily formed groups such as "Les Anciens de l'Academie Julian." The Society of American Fakirs, a satirical group associated with the Arts Students League[20], produced a children's' book satire of cubism bearing the title of *Cubies ABC* by Mary and Earl Lyall (115). In a somewhat racist condemnation, conservative art critic Royal Cortissoz called the European section of the exhibit "Ellis Island Art"[21], and his colleague Kenyon Cox in a somewhat more reasoned, yet still shocked response, confirmed his prediction of two years earlier that indeed art had "fallen into the abyss." "Deliberately and determinedly," he wrote, "these men have stepped over the edge" (Rose:1975: 73).

Former President Theodore Roosevelt (1859-1919), took the opportunity to pen a "layman's view" of the exhibition, dubbing the work as "extremist," and comparing it with the fake spectacles of P.T. Barnum.

> Probably we err in treating most of these pictures seriously. It is likely that many of them represent in painters the astute appreciation of the power to make folly lucrative which the late P.T. Barnum showed with his fake mermaid. There are thousands of people who will pay small sums to look at a faked mermaid; and now and then one of this kind with enough money will buy a cubist picture, or a picture of a misshapen nude woman, repellant from every standpoint. (70)

And even the great tenor Enrico Carusso staged his own critique of the show by doing graphic satires of the paintings he deemed most offensive on the back of Armory Show post-cards and distributing them as souvenirs (Brown, 117). A few newspapers ran stories and photographs of a donkey painting a canvas with its tail revealing that this resulting work was part of the show (120). A New York Sun cartoon by Bailly closely resembling earlier Punch efforts, represents an old woman quilting with the headline THE ORIGINAL CUBIST and the old woman's rustic statement as a caption: "I tuk the fust prize at the fair last fall."

Brown suggests that most of the jingles jokes and cartoons, were "neither good nor funny," quoting one editorial writer who wrote "you can't spoof what you don't understand" (110). But the point is that non-comprehension becomes a stimulus to the critical humorist—the ironists, parodists, and satirists—and as such motivates their desire to produce humorous criticism. Brown even undermined his own objective position on the public responses to the Armory Show,

---

20. An exhibition of this work under the title *Parodies of the American Masters: Rediscovering the Society of American Fakirs, 1891-1914* was organised recently by the Art Museum at Stony Brook, New York. A history of the Art Students League, which includes information on the Fakirs, is being prepared for publication by Raymond J. Steiner. Review Steiner R.J., Art Times 10:6 Jan/Feb 1994:8-9. I am indebted to New Yorker cartoonist Anatol Kovarsky for sending me this information about the Society of Fakirs.

21. Cortissoz, Royal, *American Artists* New York: Scribners and Sons (1923:18), requoted in Rose, B. *Readings in American Art 1900-1975* New York: Holt Rinehart and Winston, (1975:27).

by stating that "A sense of outrage underlay the hysterical vituperation of many spectators and critics" (113).

Further evidence of the complexity of the public response to the shock of modernism is provided by the sales records of the exhibition. Many of the most radical works in the exhibition sold, interestingly enough, to lawyers: John Quinn, Arthur Eddy and John G. Johnson, their acts contradicting somewhat the conservative fiber of a profession not known for its strong support of avant-garde activity. Perhaps this is another instance of inversion. After the attack on its superstructure the dominant group does what it has to immunize itself against its subordinate attackers…it buys them off! After all co-optation is better than confrontation. The wealthy lawyers" avant-garde purchases accorded them a certain cultural cachet and guaranteed them a certain notoriety on the cocktail circuit. Few of them knew at the time the potential value of their investment and must have kicked themselves solidly after selling them soon after purchase, when two decades later their works were worth over 50 times what they had paid for them.

The New Yorker

By any standards, The New Yorker has been a phenomenally successful magazine. The history of this success has been documented in several books and essays.[22] In his biography of founder editor Harold Ross (1892-1951), James Thurber suggested that Ross, whom he described as benevolently authoritarian and wonderful eccentric[23] would have been both pleased and appalled that one November issue of 1958 ran to 248 pages, revealing that while other magazines were losing from 8-25 percent of their paid advertising, The New Yorker actually increased its revenue by 3%. During this time, it annually rejected a million dollars' worth of advertisements its editorial staff regarded "as distasteful, or not up to New Yorker standards" (Thurber, 1959: iv). While the magazine has had its ups and downs since the fifties most recently during the 1980s it has maintained its high editorial standards, and a relatively loyal following through to the present.

---

22. Routledge, Howard and Peter Bart "Urbanity Inc" Wall Street Journal June 30, 1958.

23. The New Yorker was founded in 1925 by Raoul Fleischmann and Harold Ross. Like Punch, it had its first-year difficulties in getting afloat. In 1925, which Thurber describes as a year of ups and downs, the magazine copy ran from a high of 15,000 in February to 2,700 in August of that year.

Separated by geography, and almost a century of history, Punch and The New Yorker are in some respects very close. However, in contrast to the politically peripatetic Punch, The New Yorker, throughout its history, has remained what Dwight MacDonald termed, a "mid-cult" magazine. Without the effects of the rigid class system of Britain, its ideological battles have been less pronounced than those at Punch. The chronicles of the time record some close contacts and idea trafficking between the two journals; for instance, in November 1952, the staff of The New Yorker entertained the editors, and some of the artists and writers of their sister publication in England (Thurber, 1957:3).

Harold Ross was aware that European journals could provide the fledgling New Yorker[24] with some powerful models and he therefore consulted them frequently. As Kramer writes:

> Living in Greenwich village, the art colonies, or in the country, they knew little that went on outside their immediate circles. Ross was aware that to get something new he would have to develop new people or re-educate the old. Handicapped by not knowing what he wanted, he had no idea where to begin. The best he could do was to leaf furiously through Punch and the German (Simplicissimus) and French humour publications (Le Charivari) and, when he found something he liked, show it to (Rea) Irvin and tell him that it was the sort of thing that he was after. (125)

In this way, many of the Punch cartoons or cartoon features, satires, and parodies, became direct models for the New Yorker. For instance, Punch's "Our Social Outcasts" became "Social Errors" in the New Yorker. The English magazine often provided the cartoon models for its younger American counterpart and occasionally vice versa. Writing about this special relationship between the magazines, Kramer (1951), a contemporary commentator, argued that The New Yorker advanced the art of cartooning by moving the captions from several lines to one, thus conveying the bulk of the information in the visual, where previously Punch and other European humour journals, had tended to be text heavy. For at least the first ten years of its existence, New Yorker production was quite hierarchical, with Ross "rarely missing a beat." Thurber recounts how, at art meetings held then, on Tuesday afternoons, a continuing tradition,

---

24. The Dandy on the cover of the first New Yorker (February 21, 1925), subsequently christened Eustace Tilley by Corey Ford, was drawn by Rea Irvin, New Yorker art director from 1925-1939. Many scholars have noted the resemblance of the figure to The Chicago literary magazine The Cap Book 18. See Inge, Tom, *Comics as Culture* (1990:109).

> Ross rarely laughed outright at anything. His face would light up, or his torso would undergo a spasm of amusement, but he was not at the art meeting for pleasure. Selecting drawings was a serious business, a part of the week's drudgery, and the back of his mind ever held the premonition that nothing was going to be funny. Just as he searched writers' copy for such expressions as Dorothy Parker's once celebrated "like shot through a goose," he scanned drawings for phallic symbols and such, and once found one, he thought, in a hat I had drawn on a man in one of my covers. He was imagining things, but I had to change it anyway (48).

Thurber gives another example of the kind of cartoon detail which upset Ross. In an issue of December 20, 1930, a cartoon by Garrett Price showed a young woman on an operating table exclaiming to the surgeon entering the room "Why Henry Whipple, I thought you were still in medical college!" The scrub nurse in the drawing is holding a tray containing a double spoon curette used for female medical procedures. Ross exploded, thinking that the artist was trying to, as he said, "put one over us." But Price, whose father was a doctor, was not aware of the use of the instrument. He had simply drawn the object from his memory of the instruments used in his father's office (48). This sense of morality was so ingrained into the magazine's editorial fabric, that it was not until 1992, that the figure of a cartoon male with an erection (a stick figure drawn upon a cave wall by a stone age artist) made it to the pages of the magazine.[25] Art editor Lee Lorenz's cartoon beautifully satirizes those criticizing the National Endowment for funding so-called obscene art: the work of Andres Serrano, Robert Mapplethorpe and Karen Finley.

While Ross respected a number of his artists, particularly Peter Arno and Helen Hokinson, his opinion of many others was low. Artists were difficult creatures who required, he said, "handholding."[26] According to Thurber, Ross maintained his distance from many of the writers and artists working for the magazine, but was "socially close" to: Arno, Al Frueh, John Held Jnr., Rea Irvin, Lyuas Williams, Rube Goldberg, Wallace Morgan, Ralph Barton, and Thurber himself.

Like Punch, The New Yorker has had very few art editors. During the first year of economic turmoil, the first art editor, a woman, was fired, partly because, according to Thurber, she, like most women, made Ross nervous. Philip

---

25. I am indebted to Lee Lorenz, former editor of The New Yorker, for telling me this during a conversation I had with him in 1993.

26. Artists who worked for The New Yorker in the first decades of its existence included: Helen Hokinson, Al Frueh, Barbara Shermund, Reginald Marsh, Johan Bull, Covarrubias.

Gordon Wylie who was given the job of firing her, assumed her role briefly before relative (masculine) stability descended upon the art department. From the years 1925-1994, The New Yorker has had only three art directors: Rea Irvin (1925-1939), James Geraghty (1939-1973), and Lee Lorenz, from (1973-1994).[27] This continuity, as impressive as its English cousin, maintained a high level of consistency in the magazine design and its contents. And with little editorial movement in the art department New Yorker production methods were also consistent. It was not easy, then and now, for a new artist to break into the magazine. Many tried for months, a few for years. And those who made it often worked for the magazine for decades, sending in their visual's week after week, having a few published, if lucky, and the remainder returned. In the first decades, the cartoon caption and drawing were usually the result of a collaboration. A few artists worked on both; Mary Petty, for example, never worked on any ideas other than her own. But Helen Hokinson's cartoon captions were written by James Reid Parker, and many of the other artists worked with captions provided, and developed, by the staff. Sometime editors, Thurber and Andy White sent scores of captions and ideas to the meetings. But Ross, who always had a strong proprietary interest in the magazine, remained the "chief tinkerer at the art meetings." "One week, during the thirties, finished drawings, rough sketches and typed suggestions reached a total of some twenty-five thousand" (Thurber, 1957:44).

The New Yorker cartoonists explored a wide range of subjects but there were a few that occupied their time more than others: the legal and medical professions, the theatre, the art world, family, gender relations, sports and pets became favourite subjects. Over the years hundreds, in a few cases thousands, of cartoons on a single subject were produced, resulting, as was the case with Punch in the publication of several special Album anthologies[28] and theme publications. It is not difficult to understand why the art world became a popular subject for The New Yorker cartoonists. For a start, the magazine's basic raison d'etre was Culture, and moreover, since the late 1930s New York had been replacing Paris as the dominant centre for western culture in the world, making it a vital city in which to live and work. After the end of WWII and certainly by 1950 this geographic shift in cultural power had become a reality (Guilbaut 1984, 1992). As the newly dominant centre, New York provided a virtual cor-

---

27. See Lorenz's publication *The Art of the New Yorker* (1995).

28. *The New Yorker Album of Art and Artists* New York, Graphic Society (1970), *The New Yorker Album of Sports and Games*. New York, Harper Brothers (1958). See bibliography for additional entries.

nucopia of figures and cultural events, in all fields and professions, to respond to. Many of The New Yorker cartoonists were high culture artists painters usually but for a variety of reasons, some related to inclination, training, economics, they chose to place their primary emphasis on their work as cartoonists. A few, Alain, for example, whose proper name was Daniel Brustlein, chose to divide their time between painting and cartooning, the cartoon work often providing the economic support for their high art pursuit. Some gave up high art altogether to pursue cartooning and some, Anatol Kovarsky, is a good example, after a long-standing struggle, suppressed their cartooning interests to promote their high art vocation.

As a result of its status within culture generally and the institution art specifically, cartooning was perceived by many as a subordinate activity, but because it provided the artists with the proverbial "bread and butter," it often became, by default, their major occupation. While few cartoonists would admit to the fact, this must have become a source of some tension and/or anxiety. It was a problem too that their art college colleagues who continued to work within their high culture boundaries, had the potential at least to make as much from the sale of one abstract painting, as they could from a year, or more, of continuous free-lance employment as a cartoonist. Even working for one of the most successful magazines in the world, their roles as cartoonists were still perceived to be subordinate to the world of high art, where success at the highest level could reap enormous rewards, far beyond those the most successful cartoonist could expect to receive, unless that is, like Saul Steinberg, and a few others, they were admitted into the elite spaces of the world of high art.

The situation, however, is not quite as black and white as it seems. While there are distinct differences in their work, remuneration, roles, behaviour and identity, and career expectations, the institution of cartooning has a hierarchy which is similar in many respects to that operating in the art world. The cartoonist's world has its own systems of legitimation, valorization, rewards and honours. But few cartoonists, in their own lifetimes, can expect their work to be collected by major museums, auctioned by Sotheby's, and bought, sold and traded at the highest levels within the art market; fewer still can anticipate some critical and art historical interest in their work which would naturally lead to a monograph or two and subsequent permanent installation in the art historical registers. A Pulitzer prize for cartooning may be the pinnacle for a cartoonist, but it is certainly not a full dress retrospective at the Guggenheim, the Metropolitan, the Museum of Modern Art, or an invitation to the White House for dinner...rewards and honours which would be accorded a Rauschenberg, Warhol, or a Lichtenstein, as a natural consequence of their international success in the world of art.[29] Of course these honours and rewards are not bestowed upon more than a minority of high culture artists either, but the *potential* is there for this to occur. One could argue that extraordinary success in any field or human endeavor—or simply, as is the case in North America, *celebrity*—can lead to significant rewards and honours (perhaps the White House is less than discriminating), but the structural features of various professions, and institutions regulate the forms of legitimation, and valuation, including the rewards. In western culture, greater cultural capital still accrues to the exemplary high culture artist even before, and occasionally, in spite, of success. While it is true that during their career, a cartoonist may earn more than a painter, the painter's status within the culture is significantly higher. This is as much the result of history (and convention), as it is the structural, and determining, features of the art institution, its systems of education, legitimation and valorization. This is the logic of distinction, of constructed class (Bourdieu 1984: 106-8); a logic that marks ideological difference and all that emanates from this, with respect to societal expectations of performance, institutional legitimation, public rewards, and honours, including academic scholarship that is subsequently entered into the permanent register as art history. Keeping these points in mind, we should now take the opportunity to explore briefly the life and work of a few of the most prolific art satirists for The New Yorker. This will provide us with some further insights into the distinguishing characteristics between high art and popular culture and how this bears upon the contest of cultural meaning, and the symbolic representation of class conflict.

Anatol Kovarsky is the most prolific New Yorker art satirist in the history of the magazine.[30] He was born in Moscow into a conventional middle-class family, and had an early education in Warsaw, followed by college in Vienna and the Ecole des Beaux Arts in Paris. He emigrated to the United States in 1942 and began producing cartoons for a number of magazines including The New Yorker which remained his principal publisher until the early 1980s. He travelled widely throughout Europe, parts of Asia and Africa, his travels providing

---

29. Commenting on social and cultural hierarchies in 1996, *Peanuts* creator Charles Schulz was quoted as saying that even with the world wide popularity of *Peanuts*, its syndication in hundreds of newspapers, and magazines, a T.V. programme, publications, as well as the honours bestowed on Schulz himself: prizes, honorary degrees, publications, and retrospectives at major international museums; this was still not enough cultural cache to get him a place in a celebrity golf tournament!

30. I was fortunate to have some extensive, and very useful discussions with Kovarsky, who as the most prolific modern art satirist of all of the New Yorker artists, was a most useful informant.

him with some of his other principal subjects including the far east, world religions and mythology. During the period Kovarsky (Akov) worked for The New Yorker he produced cartoons under a number of themes or "worlds" as he called them, which are documented in his collection *Kovarsky's World* (1956).

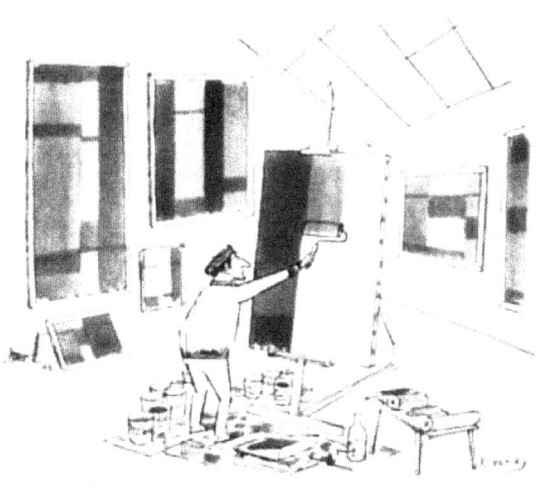

Figure 26: Kovarsky, A. New Yorker 6th April 1955.
© New Yorker Cartoons, Conde Nast.

For many years, the art world represented a special subject for him. In fact for thirty years he remained one of the most astute satirists of the art world, producing during between 1945-1975, over 60 art world satires.[31] Asked by the author why he devoted so much time to the art world, he replied "quite frankly I have this conflict between painting and cartooning" (interview 17.10.93) I published a number of satirical cartoons in Playboy and would have done more cartoons of a social nature, but I got cold feet, I chickened out...if this is the right phrase. I would get all kinds of ideas for social commentary in my cartoons, but this was taking my time away from painting."

---
31. Some more examples of Kovarsky's art satires will be discussed in Chapters 6 and 7.

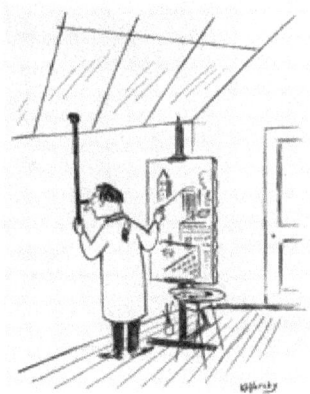

Figure 27: Kovarsky, A. New Yorker 4 June 1955.
© New Yorker Cartoons, Conde Nast.

Three of his most insightful satires target abstract painting. One shows a modernist painter in typical studio attire, painting with a roller, reproducing one of the common stereotypes about hard edge abstracts, the work of Barnett Newman for example, that it was executed with a house painter's roller (Fig. 26). This kind of graphic satire depends for its success upon the technical comparison between functional painting—non-art—and artful but useless painting. Another cartoon reveals the process of abstraction in modernist art as the result of excessive drinking on the part of the artist.

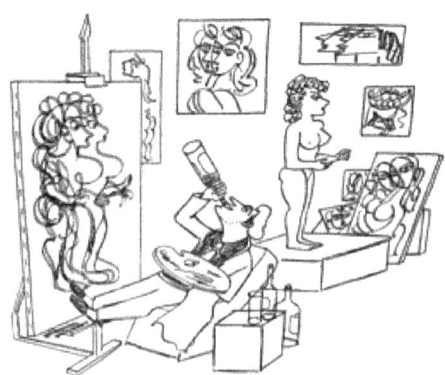

Figure 28: Kovarsky, A. Alcoholic artist in "The Artist's World" *Kovarsky's World*.
Alfred A. Knopf, New York 1956. © New Yorker Cartoons, Conde Nast.

The intoxicated painter appearing in this cartoon (fig. 28) with his nude model, produces doubled images resembling Picasso paintings because he cannot see straight. This kind of satire uses a variant of the technical critique with the essential difference that this time technical deficiencies are the result of the painter losing his locomotor control through excessive drinking. "The guy's drunk and cannot see straight!"

A third example (Fig. 29) from "The Artist's World" section in *Kovarsky's World* (1956) publication targets non-objective abstract work. This cartoon shows a painter taking a break from his dot painting on a large square canvas, sectioned off Mondrian-like into four unequal rectangles by two lines, one horizontal, one vertical. Reaching an impasse and requiring a break, the painter lays down his tools, puts on his coat and hat, walks down the road, but stops, obviously reflecting on the condition of his painting. He returns to his studio and adds one dot to the lower left of the canvas, and then exits again, satisfied. This cartoon represents an aspect of the creative process the intuitive flash common to many artists. The extremely reductive form of the painting enhanced, ironically, by the addition of one dot, produces the humorous response here.

Like Kovarsky, Barney Tobey, the second most prolific New Yorker art world satirist (28 art cartoons from the period studied), also has a wide range of subjects, but his art cartoons represent an important segment of his work. Like many artists he credited his early interest in art to some of his grade school teachers. "In school I was lucky with my teachers. I was awarded a scholarship to Parsons (School of Design) but left after a year to work at Batten Barton Durstine and Osborn's advertising agency." He stayed for six years and eventually was made head of the agency's Art Dept. During this time, he produced three covers for the New Yorker which were accepted, and

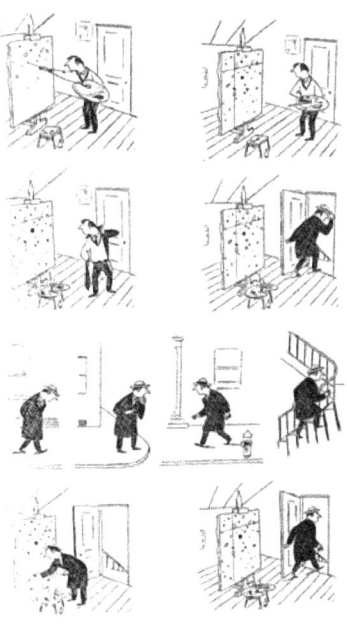

Figure 29: Kovarsky, A. Dot Painter, *Kovarsky's World*. © New Yorker Cartoons, Conde Nast.

this encouraged him to begin freelance contract work, cartooning, while maintaining, for economic security, his commercial art contacts. Again, like so many other artists from the turn of the century on, he attended night classes at the Art Students League, then, as today, an important training centre for cartoonists.

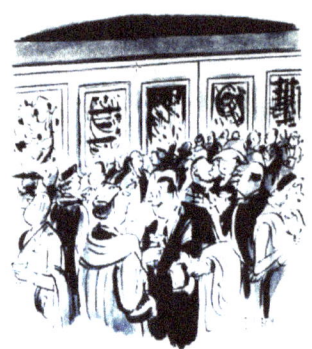

"I don't know anything about art, but this is a damned good Martini."

Figure 30: Tobey, B. New Yorker 1 Dec 1956.
© New Yorker Cartoons, Conde Nast.

Some of the best examples of Toby's work simultaneously satirize abstract art, minimalism and gender relations. Three cartoons from his 1983 publication show women instructing their male companions in the symbolic meaning of late modernist art. Sitting on a park bench a woman whose partner's arm is around her, turns to view the menacing open-mouthed Liebermann snake like sculpture and says "George, would you mind if we ate somewhere else?" It is hard not to read this (through a Freudian lens perhaps), as sexual innuendo. But as one reads the image its 'deconstructs' itself. This androgynous phallic object turns from a sucking snake into a monster vacuum cleaner. To the literate New Yorker reader, the nervousness of the woman owes something perhaps, to a suspense sequence from a Hitchcock film. But the base theme is the ironizing of modernist art. In another cartoon, a middle-class gallery going couple inspects a generic lyrical abstraction. The middle-aged male viewer exhibits a non-plussed air, a shrug of indifference perhaps, to which the neat woman with handbag replies "Of course *you* don't understand it. He's an artists' artist." Another cartoon shows a classy cocktail party hosted by a rich collector who, glass in hand, is pointing out the blue chip sculptural works in his collection "Starting at left, Marini, David Smith, Giacometti, Stanciewicz, Calder, Nevelson, and, good Lord, my wife and Harvey Peterson!" This hilarious image, worthy of Playboy as much as The New Yorker merges the viewing, collecting of contemporary art with adultery. Each of the sculptures is correctly identified and very close to originals by the artists mentioned, which for art literate readers further intensifies the joke.

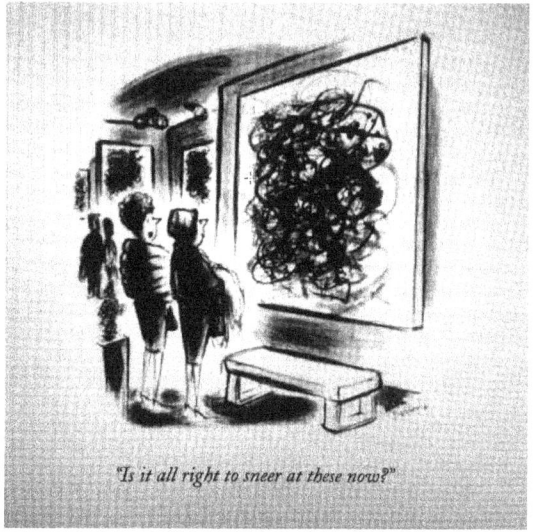

Figure 31: Darrow, Whitney Jr. New Yorker, 6 June 1959.
© New Yorker Cartoons, Conde Nast.

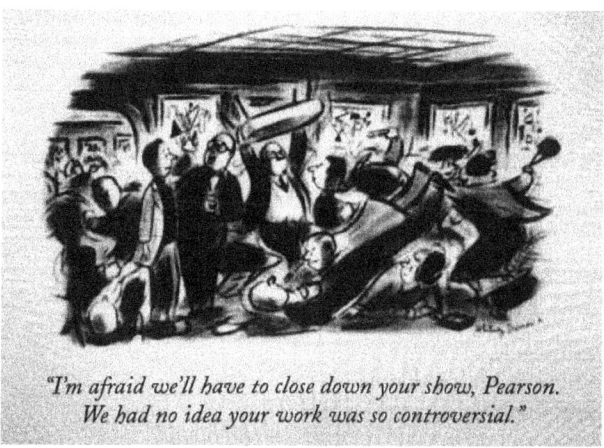

Figure 32: Darrow, Whitney Jr. New Yorker, 31 October 1953.
© New Yorker Cartoons, Conde Nast.

Whitney Darrow Jr., third on the list of active art satirists for The New Yorker, was born in 1909 and raised in Princeton, New Jersey. After high school he entered Princeton University and majored in literature and history. His cartoon doodles encouraged a colleague to suggest that he submit them to Princeton Tiger, the University humour magazine and with a few published drawings as a stimulus, he decided to shift his majors to art and archeology. He studied drawing in summer classes at the Art Students League and finally graduated from university during the early years of the Depression. With few job prospects and little inclination to continue study, he decided to try selling his cartoons and had limited success with several magazines: Judge, Life and College Humour. His second group of submissions to The New Yorker was successful and his first published cartoons for this magazine appeared in 1934. Darrow's attitudes toward contemporary art are clearly evident in many of his satires. While he counted himself a friend of Jackson Pollock,[32] his relationship with the world of avant-garde art was, at best, peripheral. And although he used modernist art frequently as a subject for his cartoons, he did not attend art openings regularly or fraternize with many members of the New York avant-garde. High culture artists and cartoonists tend to have their different social gathering places, their own bars and pubs. While some cross-over and intermixing occurs, separation is the norm. Discursive communities can be quite exclusive, making boundary crossing a difficult affair.

Questioned about his hilarious cartoon of a rumble at an art gallery opening featuring abstract expressionist painting, bearing the caption "I'm afraid we'll have to close down your show Pearson. We had no idea your work was so controversial" Darrow offered the following responses: to the question "do you think the cultured classes enjoy controversial art?" he replied "No"; and to the follow-up question "is there any art you have seen which you feel is too controversial for exhibition?" he answered "no." But in response to the question "in your opinion has abstraction enjoyed too much success?" he answered affirmatively. Many of his cartoons reinforce Darrow's admitted antipathy toward abstract expressionist art including the following examples: two fur coated women are shown before a generic Jackson Pollock painting, and one says to the other "Is it all right to sneer at these now?"[33] Another published a week later on June 13, 1959, shows a bright-eyed kid who has just delivered some

---

32. Correspondence with the author, 1993.

33. An interesting parallel is provided in T.J Clark's (1989) discussion of the use of Pollock's work as a backdrop for Cecil Beaton's photographs of models for Vogue magazine. (see Guilbaut, S. 1990:172-243).

smart pejorative—perhaps, "I hate your art Mister"—to the artist peddling his abstract works on the street who replies: "It just so happens I don't care *what* you think!"

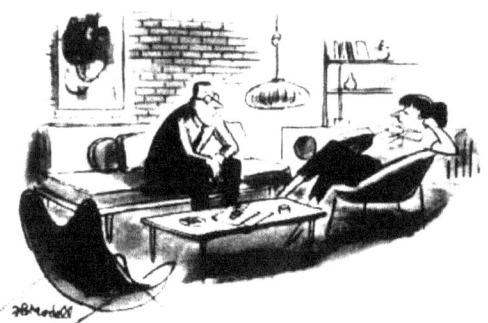

"I thought when we got all this modern stuff it would do something for our lives. But it hasn't."

Figure 33: Modell, F. New Yorker 17 May, 1958.
© New Yorker Cartoons, Conde Nast.

Frank Modell (1917-2016), born in Philadelphia, Pennsylvania, studied at the Philadelphia College of Art, from which he graduated in 1939. After his first cartoon success with the Saturday Evening Post he began regular work for The New Yorker, first as a gag line editorial assistant and then, after military service in the U.S. Signal Corps 1941-45, he worked as a contract cartoonist. During the period studied, he produced over 26 art satires. Modell is unusual among his New Yorker cartoonist colleagues; in that he also sustained a career as a stage and movie actor. Like many of his comic art colleagues throughout the decades, he cites the influence of the Sunday newspaper comics on his early development. From kindergarten age he was interested in copying cartoons from the comic pages. He admits that he is a "method artist," saying "I'm every dog, man, woman and turkey I draw" (Horn, 1981:149). His model was the early New Yorker cartoonist Peter Arno, and many of their cartoons work from the same ironic premises. In correspondence with the author Modell provided some quite revealing responses to questions regarding three of his cartoons. One cartoon shows a generic sculptor-type with beret and beard—a Rodin stereotype—carving a standing nude woman from a block of granite or marble. Upon completion, he has it crated and shipped it to the annual sculpture show at the local museum only to discover that the work adjacent "Mass," is exactly the same as the raw rock he began with, and worse, it has won first prize. I asked him the following questions about this cartoon. "This is a very ironic cartoon representing clearly the struggle between the traditional and the modern, between the fashionable, and the out of fashion. Was this a struggle which you personally identified with, either in your earlier art school training, or during your work as a cartoonist for The New Yorker?" to which he replied "Yes." My second question elicited a response which is reflective of the common attitudes toward the vanguard art of their time held by many New Yorker cartoonists. Question: "Thinking back to the late 1940s and early 1950s, was the success which abstract art enjoyed a subject of concern for you and your peers, and how do you feel about that time in terms of your own career? He replied, ironically, "I escaped it by sticking to cartoons." Escaping modernist art and sticking to cartoons may be a matter of personal choice, but it is also a result of the constructed conditions of the institution art and the divisions between high and popular culture which reinforce and in fact regulate difference. Modell's response is a kind of ironic disavowal, but it betrays a certain cynical detachment as well; and the knowledge perhaps that while a few of his art school peers may have made it in the world of high art, he is better off than most. This is the proverbial "Catch 22" of art school education. The potential is a good life, excellent wine, beautiful lovers, celebrity and everlasting fame. The reality is typically Hobbesian in the extreme. Modell and his colleagues know this only too well. Bitterness does not enter their vocabulary, although it could. If they have feelings of bitterness, they are more likely to become sublimated in their work.

CHAPTER 6

The Pile of Junk

> The basis of everything for me is the universe. The simplest forms in the universe are the sphere and the circle. I represent them by disks and then I vary them. My whole theory about art is the disparity that exists between form, masses and movements. (Alexander Calder)[1]

Within the history of western culture, there are only a few artists who have achieved the status of popular icons, but like their fellow icons—Mickey Mouse, Marylin Monroe and Elvis Presley—the names Leonardo Da Vinci, Vincent van Gogh, Edvard Munch, Pablo Picasso and Piet Mondrian have become the focus of every form of, honorific and money making venture imaginable. As a result of their cultural and economic power, these icons also became the target of every iconoclastic gesture and subversive trick that media agents working within the domains of popular culture could produce. Less recognizable as icons within popular culture, but established as such within the art history canon, the work and identity of a larger number of artists: Courbet, Manet, Monet, Duchamp, Klee, Calder, Moore and Pollock, has been subjected to the subtle critiques of the ironist and the satirist's sharp barbs of invective.

How and why did this occur? This is a complex question, but it appears to be the result of a dynamic social process that has several components and stages of development. First, certain features of the artwork provided cues for the artist's admirers and critics. Millions now recognize the asymmetrical eyes in a Picasso painting, Duchamp's mustachioed Mona Lisa, Klee's stick figures, the severe non-objective reductivism of Mondrian's late abstract paintings, and the dribbles and drips of Jack (the Dripper) Pollock. Second, any controversial aspect of the artist's personality or behaviour could also be used to reinforce the public perception of the shocking and outrageous character of the work. Picas-

---

1. Kuh, K. "Alexander Calder" in *The Artist's Voice*. New York: Harper and Row (1960), requoted in Rose, B, *Readings in American Art 1900-1975*. New York: Praeger (1968, 1975:243).

so's reputation as a great lover and seducer of women, enhanced his reputation in some constituencies, while in others, it reinforced public negativity toward him and his work. Pollock's reputation for being a heavy drinker with a volatile temperament—once pissing in a fire place at a swank party organized by New York socialite Peggy Guggenheim—did much to enhance his reputation after his tragic death in a car accident but during his lifetime, lead to his virtual ostracism.

Popular media representations involving substitutions and exaggerations of an artist's work (and personality) provide the base upon which subsequent critical responses are constructed. Symbolic reductions of an artist's work operate in two ways. They facilitate public recognition of an artist's artwork, and this then encourages stereotyping and iconicity to occur. Reductive substitutions (from a whole to a part), can result in misreading and misunderstanding, as often as they may encourage a more positive and critically neutral appreciation of the artist's work in question. The artist's name and the labelling of his or her work further assists in the production of cultural stereotypes. Significant sections of a popular image; for example, the Mona Lisa smile transported to another context, may encourage popular recognition to occur. The substitution of the part to a whole is a phenomenon that has occupied perceptual aestheticians and gestalt psychologists for years[2] and does not require extensive elaboration here. It may be suggested however, that the complex cognitive process underlying some of the gestaltists' claims—dubbed in the literature as completing the incomplete—may have its corollary in the reduction of complex semiotic constructions to common levels of intelligibility. This may explain why popular critical representations of images are reproduced over extended periods of time. Mass familiarity with the whole of a popular image may explain how representations of any of the parts: for example, the eyes, lips, legs or voice of Marilyn Monroe, come to symbolize her total presence. In a similar manner, the legs, a phrase, the hair of Mae West or Marlene Dietrich, the eyes of Elizabeth Taylor; the nose of Streisand; the voice of Duranty; Churchill's cigar; the biceps of Stallone; Michael Jackson's white glove, affirm their individual status as icons. The tiny signals which are able to be so successfully employed in a game of charades, become the basic units of a complex process of fetishization where

---

2. See Arnheim, R. *Art and Visual Perception* New York and London: (1956), *Towards a Psychology of Art* New York and London (1966), *Visual Thinking* New York and London: (1970); and Ehrenzweig, A. *The Hidden Order of Art* London: Paladin (1970) first published (1967).

only the tiniest of details may be required for the identification of the whole. In semiotic terms, the detail as signifier provides the signified for the whole; the index, its referent. Even in the absence of a context and key framing information, such as a name or part of a name, the representation of a tiny, yet significant detail, may permit public recognition of the icon. The same could be said of other generic (often misogynistic) stereotypes in popular culture such as: the dumb blonde/bimbo, the drunk, the *femme fatale*, the hood/criminal/gangster, the fat capitalist pig, the gigolo and the cute kid. Humorists, cartoonists and caricaturists typically exaggerate and fetishize those features that are perceived to be beyond the norm. These exaggerations can then be employed as signatures to reinforce resemblance and therefore recognition. Within the extensive literature on caricature, a portrait drawing's similarity to its subject and its subsequent exaggeration in a caricature become necessary preconditions for the construction of a parody or satire. The success of a parody or satire may depend on a number of other complex factors, including the reader's identity and reading/viewing contexts, to give the two most obvious and important conditions. Finally, the form of the work must contain elements that can stimulate immediate recognition and comprehension to occur in the mind of the viewer.

In earlier chapters, I noted that the incidence of cartoon satires may increase during exhibitions of an artist's work, particularly if the art provokes a controversy of some kind. Satirical cartoons, ironic commentaries and parodies identified previously as exogenous criticism (generated from outside the artworld centres of critical and legitimating discourse), may begin to appear in the media soon after the appearance of extensive publicity promoting a major artist's retrospective, a group exhibition, the unveiling of a major artwork, publication, feature article, sale, auction of a work, or awarding of a prize. The social and political meanings attaching to the extraordinary production of cartoons attending a specific artist's work are complicated and cannot be reduced simply to a primary level semiotic analysis, a psychological, or psycho-social reflex. I have argued, however, that the presence of a large number of satirical and parodical responses to the oeuvre of a relatively small number of artists, is related to the distinctive stereotyping of certain forms of art, itself the product of a nascent or developing negativism projected, inflected from one social group or class fraction, to another. While it is unwise to provide separate categories for a linked system of constructed meanings within a discursive field, it is evident that the artists, their personality, behaviour, and in most instances, their works, become the targets, ultimately the repositories, of such criticism. The features of the artworks that are usually marked for stereotyping by the cartoonists of the popular press, are those representing a range of cues which are alien, illegitimate, or simply, suspect. Through their various graphic responses, the cartoonists participate in, and may even lead, the production of stereotypes, which then become accepted as part of a class discourse. To members of the marginal classes and class fractions; that is, those who do not share the assumptions, premises, or ideologies operating within the discursive fields of modernist art, the popular (stereotyped) conception and representation of the generic Alexander Calder sculpture is simply a pile of junk. To non-art literate viewers, who lack "cultural competency" (Bourdieu, 1984:66), Calder's junk is a primitive and dumb artwork constructed from elements of detritus and industrial waste. In a similar manner to the popular reduction of Calder's art, the popular stereotype for a Henry Moore sculpture became the "rock with a hole." During relatively distinct periods of time, these reductions of the artist's work to a single image with limited referents, begin to proliferate. Critical reductions frequently originate in the sites of reception, the galleries and museums where the artists' work first meets the public gaze. The opinions negotiated here are later confirmed and reproduced in the editorial and review pages of the popular press, and echoed as visual representations in the cartoons attending, occluding, sometimes precluding, such commentary.

To obtain some further insights into these *dynamics*, in this and the following chapter, I will begin a more extensive elaboration of this process. This discussion will focus upon the various popular responses to the sculptural works of Alexander Calder and Henry Moore. For almost twenty years their sculpture remained a popular target for cartoonists bent on satirizing contemporary art, far beyond the usual time period reserved for artists of international stature. From 1935-1955 for Calder, and 1940-1960 for Moore, the work of both artists exhibited the quintessential elements, the indispensable conditions for the construction, destruction, and in some instances, critical deconstruction of popular meanings for modernist art. Using the rhetoric of contemporary art discourse, I will suggest that the cartoons of the two artists' work represent popular responses to the *paradigmatic* forms of modernist sculpture, the values pertaining to modernist art in general and the ideologically dominant position of high culture within classed society. Popular critical responses to advanced art may not encourage us to understand, absolutely, the manner in which specific class fractions, groups, communities viewed, interpreted and understood the work of these modernist artists. The cartoonists' responses do reveal however, how the meanings of modern art were being contested within various discursive communities, especially by those critical agents working outside of the venues of official art discourse and institutional sites of cultural power. In these two chapters, the discussion will concentrate upon the twenty-year periods during which Calder and Moore were confirmed officially as major contemporary artists, producing and exhibiting work, that on specific occasions during these periods, and in distinctly popular terms, was respected, feared and rejected.

Most of the cartoons of Alexander Calder's art date from the middle to late 1940s. They began to appear in large numbers after his first major retrospective exhibition at the Museum of Modern Art in 1943, and the production and wide distribution of a short documentary film about his life the following year.[3] Calder had received a measure of attention in Europe during the nineteen thirties and some success in his native U.S. in the early nineteen forties, but in many respects this was marginal in comparison to the boost given his reputation by the retrospective, the film and eight years later in 1952, a feature article in LIFE magazine[4] that must have been read by millions of people. During the years spanning 1940-1952, Calder showed his work in no less than thirty major exhibitions, in venues throughout the United States, Europe and South America. His reputation was secured further with the sale of major works to many of the institutions in which he exhibited, including MOMA in New York, the Museu de Arte in Sao Paulo, the National Museum of Sweden, Stockholm and the Musee d'Art Moderne in Paris. These years witnessed as well, the publication of approximately twenty major articles on his work in the leading art magazines and journals of the day. Some two decades after the terms *stabile* and *mobile* to designate his art had been coined by the leading French avant-garde artists Jean Arp and Marcel Duchamp[5], Calder had been canonized, the toast of the international art set and thus a ripe target for the pillorying proclivities of the popular press.

---

3. The Museum of Modern Art catalogue, *Calder* (1943), contains an introductory essay by James Johnson Sweeney, a full biography and bibliography up to this period in Calder's career.

4. Sieberling, J. "Calder: His Gyrating Mobile Art Wins International Fame and Prizes," LIFE August 25, 1952.

5. The terms *stabile* and *mobile* were coined respectively by Jean Arp (1930), and Marcel Duchamp (1931), after Calder's Galerie Percier, and Galerie Vignon exhibitions.

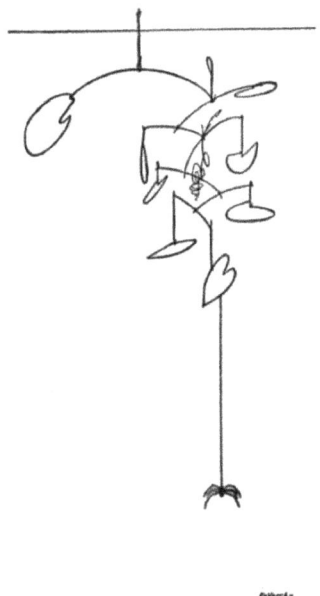

Figure 34: Kovarsky, A. The New Yorker Nov 6, 1948.
© New Yorker Cartoons, Conde Nast.

The popular conception upheld during the late nineteen forties that Calder's art was constructed from the refuse and junk of modern society[6] is confirmed in many cartoon satires from this period, including the example illustrated one of many produced of many years by Anatol Kovarsky for The New Yorker.[7] In Kovarsky's cartoon, the art thieves—instantly recognizable from their conventional dress and demeanor—are shown in the act of stealing a hoard of high culture art from the well-stocked domestic interior of a haute bourgeois household. One thief is shown casually removing a painting from its frame with a knife, while the other is standing on a chair carefully snipping the Calder mobile from its ceiling wire support with a pair of shears. The irony of this image which shows the art thief artfully snipping the kinetic work away from its wires with a pair of kitchen, gardening or workshop shears, provides the humour here. Viewers recognize that the Calder piece is constructed simply from odds and ends (junk) and with a group of similar materials and a little knowledge of the

---

6. During the height of his career, Calder actually recycled few elements of industrial waste into his sculpture.

7. Kovarsky produced several cartoons of Calder's work. During a twenty-year period, he produced over sixty-five cartoons with art related themes for The New Yorker magazine.

artist's methods, they may think that this piece of sculpture could be as easily forged, in the relative safety of the thieves' own home. The popular perception provided by Calder's art that it was produced by an unskilled handyman, or *bricoleur*, to use a term adopted by Levi-Strauss[8], is represented in many of cartoons of this type that are overtly critical of the perceived arbitrariness of the economic value and general uselessness of the modern art object.

The stereotypical sub-texts that could be attached to Kovarsky's cartoon are: "my kid could do better than that," or "you have to be out of your mind to: (a) produce that (useless junk), or: (b) "to buy that useless junk." The non-art literate response may be: "garbage!" or the ultimate put-down to the self-assured and superior human animal, the likening of the human creative project to that demonstrated by lower order primates, for example: "a monkey could do better than that!" This last critical reduction became the frequently attached by-line to the productions of abstract artists (see Chapter 8), after the Kellogg's bio-social studies of the 1930s had made favorable comparisons of human infant locomotor development and skill acquisition to those of the chimpanzee.[9] One of the funniest examples from this genre is an Alan Dunn cartoon from The New Yorker (c.1955), which shows a chimpanzee wearing an artist's beret, champagne glass in hand, basking in the success of his own one-man show of abstract expressionist paintings.

Both of these cartoons represent the modernist project from the position of an outsider, which is not to suggest that the cartoonists themselves are necessarily outsiders, although they may lack the high degree of cultural competency that would make them definite insiders. From the outsider's position the cartoons symbolically represent avant-garde art as *other*, as essentially alien. The cartoonists employment of visual parody, irony and satire, enable modern art to be perceived by their readers as degenerate, pretentious, nonsensical, silly, stupid, or just plain dumb. Modern art, therefore, is to be disavowed, repudiated and rejected. The artists, and by extension the institution of art itself, become objects of popular derision. For every cartoon irony, parody or satire that represents the

---

8. See Charbonnier, G., *Conversations with Claude Levi-Strauss*. London: Jonathon Cape Editions 1969, and Levi Strauss, C. *Totemism*. Trans. Rodney Needham, Harmondsworth: Penguin Books, 1969:50-2.

9. See Kellog, W.N. and L.A. *The Ape and the Child* New York: McGraw Hill 1933, and Morris, D. *The Biology of Art* New York: Knopf, 1962. Morris discusses his research work of Congo the chimpanzee painter. One of the most celebrated ape painters ever to wield a paint brush was the chimpanzee Pierre from Sweden, whose works were exhibited in 1964 under the name Pierre Brassau. His paintings received serious critical attention, and several were actually sold before the hoax was discovered. For its March 1958 issue (no 38) MAD magazine produced a cover "Special issue: A Chimpanzee painted this cover of MAD" and inserted the image of the chimp himself. (see chapter 11) for further discussion of the mad artworld of MAD.

philistinism of the outsider classes with respect to the vanguardist project and that is most of those groups excluding the avant-gardists (initially) themselves, there are others that support an insider's critique, which arguably, provides reinforcement and support to the critical assault against convention. It is ironic that conventional insider critiques are also assumed by the modern artists themselves to be the locus of their avant-garde intentions. This is probably a function of "empathetic reaction," a process referenced to earlier with respect to Dwight Macdonald's discussion of the differences between parody, burlesque and satire. Given the contrary functions of irony such cartoons as the Dunn example may be considered more ironic, affirmative and accommodative, than satirical, that is, negative and rejective. It should be acknowledged, however that aesthetic judgements themselves are dependent upon the cultural capital and class ideologies of the readers of the image. The Dunn image is a cartoon of this type. It may not necessarily reinforce the standard range of philistine positions proffered by subordinate classes who lack competency in the reading of contemporary art, neither does it approve of the bio-social primate comparisons of the Kellogg's. In fact, a reader looking at the Dunn who has been previously convinced by the Kellogg creative ape studies, may take it as an assault on the scientific methodologies of the biologists, not necessarily as an insubordination directed towards the artworld or abstract expressionism, although this, for most New Yorker readers, is most certainly the target. Here the ambiguity of the image becomes subjected to the politics and the judgement(s) of the reader, who may recognize that Dunn's cartoon employs a dual functionality that enables it to serve two ends: Dunn's extraordinary visual irony provides the vehicle for the satire of both abstract expressionism and socio-biology.

A Sam Cobean cartoon (The New Yorker July 22, 1950), provides a mildly ironic class critique, visually articulated in the collision between bourgeois patronage and the projects of the avant-garde. This cartoon depicts a Calder mobile hanging resolutely in the picture window of an upper middle-class household amid other blue-chip examples of contemporary art by Arp, Archipenko, Braque and Picasso. The respectably dressed woman says to her indifferent and cigarette smoking husband: "George, I don't know how you're going to take this, but I've grown tired of modern." One reading of this cartoon lays bare the complete arbitrariness of the nouveau riche collector's taste; an expense account mentality that bases the decision to acquire art on a mere fancy or whim. The woman's offhand comment could just as easily be referring to her clothes. And one suspects that her clothes would receive better treatment.

Other cartoon examples indict the Calder by association. A Goldstein image (The New Yorker Nov. 8, 1952), shows a puzzled gallery visitor staring vacantly, hat in hand, at a ready-made vertical "this way" sign, while a Calder stabile dances cheerily in the background. To the viewer, the confusing polysemy of the Calder sculpture dancing in all directions, is contrasted to the severe presence of the readymade one-way sign, a Duchamp inspired ready-made (aided), framed as contemporary art. In a somewhat more perverse cartoon, a museum guard about to commit suicide with the aid of a Calder mobile hanging from the ceiling, is restrained by a colleague who tells him "hold it…you've been shifted to Flemish Renaissance." The allusion to Flemish Renaissance, the very epitome of bourgeois (middle class) rectitude and protestant restraint, is hilarious, clearly establishing in the reader's mind, the difference between modern and traditional art. The cartoon beautifully contrasts the art of historical importance—that of the Northern Renaissance or Baroque (Vermeer, Rembrandt)—to the art of less historical and thus popular significance, modernist abstraction (Pollock, Rothko). Ironically, the information missing here, of which the cartoonist is presumably aware, is that many of New York's museum guards are themselves artists and may therefore share in the discourse relating to the most advanced modernist projects of the day. This does not alter the implicit criticism of the cartoon itself but may allow us to consider how the addition of such contextual information can alter the meaning of an image.

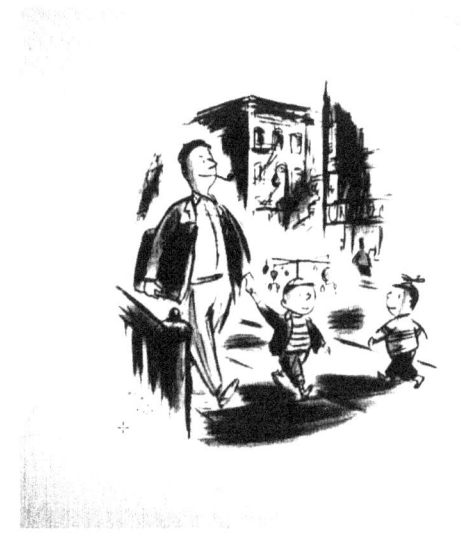

Figure 35: Darrow, Whitney, Jr. The New Yorker April 4, 1953.
© New Yorker Cartoons, Conde Nast.

Many of the cartoons of Calder's work exist as satirical responses to specific showings of his work and may not exhibit therefore, the same degree of ironical polysemy of the Dunn chimpanzee cartoon and others like it. A large number of cartoons of Calder's work appeared in The New Yorker and Punch during the five-year period 1950-1955. Whitney Darrow Jr., a producer of many art related cartoons, drew the example illustrated (Fig. 35), shortly after the Curt Valentin Gallery retrospective of Calder's work opened in New York in early 1953, although in correspondence with the author he did not remember the exhibit. In this image, the artist—note the give-away clues of the beret, pipe and art folio (reminders of late 19th century French stereotypes)—is promenading with his son wearing the latest beany fashion, a Calder mobile replacing the less fashionable propeller modeled by the boy adjacent. In answer to the question "What did you think of Calder's art at this time and have your thoughts changed today?" Darrow affirmed, with some degree of irony perhaps, that he "loves the stabiles."[10] Richard Decker's cartoon from this period shows a depressed artist, a common cultural stereotype,[11] surrounded by post-Calder/ Calders, while his supportive Wife offers her best friend a one-liner reason for the artist's depressed state: "His blowtorch is on the fritz."

Dana Fradon's cartoon (Fig. 36), represents a close approximation of an actual Calder work, *Lobster Trap and Fish Tail* (1939)[12]. framed by the hilarious question offered by the woman in the image: "Did I ever tell you I was born in Mobile?" Any high culture reader of The New Yorker familiar with the use, if not perhaps, the genesis of the term mobile, would have recognized the pun for what it is not, the naive response of the member of the un-cultured, naive, philistine lowbrows, in this instance represented by the provincial southerner, who while she exudes the confidence bestowed by privilege and new money wealth—possibly good 'ole gal' breeding—is still non-plussed by the meaning of the sculpture. She free associates on the label and 'domesticates' it by

---

10. Correspondence with the author, January 1993.

11. See Pelles, G. *Art, Artists and Society: Origins of a Modern Dilemma. Painting in England and France 1750-1850*. Englewood Cliffs, New Jersey: Prentice Hall (1963), and Wittkower, R and M. *Born Under Saturn: The Character and Conduct of the Artist from Antiquity to the French Revolution*. New York: Wittenborn (1968). The psychopathology of the artist has a long and powerful history from Lombroso to Freud, Ernst Kris and beyond, and is partially responsible for the enduring status of the subjective *hagiographic* approach to the writing of art history from the mid-19th century to the present day.

12. Fradon did not remember whether this was an actual work by Calder, but he said, "I was certainly thinking Calder." Asked whether he viewed Calder's work at the MOMA, or at any other location, he said "Oh, Yes! I'm very fond of his work." Correspondence with the author, March 1993.

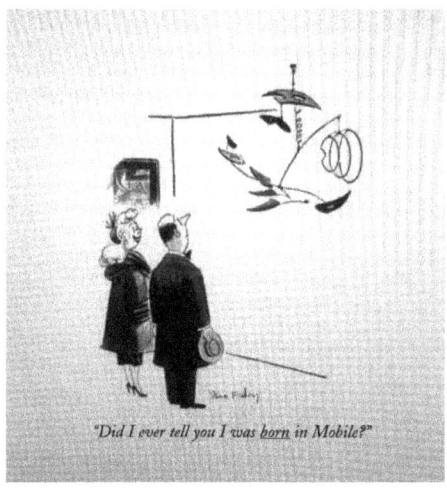

Figure 36: Fradon, D. New Yorker March 3, 1956.
© New Yorker Cartoons, Conde Nast.

projecting on to it her own origins in Mobile, Alabama.[13] Here the projection of self-knowledge in the face of potentially alienating or disorienting circumstances eases, if not erases, the tension invoked by her cultural incomprehension. For this refugee from Mobile, the world possessed is a world known. And if we took the cartoon to its logical limits of psycho-social intelligibility and subjected it to a more rigid interpretation, we could suggest that the woman's solipsistic tendencies have allowed confirmation of the object's presence and absence, thus rendering it transparent and politically benign. The male in the cartoon demonstrates an abject puzzlement, either at the woman's comment, the sculpture, or both. Her statement is performed as a dismissive, one that simply confirms (existentially) her own birth and place origin. The woman's statement is a simple confirmation of Bourdieu's arguments about cultural competency, that "when faced with legitimate works of art, people most lacking the specific competence apply to them the perceptual schemes of their own ethos, the very ones which structure their everyday perception of everyday existence" (1984:44). But in a curious way, the cartoon may be read as both acceptive and rejective of modern art. The transcendental call of modernism—the bait of entrapment—is here rejected in favour of an affirmation of self and place (home).

---

13. In answer to a question regarding the lower-middle class positions of the couple, Fradon suggested that they were "sort of–the vacant headed woman could not be safely depicted today. I think it sort of indicates the public's rather shallow interest in art." Correspondence with the author, March 1993.

130   Popular Modernisms

In its institutional museum setting, modern art is represented here as something that one partakes in order to be called "with it," fashionable and cultured. If the experience of the artwork itself is alienating, then other associations, relational positions, or simply, modes of address, can be used to render the work intelligible, non-threatening, and comfortable. In this sense the work of avant-garde art can become the occasion, according to the aesthetic philosophy of John Dewey[14] and others[15], for the acquisition of new knowledge.

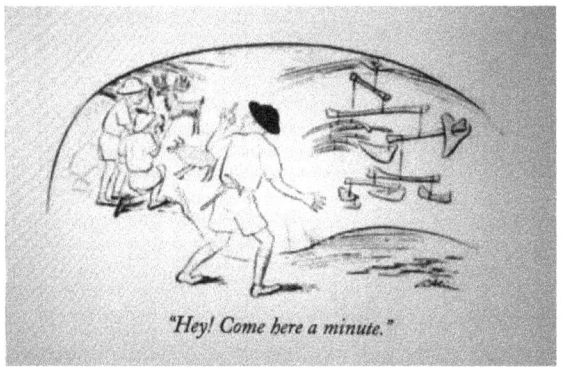

Fig. 37: Alain, The New Yorker Dec 8, 1956.
© New Yorker Cartoons, Conde Nast.

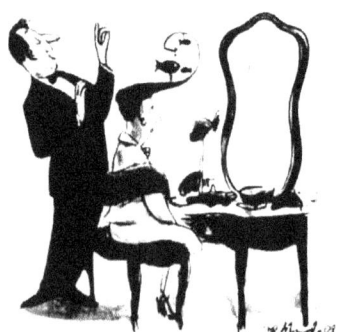

Fig. 38: Modell, F. The New Yorker Aug 14, 1954.
© New Yorker Cartoons, Conde Nast.

---

14. Dewey, J., *Art as Experience*. New York: G.P. Putnum's Sons, 1934.

15. Langer, S.K. *Philosophy in a New Key* Cambridge, Mass: Harvard University Press, 1942, and this author's *Feeling and Form: A Theory of Art*, New York: Scribner's and Sons, 1953.

The connection between so-called 'primitive' art and abstraction will be discussed in Chapter 8. There are a number of cartoons however, that represent Calder's work in a primitive context that can be discussed briefly here. These associations effect a somewhat more negative rejection of Calder's art than those discussed earlier. One such example, (Fig. 37) by Alain (the painter Daniel Brustlein),[16] shows an archaeologist, coincidentally a common New Yorker and Punch cartoon archetype, beckoning to his colleagues working near the entrance of their cave site to view a Calder mobile that has been constructed from the bones of birds and mammals tied together with some type of twine. This parodies Calder's own penchant during the thirties and early forties for using bones and other natural objects for some of his works, possibly also his publicized trip in 1950 to the caves of Lascaux. Alain could also be referring to the many essays and reviews appearing at that time in the specialty art press that associated Calder's work with primordial elements and natural flux: the body, earth, wind and sea. As a practicing high culture artist himself, Alain was very familiar with the discursive field surrounding Calder's work which related it to history, biology, technology, space, time and change.

Many cartoon satires representing the relationships between primitivism and nature in Calder's sculpture appeared in the 1940's and 50's. The prevalence of these cartoons may have been initiated by the artist's titles for his works, which range from the fantastic and surreal to the conventional and mundane. Given titles such as: *Black Beast* (1940), *Apple Monster* (1938), *Black Thing* (1942), *Spiny* (1942), *Morning Cobweb* (1945), *Bayonets Menacing a Flower* (1945), and *Gypsophilia* (1950), it is not surprising to find Calder cartoons that also represent natural and surreal associations with the material world. Frank Modell produced a Calder hat design variation (fig. 38), shows an upper-class woman at her local milliner's shop trying on a hat bearing a fish mobile while the designer announces proudly…"It came to me in a dream one night." In correspondence with Modell about his appreciation of Calder's art, he confirmed that he "liked it then, and likes it now." Asked why so many New Yorker cartoonists produced cartoons of Calder's work, Modell suggested that "It wasn't because of the work itself…it was, I think…because of the reaction it drew from some people who viewed it, being as it was so

---

16. Daniel Brustlein, was a close friend of Ad Reinhardt one of the first generation New York abstract expressionists. It is revealing that he used a pen name, Alain, for his work as a New Yorker cartoonist yet reserved his given name for his artwork.

strange and unfamiliar to them."¹⁷ Modell's comment is interesting because it places The New Yorker cartoonist in the position of affirming the work of the avant-garde artist by satirizing the public response. This is a typical response of the high culture critic who shares to some extent the progressive projects of the modernist avant-gardes, but it may also be a mature and successful artist reflecting upon the impetuosity of his youthful dislikes.

There are many examples of cartoon mobiles that simulate Calder's own sculpture designs. Anatol Kovarsky's cartoon spider dangling naturally from a mobile web resembles many of the artists metal and wire constructions. One of hundreds comparing Calder's work to spider webs, Kovarsky's cartoon closely parallels a Calder title, *Morning Cobweb* (1945). Chon Day's cartoon shows a stereotypical shipwrecked sailor on his desert island artfully constructing fish bone mobiles, leftovers from his survival catches. Each of these cartoons attempts to reintroduce Calder's art to a familiar setting, to lifeworld contexts beyond the art system. Surface readings of these cartoons—particularly the desert island mobile example—suggest that these are similar to those discussed previously with respect to other modernist artworks. Lack of aesthetic competency demands that the viewer naturalize or domesticate the non-objective abstract forms before they can become meaningful. The work can only have meaning and interest for someone who possesses the cultural competence, that is the code, into which it is encoded. The cartoonist may have the code or be representing or stimulating it absence on the part of the viewer. Day's skeleton mobile produced by the shipwrecked sailor implies that this new kind of simplistic art would only amuse someone with plenty of leisure time on their hands, someone stranded on a desert island with nothing better to do than attend to basic physical needs and await rescue. The Modell cartoon illustrating a Calder hat mobile, alludes neatly to the appropriation of high art by popular culture—the result of a natural dream in this instance—of avant-garde culture to the fickle domain of fashion, a process that has been around since the birth of modernism.

The hundreds of spider web parodies of Calder's mobiles can be considered a sub-genre of satirical activity. One such cartoon (The New Yorker circa 1955), shows a beat-poet type, or artist, seeking divine inspiration by medi-

---

17. In his correspondence with the author, Modell wrote that he did not know whether Calder responded to The New Yorker cartoons of his work. He said that he "met Sandy Calder once at the home of Murdoch Pemberton (or his brother Brock's), I don't remember which. Murdoch was covering galleries in New York." Asked whether he enjoyed using the New York art world as one of his subjects, Modell said "yes. Why Not? But not particularly." Noting that he never really felt part of the art world, or any other…just an observer." Correspondence, January 1993.

tating in a half-lotus position before a spider web mobile, with several spiders providing the key to a seamless mantra. A cartoon by Punch cartoonist Smilby (F.W. Smith, Punch July 18, 1951), shows the mobile sculpture providing the architecture for four webs, thus reinforcing the integration of art/life, the implicit utilitarianism of this useless art object which must be transformed and naturalized for it to assume any importance. A major difference between the English and the American cartoonists in their response to the Calder works is represented in the British urge to turn the kinetically mobile, machine-like, yet essentially useless art, into something useful, that is to integrate the functionless object of contemplation into the praxis of everyday life. There are some powerful ideological messages being reproduced in this primary transformation that after Benjamin (1934), we must acknowledge in economic terms, as a substitution of exhibition value into use value.

But beyond the economic reductionism implicit within the Marxian transformation model alluded to above, some of the broad discursive features of this ideological structure are as follows. Art serves a limited function if it represents commonly held perceptions/positions as to what constitutes professional behaviour in the art world. In aesthetic terms this directive requires that art should be well drawn, well-made or artfully produced. It should be technically complex and therefore beyond the scope of the everyday skills of the untrained, those without talent, or the non-gifted. In contrast to the professional role of the high culture artist, the work of the average housewife or handyman is labour intensive, service oriented and therefore subject to the extreme division of labour common to those in the service sector, petty commodity, and large-scale industrial production sectors of the economy. To these ordinary folk—outsiders—art is, or should be, beyond their own *ordinary* capabilities. Outside of those agents operating at the official valorizing level within the museo-critical art nexus (artists, critics, art historians, curators), Calder's work did not represent the products of someone who was necessarily gifted, talented or well trained. Instead they appeared much closer to the techniques of the backyard folk artist, the amateur, handyman (*bricoleur*) than most members of the underclasses would wish to admit or accept. In other circumstances perhaps, the very simplicity of Calder's methods and materials, in company with the no-nonsense rhetoric associated with his work (some of the time), could have endeared his art to many of his popular critics, but these attributes actually rendered it totally suspect. This naive, wholesome and folksy image of Calder's work was the very antithesis of what the middle and working classes wished for *their* art. Those who were antagonistic towards modernism expected their art to be mimetic, naturalistic, up-lifting, transcendent, comfortable, and accessible. Typically, the art outsider classes see and experience that does not conform to their acculturated tastes or world view, is ignored, denied and rejected. The expectations that the viewers brought to the works determined to a major degree the manner in which they would respond. When these expectations were not met, conflict became the obvious result. Acting under the power of a kind of false consciousness[18] when confronted with the work of the avant-garde, the cartoonists confirm the opinions of the outsider classes and ironize, parody, satirize or in other ways humorously critique the work of the high culture artists, and occasionally their audience. It is somewhat ironic that the artists of the avant-garde producer class fraction represent in their work and behaviour an antagonistic relationship to the conventionality of art practice, and in many cases, *all* art practice, but they become *defined* as high culture artists by virtue of their close attachment, either during or after the formation of the avant-garde sub-group, to the institutions, the sites of cultural production and consumption, legitimation, valorization. These are site(s) where, in a word, control is exercised; and where control is exercised and maintained, so too is it contested. The struggle is directed towards the identity, configurations of the sign(s) of, in this case, modernist art, and/or the right to the ownership and demonstration of cultural capital that the sign(s) may represent.

Punch magazine cartoon satires of Calder's mobiles began to appear shortly after the first major exhibition of his work in January 1951 at the Lefebvre Gallery in London, England. An earlier and much smaller exhibition of his work at the Mayor gallery in December 1937 did not incite quite as much critical commentary in the press, neither did it produce the volume of cartoons of the Lefebvre exhibition. A few of the cartoons, however, did appear before the opening of the Calder exhibit at the Lefebvre, indicating the extent of prior knowledge of Calder's sculpture and "other (awful) modern art stuff!" within the offices of Fleet Street and beyond.

---

18. It was suggested in Chapter 3 that while the artist/cartoonists may have the benefit of close affiliations with the producer class fraction i.e. birth, education (artistic training) economic arrangements, engagements and other social ties, they are nevertheless technically outside of the specific social relations and discursive fields that characterise the class fractions of the dominant culture, including the sub-cultural avant-garde itself. In its early stages of formation, the avant-garde is a fairly closed shop. Participants in the discourse at this level are closely screened by those with a controlling influence over the structure of the discourse. The entrance of new-comers to the field is subject to an arbitrary, yet ultimately decisive, selective and exclusive, process.

The Pile of Junk 135

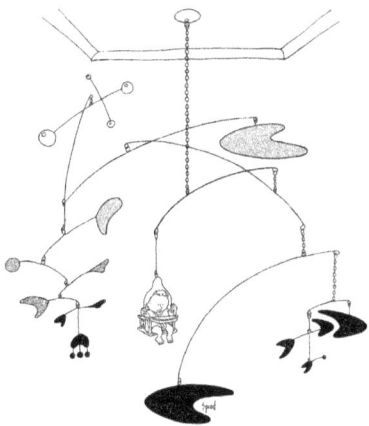

Figure 39: Sprod, Punch July 18, 1951. © Punch Cartoon Library, Top Foto.

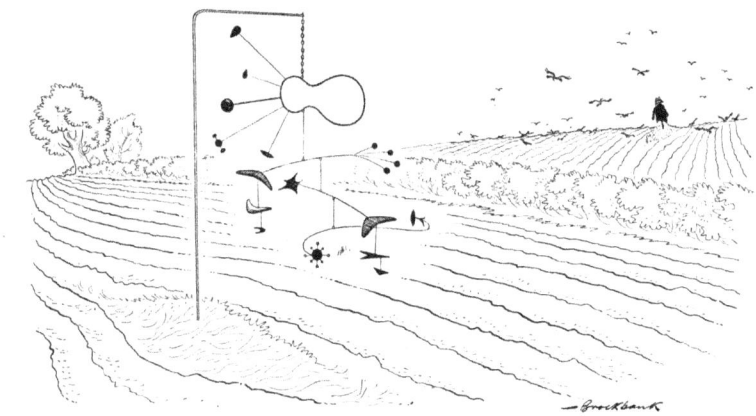

Figure 40: Brockbank, Punch Sept 5, 1951. © Punch Cartoon Library, Top Foto.

After the Lefebvre show opened, cartoons of Calder's work appeared in Punch at the surprising rate of one a month, which translates into one every third or fourth issue. The implicit or explicit utility, that I suggested earlier, differentiates the British responses from those of the American, can be seen in the examples illustrated which appeared in the pages of Punch from July 18, 1951, to December 17, 1952. The first example drawn by George Sprod (fig. 39), shows a baby balancing in a seat that provides one of the elements of the Calder mobile. This cartoon is particularly interesting because it appears to precede by a few years the vogue for baby centered mobiles used to amuse and educate the pre-toddler set. A cartoon by Hewison reveals that the Calder mobile can be transformed into a Lazy Susan for the dining room table. Oblivious to his wife who instructs him to "Push me the sugar," the bearded husband (an artist perhaps?), is berated for pushing her the milk instead of the sugar.

Within the corpus of art related cartoons there are many examples which transform modernist sculpture into scarecrows.[19] The number of Calder works satirized in this way are few yet important, for they represent another popular critique of the artist's work. Brockbank's[20] satirical transformation (fig. 40), is a classic example within this genre. The meaning of this cartoon is dependent on the re-contextualization of the useless *objet d'art*, out of the gallery and into the field or, to borrow a useful transformative from structuralist thinking, from culture to nature. This new (modern), scarecrow is truly ugly enough to scare the birds away from the newly planted seed, a fact underscored through the ironic comparison offered in the field adjacent, where a more conventional scarecrow, presents no threat whatsoever to the birds who feed around it with impunity. The answer to the bird problem of farmer Brown and his neighbours...this outlandish piece of modern art! Once again, the activist provocations and anti-bourgeois strategies of the avant-garde artist are rendered innocuous by the simple act of relocating the piece of modern art from the art museum to the farm.

A William Scully cartoon that depicting a middle-class domestic interior reveals how the thoroughly modern exhibition of art may be rendered less convincing because the telephone has been left in its natural condition as a functional object. The possibly culturally competent female viewer demonstrates an ironic if somewhat contradictory disdain at the inclusion of the telephone in this collection. This is similar to the social dynamic discussed earlier with respect to the expectations of the *bourgeois* art viewer regarding the conventional experience of art in a gallery or museum space. Here the woman simultaneously reveals and denies her (mis-)understanding of the work on exhibit. She feigns insider knowledge or with-it-ness, by criticizing the one object in

---

19. This use of the scarecrow metaphor may derive from the use in popular speech of the comparison between someone who is fashionably well dressed, attired, or *coiffed*, and someone who "looks like a scarecrow," a shorthand description of an individual dressed in 'odds 'n ends', unfashionably untidy, or unkempt; in Cockney and North Country parlance "fit to scare the birds away."

20. Russell Brockbank was for a time an art editor for Punch. From 1945 until the end of this relationship with the magazine, he published some 12 art satires.

the room—the telephone—that permits such recognition to occur. Even in the absence of a Duchampian ready-made aesthetic as a discursive support, the woman's framing of "the telephone-as-art" domesticates the art, confirming the ordinariness and banality of the exhibition itself. The humour results from the ironic incongruity of contrasting with its modernist abstraction and traditional (old hat) utility. The humour results from the reader's recognition of the irony contained in the inherent negativity—if perceptual correctness—of the woman's statement. Amid the mélange of forties and fifties abstract styles collected together in this room: art deco, Bauhaus, post-Bauhaus, constructivist, fifties modern, organicist and functionalist, the telephone, in fact, is the only thing that does stand out. Like the Zulu outworker who stumbles into an Afrikaner cocktail party, the mere presence of the telephone, announces *difference*, and as a result, becomes suspect.

Another Smilby cartoon shows a couple decorating a Calder mobile Christmas Tree with gifts. Here again the domestication or better, anaesthetizing, of the offending object, is necessary for it to become safe. From the high culture perspective, the humour is stimulated through the recognition of the conflicting aims of the functional and the (non-functional) aesthetic offered in the kitschification and banalising the conflation of the popularization of art. In another cartoon (Fig. 42) Smilby shows a fisherman using a Calder fishing line with Calder flies, an allusion perhaps to the luring of the innocent to the disreputable pleasures of art. Is the fisherman represented here a modernist artist indulging in his leisure time pursuits?

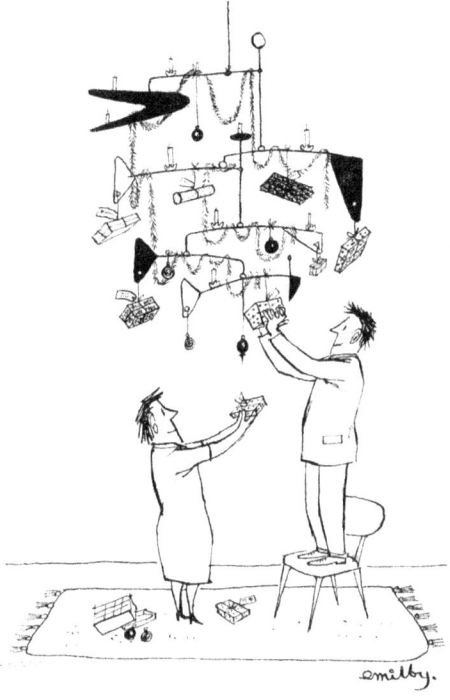

Figure 41: Smilby, Punch Apr 9, 1952.
© Punch Cartoon Library, Top Foto.

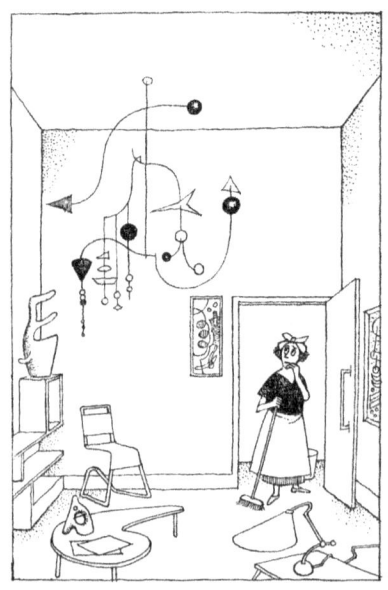

Figure 42: Smilby Punch Dec 17, 1952. © Punch Cartoon Library, Top Foto.

Figure 43: Brockbank Punch May 14, 1952. © Punch Cartoon Library, Top Foto.

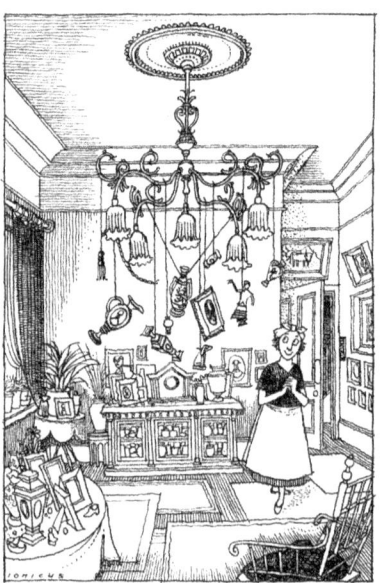

Figure 44: Ionicus Punch. April 9, 1952. © Punch Cartoon Library, Top Foto.

Perhaps the most successful satires of the Calder mobile sculpture from a class specific perspective, are the three illustrated (figs. 42, 43, 44), the first by Smilby again, who by this time must have acquired a veritable 'bee in his bonnet' about Calder.[21] In this next example (fig. 45), Smilby shows his satisfied middle-class consumer exiting the Galerie Lavere (read Lefebvre), having acquired and had gift wrapped, one of the Calder mobiles on display. The relationship between the timing of the announcement of Calder's exhibition and the Yuletide issue of the magazine; moreover, the difficulty of wrapping a mobile while simultaneously concealing its identity from its intended recipient, invokes the humour here. "Why buy something as useless as this anyway?" is clearly the intended question message of this cartoon. It is worth noting also the pun in the transposition of Lefebvre to Lavere which is morphologically close to the French verb *laver*, meaning to wash, wash out or perhaps its derivative lavure, dishwater. In Britain the appropriation and use of French names has often been the focus of national and classist derision. The use of French is viewed as somewhat pretentious, the product of effete, snobbish members of the upper and upper middle classes who attempt to display their 'culchah' to members of their own class and their subordinates. This may be understood as either a counter-alienating, esteem producing manoeuvre, or an attempt to appropriate the manners— the prestige and power—of the upper classes.

Ionicus' two-frame cartoon (fig. 44) depicts a cleaning woman/ maid servant viewing a Calder mobile in the contemporary apartment that she is engaged in cleaning. She is so inspired by the experience that during her next cleaning assignment she creates her own Calder, using materials available in the Victorian home of her employer. The cleaning woman's somewhat puzzled expression in the first frame gives way to the expression of self-satisfaction, the delight in creation, in the second. The humour for the literate Punch reader is the recognition of the ironic contrasting of the Calder sculpture to the class status of the woman, and the space represented in the second frame that may be read as an upper middle or upper-class living room of a Georgian or Victorian home. The class critique extends to the time-bound aesthetic character of Calder's art.

---

21. From 1950-1974, Smilby published approximately 25 art related cartoons which places him within the middle range of those Punch cartoonists who produced a large number of cartoons with art related themes.

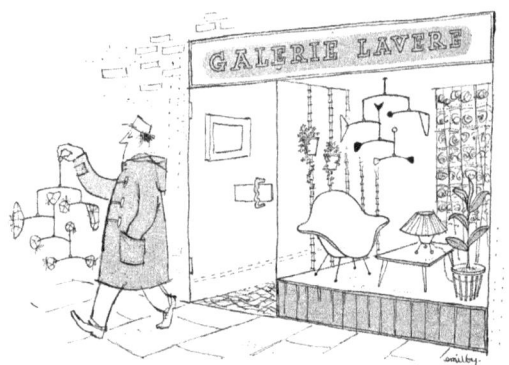

Figure 45: Smilby, Punch June 10, 1953. © Punch Cartoon Library, Top Foto.

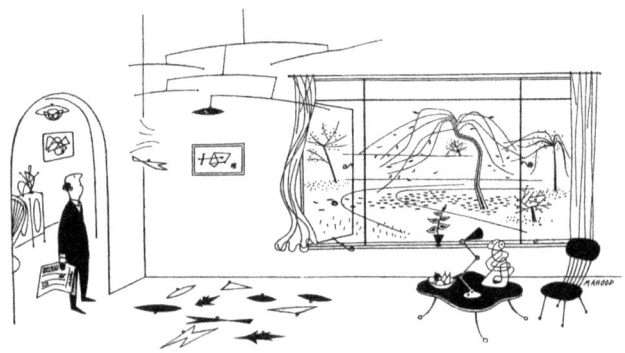

Figure 46: Mahood, Punch Oct 13, 1954. © Punch Cartoon Library, Top Foto.

Two final cartoons (figs. 45, 46), represent themes we have previously encountered, particularly the maintenance and installation problems of Calder's work calling into question again, its stability and legitimacy as an art form. The kinetic and ephemeral condition of Calder's art subverts the traditional base or architecturally dependent and historically secure sculpture. John Taylor's cartoon for example, shows an irate consumer returning his mobile to the Complaints Department because in his words, "It's gone static." Smilby's cartoon shows his character, a collector or gallery staff member, reduced to the status of servant or handyman, oiling his Calder to keep it in good working condition. The fact that it does not actually produce anything, apart from a rather dubious aesthetic experience, is of no consequence; and like other types of mechanical apparatus, this artwork must be regularly maintained. Eric Burgin's time-based cartoon shows the office worker's fan driving a Calder mobile amok. And finally, Mahood's cartoon example (fig. 46), represents his art collector's Calder sculpture shedding its leaves in a dualistic nature/culture empathy with the tree outside the window. Technologized representations of nature provide the raw material for the cartoonist who has found it expedient to give Calder some additional dynamism and use value as contemplative object. An important message conveyed in all of these cartoons is that Calder's art is too subject to the vagaries of nature and the chance occurrences of life to be legitimate!

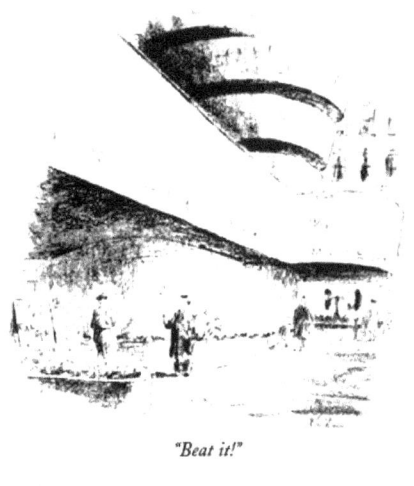

"Beat it!"

Figure 47: Dunn, A. New Yorker Nov 28, 1964. © New Yorker Cartoons, Conde Nast.

In summary, the examples discussed reveal how these representations of the stereotypical Calder artwork, functioning both as models for modern sculpture, in particular and modernist art in general, participate in the projects of both cultural affirmation and culture criticism. Many of these images reproduce publicly acknowledged antipathetic responses to the work of modern art. The cartoons undermine the role of the artist as producer of objects of value within classed society—with all that this obtains—in economic, aesthetic, cultural terms. Once the political nature of the humour vested in these cartoons is recuperated, the higher meaning of these images becomes clear. In many of these cartoons, the popular responses to the work of the dominant culture's agent—the modern artist—is outright denial, or rejection. In other examples the humour is more ironical and tendentious, closer to the types produced intra-culturally within the producer classes and class fractions themselves. Yet its political characteristics are still evident, as is its representation of the bid to govern the sign. What could be clearer as a form of rejection or negation than the Alan Dunn image which shows a museum guard (fig. 47), ordering the street vendor to "beat it!" when he strays too close to the Guggenheim Museum which he had been using to provide a classy cover for the sales of his toy propellers. The Calder retrospective provides the *raison d'etre* for the cartoon. Low culture, the culture of the working classes, the working poor and the lower middle-classes, is excluded from the elite provinces of the dominant culture. Typically, the dominant culture's rules of law: private property, no trespassing, no vending without a license *etc.* are used to distance the adventurous entrepreneurial members of the under-class. The economic structures and sustaining ideologies of two distinct classes are here pitted, one against the another. Alan Dunn's parody of the institutional structures: architecture (the museum), law (private property), policing (the guard), education—the art show and the (implied) public aims of the museum, which maintain class dominance—allow us to consider the ways in which cultural hegemony is maintained by reinforcing institutional boundaries. Beyond the symbolic representation of ideology in this simple image of confrontation, these become the conditions that permit the judgement of its significance in the more concrete social terms as an index of resistance as distinct from *accommodation*.

CHAPTER 7

The Rock with the Hole

> He is established at the age of fifty-two, not only as one of the five or six most important living modern sculptors, but as a popular symbol of the modernist movement, as is best evidenced by the fact that when a comic artist or cartoonist wants to poke fun at modernist sculptures, he generally uses one of Moore's perforated figures for his example.[1]

The critics Thomas B. Hess (1960), Clement Greenberg (1961), and Peter Fuller (1988), have each vigorously contested English sculptor Henry Moore's position as a major artist within the modernist canon, but this has not seriously undermined his status as a famous artist, or that his work attracted an extraordinary range of critical responses from the mass public—rivaling that of Picasso—from unmitigated outrage to raucous laughter. In previous chapters I argued that these were typical public responses[2] to the avant-garde strategies of modernism from its inception and accordingly it was early modernists such as Gustave Courbet and Edouard Manet who were among the first to be attacked. Public criticism was subsequently unleashed against the work of artists associated with the late nineteenth and early twentieth century avant-gardes: the fauves, cubists, futurists, dadaists and surrealists. A few members of today's 'neo-avant-gardes' have also frequently come under attack, among them: Vito Acconci, Chris Burden, Adrian Piper, Michael Basquiat, Andres Serrano, Karen Finley, Annie Sprinkle and Jana Sterbak. The art (or behaviour), of each of these artists has become the subject of severe controversy in the media, less for usurping the prevailing cultural status quo than for challenging existing codes of sexual propriety and public morality. In company with many of these contemporary artists, the public responses to

---

1. "Mostly Sculpture" The Art Galleries, The New Yorker, May 1951:74.

2. This is obviously a larger topic than is suggested by this generalization. However, within the considerable body of literature on the avant-garde, including those texts by: Pelles, G. (1963), Poggioli, R. (1981), Hadjinicolaou (1973, 1978), Calinescu, M. (1977), and Burger, P. (1984), there is considerable agreement on the types of popular responses to avant-garde behaviour. A study of the popular literature coincident with the various avant-garde movements reveals a similar range of responses to those implied here.

Henry Moore's art had less to do with his avant-gardist triple A's -- activism, agonism and antagonism (Poggioli, 1981), than with his purported rejection of commonly held opinions as to what constitutes appropriate representations of the human (female) body, intimacy, desire and sexuality. And like the strident examples of contemporary art by Acconci, Mapplethorpe, Finley, Sterbak et al., Moore's sculpture of the 1940s and 1950s challenged what were considered to be normative standards of decorum and morality.

With other famous modernists, Henry Moore's prodigious output of sculptures and drawings produced over the course of his spectacular career, spawned many parallel—parasitic—productions: reviews, critical essays, biographical writing, films, radio and television programs, lectures etc., not to forget of course, the work of legions of artists and students responding to his powerful influence. Mass media cartoons represent one extensive domain of production indicative of the public reception of his work. Cartoon satires of Moore's art number in the hundreds, possibly the thousands; many of them responding to challenges that Moore himself issued to the public: specifically, that a sculptural representation of a nude, a reclining woman, mother and child, would appear as the subject in question and not be reduced to some unintelligible abstract form.

In this chapter, I will reveal that many of the cartoons of Moore's sculpture contain a complicated image/text semiotic engaging complex notions and emotions pertaining to sexuality and desire. And like some readings of Moore's sculpture itself these cartoons represent—if only on a symbolic level—the contest between private sexuality, public morality, prurience and jurisprudence. On one interpretive register, it can be argued that it was the perceived lack of decorum of Moore's sculpture, the denial of anticipated sculptural values and thus conventional aesthetic form that disturbed viewers. At the level of the sub-conscious, Moore's sculptures engaged certain taboos, symbolically initiating his viewers to the pleasure of releasing inhibited or repressed desires, and raising, coincidentally, the dangers associated with doing so. Interpreted in these terms his sculptures become complex and extremely dynamic tropes. In the viewer's mind, they have the capacity to represent, yet often contradict, constructions of gender difference. When the public gaze first met Moore's art it had the capacity to stimulate the viewer into the unconscious negotiation of genital, oral and/or anal erotic power.

The aesthetic justifications and quasi-scientific rationalizations of Moore's critics and biographers, whose writings are based variously upon the aesthetics of Roger Fry and the psychological theories of Sigmund Freud, Karl Jung,

Melanie Klein, and F.D. Winnicott,[3] have each provided an enriched field for textual exegesis of the artist's work and life as an artist. To those unacquainted with either the pronouncements of the sculptor or the writings of his critics and their theorists however, Moore's sculptures elicited various cognitive dilemmas. Representatives of class fractions at the margins of high culture, and therefore outside of the fields of critical and art historical discourse, found that Moore's art stimulated difficult questions about the forms and meaning of modern art. On the positive side, his art enabled them to confront the publicness of sculpture, the representation of nature, the body, the family, and the 'archetypal' bond between mother and child, as well as relatively complex questions pertaining to religious belief, spirituality and God. But Moore's art also immersed his viewers into a complex set of discursive fields articulating different ideological positions with regard to the use of the human body in art, the nuclear family, and constructions of femininity, masculinity, intimacy and desire. The cartoons of Moore's art symbolically represent a wide range of positions on these topics, some of which can be interpreted as signs of mild concern for the sanctity of the human body, and others representing strong arguments for the protection of public morality. Extreme responses to his work reveal the shock and rage of a public affronted by what it perceives to be a transgression against the normative conditions for the display of the body in daily life. For these denizens of public faith, Moore's sculptures and even the artist himself were considered nothing less than dangerous.

A revealing example of this hard rejective form of popular response is represented in the following anecdote occasioned by an international traveling exhibition of the sculptor's work in 1955. This response, or "incident," as it was described disparagingly by Moore biographer Roger Berthoud, took place in a major gallery of one of Great Britain's far flung regions of The Empire, coincidentally this author's birth place, Auckland, New Zealand. The public reception to the Moore traveling exhibit installed at the Auckland City Art Gallery is well known to those who have examined overseas influences on the work of New Zealand artists during this period,[4] but they are also familiar to many constituencies in other regions of the world where Moore's sculpture

---

[3]. See for example: Neumann, E., Trans. R.F.C. Hull *The Archetypal World of Henry Moore* London: Routledge, 1959; Sylvester, R. *Henry Moore* London: The Arts Council, 1968; Fry, R. *Vision and Design* London:1920 Fuller, P., "Mother and Child in Henry Moore and Winnicott" Winnicott Studies, The Journal of the Squiggle Foundation No.2 1987.

[4]. Particularly by art historians and former graduate students at the University of Auckland, among them: Anthony Green, Michael Dunn, Leonard Bell, Francis Pound, Christina Barton, and Priscilla Pitts.

has alighted, including countries in Europe, Asia, North and South America. The ACAG exhibition contained twenty-four sculptures including the famous *Standing Figures* (Battersea Park) group of 1947. In a remarkable statement, the Mayor of Auckland, J.H. Luxford established his name in history in a more assured fashion than he did in his position as the leading local government representative of New Zealand's largest city.

> I have never seen the art gallery so desecrated by such a nauseating sight… these figures offending against all known anatomy, to me are repulsive. (Berthoud, 1987:268)

At this public confession, an unidentified man purportedly screamed at the sculpture and ran from the gallery shouting, "that man (Moore) ought to be shot!" (268).[5]

During the 1950s, at a time when Moore's work was relatively unknown, negative responses such as these were repeated around the world. Even some ten years later, in the cosmopolitan Canadian city of Toronto, Moore's sculpture The Archer was rejected as a public acquisition for an exterior site adjacent to the new Toronto City Hall. Public attacks forced the local government art acquisition committee in a narrow vote, to reject its agreement with the artist and his representatives. But this time it was an enlightened city mayor who came to the rescue by establishing an independent fundraising committee that purchased and installed the work as planned. The public outcry over the Moore commission lasted for months, precipitating heated editorial debate, cartoons and commentary from all quarters of the community. One noted Canadian academician and defender of public morality, the avowed anti-modernist Kenneth Forbes, published a poem decrying the sculpture.

> THE ARCHER
>
> A Bronze by Henry Moore
>
> What sights we see by the New City Hall
> An "Archer" monster of ludicrous shape
> Does it enthrall or does it appall?
> Or stir emotions of laughter or hate
> This clumsy thing called "Archer"
> Could just as well be labeled Vulture

---

5. Original report published in the Daily Telegraph 19th September 1956.

> How like a discard from a plumber's shed
> Does it slumber, or has judgment fled
> This bronze has a heartbeat so they say
> The world is flat so others bray
> Trends in art come fickle and fast
> Each one sillier than the last
> Used by schemers in art to dictate
> Cults have brought art to so low a state
> Art and nature has been betrayed
> By fashions whims and the greedy art trade
> For anti-art there is at the Tate
> Has Toronto deserved a similar fate
> If this is art why have I striven
> When failings are virtues praised to Heaven
> Critics praise should be suspect
> What they revile treat with respect
> Be not aware of the avant-garde stare
> Be assured there is nothing there
> To what pretense has art declined
> If this is art chaos is not far behind.[6]

These rhetorical attacks were vitriolic enough and yet the subtleties of culture criticism obviously eluded many official guardians of public morality. Subtlety, however, was the *modus operandi* of a large number of cartoonists working for the popular media. The cartoonists' satires are far less rhetorical and antagonistic than the examples of establishment criticism cited above, but in many of the graphic examples, the basic sentiments remain the same. It could also be argued that their influence on mainstream culture was far more pervasive.

Cartoon satires of Moore's art appeared in all cities throughout the world where his sculpture was exhibited or permanently installed. The discussion in this chapter is based upon a small sample of seventy-five cartoons published in the New Yorker and Punch magazines during a thirty year period.[7] I will argue that these provide a focus for how his work was viewed and received

---

6. Forbes, Kenneth *Great Art to the Grotesque*, Toronto: Pitt Publishing Ltd, 1972:65. I have been unable to find the first site of publication of this poem which was probably written sometime in 1966 when the Moore controversy began.

7. See Chapter 5. Both the New Yorker and Punch have interesting histories. The editorial positions for both magazines have changed substantially over the years, reflecting the changing social and political circumstances of various periods, as well as the beliefs of various individuals who steered editorial policy. Punch moved from being a small circulation radical opinion weekly with left wing sympathies, to a conservative magazine in the 1920s, radical again in the 1930s, liberal/conservative in the 1950s and 1960s, to a position in the 1990s of presenting some sympathy for the right wing agenda of Thatcherism. For an excellent account of Punch's changing politics to the mid 1950s see Price R.G. *A History of Punch* London: Collins, 1957.

in two culturally sophisticated metropolitan contexts, New York and London.[8] While these magazines are produced and received at what Dwight MacDonald (1961) has termed the "mid-cultural level," the readership for both is considerably wider than this categorization suggests. Graphic satires of Moore's art were produced by cartoonists who, while they may not have shared the same discourse, nor class sympathies as the artist (Moore was from a working class background and was for a time, a committed and active socialist), they do, generally speaking, value high culture and support the maintenance of the cultural *status quo*. More importantly, these artists often reflect the values of their magazine's editorial boards and to a greater or lesser extent, those of their readers. As discussed earlier, a few of the Punch and New Yorker cartoonists consistently satirized the work of high culture's avant-garde producers, a fact that will be reinforced, as I discuss these images.

The cartoon examples discussed here were published in The New Yorker and Punch over a twenty-year period. The New Yorker examples appeared between the years 1945 to 1957, coinciding with three major exhibitions of Moore's work in New York; his first, at the Buchloh Gallery in 1943, a retrospective at the Museum of Modern Art in 1946, that lead to the making of the first film documentary on his work, and five years later in 1951, another exhibit at the Bucholz gallery. The Punch cartoons span a longer period, from 1944-1972, quite possibly a function of Moore's status as native son, or the unwillingness of the English cartoonists and their public to fully acknowledge or consummate, his international success.

It is apparent from the earliest cartoon examples, that Moore's art was a relatively easy target to address. For nearly sixty years he maintained a fairly close relationship to four major themes: the female nude, the reclining figure, mother and child and the so-called interior/ exterior forms. Others have been identified, but the four principal themes, for obvious reasons, seem to have occupied Moore's satirists as well. An important feature of many of the artist's sculptures—the aperture, or hole—seems to have fascinated the cartoonists. I will argue that the proliferation of cartoon satires of Moore's art (more than for any other member of his generation), can be attributed to this important element in his work.

---

8. Pierre Bourdieu argues that merely being born in one of the large metropolitan contexts: Paris, New York, or London, has the potential to provide one with more cultural capital than if one was born in another geographical region, even if the class of one's parents was the same in both instances. See Bourdieu, P., and Passeron, J-C., *Reproduction in Education, Society and Culture*. London, and Beverly Hills: Sage Publications 1977.

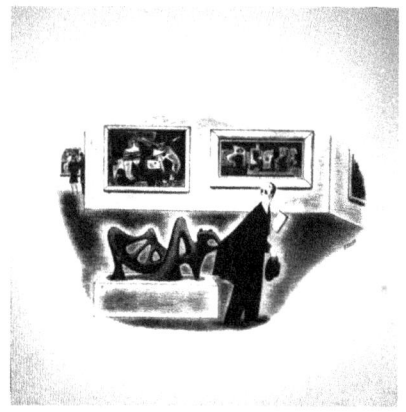 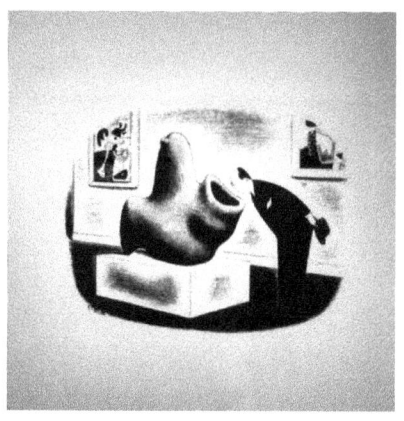

Figure 48: Taylor, R. The New Yorker June 2, 1945. © New Yorker Cartoons, Conde Nast.

Fig. 49: Taylor, R. The New Yorker Oct 12, 1946. © New Yorker Cartoons, Conde Nast.

I will use the first two examples illustrated here, both from the pen of Canadian born artist Richard Taylor (1902-1970),[9] to underline a few of the issues we will be confronting in this introductory examination of the Moore cartoon corpus. The first cartoon (Fig. 48), confirms the bio-morphic status of many of the sculptor's works from this period and attests to the ambivalent responses of many puzzled viewers confronted by these artworks, that to the uninitiated—those lacking, as Bourdieu insists, "cultural competency"—could be compared to biological hybrids or alien creatures from another planet. In Taylor's cartoon a stereotypical common man is restrained by the Moore sculpture that like Pygmalion has come to life, interrupting his passage past the sculpture with a sharp pinch to his posterior. The cartoon reverses the usual male to female harassing gesture, thus transforming the male into the object of desire. The second cartoon (fig. 49) demands a closer reading. Here, a middle-class viewer—a New Yorker cartoon stereotype—has been attracted to the interior of the slug-like form (note the foot to the left). This work is very similar to *Moore's Composition* (1933) of Corsehill stone which Richard Taylor may have seen, either in Moore's MOMA exhibition of that year, or in a review of the same. In this cartoon however, the latent sexuality of the Moore sculpture is accorded much greater emphasis. The cartoonist has exaggerated the bumps and mounds on

---

9. Taylor was born in Fort William, Ontario, and studied in Toronto under Harry Britton. At age 12 he attended the Technical School of the Ontario College of Art. His first employment was the colouring of magic lantern slides for use in Sunday schools, and in 1927 he began producing cartoons for the Toronto based magazine Gobin. He became a member of The New Yorker stable of cartoonists in 1935. A volume of Taylor works, *The Better Taylors*, was published in 1944, and a subsequent collection of 95 cartoons, was published under the title, *Wrong Bag*, New York: Simon and Schuster 1961.

the sculpture to reveal what could be described, without too much stretching of the imagination, as an erect nipple on a somewhat priapic breast. These androgynous forms increase the libidinous significance of the body orifice into which Taylor's character is innocently peering, a relationship that the cartoonist seems also to have commented upon in the paintings hung on the wall behind the sculpture. The humour is provided by our conscious or perhaps subconscious perception of the significance of the hole or mouth to which the male viewer, at any instant, may become victim. A Freudian specialist of the *ars erotica* could have a field day with an image such as this, testing the cartoon's erotic polysemy against fetishistic imaginings of the vagina dentata, the primordial breast or the anal erotic. Is it too coincidental that Taylor's middle-aged viewer is bald? The surreal humour here (can this be humorous?) is concentrated on our recognition of the juxtaposition of this naive and unsuspecting viewer of modern art to this rapacious piece of sculpture. With the absence of a text, the cartoonist has cleverly implicated the reader in the semiotic construction and translation of meanings for this cartoon and thus by extension, the Moore work itself. Armed with the post-Freudian analytic techniques of contemporary feminism and/or post-Lacanian psychoanalysis, we may wish to deconstruct the meanings of this cartoon to thereby disclose the intentions of the artist and arrive perhaps, at a provisional judgment of misogyny. The cartoonist after all, may be aligning himself with the manifest or latent eroticism within the sculpture; if not, this reading would be an example of an intentionalist fallacy. We can relate Taylor's powerfully ironic response to Moore's art as a demonstration of oppressive attitudes toward women within patriarchal society. Richard Taylor produced a large number of cartoons with sexual content, and as the statement on the fly leaf of his 1961 published collection of cartoons intimated, he was a keen student of human behaviour.

> His patiently researched character studies give deeper insights into such sociological types as the blonde and the sugar daddy, the artist and the publisher; the hunter and the counterfeiter. As nearly as anybody can tell Taylor thinks mainly about men and women–and art. Perhaps one day this will be explained. (Taylor: 1961)

Perhaps indeed! This is properly another book on the misogynistic representation of these sociological types – the blonde and the sugar daddy – and somewhat beyond the scope of the art, artist and art historical emphases in *Popular Modernisms*, although several topics and examples related to gender and sexuality are referenced in this chapter on graphic satires of Henry Moore's sculpture, and the chapters that follow.

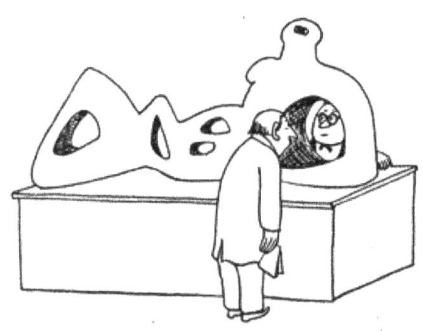

Figure 50: Kovarsky, A. The New Yorker May 1, 1947.
© New Yorker Cartoons, Conde Nast.

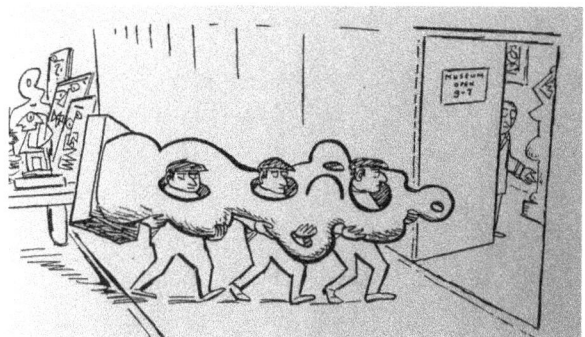

Figure 51: Kovarsky, A. The New Yorker May 17, 1949.
© New Yorker Cartoons, Conde Nast.

The next example (Fig. 50), an early cartoon by Akov (Anatol Kovarsky), resembles several of Moore's reclining figures from the 1940s, specifically the elmwood *Reclining Figure* (1945), which was shown at the Museum of Modern Art retrospective and illustrated in the catalogue accompanying the exhibit.[10] Beyond the surface similarity to the Moore work, that confirms its identity as modern art, the viewer is encouraged to ask the following questions: what are the two viewers engaged in?[11] Has the hole in the sculpture become some device for transcendence or metaphysical reflection? A Lacanian mirror perhaps?

---

10. See the catalogue *Henry Moore* New York: Museum of Modern Art 1946 which contains an introduction and commentary by Herbert Read.

11. This image is very similar to one that appeared in Punch October 26th, 1949, with the exception that in this example one of the men thrusts his hand through the hole to grasp the other in a handshake. The caption accompanying this cartoon reads: "Why Rawlings, fancy running into you!" It was common at this time for Punch cartoons to influence New Yorker artists and vice versa.

Is the figure in the foreground asleep or are his closed eyes and puckered lips signifying something else a stolen kiss perhaps? And is the perturbed look on the face of the upright citizen behind the sculpture a reflection merely of puzzlement or disdain for the perversity of the act performed before him? Beyond this form of questioning which could continue in an endless, perhaps perverse pursuit of interpretative veracity, is it the simple recognition of the ambiguous status of the hole that renders the work suspect? This ambiguity encourages the magazine's readers to interpret the image in several ways. In correspondence the artist offered a number of interesting responses to some of these questions and interpretations. For instance, in response to a question about his familiarity with Moore's work and whether he had visited either the Bucholz gallery exhibit in 1943, or the MOMA show of 1946, Kovarsky offered the following observations: "I've been familiar with Moore's work and admired many but not all, of his sculptures. Also, the great drawings of people in shelters during the 2nd World War," with later, "I didn't visit the Bucholz gallery in 1943 or the MOMA show." Kovarsky also stated emphatically that "the drawing is not a representation of an actual Moore work" and "there is no erotic significance to this drawing. It satirizes sculpture with holes in it but not specifically Moore's."[12]

Notwithstanding Kovarsky's guarded comments regarding this cartoon, many of his other cartoons and paintings evidence a keen interest in representing gender difference and eroticism, as well as various sexual codes and transgressions of public morality. The semiotic status of the hole is an important feature of the meanings in several other examples (figs. 50, 51), and from The New Yorker issues of September and November 1948. In these cartoons, the hole(s)—through a process of negative substitution—confirm the uselessness of the objets d'art represented. Kovarsky's image (fig. 51) shows a three-man art moving team using the holes in purely practical fashion to carry the sculpture, "a generic piece satirizing modernist art in general,"[13] from the studio to the gallery. In such a compromised position the three workers remind us of the three simians of "hear no evil, see no evil, and speak no evil."[14] And in their trapped (breached), position, they offer further confirmation of the erotic significance of the hole in contemporary sculpture, although here once again, Kovarsky would not admit

---

12. Correspondence with the artist, March 20, 1993.

13. Corrrespondence with the artist, 1993.

14. Kovarsky was "not sure whether this (was) the right interpretation" Correspondence with the artist, March 20, 1993.

to this as his intention, maintaining a suitable ironic propriety, which allowed him to keep his distance from any direct engagement with the topic of sexuality in his Moore cartoons. For instance, when asked again whether this image could be interpreted as a satire on the erotic significance of the hole he replied "no, I don't think so." In the context, however, of Kovarsky's work both as a cartoonist and a painter, and also considering the large corpus of cartoons of Moore's work, it is my belief that this image can sustain a semiotic complexity without over-burdening it with the interpretative (and possibly salacious), powers of a reader. A deep reading of this image would also have to account for the embarrassed, effete, or is it simply a deferential wave of the gallery doorman, attendant (gallery director?), that signifies some ancillary and possibly alternate meanings.

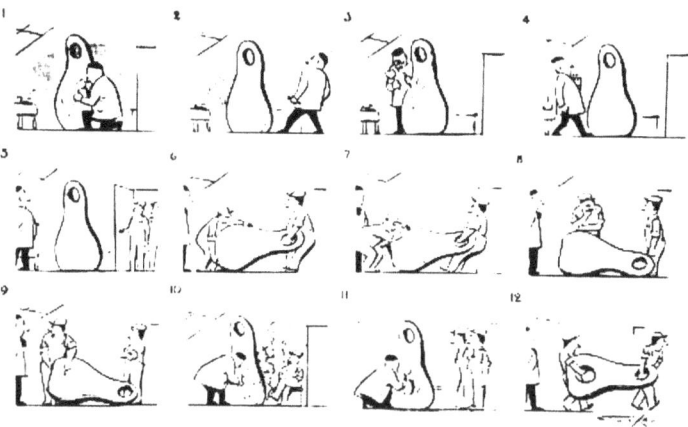

Figure 52: Leslie Starke, New Yorker Nov 27, 1948.
© New Yorker Cartoons, Conde Nast.

A multi-panel cartoon strip by Starke (Fig.52), represents the sculptor happily complying to the requests of the art movers to equalize the pleasure, or at least re-distribute the pain represented in the unequal distribution of the sculpture's mass. Here the apparent arbitrariness of the placement of the original hole gives way to the more mundane considerations of weight distribution and ease of removal implied in the exact placement of the second hole.

In the copious literature on Moore—over forty books and catalogues, at last count, including hundreds of essays and reviews—the significance of the hole in his work is usually discussed in purely formal terms. Early charges directed against his work, that it was both "immoral" and "Bolshevik"[15] were soon lost in subsequent interpretations, which taking their cues from Moore's own guarded or re-interpreted pronouncements, tended to obscure or downplay the eroticism of his sculptures, burying it in the arcane language of form. And just as the overt eroticism of some of his art was being erased or subordinated, the cues establishing parallel conditions for interpreting the works, and moreover, the fecundity of Moore's hand, were being reinforced.

Much of the writing on the function of the hole in Moore's art is based upon his own writing, in particular the early "Primitive Art" article published in The Listener[16] in the summer of 1941. In this short essay he affirmed some basic aesthetic positions obtained from Roger Fry's book *Vision and Design* (1921) and asserted the relationship between sex and religion as the "main interacting springs of life for the Negro and other primitive peoples." "All art," he wrote, "has its roots in the primitive" and, he continued, "it is something made by people with a direct and immediate response to life"; "the channel for expressing powerful beliefs, hopes and fears" (35). Moore followed these ideologically loaded sentiments with a specific passage to which many of his subsequent critics and biographers refer. It deserves to be quoted in full:

> A piece of stone can have a hole through it and not be weakened if the hole is of a studied size, shape and direction. On the principle of the arch, it can remain just as strong. The first hole made through a piece of stone is a revelation. The hole connects the one side to the other, making it immediately three dimensional...the mystery of the hole the mysterious fascination of caves in hillsides. (39)

The meaning of the hole has been of great importance to a few of Moore's critics. David Sylvester is convinced that the erotic is the deepest meaning in Moore's sculpture.

> It is worthy of note that when discussing the formal value of holes, Moore considers the hole as an aperture piercing a form, but as soon as he refers to its poetic value, he suddenly identifies the hole with the cavern. (Sylvester, D., 1968)

Sylvester's statement can be compared to one made earlier by critic Erich Neumann, who published a Jungian influenced study of Moore's work in 1959.

---

15. According to Herbert Read, these remarks were attributed to the art critic of the Leicester Morning Star in his review of Moore's 1931 exhibition at Leicester Gallery. Read, H. *Henry Moore, a Study of his Life and Work*, London: Thames and Hudson 1965.

16. The Listener, 24 August 1941, pp 35-39.

> Moore can hardly be described as a psychopathic personality who is obsessed with sex and sees holes everywhere even where none exist in reality. (Neumann 1959: 41)

Hardly, and yet the evidence in Moore's statements, particularly the written accounts of his early work, have militated against Neumann's post-Jungian account and tended to substantiate Sylvester's position, and the popular, more vulgar readings, of Moore's art. It is interesting that Neumann himself capitalizes on some of the features of Moore's biography for his own, what he termed, "depth psychological analysis."

Although there is not space to do so at great length here, it is fascinating to trace the origins of the debates about sexuality and the erotic as these have been raised, only to be, for the most part, simultaneously repressed by Moore's critics and biographers. They can provide an appropriate background to our discussions of the more popular readings of the sculptor's art represented in the cartoons. But this is an elusive quarry, particularly when, as is the case in many of these cartoons, the topic of sexuality is regarded as somewhat of a taboo. Even where a cartoon can be read clearly as a representation of human sexuality, as in the Taylor and Kovarsky examples discussed above, the artists themselves, as Kovarsky's comments serve to demonstrate, often remain silent on the issue.

Herbert Read's biography of Moore (1965) contains many anecdotes relating both directly and indirectly to the sexual themes of the sculptor's work. It could be argued that Read's early supportive essays and his biographical study of Moore established the foundations for the artist's subsequent canonization as a major figure in the history of modernist art. In common with many art history monographs, Read's anecdotes confirm that Moore's success and his international stature as an artist was intimately related to his origin. In Moore's case this was the working-class mining town of Castleford. Herbert Read advances a comparison with writer D.H. Lawrence—Moore's Castleford to Lawrence's Eastwood—as he discusses two key formative experiences on Moore's induction into the life of sculptor. He cites the young sculptor's early Sunday school exposure to the work of Michelangelo and the massaging of his mother's back with homemade liniment to relieve her of rheumatic pains, as being particularly formative experiences. Read paraphrases liberally from personal discussions he had with Moore, and includes the following revealing anecdote:

> When Henry was old enough and strong enough, she would ask him to rub her back with the strong-smelling liniment which she herself made. The liniment smarted and brought tears to his eyes, but what was to endure all his life was the physical sensation conveyed by his fingers as they came in contact with the bones beneath the flesh. To the boy, the expanse of back—his mother was quite a large woman—seemed to be immense, and full of subtleties of yielding flesh and resisting bone that combined to give him a unique sensation which later he was to recognize as a specifically sculptural sensation, especially that sensation elicited by the human body. (Read, 1965: 21)

This "awakening of the plastic sensibility," as Read termed it, was further confirmed by other formative experiences that Moore had at school including one key aesthetic experience which as Read suggests, reinforced Moore's early "sensitivities to the plastic."

> As an indication of the awakening of his *plastic sensibility*, at an early age Henry Moore once described to the author how he was able to recognize the girls in the school by the shape of their legs. "If their bodies and features had been hidden by a board below which only their legs showed, I could still have given a name to each pair. (25)

Read permitted some intimacy to this story yet distanced himself from the telling. It is tempting to suggest that this enabled a proper sense of propriety and decorum to be maintained, so that neither man's reputation could be sullied by the sexist epithet, "leg man." We are, after all, dealing with "plastic sensibility" not ardent sexuality. These anecdotes established the subsequent bias of his hagiographers and perhaps Moore's own later reflections upon the meaning of his life and work.

These historiographic anecdotes can provide a context for a discussion of the cartoons of Moore's art that appeared in the media. From a larger corpus of seventy-five examples I limit my discussion to six representative examples respectively from The New Yorker and Punch. These groups of cartoons further confirm the implicit sexual characteristics of the hole in Moore's sculpture that the cartoonists in their drive to satirize his work, have capitalized upon.

A Dana Fradon cartoon (Fig. 53) plays the sexual morality issue to the proverbial hilt. This six panel caption less gag shows a balding man of the cloth passing a generic piece of 'holy' modernist sculpture, perhaps a Moore but it could also be a Hepworth or Archipenko. With his interest suitably engaged, the priest takes out his spectacles to read the museum label *Nude* to suffer, as a result, the acute pain of embarrassment.

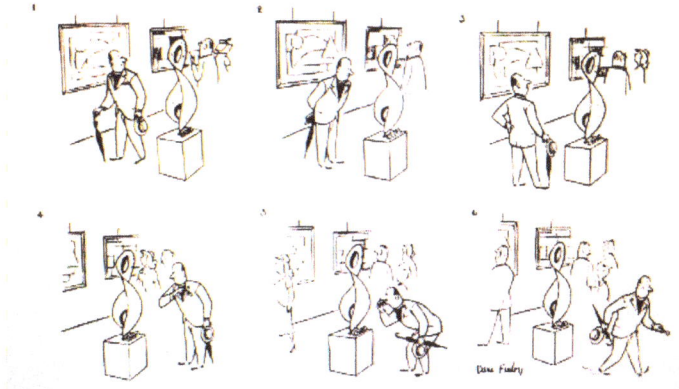

Figure 53: Fradon, D. New Yorker Oct 20, 1951.
© New Yorker Cartoons, Conde Nast.

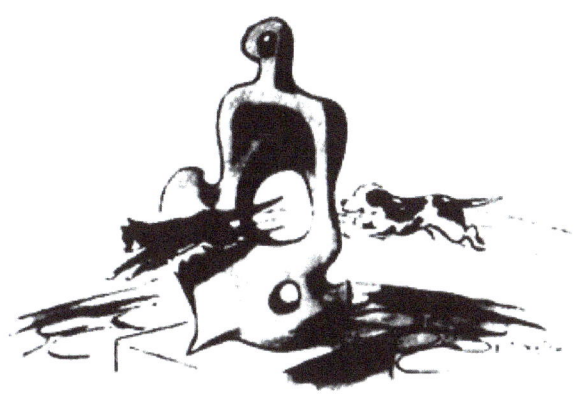

Figure 54: Tobey, B. New Yorker Jan 1, 1955
© New Yorker Cartoons, Conde Nast.

Barney Tobey's cartoon (fig.54) shows another generic Moore (*Standing Figure*) sculpture with a dog in hot pursuit of a cat flying through the hole. This image seems innocent enough, until we place it in the context of the symbolic use of dogs and cats in art history. Historically cats in art, especially black cats are associated with female promiscuity, and dogs of either gender, with fidelity. With the sculpture providing the subconscious vehicle for the animation of animal desire, it is possible to read this benign chase allegorically as a male/female pursuit with perhaps rape as the final goal. An equally 'benign' cartoon from four years earlier satirizes the generic Moore sculpture through a subtle association with a phallic symbol. In this example an innocent looking broom resting against the Moore sculpture perforated with a single hole, could be read in priapic terms, as an erect penis. It is noteworthy in this context that New Yorker cartoonists were often accused of trying to put something over their editors. Thurber's biography of The New Yorker managing editor Harold Ross suggests that he and other editors often had to counsel Ross against his desire to mis-read cartoons for their erotic content. But in many cases, as a moral inquisitor and chief censor of his magazine Ross may have been right! As recently as 1993, Lee Lorenz, art editor of The New Yorker for twenty years, suggested to me in conversation that he may have had the honor of publishing the first male erection in the history of The New Yorker with his satire of the Mapplethorpe, Serrano, Helms NEA (National Endowment for the Arts) affair, a cartoon that shows two primitive artists examining a stick figure drawing complete with a tiny erect penis on the wall of their cave. The caption reads "Whoops…there goes my NEA grant!" But the first cartoon 'erection' in the magazine can more likely be traced to the 1940s and 1950s, with even more subtle and ambiguous cartoons such as the two discussed above.

A William Steig cartoon from a 1955 issue of The New Yorker invokes a regrettable interpretation of the Pygmalion myth by representing a bearded sculptor embracing his sculpted woman with a hol(e)y body. And in a three-frame cartoon strip Ton Smits, depicts a young boy mischievously—misogynistically?—examining a sculpted reclining figure with two large holes, one in the head, and the other in the trunk of the body near the genital area. In the second frame the boy looks around guiltily to see if he is under surveillance. The final frame shows him exiting, having left behind a moustache below the hole in the head of the sculpture, a direct reference to Duchamp's famous addition of a moustache to a reproduction of Leonardo's Mona Lisa titled *LHOOQ*, 1919.[17] A hilarious cartoon by Wiseman represents a mother frantically summoning a museum guard to retrieve her screaming son whose head has been caught fast in the hole of the Moore sculpture he was inspecting. One can read this as a simple misadventure on the part of the child, but the implied reference to a woman giving birth, provides a satirical indictment of modernist art, without which this disaster would not have happened.

---

17. When pronounced in French the letters *L.H.O.O.Q* (*Elle a chaud au cul*) translate as "she has a hot bottom," a reference to Freud's famous study of Leonardo that contains a discussion of the artist's purported homosexuality.

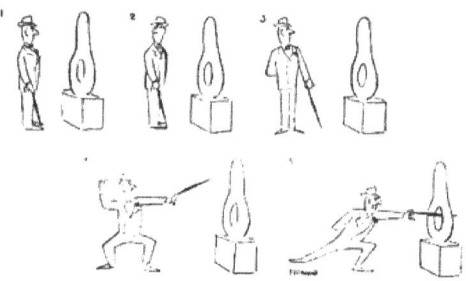

Figure 55: Modell, F. New Yorker June 25, 1955.
© New Yorker Cartoons, Conde Nast.

The final New Yorker cartoon from this group of six cartoons, is a strip drawn by Frank Modell (fig.55), that depicts a well-dressed male gallery visitor with hat, suit, bow tie, and what appears to be a flower in his buttonhole. Over the course of the first three frames the man contemplates a biomorphic sculpture with a hole, a generic Moore, or perhaps a sculpture by Noguchi.[18] He peers to the right to check on potential surveillants, and then assumes a full frontal *en garde* fencing posture with his umbrella. In the final frame the fencer, now exhibiting a sneer of defiance on his countenance, is shown thrusting his umbrella through the hole.[19] Once again, an innocent reading of this cartoon would see this simply as a humorous interlude. With different discursive reference points however—with the aid, for instance, of Freud and Jung on the psycho-sexual significance of umbrellas—this strip convicts the modernist sculpture by its erotic associations with masculine desire and androgynous sexuality. No innocent thrust this, but one that engages, in a deeply ironic manner, the taboo areas of the *ars erotica*. When Frank Modell was questioned on the erotic significance of this cartoon, he answered both ironically, that is, turning the question back to me, and contradictorily, with a defensive qualification.

> The erotic significance is in the eye of the beholder. I am not aware of my own subconscious thoughts.

In the previous chapter, I suggested that the major difference between the approach of The New Yorker and Punch artists to the satirizing of Calder's art,

---

18. Correspondence with the artist, March 1993.

19. The fencing image is similar to a famous Thurber cartoon in which one fencer 'innocently' decapitates his opponent.

is that the Punch artists domesticate the work. A similar attitude prevails with respect to cartoon images of Moore's art. The Punch artists again seem to have a penchant for domesticating the work, of turning the useless *objet d'art* into an object of utility. A cartoon by Emett, published in Punch October 13, 1948, is a perfect example of this process. An exhibition of Garden Sculpture by the fictional artist Cedric Chippynge shows two adjacent works on pedestals. A granite figure with a large hole on the left of the image is shown holding a fish and wrought iron flower titled the *Spirit of Indolence* bearing the ticket price 250 pounds. This is contrasted with the *Useful Granite Roller* adjacent at the lower price of 49 shillings and sixpence. The granite cylinder is the positive (cut-out) residue, of the earlier useless figurative work. And in a typical Punch overkill the caption announces,[20] "I must say, this modern trend DOES give one an opportunity to combine Art and Utility."

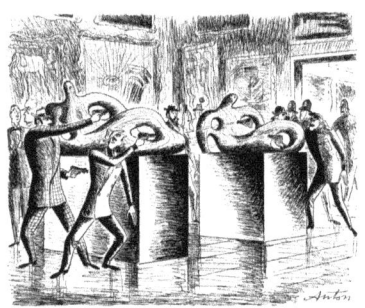
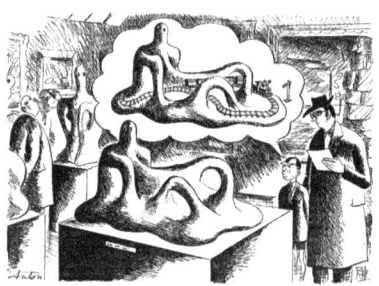

Figure 56: Anton, Punch Nov 12, 1947. © Cartoon Stock

Fig. 57: Anton, Punch Mar 16, 1949. © Cartoon Stock

The British artists also engage the Freudian potentialities of the apertures in Moore's work. Anton's brilliant cartoon (Fig. 56), for example reveals a cops and robber's museum shootout—the Moore reclining figures being used as cover—and the holes functioning as shooting gallery apertures. Another Anton cartoon (Fig. 57), exploits in very subtle ways the erotic potential of the Moore sculpture by illustrating a young boy's thoroughly surreal thought balloon, which takes up a major portion of the image, showing a train moving

---

20. Often this 'overkill' was the direct result of a collaboration (competition) between a caption writer, and the artist. For many years, both Punch and The New Yorker employed gag writers with artists, the writers providing the captions for the artists to illustrate or providing captions to the illustrations sent in by the artists.

upon railway tracks through the orifices made by the arms and legs of the body. Framed by a Freudian or Jungian dream hermeneutic, and the many symbolic uses of train imagery in both high and popular culture—from the Surrealism of Magritte and Balthus, to Alfred Hitchcock, Fritz Lang and Ingmar Bergman, to today's elaborate music video's displacements and condensations—one could read this cartoon from many different positions; variously, as an allegory on childhood fantasy, to adult transcendence, and consummation of sexual desire.

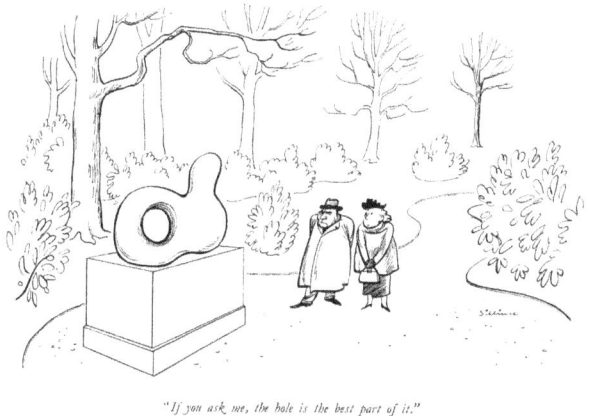

"*If you ask me, the hole is the best part of it.*"

Figure 58: Sillince, Punch Nov 14, 1951 © Cartoon Stock.

Punch cartoonist Sillince's satire of Moore's work provides a vehicle for several contrary readings. His cartoon (fig. 58), shows a couple before a large generic Moore sculpture (biomorph with hole) in a park, probably Battersea, which contains a large number of Moore sculptures. The man with a disgruntled look on his face contemplates the sculpture while the woman says, "if you ask me, the hole is the best part of it." Similarly, a Siggs cartoon shows a mother shrouding a young boy's eyes as they pass a Moore sculpture bearing the title *Nude*. The irony here is that while the young child would not have recognized this as a potential site for 'perverse' thoughts, the mother does, and not simply, one suspects, because it is labeled nude. It is interesting to contrast this with a later cartoon by Siggs that places a mother and child (mother spanking child), on the pedestal which recently held a sculpture titled *Mother and Child*, now showing a natural-looking male torso on the left, and a generic Moore on the right.

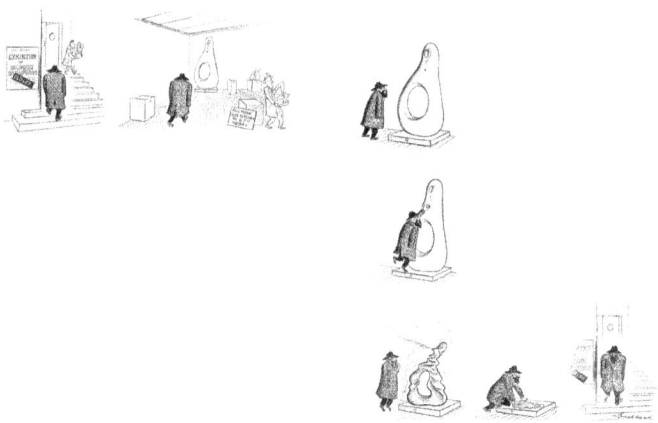

Figure 59: Brockbank, Punch Nov 12, 1952 © Cartoon Stock.

Finally, an extraordinary cartoon example by Brockbank (fig. 59), invokes both the elicit pleasures of a kinky sexual fantasy and frustrated onanism. This six framed panel follows the path of a sculptor who has come to collect his work from the Exhibition of Modern Sculpture. The second frame states that "All Work Must Be Removed by Six P.M. Today." Dressed in a long plaid coat, the sculptor presents a stereotypical shady character. When he moves to retrieve his work, he simply pulls the plug to deflate the Moore rubber sculpture then rolls it up, tucks it under his arm and exits. The humour here is very subtle, engaging us in quickly dismissed thoughts of flashers in raincoats and inflatable sex aids purveyed in sex shops and on the internet. Placed in the context of the popular resistance to Moore's erotic signals, it is difficult not to interpret this image in terms of sexual politics. The problem is where to locate sexual politics within class politics. But after Foucault's *History of Sexuality* (1978), and the last thirty years of feminist scholarship on these matters, it is not too difficult to locate expressions of sexuality, their management and prohibition, as indices of social and political power. As Foucault has suggested in a surprising passage:

> May I be forgiven by those for whom the bourgeoisie signifies the elision of the body and the repression of sexuality, for whom class struggle implies the fight to eliminate that repression; the "spontaneous philosophy" of the bourgeoisie is perhaps not as idealistic or castrating as commonly thought. In any event one of its primary concerns was to provide itself with a body and a sexuality–to ensure the strength, endurance and secular proliferations of that body through the orga-

nization of a deployment of sexuality. This process, moreover, was linked to the movement by which it asserted its distinctiveness and its hegemony. (Foucault, 1978: 125-6)

Both Moore and his respondents can be seen in the context of a Reichian or Foucauldian "repressive sexuality hypothesis"; a context within which the enunciations of sexuality are subjected to forms of control, and where meanings are within a field of shifting and evanescent textuality. By way of an imperfect, yet perhaps appropriate closure to this whole topic, I will leave the last word on Moore's holes to Punch Literary satirist–and the poem AN ULTRA MODERN SCULPTOR, August 10, 1949.

<blockquote>
All his concepts were too rarefied
for matter,
So, he crushed a chunk of marble
into dust
And dispatched it, on a complicated
platter,
To a gallery, with a label, as
a bust.
All the critics gaze with ecstasy
unfailing,
At this whole without a sole
coherent part,
And, on windy days, they stand
in groups inhaling
Little puffs of airborne particles
of Art
</blockquote>

CHAPTER 8

Even A Monkey Could Do It!

> Abstract art? A product of the untalented, sold by the
> unprincipled to the utterly bewildered. (Al Capp)

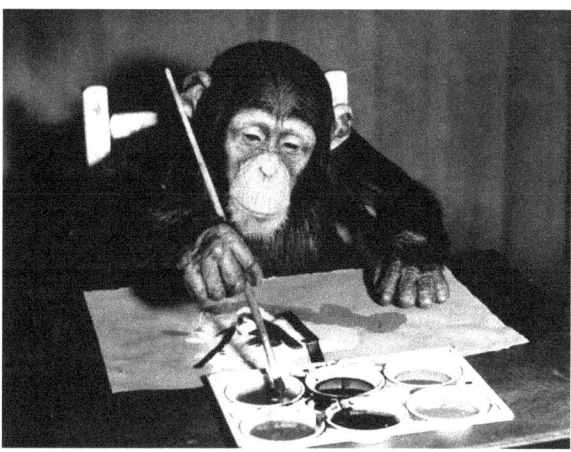

Figure 60: Chimpanzee 'Congo" painting a picture at London Zoo, 1958. World History Archive / Alamy Stock Photo

Abstract art has been an important target for producers of popular criticism for nearly a hundred years. Examples of these attacks are evident from the very beginnings of the so-called "crisis in representation" coincident with the mid-nineteenth century introduction of the photo-mechanical means of reproduction.[1] In this chapter I will discuss a range of critical responses, to the modernist avant-gardes from the birth of modernism to the present with special attention given to satirical attacks directed against the work, behaviour and institutionalization of the

---
1. Walter Benjamin was one of the first to recognise the political implications attending the change in production methods initiated with the invention of photography. His famous essay "The Work of Art in the Age of Mechanical Reproduction" is the obvious reference here. See Benjamin, W. *Illuminations,* edited and with an introduction by Hannah Arendt, H. Zohn, Trans. New York: Schocken Books (1969):217-252.

first generation Abstract Expressionists of the so-called 10th Street, or New York School. This discussion of popular critiques of abstraction will engage various topics relating to the public reception of modernism including aesthetic freedom, primitivism, gender, sexuality, religion, biology and politics. The critiques will also provide some entry into various aspects of the cultural stereotype of the artist as hero: the fecund, mystical, poverty stricken and supremely misunderstood creative magus and mad genius figure of popular consciousness. The chapter will conclude with a discussion of a representative collection of cartoon satires of abstract art that conform to nine categories of rejection, nominally subsumed under the following subject headings: politics, psychology, physiology, aesthetics, philosophy (ethics/morality), law, economy, gender, and technology.

Graphic satires aimed at the work of the proverbial "daubers," "fakes," "phonies" and "miscreants" of modern art appeared before the early twentieth century discourses associated with abstraction became fashionable among the cognoscenti of Paris, London and New York. A 1912 Punch cartoon drawn by M. Smith, provides an example of this type of critical response to proto-abstract art. The image depicts a group of gallery goers admiring a very contemporary looking black monochrome painting in an ornate frame. The caption below the cartoon reads:

> The late coal strike has caused extraordinary interest to be taken in the picture entitled "A Deserted Coal Mine," by Mr. Inkerman Knight, the Miner artist. The simplicity, breadth of treatment, and tranquility of coloring of this picture make it appeal to all true lovers of art, peace and cheap coal.

From today's vantage point this wonderful spoof of English social realist painting can be compared to more recent graphic satires of abstract art. The non-objective monochromatic painting in the cartoon strikingly resembles *Black Quadrilateral* (1913), by the Russian Suprematist Kazimir Malevich, a work produced a year later than Smith's cartoon. Mr. Inkerman Knight's deserted coal mine painting may also be compared to other more recent monochromatic abstractions within the modernist canon such as Ad Reinhardt's majestically minimal square black paintings of the late 1950s and early 1960s, and Alan McCollum's tight conceptual arrangements of his small black paintings in the 1980s. But the appearance of the Inkerman Knight monochromatic painting in a Punch issue of 1912 is totally fortuitous and therefore unrelated until now perhaps to popular criticism of the abstract paintings of these later artists. Smith's satire of abstraction is really that only by default. His target was the *fin de siecle* socialist realism of the kind made popular by Ford Madox Brown and his circle in the late Victorian era, and unless one believes in prophecy, the similarity of this cartoon to later cartoon satires of abstract painting has to be treated with some caution.

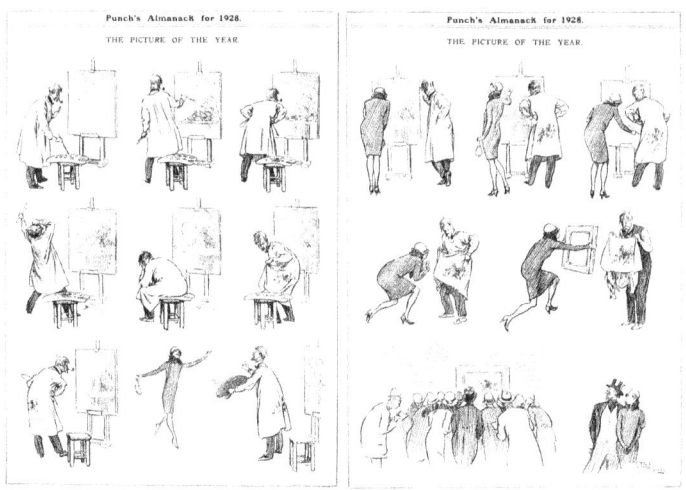

Figure 61: Reynolds, F. *Picture of the Year*, Punch Nov 7, 1928 © Cartoon Stock.

Frank Reynolds' hilarious *Picture of the Year* (Fig. 61), another prototypical satire of modernist abstraction, demonstrates how an artist's paint splattered smock *a la* late 1940s Abstract Expressionism, can become an award-winning artwork at least two decades before action painting's drips and splatters became *de rigeur* and Harold Rosenberg's "arena theory" of painting the encyclical for all would-be members of the expressionist avant-garde. The cartoons by Smith and Reynolds are not prophetic examples of the outsider criticism of the modernist avant-gardes, but it is important to recognize them as images linked to the crisis in representation issuing from mid-19th century debates, coinciding with the invention of photography, about the artist's role in society, in which the business of representing the material world was beginning to undergo rapid redefinition.

During the past ninety years modernist art has spawned literally thousands of cartoons similar to the two illustrated. Many parodies, satires and burlesques of avant-garde art and artists, have also appeared in forms beyond the newspaper and magazine. In literature, there are examples of satires of art in mid-nineteenth century novels such as Theophile Gautier's *Mademoiselle Maupin*, and more recent ones, such as Bernard Malamud's *Pictures of Fidelman* and Janet

Steinberg's *Death of a Post-Modernist* (Was it art or was it murder?). In film there are also many examples including: The Marx Brothers' *Animal Crackers*, Fritz Lang's *Scarlet Street*, Roger Corman's two versions of *A Bucket of Blood* and Tim Burton's *Batman*. In television, William Asher's *I Love Lucy*, and David Silverman and Matt Groening's *The Simpsons* have continued the public assault on modernist art. If much of the criticism directed towards abstraction in modern art has emerged from outside the borders of the art world, some of it, as we shall see in the next chapter, has its origins within the very inner circles (cenacles), of the art world itself. Culture criticism can originate from any institution, space or place where people congregate to discuss the cultural views and news of the day. Attacks directed towards the high cultural avant-garde can originate in the media, academe, the business world, the scientific community, the medical and legal professions, as well as government. Criticism may circulate for a time as an integral element of general discourse and then (re)enter the media in the form of crystal-clear cartoon satires and textual parodies. Powerful satires and parodies circulate and stimulate the production of others.

What is it about abstract art [2] that has made it such a popular target for cartoonists and writers to satirize? And what are the political meanings behind such stock phrases as "even a monkey could do it!" or "my six-year old could do better than that!"? These related questions are at once difficult and easy to answer. During the early years of the twentieth century abstract and non-objective tendencies in art began to submit to the critical scrutiny from various constituencies within the art world, particularly from those individuals who believed that the prevailing status quo—privileging mimetic, naturalist or realist modes of representation—was in the process of being usurped. Sometime later, modernist abstraction was subjected to the critical judgements of those members of the non-producing public—with little "cultural competency," in Bourdieu's sense—to whom art was, or should have been an illustration of reality, or some form of naturalistic representation; one moreover, that in the age of photo-mechanical reproduction, could successfully compete with the *truth* of the photograph. Abstraction's difficulty for the public of the first decades of the C20th was directly related to the inaccessibility of the principal features of the discourse associated with abstraction circulating between the critical players in the field of production. Pierre Bourdieu has described this competition in sociological terms as a type of communication divergence between producers

---

2. Abstract Expressionism was the term given to this new school by Robert Coates, art critic for The New Yorker Reference from Guggenheim, Peggy, *Confessions of an Art Addict* London: Andre Deutsch Ltd., (1960):104.

and recipients about the meaning of the coded messages contained within the discursive field of reception.

> a divergence between the *level of emission*, defined as the degree of intrinsic complexity and subtlety, of the code required for the work, and the *level of reception*, defined as the degree to which this individual masters the social code, which may be more or less adequate to the code required for the work. (Bourdieu, 1993: 224-5)

The struggle over meaning occurs in the discourse surrounding the work of art as well as internally in the consciousness of the receiver of the work itself. For example, within the shifting borders of the art world of the 1850s and 1860s arguments about representational veracity—an expected value within conventional art practice—often coalesced around the question of whether an artist had worked with photographic *aides de memoire*. These debates were precipitated by nineteenth century theories about the relationships between art, science and technology written by many leading intellectuals of the day. In France this group included Fourier, Gauthier, Zola and Baudelaire; and in England, Ruskin, Morris and Wilde. It is well known now that many mid-19th artists—Delacroix and Manet—for example, used photographic aids for their work. Even the exemplary *plein air* painters of the Barbizon School, of whom Corot is the prime example, were not immune to the use of the new photo-mechanical apparatus to enhance their powers of observation and memory.[3] According to his biographer, after Corot's death some six hundred photographic plates, many documenting his favourite subjects, were found in his studio. This large number of photographs demonstrated that his exemplary paintings from nature which reveal the effects of halation (the destruction of form by light), far from being the products of direct observation, were modelled after subjects frozen in time on the photographic plate. But at the time, scientific debates about the use of technical aids for representation were subordinated to the business of appreciating the work for its assumed veracity to the subject represented.

The early 1900s witnessed the entry of the work of the Fauves the wild beasts and Cubism, renewing the angry public debates about the madness of contemporary art that had begun in earnest in the early 1860's with the exhibition of Manet's scandalous paintings *Dejeurner sur l'herbe* (1863), and Olympia (1863). For some historians 1905 is acknowledged as a key starting point for the origins of the critical discourse around abstraction in art. This year marked

---
3. See Scharf, Aaron, *Art and Photography* Harmondsworth: Penguin (1968).

the showing of Cezanne's *Les Grandes Baigneuses*, Matisse's *La Joie de Vivre*, the publication of Einstein's first theory of relativity, and Freud's *Three Treatises on the Theory of Sex*. For others, the year 1907, is the key date within the related histories of modernity and modernism, and certainly a better candidate for the origins of the public dates about abstraction, for it was in this year that Picasso's shocking masterpiece *Les Demoiselles d'Avignon* was painted and seen and discussed by his friends and acquaintances, although it was another nine years before this controversial work was unleashed onto an unsuspecting public.[4] Discussed in the art historical literature as Picasso's response to his "revelation" about African sculpture (Rubin, 1980:87), this canvas more than any other from the first decade of th 20th century, reveals dramatically the shift from representation into a primitive abstraction, shocking a bourgeois public which even by 1917 was beginning to believe it was unshockable. More than any artist of the period, with the possible exception of Marcel Duchamp, Picasso's work hardened the French public toward the avant-garde assaults on their consciousness that were to appear at regular intervals throughout the following decades of the twentieth century.

By the time of the publication of Marinetti's Futurist Manifesto in Le Figaro on February 9th, 1909, several separate and competing discourses attended the work of those artists of the avant-garde who were producing abstract art. The development of post-cubist aesthetic movements in Europe: Futurism, Constructivism, Productivism, Suprematism, Dada, and Surrealism, and the entry of these into the British and American contexts, produced further complexities in the discourses of abstraction.[5] Art exhibitions containing representative works from any of these modern art movements were often satirized in the popular press, a result of cultural lag in the dissemination of key elements of the aesthetic discourse used to legitimate the practices and strategies of the avant-garde, for reading, comprehension and reproduction by a suspicious and often incredulous public. As a result of the mismatch between the various levels of competency operating within the field(s) of reception, popular criticism attending these movements reduced the complexity of the theoretical discourse functioning at the high cultural level to simple oppositional tropes. By the early 1920s, inside the art world centres of advanced discourse abstraction had become the subject of intense aesthetic and critical discussion, but outside these

---

4. The painting was given its present title by Andre Salmon in July 1917, when it was first publicly shown in the "Art Moderne en France" exhibition at the Salon d'Antin, Paris.

5. Barr, Alfred H. Jr. *Cubism and Abstract Art* New York: Museum of Modern Art, 1936.

centres of privileged interpretation, abstract art was subjected to acrimony and dissent. Within the art world the contest of meaning and value about abstraction was typically reduced to conflicts over the interpretation and privileging of various aesthetic philosophies, but in the public sphere the debates were simplified to a struggle between the good, the bad, and the ugly.

From the early years of the twentieth century, graphic satires focused upon those elements of modernist art that were easily identifiable to the public as essentially alien or other. Art cartoons satirizing abstraction took several forms, each of which can be categorised loosely under the headings listed previously (technical, psychological, aesthetic etc.), and tied to ideological positionings upheld by various classes and class fractions. Before I begin to discuss the distinguishing characteristics of each cultural critique category however, I will explore the broad features of the attack against abstraction as these were advanced by social critics, artists, and cultural historians working within the domain of popular culture characterized by Dwight MacDonald as mid-culture. The mid-culture critical discourses of abstraction reveal many aspects of the complexity of the debates around representation, that remain somewhat hidden in the graphic work. In order to provide the reader with access to the broad characteristics of the critical attacks on abstraction, I will engage in a close reading of three texts published in Tulsa, Toronto and New York, in 1952, 1972 and 1975 respectively. Each of these books: *Are You Fed Up with Modern Art?* (1952),[6] *Great Art to the Grotesque* by academician Kenneth Forbes and *The Painted Word* (1975), Tom Wolfe's celebrated broadside against Abstract Expressionism, symbolically reproduce the popular negative categorizations of abstract art apparent since its inception.

Are You Fed Up with Modern Art? (1952), edited by Clarence Canning Allen—art director and promotion manager of the Tulsa World and Tulsa Tribune Newspaper Corporation—is one of the least celebrated, yet probably in some constituencies, one of the most influential books to ever attempt to undermine the cultural supremacy of modern art. Without the brilliantly cynical wit that characterizes Wolfe's famous art world satire twenty years later, Allen's book contains many of the standard critical positions adopted from the early years of the twentieth century by those who thought that modern art had, as he put it, "gone too far!" As the book's editor, Allen employed a quasi-objective debating model—more Texas high school than Oxbridge Socratic—that propelled him

---

6. Allen, Clarence Canning (ed) *Are You Fed Up with Modern Art?* Tulsa: The Rainbow Press (1952). I am indebted to Anatol Kovarsky for bringing this book to my attention.

to align his contributions into two sections, offering diametrically opposed positions—both for and against—modern art. This editorial strategy was devised presumably, to place the reader in the position of assuming the role of impartial judge to the merits, or lack thereof of modern art. Despite claims to objectivity offered in the introduction, Allen's book reveals that The Contraries in this great debate held a decidedly stronger position than The Fors, thus heavily biasing the case against modernism.

The book contains letters, documents, *bon mots*, short articles and reviews, interspersed liberally with cartoons, paintings and photographs representing both sides of the debate. The frontispiece opens with a preface outlining the editor's reasons for the existence of the book.

> This book has been compiled through the earnest desire of the editor to find satisfactory answers to the many questions from friends and correspondents regarding modern art. Privately and among friends one hears the constant muttering and grumbling about modern art in the annual exhibitions, how much crazier it becomes each year, how it has taken over our colleges, universities and museums. Have we bone fide grievances? Why? (Allen, 1952:5).

The inside cover contains a Robert Capa photograph (Look, Jan. 4, 1949), that shows Pablo Picasso with his hand resting, proprietarily, upon the hip of one of Michelangelo's sculptures. Hanging on a wall in the background are two drawings by Picasso accompanied by what must have been to Allen and his friends, the shocking revelation that "Picasso's works will displace Michelangelo at the Antibes Museum."

Part I begins with a somewhat ingratiating editorial, a Dedication to all "Modern Artists, the creative trail blazers of the creative fields—They have everything against them; AND FOR THEM, only their faith in themselves." In a similar effulgent style, the Foreword extols the virtues of originality and creative freedom; of the artist being him/herself, but it underlines also the reason why the young artist should learn the rules before he/she breaks them—"Of course it is good to know the principles in order to know when, where, and why one is breaking one." (11) This statement is followed by a potted and repetitive lesson on the importance of a type of modernism that while new and progressive, is tied to tradition. For the young artist, Allen extols the virtue of learning thoroughly the rules of his craft. And least we miss his aphorisms in our haste to know why we too are fed up with modernist art, his text is studded with capitalized bon mots such as: "MAN'S ETERNAL WARFARE IS HIS BELIEF IN

HIMSELF AGAINST THE QUAGMIRE OF MASS CONFORMITY." This is followed by a now familiar discussion of how modern (specifically abstract) art, the quest for originality and creative freedom, can represent the highest political ideals of democracy.[7]

> It is most fortunate for those who desire to develop that spark of originality within them that they live in FREE, DEMOCRATIC AMERICA. Here the individual rights of the people are considered. HERE ONE CAN HONESTLY BE HIMSELF, be original. Which is the only way to fully enjoy the privileges of his birthright; INDIVIDUAL LIBERTIES AND FREEDOM OF EXPRESSION. (12)

The editor concludes his forthright introduction with encouragement to the intelligent reader to seek out similar ideas in books such as Ralph M. Pearson's *The New Art Education* (1950).[8] This first section of Allen's book contains some seventeen contributions, including for comparative measures, a short excerpt from MOMA curator James Thrall Soby's *After Picasso* (1935). As was common to many participants at the cultural margins tending the interpretation and reproduction of modernist discourse, Allen's arguments are somewhat out of character with the manner in which these debates were being played out in key high culture venues such as the Partisan Review, Art News, The New York Times, The Nation, and The New Republic.[9]

The paintings illustrating the 'for modernist art side' of the debate in this odd anthology include works which for the time, could hardly be described as contemporary. Examples of abstract expressionist painting that was beginning to shock members of the public in New York at this time do not appear in the book. In their place were art works produced some twenty years earlier: Picasso's *Seated Woman* (1926-7, MOMA), and *Girl Before a Mirror* (1932), John Marin's *Lower Manhattan* (1922, MOMA), and Katherine Dreier's *Portrait of Marcel Duchamp* (1918). The writers aligned to the pro side, however, did occasionally demonstrate a knowledge of abstract art and included oblique references to expressionism in their statements. Mortimer Borne of the New School

---

7. For a thorough discussion of this premise for modernism consult Serge Guilbaut's *How New York Stole the Idea of Modern Art* Trans. (Arthur Goldhammer) Chicago and London: University of Chicago Press (1983).

8. Pearson, R.M. *The New Art Education* New York: Harper and Bros. (1950). For its time, this was a very popular book and appeared in over ten editions. Pearson was a founding member of the progressive American Artists Congress and the author of a number of other books on American modernism including *Experiencing American Pictures*, New York: Harper and Bros., (1943), and *The Modern Renaissance in American Art*, New York: Harper and Row, (1954).

9. See Guilbaut, S. (1983) and Frascina, F., ed., (1985)

of Social Research, New York and Alexandre Hogue, Head of the Department of Art, University of Tulsa both responded negatively to Allen's question of "are you fed up with modern art?" In response Hogue writes "No I am not fed up with modern art, but I do reserve the right to criticize its weaknesses," and curiously, "It 'ain't like Caesar's wife." (16) Allen includes an excerpt from Eliel Saarinen's *Search for Form* as if to counter the ambivalence of advertising executive Joe Russakoff's "Opinion of Modern Art," who wasn't sure whether he was "jumping on modern art or approving it." For a long time, he confessed, "I have been baffled by it—not knowing what it's all about. And I am still in ignorance of many of these forms of modern expression." Russakoff concluded however, that because abstract artists are trying to see "beyond the surface of things," then they must indeed "have something to say." (18) His short statement is followed by a more up-beat 'manifesto' from Craig Allen, a student of architecture at the University of Texas, and the son of editor Allen, casting a slightly oedipal shadow over the entire project. In contrast to his father's avowed liberal position on modernist art, the younger Allen's opinion is youthfully idealistic, pragmatic and progressive. Taking a historical perspective, Craig Allen suggests that as modern art has been around for a while "we can no longer do away with [it] any more than we can do away with television antennas on roof tops." But because modern art was "in its infancy," he wrote, it required time to develop "a philosophy of purpose" which he further suggested should be both liberal and progressive. C. Edward Cerullo, Art editor of Today's Woman magazine, declared his position on the question after serendipitously tripping through the history of modernist art, tipping his hat this way and that to those he termed the "adventurers" and the "greats" of the modern heritage. He opined that the "American illustrator of today is fully aware of these traditions and influences," or, he warned, "should be!" (21). Cerullo concluded his opinion by suggesting correctly that modern art has not only "revolutionized gallery painting," but it has also influenced and changed "the printed page, the way we live at home, at work, and in our whole visual way of life" (22). Comparing scientific progress with modern art Cerullo writes "A stated science with intuition, is for today and tomorrow; we must go forward. That is modern art" (25). After Cerullo, William Rexford Garey, a Kansas based artist/numerologist offered his somewhat eccentric approach to art. Basing his comments upon his admiration for Kandinsky, Klee, Miro and Mondrian. Garey mentions a short excerpt included in the book from James Thrall Soby, author of *After Picasso* (1935) which confirmed his own somewhat conventional approach to cultural progressivism.

Garey is followed by Albert Dorne, introduced as President of the Famous Artists Course, of Westport, Connecticut., appearing in this context as a somewhat unrepresentative modernist. Allen suggests that his interview with this artist is for "those who aspire to become illustrators and commercial artists." Dorne is quite candid in his opinion of recent graduates of art schools, whom he says, "simply aren't equipped to take their places as practical, trained artists." His guiding principle is hard work, and he cheerfully presents his own protestant work ethic as a model. Once, he said, he worked "a straight thirty-eight days with less than two hours sleep a night." He follows this pronouncement with an unapologetic endorsement of capitalism: "Say what you like, money is one good, hard mark of success, and its contribution to the enjoyment of the cultural aspects of life is not inconsiderable." More than other representatives for the Pro side, Albert Dorne confirms his firm belief in what he calls "the modern art movement" even if his version of modernism falls somewhat short of that extolled by contemporary champions of the avant-garde, Greenberg, MacDonald, Shapiro et. al, writing in the pages of The Partisan Review.

The following eight pages of Allen's book are given over to the reproduction of a New York Times article written by the peripatetic modernist Ralph M. Pearson, in which he espouses the "Five Qualities of Modern Art: creation, expression, design, adventure or dramatization" and something which he terms mysteriously "non-literal penetrating vision." Pearson was less than charitable to those engaging in what he termed the "debacle of art values" who he suggests had abandoned content and form in art, supplanting these with the "noisy embracing and honoring of chaos, or the beginning of the emergence there from." And "since chaos is not art," he continued, "this marks the low ebb of the historical tide." The final contributors for the for side included Tulsa-based architect Bruce Goff, and provincial art critic Martin M. Weisendanger who provides an ecstatic review of the work of Bernard Frazier whom he certifies as a representative modernist. Goff's "Contemporary (sic) Art" exposes his problems with cultural lag and what he calls the three enemies of modern art, whom he identifies as the critic, the artist (his own worst enemy), and the public. "Today, as always," he concludes, "we have good, bad and indifferent modern art, but we have it in greater quantities than ever before." (43)

The pro-modern section of the book closes with critic Martin M. Weisendanger's reviews of artist Bernard Frazier's faintly modernist allegorical bronze war memorial plaques: *Achievement, Sorrow, Courage, Mediation, Aspiration and Silence* for the University of Kansas, which he claims—somewhat adventurously—are "the most important bronzes of the first half of the 20th century." He waxes eloquently over artist Fred Conway's "famous" 75x25 feet mural The Birth of Oklahoma commissioned by the First National Bank of Tulsa, another work of somewhat dubious cutting-edge distinction, when compared to the hot modernism practiced in the cultural centres of New York, Chicago and Los Angeles. A cartoon satire of modernist art instruction by New Yorker cartoonist Anatol Kovarsky, appears to bridge the For and Against sides. Kovarsky's cartoon illustrates a life painting class in the 'typical' modernist academy. The image shows all of the students diligently painting the same generic Picassoesque cubist image of the female nude. Kovarsky's cartoon predates by some three years a similar although much more celebrated one by Alain, published in Ernst Gombrich's *Art and Illusion: A Study in Pictorial Representation* (1960). Alain's cartoon shows Egyptian art students in the process of learning to draw paratactically—without the benefit of monocular perspective—from a female nude who is engaged in "walking like an Egyptian" The venerable art historian uses Alain's cartoon to discuss the "riddle of style" (2), and historical progression of "schema and correction." Alain's cartoon demonstrates that the Egyptians only drew what they knew, not what they saw. The cartoons underline the standardization of conventional art education instruction that turns fashion into convention.

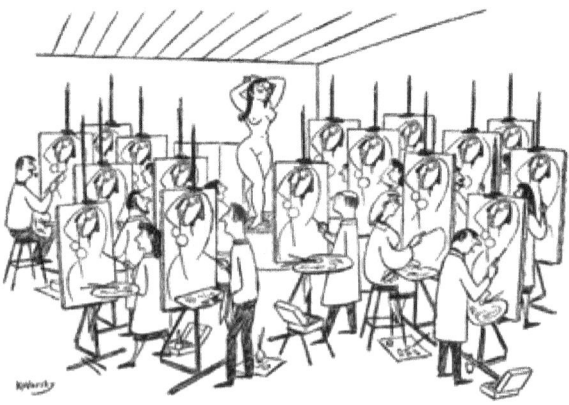

Figure 62: Kovarsky, A. *Picasso Life Class*. The New Yorker.
© New Yorker Cartoons, Conde Nast.

The book's second section, Against Modern Art, contains some extraordinary if predictable, indictments of modernism. In his introduction to this section, Allen employs various criteria for judging modernism's lack of value and as prophetic entree to Tom Wolfe's satire, he suggests that abstraction is "theory driven" and that its success is dependent totally upon the critic whose "skill of word and phrase juggling, explaining and justifying (sic) these abortions, is not only indispensable but much more clever than the artist's own work" (53). Here, laced with hyperbole, Allen reveals his true prejudices against modern art, which he vilifies as the "RED! DEAD END" of art trying to make "TWO and TWO look like THREE." And "A DARK AGE, SIDESHOW, HANGOVERS, JOHNNY COME LATELY." These "SIDESHOW FREAKS…Picasso, Braque. These self-anointed missionaries of modern art…." He goes on to decry modern art as an "infection," "addiction"; that abstract artists are "drugged," "decadent…" In two blistering pages, Allen trots out every epithet that has ever been used to attack modernism, the work and behaviour of the abstract artist.

In a confident follow-up to this introduction, Kevin Lynch, the first contributor to this section, critiques the conservatively 'modernist' First National Bank mural discussed in the previous section, with the very quotable "All the good artists are dead, and all the live ones ought to be." (59) This is followed by a contribution from Jenkin Lloyd Jones, editor of the Tulsa Tribune, Allen's employer, who suggests that it is time that "we had a revival of *real art* in America," art which he boldly asserts, should be defined as "something that looks like something." (60) Both pages of Jones' invective had caught Allen's attention when published previously as editorials in the Tulsa Tribune.[10] Jone's redneck critique of modern art is endorsed by another contributor, Dale Nichols, whom we are informed is a famous artist from Tucson, Arizona. Nichols believes that the lunatic fringe has seized both modern art and criticism, and that it is now "time to blow the whistle on this stuff!" His biography states that he spent twenty years as a farmer, then studied art and aesthetics in Chicago and Vienna. His book *A Philosophy of Esthetics* promotes his powerful credo that "perfection comes through obedience to and practice of natural laws." His over the top broadside exposes Modern Art as a movement with no lesser intention than to destroy western civilization simply by, 1) "destroying the old master painters who illustrated the lives of Christ and Moses. 2) by popularizing an unreal form…3) by popularizing the "abstract." And in what must count as once of the first uses, after historian Arnold Toynbee, of the term postmodern, he suggests

---

10. Jones, J. L., "Isn't Modern Art Awful" Tulsa Tribune May 16, (1947), and "In Defense of Beauty," July 18, (1952).

that he is launching "A *Post-Modern* movement which will be nothing more than a modern artist's movement *for*, instead of against, Western Civilization" (66) (emphasis added).

Nichols' contribution is followed by another trenchant critique of modern art's bolshevism by the infamous Republican congressman from Michigan, George A. Dondero. The Dondero contribution consists of a reproduction from The Congressional Record of his famous speech against modern art titled clearly "The Communist Conspiracy in Art Threatens American Museums" delivered before the second session of the 82nd Congress in March 1952, an event of enormous significance for millions of people like Allen who felt that there was more to modernist art than met the eye; that in essence, it was a Bolshevik conspiracy aimed at nothing less than the dismantling of western civilization!

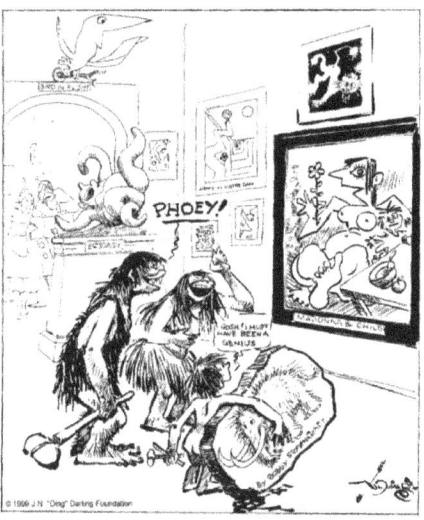

Figure 63: J.N. (Ding) Darling, *Stonehatchet Family Visits Modern Art Exhibition*. Des Moines Register Cartoon

The next group of contributors against modern art: author, George Mathew Adams, journalist Lucia Ferguson, Billie Thaxton, Westbrook Pegler, Frank Tripp, August Derleth, art critic, C.L. Newcomb, art director, Clair V. Fry, Dale Carnegie (of Institute fame), and radio personality Art Linkletter, outline in quick succession why modern art is "primitive," "generally of little merit," "beyond the pale," "dangerous," and "the epitome of evil itself." From this group of contraires, naturalist painter, William R. Leigh reduces modernism down to a comment that suggests that "the whole sickening sham induces revulsion, horror, despair, a shuddering distrust of humanity itself." (77) These contributions espousing the dangers of modernism are interspersed with several graphic satires. One by J.N. (Ding) Darling from the Des Moines Register headlined "Stonehatchet Family Visits a Modern Art Exhibition" (fig. 63), shows Bobby, a stone age child with his huge stone tablet drawing of a mammoth, exclaiming "Gosh I must have been a genius." The object of his identification is a generic cubist *Madonna and Child* by Picasso. In attendance his cavewoman mother hoots and his father blasts...PHONEY! Another cartoon by Wilson McCoy, comic artist of *The Phantom* shows an artist congratulating himself on his abstract artwork announcing "Gad! This is good, I don't get it myself!"

Both contributions by Senator Dondero and Eleanor Jewett, art critic for The Chicago Tribune denounce modern art as a tool of communist extremism. She writes:

> The greatest argument against modern art is the fact that it has been and is being used by Moscow as a tool of communism. Modern art has neither standards nor traditions. It began as a spirit of revolt and has continued its aggressive mood into today. The State Department has admitted there are communist artists in government positions but "not in places of importance." (79)

Jewett details how the major show of avant-garde art sent to represent American culture by the State Department to Europe in 1947 was recalled by President Truman. She quotes Fulton Lewis Junior, who in his talk of October 30, 1952, showed reproductions of work by twenty communist artists, suggesting that these represented a good half of the artists participating in the exhibition. In her short one page statement, this defender of the faith negated the modernist project with at least eight of the negative categories of popular rejection: these artists only do it to shock the bourgeoisie; they are doing it for money; to develop the cult of the accidental and the ugly; and to spawn irreligion and blasphemy. To Jewett modern art lacks spiritual values, is monotonous, boring, one-dimensional and ugly; modern art is communist, Bolshevik, hoaxed by animals (even a monkey could do it!), and base amateurs. Cartoonist Dallas Meade provides another anti-communist Cold War position. He writes that "Modern Art is an import from Europe. They have a philosophy over there that creates confusion. I refer to communism. Could modern art be one of their tools to create more chaos?" (85) Meade's cartoon shows a blindfolded painter, with his hands tied behind his back working on a canvas, with his paintbrush held between his toes. The accompanying caption "Painting Modern Stuff" demonstrates that the modern idea is not to "paint what you see, but what you feel." Allen concludes his book with the hope that his readers have been encouraged to consider both sides of the debate, and not merely their own prejudices. The balance, however, is more in favour of Allen's prejudices and his biased colleagues who are "fed up" with modern art and have absolutely no problem with announcing it.

The socio-political significance of the promotion of abstract painting by the U.S. Department of State and the USIS in the early Cold War period has been discussed extensively by Cockroft (1974), Tagg (1976), and Guilbaut (1983). These writers argue that the promotion and circulation of American Abstract Expressionist painting by institutions like the Museum of Modern Art in collusion with the U.S. Information Service served several ideological purposes: the promotion of freedom, democracy, capitalism, and generally to convince Europe and the rest of the world, of the omnipotence of American cultural power in the post-war era. Guilbaut argues that the introduction of "Schlesingerian liberal politics of the vital centre" after the presidential elections of 1948, assisted in the development of a new kind of liberalism, which "unlike the ideologies of the conservative right and the communist left, not only made room for avant-garde dissidence but accorded such dissidence a position of paramount importance." (Guilbaut, 1983:3) The Allen book among others like it, demonstrate the spirited character of the cultural debates in regional centres by members of the middle-classes and regional intelligentsia. Marginalized from the sites of real cultural power and with less cultural capital upon which to base their arguments, Allen and his various contributors resort to time-honored political broadsides laden with invectives, slurs and oaths stereotyping, satire and burlesque, aimed at underwriting the claim that modern art is a communist plot aimed at derailing the great freight train of civilization.

The pages of Allen's book exist as a testament to the contest of meaning over the value of modern art and demonstrate the attempts made by various constituencies to both achieve cultural hegemony and resist the presence of destabilizing influences in their domain. At the same time that the denizens of cultural power in New York were engaging in a spirited defence of modernist avant-gardism, which according to Greenberg (1947), involved turning their Stalinist inclinations into a softer Trotskyism that would pave the way for an heroic apolitical arts for art's sake for a free and democratic future, the regional and class based responses to modernism's entry into the public sphere were solidly right wing, macho, jingoistic, racist, anti-communist and fundamentalist in tone, heroic Jeremiads aimed at bringing 'God's truth' back to the cultural foreground where it belonged. As the efforts of Allen's writers Against Modernism provide ample testimony, abstraction and modern art in general were undermining fundamental democratic values and rights, the kind of rights enshrined within the American constitution: Freedom, God, Good Government—and probably the right to bear arms—values that common Americans espoused to be the basis of their strength and indeed the moral bases of western civilization itself.

Twenty years after Allen's book had become the talking point of Tulsa high society, Pitt Publishing of Canada published another virulent attack on modernist art in a strange little book titled *Great Art to the Grotesque* authored by Kenneth Forbes, a member of the Royal Canadian Academy. Forbes raged against modern art for most of his career, quitting in 1951, the Ontario Society of Artists, as well as his membership in the Royal Canadian Academy for their acquiescence to what he believed to be the fraud of modernism. In the short chapters of his book Forbes, like many before him, rails against modernism in general, abstraction in particular, the modern artist, his critics, dealers and other institutional bastions of modern art, for they are all engaged, in "putting it over." Institutions of contemporary art perpetuate what Forbes called "*the grotesque*" in art. And like Allen and his friends, he spends little time in unveiling a sinister plot that is out to hoodwink the naive and unsuspecting public; a plot to destroy the history of *good* art and the work of the masters within the western canon.

The key arguments and examples Forbes uses in his book reproduce in heightened form the popular criticism of abstract art evident from its inception and still circulating within society at large fifty years later. Much of Forbes thinking on these matters was hardened in the 1930s and 1940s but until the 1970s most of his attacks against modernism appeared the form of letters and short poems. The book chapter titles reveal the major thrust of his attack, even if the two-and three-page contents of each chapter fail to deliver conclusively the harsh critiques of modernism which are implicit in each title. His first chapter is provocatively titled, *The Swindle of* (sic) *Modernistic Art*: *The Cult of the Ugly*. In this chapter, Forbes colorfully argues that "the beautiful mansion of art" has been "attacked by termites" .and its utopic garden has been "overrun with noxious weeds." He goes on to attack the "hordes of charlatans, neurotics and incompetents who have invaded the world of art with pretentious claims to justify the doodling, the fads and nonsense that they call art.(11) He lays the blame for modern art's "cult of the ugly" squarely upon the shoulders of ideologues, the architects—critics, theoreticians and artists—of modernism, among them: Apollinaire, Max Jacob, Cezanne, Picasso and Braque, who "lowered the standards" established by the great technicians—Raphael, Michelangelo, Leonardo—of the High Renaissance. "The explosion of cubism," we are told, "was a staggering blow to genuine art–one from which art has not recovered." Forbes asks whether this appalling state of affairs is part of a sadistic impulse, or even "an urge to debunk the human race." (2)

In his second chapter, How They Put It Over, Forbes suggests simply that the public has been brainwashed into admiring modernist art. He compares the propaganda techniques used in this swindle to those used in the Hans Christian Andersen tale of *The Emperor's New Clothes*, suggesting the public have been hoodwinked into believing grotesque modernism worthy of admiration. The critics, he suggests, have used "incomprehensible mumbo jumbo" and jargon to put it over. He cites the following examples: a "charlatan," writing about an "incomprehensive mess of paint" who states "that it has plastic disintegration of rhythmic essence." Another critic he opines, praises a childlike painting for "having a phenomenal degree of micro-cosmic synthesis, or three-dimensional reality." (4-5)

The third chapter of Forbes's book, *The Weird World of Modernistic Art*, provides some further details about this flagrant "art of the grotesque." He cites examples of 'convincing' modern art produced by animals, children and mental patients which have been passed off as legitimate. Lola the donkey, rails Forbes, was coerced with a bunch of carrots to paint a canvas with a brush tied to her tail. Forbes rages that one of her efforts titled "And the Sun Sank to Sleep on the Adriatic" was praised by critics when it was placed in a salon exhibit! And in Bournemouth, England, a winning collaborative work was created when the daubs of the six-year-old son of an English Academician were joined by the pot of paint spilled by the family cat! With the perceptive addition of some twigs, dirt and rubbish from the garden, Forbes writes, this effort was sent off to the Academy to win rave reviews from the critics. And as if this is not evidence enough to rest his case on the modernist(ic) grotesque, Forbes includes the celebrated case of Peter, a 4-year-old West African chimpanzee from Sweden's Bora Zoo, whose paintings were hung in a gallery under the name of Pierre Brassau. One of his oil paints sold for $90.00 and a reviewer of the exhibit wrote "Pierre Brassau paints with powerful strokes but also with clear determination. His brush strokes twist with furious fastidiousness. Pierre is an artist who performs with the delicacy of a ballet dancer." (8)[11]

In his fourth chapter titled *Deceiving the Experts*, Forbes discusses several examples of fake work which deceived both the curatorial experts of National Galleries, both in Canada and England, as well as respected art historians like Sir Kenneth Clark. He suggests that had "real experts"—presumably academic painters such as himself—been asked to offer their opinions on the authenticity of certain works, they would not have been purchased. After an inspection of a van Dyke oil painting owned by the National Gallery of Canada, he suggested that he knew that it was a fake because *his* examination of the work proved that he could have done better himself and therefore, it must be a fake! In Chapter 5, *The Ignorance of Critics*, he argues that critics are responsible, along with disreputable dealers and professors of art and art history, for the art of the grotesque. To Forbes (and many other anti-modernists) critics and art historians are failed artists, parasites who should be made to pass exams before they are allowed to practice.

In Chapters 6 and 7, again bearing provocative titles—*The Strongholds of Sanity*, and *The Standards of True Art*—Forbes pays homage to those few high culture institutions, the guilds, academies and museums that, with the support of a few high minded artists like himself, have resisted the art fads and the cult of the ugly to pursue the righteous paths of truth and beauty. And in the following chapters, *Recognition* (Chapter 8), *The Atrophy of Beauty* (Chapter 9), and Chapter 10 (*The Crime against Sanity*), Forbes further articulates his naked antagonisms toward modernist art which he established in the first pages of his book. Finally, in an ecstatic flourish, Forbe's appendix printed on the back page, reproduces the "revelatory research" of Paris based Greek physician Dr. Elie Bontzolakis, alongside a photograph of the good doctor, who divides abstractionists into two classes:

> By far the larger: the poseurs attracted by snob appeal laziness, money, or mere lack of talent. These he finds are rarely neurotic. But about one third of his patients (the second group) are passionately sincere [but] they have both emotional and physical symptoms. (67)

Given the biased content of his book, Forbe's use of illustrations is somewhat predictable. An academic painting of a nude by the painter Orpen is compared to a reclining nude by Picasso which Forbes informs us would fetch $500,000

---

11. Requoted from TIME magazine February 21, (1964):45.

more than the Orpen in the art market. The "ridiculously overrated" painting *Poplars on the Epte* by Claude Monet is unfavorably compared to correct view of nature represented in *The Road* by Sir George Clausen, R.A.; Cezanne's *Portrait of Camille Pissarro* is compared unfavorably to a Rubens' *Self-Portrait*; a famous Giorgione is compared to the equally famous, but lesser Cezanne; A Sargeant portrait is contrasted with a Vincent van Gogh self-portrait, whose painting, we are told, is a "repulsive portrait of a man with a disordered brain. Failure at everything he attempted" (41). A Velazquez portrait is compared to a self-portrait by Matisse. Forbes leads us into an historical leap from the sublime *Spring* by Botticelli to the "repulsive grotesque" *Les Demoiselles d'Avignon* by Picasso. A reclining figure sculpture by Henry Moore is compared unfavorably to one by Forbes's Renaissance master, Michelangelo, and an untidy *Artist in his Studio* by Picasso is compared to an obsessively tidy *Studio* by Vermeer. *A Woman's Portrait*, by academy member Alfred Stevens, is judged against a grotesque abstraction by Willem de Kooning. An abstract painting by Sara, a four-year-old, is compared to a similar painting Burst by the abstract painter Adolf Gottlieb. Finally, Forbes delivers the following judgement in his comparison of an abstract work *Qualme* by modernist painter James Brooks to the efforts of Congo, a monkey,

> Forbes' idiosyncratic, yet systematic attack against modernism would be hilarious, if it were not for the fact that in the last century it has probably been endorsed by millions of people who, in similar manner, reduce their critiques of modernist abstraction to the familiar declarations: "Even a monkey could do it!," or "my kid could do better than that!"

In previous chapters, I used art cartoons produced during the late nineteenth and twentieth century development of modernism to make some conjectures relating to the public apperception and reception of the particular work of the artists and other cultural institutions and agencies associated with the promotion and development of abstraction. Abstract Expressionism represents a specific case within the development of modernism and yet, in many ways, it conforms to patterns of criticism established in earlier decades. The grouping of cartoons responding specifically to the work of the first generation of Abstract Expressionists can be traced to the early 1940s and is coincident with the developing importance of abstraction as an aesthetic strategy and the supportive theoretical and critical discourses—from Greenberg, and Rosenberg writing for the Partisan Review and other journals—that accompanied the work of the artists associated with the so-called New York School, including the major figures: Hoffman, de Kooning, Pollock, Frankenthaler, Baziotes, Motherwell, Rothko, Newman and Reinhardt.

Tom Wolfe's famous satire *The Painted Word* (1975)[12] is one of the most celebrated, if somewhat belated, attacks on modernist art. Wolfe's book simultaneously slammed home a nail into the coffin of Abstract Expressionism and solidified its author's position as a well-dressed critical icon of American contemporary culture. The ironic cover endorsements for Wolfe's book were effusive. A review, purportedly by Judson Hand for the New York Sunday News, is unequivocal:

> If you have ever stared uncomprehendingly at an abstract painting that admired critics have said you ought to dig, take heart, Tom Wolfe, in a scathing new satire, *The Painted Word*, is on your side…Don't miss it. It may enrage you. It may conform your darkest suspicions about modern art. In any case it will amuse you.

And Christopher Lehmann-Haupt of the New York Times offered: "*The Painted Word* may well be Tom Wolfe's most successful piece of social criticism to date." Wolfe opens his broadside against modernism with an ironic description of "an epiphany" he had while reading an article by Hilton Kramer for the Arts and Leisure pages of the New York Times. It was his close reading of Kramer that convinced him that without a *text*, or more specifically, a *theory*, one could neither see, or understand, a work of modern art.

> All these years, in short, I had assumed that in art, if nowhere else, seeing is believing. Well–how very shortsighted! Now at last, on April 28, 1974, I could see. I had gotten it backward all along. Not "seeing is believing," you ninny, but "believing is seeing," for Modern Art has become completely literary: The paintings and other works exist only to illustrate the text. (6)

Wolfe satirizes the moderns for declaring that art was not necessarily about anything; that all the historical avant-garde movements: Fauvism, Futurism, Cubism, Expressionism, Orphism, Suprematism, Vorticism—never mind that he had placed them slightly out of order—all shared the same premise. "Henceforth one doesn't paint "about anything my dear aunt," to borrow a

---

12. Wolfe, T. *The Painted Word* New York, London: Bantam, (1976). Original published Harpers Magazine April, (1975); First Edition Farrar, Straus & Giroux, June (1975).

line from a famous Punch cartoon. One just paints." (8-9) With a jump and a judgement from the early 20th century to the Op and Pop of the 1960s, to Minimal art and Conceptualism, Wolfe asserts that modern art is less about art than theory.

His opening chapter introduces the "apache dance," his version of primitive creative behaviour, which he associates with the antics of the avant-garde. A cartoon drawn by Wolfe shows some scruffy young hopefuls, artists "Hot off The Carey airport bus, looking for lofts." These stereotypical artsy fartsy individuals, according to Wolfe, are keeping up with their Bohemian heritage, which derived from the cenacles of Hugo, Gautier et. al dictates that they must conform to the model of the hip anti-bourgeois artist and play the game of *epater le bourgeois* and "dedicate themselves to the quirky god Avant-Garde" (17). And in two brilliant passages laced with acerbic wit, Wolfe writes that all the while these avant-gardists must keep:

> one devout eye peeled for the edge on the blade of the wedge of the head on the latest pick thrust of the newest exploratory probe of this Fall's avant-garde breakthrough of the century...all this in order to make it, to be noticed, to be counted, within the community of artists themselves,

and their other eye peeled:

> to see if anyone in le monde was watching. Have you noticed me yet? Have they noticed the new style (that me and my friends are working in)? Don't they even know about Tensionism (or Slice Art of Niho or Innerism or Dimensional Creamo or whatever)? Hello Out There!) All this activity for history because success was really only success within le monde. (17)

Wolfe continues to embellish his satire, hyperventilating over the secrets in what he calls "the art mating game," the collusion between artists, critics, dealers and museum people to put it over, for the ultimate payoff: "fame, money, and beautiful lovers." This theory of art rests on the boho dance (artworld lifestyles), and what Wolfe elegantly terms, using a sacred/sexual trope, "the art of consummation" (ibid). And all of these behaviors are directed toward obtaining success in the market place.

Wolfe's second chapter, titled Wildely, "The Public is not invited (and never has been)" continues his satirical rant against the insularity, elitism and navel gazing in-grouped ness of the international art world. He paraphrases statements by leading critics such as Lucy Lippard, by suggesting that the international art world is populated by "10,000 souls, a mere handful restricted to *les beaux mondes* of eight cities" (26). The following chapter attempts a critical deconstruction of the mating relationships between corporations, museums and the avant-garde and the art world's dependence, on the great shibboleth, THEORY. "No longer background music...," he says, it has become now "an essential hormone in the mating ritual" (37). These first three chapters are merely a warmup for his blistering attack, in chapter four, on modernist critics Clement Greenberg, Harold Rosenberg, the promotion of their "God Flat" and the first-generation Abstract Expressionists of the Tenth Street, or so-called New York School. Under Wolfe's sardonic gaze, Clement Greenberg is revealed as the prophet of Modernism who sees that art is heading through an internal logic toward a certain inevitable conclusion...

> just as Marxists saw western society as heading irrevocably toward the dictatorship of the proletariat, and an ensuing nirvana. In Greenberg's eyes, the freight train of art history had a specific destination. He called for "self-criticism" and "self-definition"—"self-definition with a vengeance," he said. It was time to clear the tracks at last of all the remaining debris of the pre-Modern way of painting. And just what was this destination? On this point Greenberg couldn't have been clearer: Flatness (49).

Parodying a Greenberg text, Wolfe reproduces this critic's Kantian reduction, if only to reinforce for the reader his sense of the absurdity of the theory sustaining abstract expressionist practice.

> It has been established by now, it would seem, that the irreducibility of pictorial art consists in but two constitutive conventions of norms: flatness and the delimitation of flatness. In other words, the observance of merely these two norms is enough to create an object which can be experienced as a picture; thus, a stretched or tacked-up canvas already exists as a picture—though not necessarily as a successful one.[13]

Wolfe argues that modernism's "other God," Harold Rosenberg's Action Painting, arrived as a solution to the problematic of contemporary art. "At a certain moment the canvas began to appear to one American painter after another as an arena in which to act" (51). In accordance with this theory,

---

13. "After Abstract Expressionism" (1962), in Geldzahler, H. *New York Painting and Sculpture 1940-1970*, New York: Dutton, (1969):369.

the action painter became the "Promethean artist gorged with emotion and overloaded with paint, hurling himself and his brushes at the canvas as if in hand to hand combat with fate." The author embellishes his satire with heroic photos of his targets, Greenberg and Rosenberg accompanying a particularly tacky image of painter Willem De Kooning's studio arena, with a full centre-fold image of Pollock's painting *She-Wolf* (1943), captioned with a hilarious reworking of the Broadway standard "That old black magic..."— "That thick fuliginous flatness got me in its spell." (57). Wolfe uses the stained canvas "Veil" paintings of Washington-based expressionist Morris Louis to demonstrate the extraordinary lengths the artist must go in order to satisfy the ambitions of the God Flat—"Did I hear the word flat?—well try to out-flat this you young Gotham rascals" (59).

Dropping in a paraphrased *bon mot* from Barnett Newman above a photo of this artist: "Aesthetics is for the artists as ornithology is for the birds," Wolfe continues to reinforce how theory, which for him, is merely the conflation of art criticism and the artist's behaviour, has superseded legitimate art practice, which throughout his book, he abstains from defining. He reserves his most acerbic commentary for Jackson Pollock, the dean of the movement whose "ugly work...began to take on a strange new glow when Greenberg pronounced him the strongest painter of his generation the most powerful painter in contemporary America the greatest painter in contemporary America" (63). But, as Wolfe dictates with relish, this is also the painter who:

> arrives drunk at Peggy Guggenheim's house during a party for a lot of swell people. So, he takes off his clothes in another room and comes walking into the living room stark naked and urinates in the fireplace (64).

For Wolfe, Abstract Expressionism was no more than a big noise made by and on behalf of, a little group, a cenacle of less than 100 people, "a club on tenth street," who had managed to hoodwink America and the rest of the world, into believing that they were producing art of the utmost importance to history and civilization. He refutes the material evidence of several hundred museums worldwide to suggest that both the number and prices of Abstract Expressionist works sold were inflated.[14] And after confirming in his book that Leo Steinberg, sometime in 1963, had pronounced Abstract Expressionism dead, Wolfe's next chapters take on Pop, Op and Minimalism. These are "new order(s)," he says,

---

14. See Crane, D. *The Transformation of the Avant-Garde: the New York Art World, 1940-1985* Chicago: University of Chicago Press (1987), for a useful discussion of the market conditions of the New York art world.

"but (from) the same mother church" (82). In keeping with his strategic hyperbole and attacks on individuals: Jasper Johns, Robert Rauschenberg, Andy Warhol duly receive the Wolfe treatment. In short measure, we are informed that Pop art's "sign system, not realism!" was too theory laden to be art and that this art movement was, "from beginning to end, an ironic, a camp, a literary intellectual assertion of the banality, emptiness, silliness *et cetera* of American culture." His final chapters summarily dismiss art movements following Pop: Op, Minimal, and Conceptual art, as "up the Fundamental Aperture."

It is possible to classify the criticism of abstraction contained in the three books discussed above and those expressed within society generally, under nine generic categories: politics, psychology, physiology, aesthetics, philosophy (ethics/morality), law, economics, gender and technology. I have chosen a representative selection of twenty-two cartoons from a corpus of several hundred that ironize, parody and satirize Abstract Expressionism according to these generic categories. In the sense that they conform to a model type, I would suggest that they are variations within a genre of cartoons that critique abstraction in art, Abstract Expressionism, and finally, modernism itself. This brief discussion of these examples provides further evidence of outsider misunderstanding of the discourses of Abstract Expressionism which include Greenberg's Kantian *ding an sich*—thing in itself—reductivism, satirized by Wolfe as the "God flat," Rosenberg's arena painting theory that privileges the expressionistic actions of the painter over the product itself, existentialism, primitivism, the creative angst of the feeling artist, alienation and ennui. The conventions of the abstract art cartoon genre provide an overarching consistency to the examples described, but there is often considerable overlap between the subject categories with some of the cartoons representing characteristics of two or more categories.

1. Politics

The first generic category assumes that abstract art has a distinct political agenda or ideology to promote; The cartoons in this category represent abstraction as the product of Bolshevik, anarchistic, communistic, fascistic, or occasionally liberal democratic ideology. Cartoons in this category often assume that abstraction is the work of dirty anarchists, left wing revolutionaries, or right-wing terrorists. Abstract art is either the result of some sort of conspiracy, state subterfuge, alien or foreign intervention. And because abstract art is foreign, it is therefore suspect.; "These people don't speak the same language as us." "We don't like their culture." "The abstract art does not represent our values" *etc*. It has been argued that abstract art in America during the 1940s represented the quixotic politics of the 'vital centre' or the new 'liberal democratic' ideology of the post-war period. As Serge Guilbaut has convincingly argued,

> Expressionism became the expression of the difference between a free society and totalitarianism; It represented an essential aspect of liberal society: its aggressiveness and ability to generate controversy that in the final analysis posed no threat.

And later, with respect to Jackson Pollock's work, he legitimates the progressive Schlesingerian democratic politics of abstraction with,

> [His] drip paintings offended both the Left and the Right as well as the middle class, they revitalized and strengthened the new liberalism. (Guilbaut, in Frascina,1985: 163)

There are hundreds of graphic satires of abstraction that allude explicitly or implicitly, to the socio-political reality outside of the esthetic proclivities of the art frame. These cartoons often endorse the progressive politics indicated in the abstract work, occasionally adding an ironic twist that accommodates and/or reproduces the politics of the reader. Examples of this include a cartoon from Punch, showing an acquaintance addressing the abstract painter with: "But I always thought you were a Tory?" A second example by Alan Dunn from The New Yorker shows a child returning from a demonstration to a bohemian looking abstract painter's loft. The child's hippy artist mother says, "He said his first words today: get out of Vietnam." Other examples allude to the political progressivism of the abstract painter without denoting the type of political ideology. A Whitney Darrow cartoon in The New Yorker for example, shows a brawl between gallery goers at an opening of an abstract art exhibition. The cartoon's caption reads: "I'm afraid we'll have to close down your show Pearson. We had no idea that your work was so controversial."

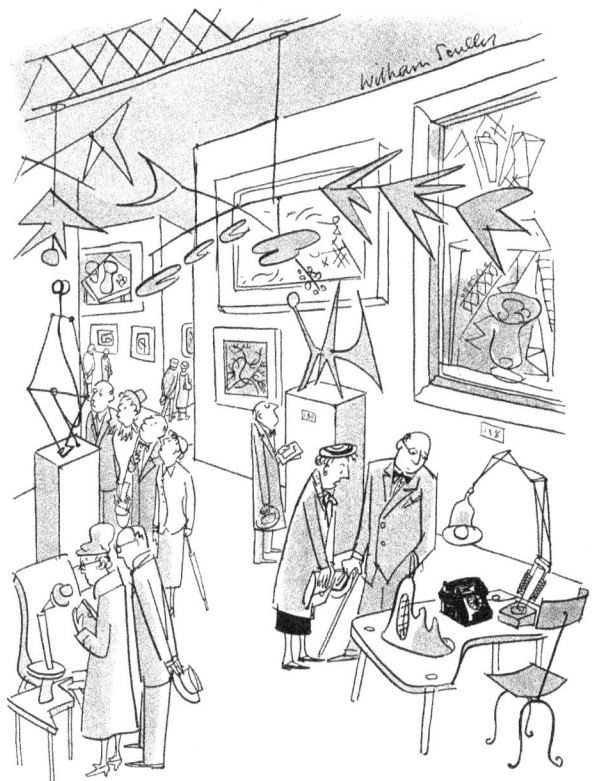

"You'd have thought they'd have done something about the telephone."

Figure 64: Scully, W. Punch August 31, 1949 © Cartoon Stock

2. Psychology

The second category, Psychology, promotes the notion that abstract art is the product of a deficient mind, the work of the insane, the psychologically aberrant personality; the result of some form of neurosis or sexual perversion. Cartoons in this category usually participate in the popular (othering) stereotype of the suffering avant-garde artist who is usually represented as abnormal: neurotic, paranoid, psychotic, schizophrenic, or simply, insane. There are a large number of cartoons within this category, including a New Yorker cartoon by Krauss showing a despondent artist addressing his partner with

"Do You Think I like to suffer?" and an example by Lee Lorenz' "Never Forget Phil," says the housewife to her artist husband "you've mastered the highest art the art of living." A cartoon by William Steig bearing the caption "I paint what I feel" underlines a common belief about the subjective origins of much abstract art. Another cartoon shows an artist's wife telling the alienated genius before his blank canvas "Time for bed, Anton. You've suffered enough for one day." A William Scully Punch cartoon, shows a stereotypical artist wearing beret and sandals, lying on his psychiatrist's couch delivering the soliloquy "...and I mix abstract with stylized romanticism. Some people don't understand what I'm getting at, but..." A cartoon by Weber shows a wife/partner of an abstract painter warning her partner as she exits to go shopping "Bye-bye. Don't go cutting off any ears while I'm gone," an allusion to Vincent van Gogh's psychological problems, and the stereotyping of the manic-depressive genius. All of these cartoons play with the suffering artist and creative magus stereotypes; the locus of the satire is invariably the genius artist whose deficient, dysfunctional or abnormal personality propels him to produce deficient, dysfunctional, and abnormal abstract art.

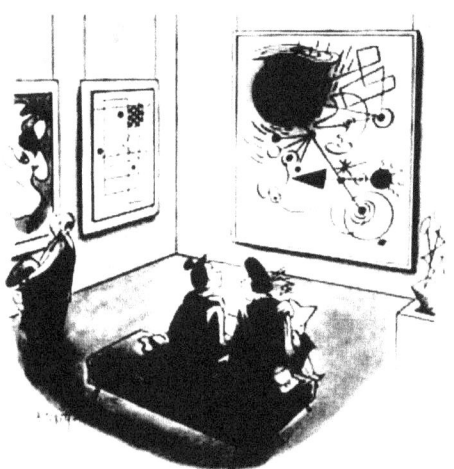

"There's probably more to it than meets the eye."

Figure 65: Tobey, B. New Yorker February 23, 1952
© New Yorker Cartoons, Conde Nast.

Even A Monkey Could Do It: 193

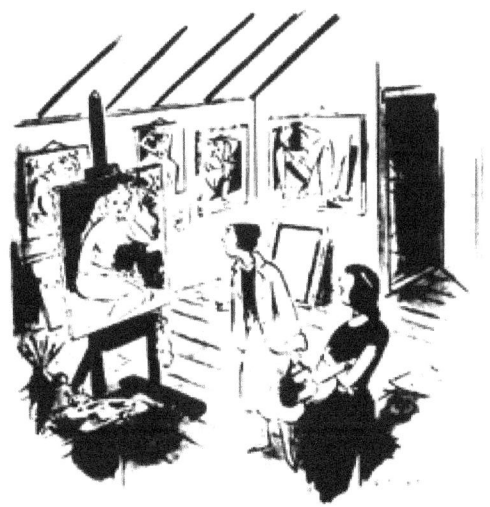

"Oh, didn't I tell you? He's got new glasses."

Figure 66: Tobey, B. New Yorker January 30th 1954
© New Yorker Cartoons, Conde Nast

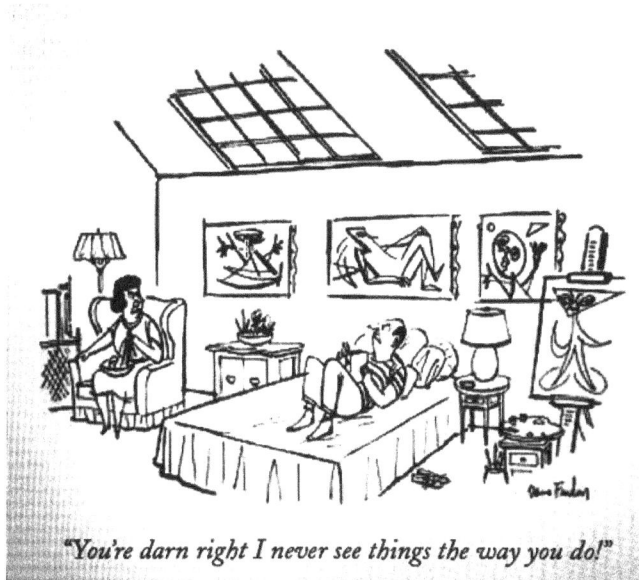

"You're darn right I never see things the way you do!"

Figure 67: Fradon, D. New Yorker 10th April, 1954
© New Yorker Cartoons Conde Nast

3. Physiology

Physiology, the third category, is similar to Psychology with the difference that cartoons in this category focus attention on the imperfections of the body, not the mind. Cartoons in this category confirm that abstract art is the work of artists with defective vision, or problems with loco-motor control that produces as a result, a distorted or aberrant representation of reality. The physiologically based cartoon satires of abstraction use sight or the absence of vision, to reveal the artist's technical deficiencies and absence of talent. The physiologically oriented cartoons may represent technical deficiency from either the position of the viewer, or the artist. representative cartoons such as those illustrated (Figs. 65, 66), by Barney Tobey, and Dana Fradon, contain revealing captions such as: "There's more to this than meets the eye" and "Oh, Didn't I tell you? He's got new glasses." Dana Fradon's museum guide, puts on his glasses to go home, implying that he prefers not to see the abstract art works he spends his workday guarding. Another Fradon cartoon depicts a puzzled viewer examining Abstract Expressionist paintings with the caption "You're darn right I never see things the way you do." Another cartoon example by Krauss (The New Yorker Jan. 8, 1955), places emphasis on an abstract artist's lack of sight. The caption reads: "I paint what I don't see." A cartoon by Lee Lorenz, (The New Yorker Aug. 8 1959), summarizes the physiological problem of abstract art and underlines it with an ideological perspective on American identity, by showing two artists selling their wares, with the indignant naturalist painter professing to the bohemian looking Abstract Expressionist on his left: "For your information, I paint things the way I see them, and I happen to see things the way one hundred and eighty million other decent, normal Americans see them." The artist's statement conflates technical ineptitude with normative models of morality and decency, which is more often than not, the subtext of many of the more explicit physiological critiques of the abstract expressionist project.

4. Aesthetic

The Aesthetic category promotes the popular idea that abstract art is grotesque, ugly, and contravenes the laws of beauty and perfection which are part of (God given) nature. Abstract art must therefore become naturalized, tamed or given some kind of aesthetic appeal. Accordingly, an Alan Dunn cartoon (fig. 68) shows a female artist painting an Op art version of a Zebra's stripes from a live Zebra model in a zoo. A Hewison's cartoon (Punch November 24, 1954), shows a male viewer examining in quick succession four generic Ben Nicholson abstracts, one of which attracts his attention because it resembles an aerial view of a soccer field. Another cartoon (The New Yorker August 29, 1964), shows a bourgeois couple relaxing on the deck of their chic modern seaside home looking at a sunset resembling a Mark Rothko painting. The man exclaims "Now, there is a nice contemporary sunset!"

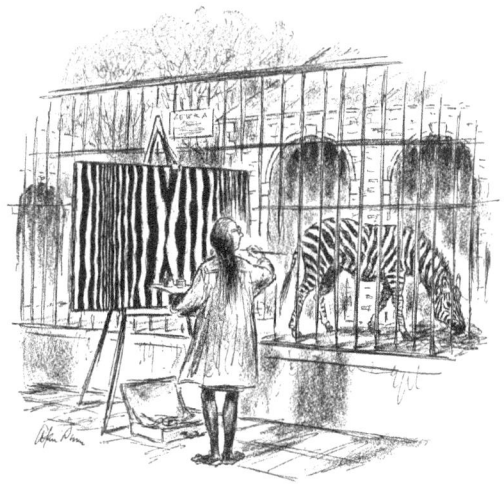

Figure 68: Alan Dunn New New Yorker Nov 28, 1964
© New Yorker Cartoons Conde Nast

5. Philosophy (Ethics/Morality)

Cartoons in this category subscribe to the idea that abstract art offends against standard canons of morality. Abstract art is immoral, offensive, dehumanizing and decadent. Abstraction in modern art is an index of social decline, ethical degeneracy and moral decay, and moreover, abstract artists are god-less atheists who aspire hate for nature, humankind and the works of God. An example by Siggs (Punch magazine, February 19, 1964), illustrates an eighteenth-century bacchanal painting with two upright women in front suggesting that "This is the sort of thing that abstract art tries to avoid Edna." Richard Taylor's New Yorker cartoon from the same period shows two elegant young women visiting a gallery. One reads a catalogue item discussing the framed blank canvas painting beside them. The text reads:

> During the Barcelona period he became enamoured of the possibilities inherent in virgin space. With a courage born of the most profound respect for the enigma of the imponderable, he produced, at this time, a series of canvases in which there exists solely an expanse of pregnant white.

The keywords here: white, virginity, pregnant, born, enigma, ironically subvert the quest for purity of modernist abstraction. Another cartoon (New Yorker April 11, 1964), shows two men, an abstract artist and his critic (or patron), in the artist's studio. As they survey the latest results on the wall, one says to the other: "See! I told you hard liquor has it all over sherry," a reference to another common behavioral stereotype for (abstract) artists, drunkenness and alcoholism.

6. Legal

This category defines the work of the modernist artist as fraudulent, a hoax intended to hoodwink the public into believing it is good, honest and legitimate art. Modernist art is lawless and therefore bound to lead to indictment or failure. This has a long history and has been the topic of many books and films including *Crack-up* (1946) Irving Rees, a crime story concerning art fakes. *Legal Eagles* (1986) Ivan Reitman Murder art fraud in which Daryl Hannah plays an artist's daughter and Winger and Redford attempt to recover stolen art. And possibly the most famous, *F is for Fake* (1973), a documentary directed by Orson Welles. A Richard Decker cartoon shows two women attending a neighbor's house fire. One says to the other "I don't want to insinuate anything, but lately Ethel has become crazy about modern."

7. Economic

The many cartoons and graphic satires in this category usually contain content that questions the economic value of abstract art. How could this useless abstract art be worth anything? How can anyone sell this? How could this become an investment? And why would anyone pay money for this trash, garbage, that any decent law-abiding citizen can plainly see is not worth the material on which it is drawn, painted or sculpted. Surely, there is more productive labour than this? Whitney Darrow Jr.'s example (The New Yorker December 15,

1951), says it bluntly: "Buy Up Now save $50,000." His cartoon demonstrates the relationship between creative success, or the ideal of same, with the (potential) arbitrary movements of the art market. The cartoon implies that if the artist becomes famous then his investors can also expect grand returns. Alain's "Closeout sale, entering new period. Everything must go" (New Yorker June 6th, 1953), satirizes the fashion conscious (fickle) art world where an artist or style is in one minute, and out the next. Dana Fradon's cartoon (New Yorker Nov 29, 1952),"Tell me John, do you really believe your paintings will become valuable after you're dead?" Bartlett's cartoon (New Yorker April 4, 1959), shows an abstract painter being delivered a message by his wife, "Somebody on the phone wants you to do something for money. Shall I tell him to go to hell?" Another cartoon for the Wall Street investor by Barney Tobey (New Yorker March 30, 1968), shows a middle-class couple informing an abstract artist at his opening that "Instead of putting money in growth stocks, we're putting it into you." A final cartoon example from this category by Saxon reveals a modernist artist encouraging the bourgeois collectors visiting his studio to examine his latest work." Believe me, for myself money means nothing. But as a custodian of my genius I must demand these prices."

8. Gender

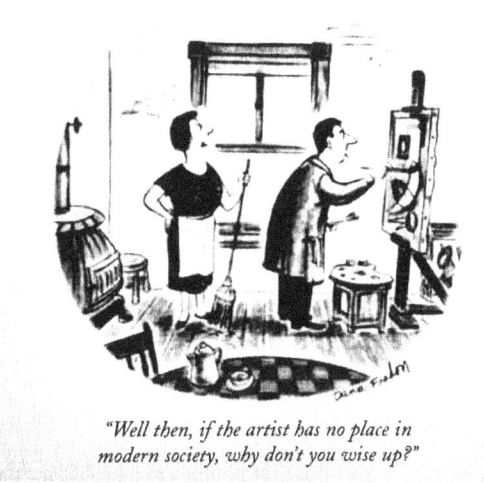

"Well then, if the artist has no place in modern society, why don't you wise up?"

Figure 69: Fradon, D. New Yorker Feb 14, 1953
© New Yorker Cartoons, Conde Nast.

There are hundreds, possibly thousands of examples in the gender category group that use domestic struggles between men and women to illustrate their point. Some would say that gendered cartoons are the stock and trade of cartooning as a whole; Certainly gender cartoons are a prominent vehicle for satires of abstract art. Dana Fradon's cartoon (New Yorker February 14, 1953), depicts a stereotypical apron clad wife wielding a broom telling her unshaven painter husband amid their impoverished surroundings "Well then, if the artist has no place in modern society, why don't you wise up?" Frank Modell reverses the gender roles in his cartoon (New Yorker February 18, 1956), which shows. the wife painting up a veritable abstract storm in the studio while husband says to male friend as he washes the dishes "it all started the day I said to her, "If you think you can do it so much better, I'll do the housework and you paint." Another cartoon by Modell, (New Yorker December 15, 1951), gives artistic inspiration a twist. The indignant wife drying dishes says to her uninspired artist who is looking out away from his blank canvas and out the window for inspiration. "Well I've got an inspiration— you go out and get a job." In a similar example by Mirachi's (New Yorker April 16, 1955), the artist's aproned wife engaged in sweeping with broom says to her abstract artist husband "Yeah? Well, you're not distracting me and I'm working," once again providing the reader with the clear implication that domestic work is productive labour and painting abstracts is not.

9. Technical

This category is also very large and contains cartoons with stock messages such as: "a child of six could do this better than this!" or "even a monkey could do it." The technical category underwrites the notion that abstract works or art are the result of fortuitous forces which have nothing to do with professional training or God-given talent. There are many graphic satires in this category that liken the abstract painter's project to the painting skills of primitive man, monkeys or chimpanzees. One of the best of these, produced with his usual extraordinary economy of means, is Allan Dunn's insouciant chimpanzee (Fig. 71) wearing an artist's beret, carefully sipping champagne at the opening of his one man show of abstract paintings.

J.W. Taylor's cartoon, from Punch shows a chimp painting with two figures in white lab coats looking on. The bearded one says to the other "On the other

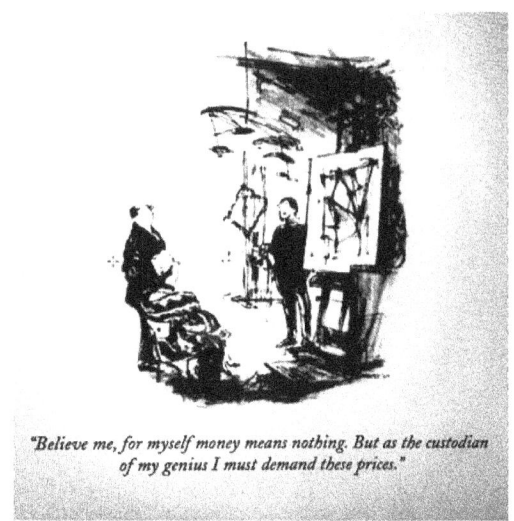

Figure 70: Saxon, C. New Yorker April 2nd, 1960
© New Yorker Cartoons, Conde Nast.

hand, it may be just a dodge for keeping out of rockets." This cartoon coincides with the frequent use of test animals in space flights and the socio-biological studies of infant development in mammals.

There are many examples of cartoons that show abstract art being made with a domestic painter's roller, a typical critique of Barnett Newman's 'zip' paintings and hard edge abstracts in general. Other examples demonstrate the grotesque and ugly side of abstraction. Anatol Kovarsky's eight frame cartoon shows a dissatisfied burglar returning his ugly modernist painting to the museum from which it had been stolen. Other examples show the action painter's art: An example from Punch (April 8, 1959), shows a painter hurling paint at a canvas while a figure delivers the one liner "When I asked him what his aim was, he said it was improving." Frachetti's Punch cartoon from the same year (May 27), shows an expressionist painter with his latest creation bearing the tire marks from his bicycle propped against canvases to the rear of his studio while a collector/critic delivers the crushing line "I think it's been done before." Holland's captionless example from Punch (February 21, 1962), represents a painter whose recent splatters and splotches have covered the whole rear wall of his studio, leaving his canvas on the easel blank. Folon's cartoon, a variation on a Rorschach test, shows an artist who blots, rather than paints his large canvas creations. He stares in absolute consternation at an accidental ink blot which he has made on the letter of the desk before him. And cartoonist Barry's example (Punch December 19, 1962), shows a painter's thought balloon containing nothing but blots holding a can of paint before a large blank canvas. Finally, an example by Dan Piraro inverts the ironic critiques of the conventional technical examples. His abstract expressionist artist is busily painting over a scribbled section of his large painting because it accidentally looks like a bowl of fruit. Popular culture's reverence towards abstract expressionist art continues to be as popular as ever. Volume 1 No I of *Vanity Furs Art Dogs,* a parody of Vanity Fair, introduces (sic.) Jackson Pawloc who was:

> best known for his innovative "drip" technique. His first painting was inadvertently created when he returned home from a walk in the rain and shook off his muddy coat on a white carpet. Art critics were taken with the power of his work and its monumental scale, which they attributed to the vigorous action of the whole body. Well-heeled art collectors, the movers and shakers of the dog world, identified with this bold new movement and coined it "abstract destructivism." White carpets have never been the same!

Sally Swain's book *Great Housewives of Art* (Grafton Books 1988) includes her satirical feminist paintings of the work of dead white male artists from the modernist canon. Her paintings bear titles such as: "Mrs. Pollock Can't Seem to Find Anything Anymore: "Mrs. Malevich Bleaches the Sheets," "Mrs. Kandinsky Puts Away the Kids Toys," "Mrs. Rothko Scrubs the Floor" an "Mrs. Mondrian Mops the Floor."

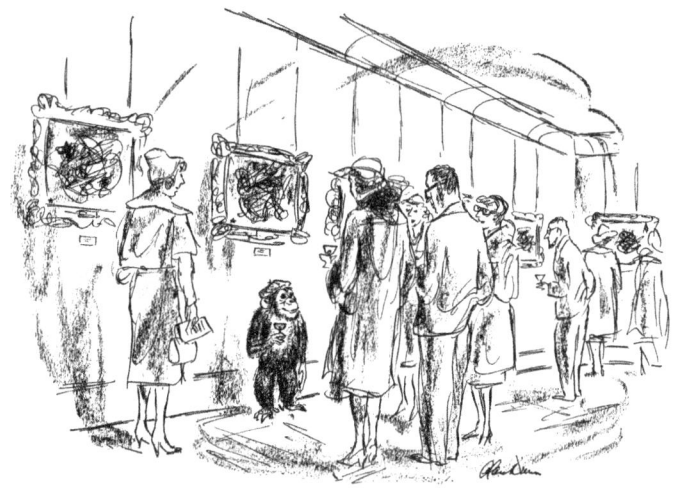

Figure 71: Dunn, A. New Yorker 21st Dec.1957 © Conde Nast.

CHAPTER 9

The Art Comics of Ad Reinhardt

> One of the points to bear in mind when looking at Reinhardt's satires is that they were produced in, and about, a compact, highly intellectual, articulate milieu in which all his nuances were appreciated, and puns and allusions understood. (Hess, 1974:46)

> Reinhardt's collaged PM cartoons in the forties were genuinely devoted to making people understand, as the black paintings were devoted to making people look and see. (Lippard, 1990:124)

In earlier chapters, I argued that it is possible to understand the process of cultural in/subordination through interpreting the ways in which social groups—classes and class fractions—represent their differences symbolically in cartoons and comics. Until now however, I have examined the relative position of graphic satires of modernist art produced by those who are technically outside of the avant-garde boundary, and not within this producer class fraction itself. Ad Reinhardt is an artist who was both *inside* and *outside* the avant-garde producer class fraction. As an artist and teacher, he was severely critical of art world institutions and of the elite culture's dominance over working class culture, but he was also, to paraphrase some of his critics, one who benefited from the very system he condemned. But those who charged Reinhardt with hypocrisy[1] have often failed to acknowledge the historical specificity of his comic strips and art cartoons and their close theoretical, if not formal relationship, to the paintings for which he is now accorded a major place within the modernist canon. On a far deeper level, Reinhardt's comics and cartoons, his painting, writing and teaching, reveal the problems he had in identifying with a social class from which he felt apart, emotionally, intellectually and politically. His aesthetic philosophy

---

1. There were many, particularly during the 1960s, his major years of success before his death on August 31, 1967.

and the attitudes that he displayed towards his profession and colleagues reveal a man often at odds with himself and his social *milieu*. Reinhardt had contradictory and, at times, severely conflicting attitudes about both his profession and the politics of the art world that in some crucially important senses, he failed to reconcile. Instead of seeking a way to rationalize these conflicts and inconsistencies within him, Reinhardt sought to transcend them entirely, through humour, criticism and negation, and in this, I believe, he was successful.

Within the history of modernism there are many examples of avant-garde artists who had, like Reinhardt, feet in two camps. These artists managed to transcend their working origins through the obtaining of education and other forms of symbolic capital, but in their work and behaviour they retained some of the formative ideologies of their class. Lacking the means of economic support (allowances, studios, equipment), provided to upper class artists by their families, less privileged artists were forced into seeking means of employment that would enable them to continue their often-non-remunerative activities as artists. Accordingly, they undertook any paying jobs, preferably part time, that would enable them to continue their practice as artists. If they were lucky, they managed to obtain positions related to their training such as various forms of design work, window dressing, illustration, or the production of cartoons and comic strips for daily or weekly newspapers and journals. But these were jobs that they and others, believed were less important than the production of high art and inconsistent with the role that society had conferred upon them. From the early 18th to the late 19th century there is much evidence to suggest that an artist's production of illustrations, cartoon or comic type images for popular consumption was relegated to a subordinate position within the art hierarchy. Even within the highest realm of the art world as it was then constituted, some types of art—history painting, mythological themes, and religious themes from the Bible—assumed greater importance than others such as genre painting: portraits, still lives, and animal paintings. Even today, the production of images for the mass market is often viewed as a subordinate and illegitimate activity for a high culture artist to engage in; that is until he or she acquires a reputation and everything they produce becomes grist to the commodity mill.

The development of public exhibitions and markets for the buying and selling of art in the early nineteenth century began to influence the modes of production and consumption at all levels within the system, subsequently developing those features that characterize and govern the art world today.[2] The effects of these market influences can be detected in the behaviour of artist producers, and other agents within the art system including: gallery dealers, reviewers, and critics. Artists working within the system reproduced pre-existing cultural behaviors, including key ideological concepts sustaining these, such as the relationship between madness and genius, individualism and creative freedom, beliefs that had their origin in early Renaissance debates about the role of the artist in society.[3]

For the benefit of those collectors, critics and historians with material investments in the art world economy *and* ideological ones in the history of art, the representation of an artist's class background in monographs and biographies could be softened, subtly altered to represent him—usually, at least until the feminist critiques of the late 1960's—and his art in a more palatable form; one moreover, that anticipated and reinforced previously accepted models of artistic vocation. Within the history of art, the representation of the *lives* of great artists within the canon have provided various and at times contradictory models for the induction /instruction of others into the art pantheon. From the time of the Renaissance critics and historians, Vasari and Bellori, to those working today, the exemplary artist's life could become the model for the representation of the stellar career, a monograph, and by extension the progressive studio direction and significant art practice. If an artists' personal history did not exactly fit the prescribed model provided by the art institution for the successful reproduction of itself, this could present a dilemma to the collector, critic, historian or biographer. As a result, these professionals occasionally took it upon themselves to subtly alter the terms of reference for the construction of the artist's *life* narrative in order to facilitate its easy entry into the historical register. Often this did not require major revision, re-writing or extreme deception on the part of the authors of the art historical text, but merely the slightest alteration, textual nuance (re-emphasis or slight reinterpretation), to the historical record could achieve the desired results. Artists also may have provided the necessary ingredients for the re-interpretation of their life narratives in order to invest them with more substance and meaning—symbolic capital—and thus ensure a place

---

2. See Holt, Elizabeth Gilmore (ed.), *The Triumph of Art for the Public: The Emerging Role of Exhibitions and Critics* New York: Anchor Press, Doubleday (1979), passim for documentary evidence of the changing role of the artist in adapting to the institutional challenges of the developing art world.

3. For a more detailed exposition of this see: Pelles, G, Art, *Artists and Society: Origins of a Modern Dilemma: Painting in France and England 1750-1850* New Jersey, Englewood Cliffs: Prentice Hall (1963); and Wittkower, R. and M., Born *Under Saturn: The Character and Conduct of Artists. A Documented History from Antiquity to the French Revolution* New York: Norton, Random House (1963) especially chapters 9,10,11 (209-278).

within the art history register. We witnessed in Chapter 7, how this occurred in Henry Moore's biography to the ultimate benefit of the artist himself, his historians and critics, art buyers, institutional and corporate sponsors, and most recently the State, which has seen fit to privilege its own priorities at the expense of those of Moore's heirs.[4]

The process of *ordination*, however, is infinitely more subtle and complex than I have described it above. A few examples may indicate the interpretive complexities associated with critical valorizing and creative hagiography or pathography[5]. The attaching of cultural capital to an artist's life and work in order to secure and maintain investiture in the canon can occur in many ways. The class origin of the artist may be valorized or enhanced. Henry Moore's working-class origin for instance, was romanticized by his critics and biographers to both his and their benefit. Herbert Read's favorable comparison of Moore's working-class background with that of author D.H. Lawrence, provided the necessary ideological and symbolic nuances to the representation of Moore's *life* in the history of art as a parallel to Lawrence's in literature. An artist's class origin and family background can also be "reframed" in order to better represent the elevated position that the high culture role accords him or her. A good example of the changing status of an artist's life at the hands of his biographers can be found in monographs on the great French artist Honoré Daumier. The facts surrounding Daumier's early life are unclear. In all probability they have been made more so. In Roger Passeron's impressive Daumier monograph for example, we are told much about the artist's early life in Marseilles. The author establishes that the profession and interests of Daumier's father were crucial to Daumier's induction into the art world. In the first chapter, Daumier's birth and baptismal certificates are presented to us as legitimate sources for information on his background. We learn for instance that he was born on the 27th of February 1808, to Cecile-Catherine Philip and Jean-Baptiste Daumier, a glazier. The signatories to the birth certificate included as first witness, one Joseph Boudes, tailor, aged 53, and the second witness, Francois-Joseph Lagrange, painter aged 30. After dispensing these facts, Passeron digresses to a discussion of Daumier's father and his employment. "According to civil and church registers, Jean-Baptiste Daumi-

---

4. Henry Moore's daughter lost a claim to move some of her father's work from his studio estate so that it might be sold on the open market. Associated Press Report, 1993.

5. This is a term coined by Joyce Carol Oates to describe a form of biography that overemphasizes the negative aspects of a person's life and work, such as failure, unhappiness, illness, and tragedy. "[It] *falls into pathography's technique of emphasizing the sensational underside of its subject's life.*"

er was a glazier (*un vitrier*)" (Passeron 1979:11). Establishing this, the author draws on the knowledge of an expert in artistic labour:

> Jean Adhemar, former Chief Curator of the print room of the Bibliotheque Nationale has explained what we should understand by 'glazier'. We must not think of an itinerant workman carrying a box of window panes on his back, a street crier offering his wares to any citizen who happened to be in need of them, but rather of a craftsman, the equivalent of a frame maker today, who might be called upon to look after, and repair engravings and paintings entrusted to him for framing. In short it was a job which would bring him into close contact with works of art, in particular drawings, and the care he bestowed on them would foster a taste for what we call the fine arts (13).

After distancing himself somewhat from Adhemar's expansive description of the trade of Honoré's father, Passeron proceeds to invest the glazier's trade, (the same trade incidentally, as Jean Baptiste's father, Honoré's grandfather had before him), with somewhat more professional significance than it held within French society at the time; in fact, the proper trade name for an arts framer, *un encadreur* was well established. Without substantiation beyond Jean Adhemar's allusion toward the "foster(ing) of taste for what we call the fine arts," he suggests that there was some development in the pattern of work, from the simple task of fitting new panes or replacing broken ones in doors and windows, to the tasks of an art framer. The historian suggests that Daumier came in contact "with engravings and drawings his father had been framing" and that this helped him acquire a *taste* for fine art. Somewhat surprisingly, the historian offers the example of his own induction at the age of seven into the world of high culture as a basis for the irrefutable nature of his claims.

> He (Daumier) was seven years old when his father gave up the shop and moved to Paris. I myself at that age was already familiar with Daumier's lithographs, for I often watched my father in his shop working on or selling prints for the great collectors of the period (13).

Passeron's example may have much truth to it. The manner in which the historian has imbricated his own early life experience on to his subject, however, gives some cause for suspicion, as do the claims made about the work and extended roles of the glazier that intersect all too neatly with those of the professional artist.

At an early age, many artists from working class backgrounds begin their unofficial drawing education by copying examples of comics, cartoons and illustrations from newspapers, magazines and books in their home[6]. Upon entering an art school for their official fine arts training they may seek to continue cartooning with the view to providing support later for their professional vocation in fine art. It is ironic indeed that many art school foundation programs actively discourage and, in some cases even penalize, their entering students from continuing their comic and cartoon drawings (or graffiti), in class. Subjected to a rejection of the very work that encouraged them to seek an art school education, many artists just give up and drop out. Others change their ways of working and still others surreptitiously continue to produce their "low" work alongside of their directed "high art" projects. Upon graduating those artists who have been reconditioned away from their interest in cartoons and comics will resort to producing their "low" work in order to pay the rent. As a result, they may try to produce work for both "high" and "low" venues. A cursory study of the careers of many cartoonists educated in the 1900s through to the 1950s, demonstrates that many artists decided to give up high art production altogether, to pursue the economically more secure occupations of cartooning, comics, and illustration in an industry that grew expansively during the 1950s and 1960s. With respect to official education, a purview of artists' biographies in *The World Encyclopedia of Comics* (Horn, 1976), reveals that some 60% of the artists listed had what could be described as less than conventional art educations, when compared to the similarly encyclopedic *Who's Who* in (high) Art registers from around the world. Fewer artists from upper and upper-middle class backgrounds begin cartooning or drawing comic strips as a preliminary introduction to their education in fine arts. The reasons for this may have much to do with the long-standing stigma associated with the funnies and indeed much popular culture that is still evident in many middle-class homes today. Bourdieu's research demonstrates that most wealthy parents provide high culture models for their children to enjoy emulate and learn from. For those parents with a university education, taking their children to The Nutcracker usually takes precedence over renting the Disney movie version of *A Christmas Tale*. Taking a trip to MOMA, the Guggenheim, the Metropolitan Museum, The Tate Gallery or the Musée des Beaux Arts takes precedence over going to the movies, the zoo, or watching

---

[6]. In his biographical notes, Reinhardt cites that from the age of two he copied the "funnies," Moon Mullins, (Frank Willard), Krazy Kat (George Herriman) and Barney Google (Billy De Beck). My early entrance to the field of art and subsequent experiences as a university art teacher for over thirty years working with hundreds of students from diverse backgrounds, verify this relatively familiar route to the role of artist, especially for working class students, but I would add that there are always exceptions to the rule.

television as venues for creative education. Music lessons take the place of visits to Disneyland, or at least, 'the ghetto' of morning and afternoon children's' T.V. The ubiquity of mass culture and social media today may suggest that children consume across taste and class boundaries and of course, there are many exceptions to the sketched patterns above. It is perilous to bracket culture distinctiveness as an absolute condition of class differentiation. Class conscious parents particularly those who have the means to pay for it, may want their children to become used to a wide range of social and cultural events as part of their education. These parents tend to emphasize cultural production and a *monitored*, as opposed to uncritical consumption of mass culture. Sociological research into these matters by Bourdieu (1977, 1984), Willis (1977, 1990) and many others, demonstrates that institutions, beyond the family, such as religious institutions, school, and daily exposure to social media provide further conditions for ideological training and induction into specific life and work options. Class distinctiveness is less the result of active choice than of ideological immersion.

> Thus one finds that the higher the level of education, the greater is the proportion of respondents who, when asked whether a series of objects would make beautiful photographs, refuse the ordinary objects of popular admiration—a first communion, a sunset or a landscape as 'vulgar', or 'ugly', or reject them as 'trivial', silly, a bit 'wet', or in Ortega y Gasset's terms, naively 'human' (Bourdieu, 1984:35).

The history of caricature reveals that the induction of some individuals into the artist's role begins with their production of 'charged portraits' of family and friends. There are artists whose career fortunes have been directed by the vicissitudes of the art world and the needs of the families they are supporting who for economic reasons, have either dropped cartooning or picked it up. Lyonel Feininger the German/American creator of the famous *The Kin-der-Kids* and *Wee Willy Winkies World* spent a few short years cartooning and drawing comic strips for a living and then, soon after being hired by the Bauhaus, stopped this activity to pursue the art work (paintings and graphics), for which now, at least within the art world, he is better known. His relationship towards popular culture was somewhat ambivalent, and yet he was quick to acknowledge that he had learned much from cartooning as a young man.

> I am far from underestimating in my development the very important years, which I spent as a draftsman of 'funny papers' (Shikes and Heller, 1984:93).

But later in life, he was still clearly less attached to his work as a cartoonist than to his *life* as an artist[7]. There is not space to pursue Feininger's career in this chapter, but it is noteworthy also that he took great care to distance himself from the base pecuniary aspects of the art business, perhaps because it reminded him too much of his subordinate role within the low culture world of the newspaper industry.

Like Feininger's comics in relation to his total production as an artist, Ad Reinhardt's comic and cartoon satires represent a small, yet extremely important part of his total work. As I have suggested above however, they are a key to both understanding his life and valuing his important contributions to modernist art. I will frame Reinhardt's life and work in class terms, not to subscribe to a reductive model of false consciousness or to indulge in some spurious psychologizing. Instead, I will adopt several positions that may serve to illustrate his extreme, critical consciousness, for perhaps more than any other artist of his generation; Reinhardt represents an extraordinary understanding of the extreme conflicts—political/aesthetic, philosophical, ethical—as well as the race/class and gender divisions of the art world of his time. He was especially sensitive to those struggles occurring within the class fraction of the sub-cultural avant-garde itself, of which he was both a willing and unwilling member. I argue that these divisions and conflicts, specifically with regard to creative behaviour, role acceptance, status, modes of work, art discourse, philosophy, criticism, politics—his *weltanschauung*—represented for Reinhardt, an alienating set of conditions that necessitated his constant monitoring and control. His efforts to control his situation however, left their marks on him, and those with whom he came in contact.

As Thomas Hess writes:

> Reinhardt often was accused in public of being a solipsist and of reading everybody else's problems through his own distorting spectacles (Hess, 1975: 31).

This contrary behaviour has been described (not uncritically), within anthropological and sociological literature, as one of "the hidden injuries of class." I hope to demonstrate that Reinhardt suffered a certain "status incongruity" (Sennett and Cobb, 1973:71), that was represented symbolically both in his cartoon and comic art as well as his writings. I will argue that his life and work reveal

---

7. This is a common sentiment among some of the cartoonists interviewed. They thought of cartooning as a *job*, a *career*, but not, as do many artists, *a Life*.

him to be an individual whose elevation to a different register within the social hierarchy—simply, class transcendence—precipitated conflicts within him that resulted in both his accommodation *and* resistance (in/subordination), to the prevailing order(s) of the dominant culture. This is perhaps the province, or the 'stuff' of biography[8], but I believe that one cannot understand the full measure of Reinhardt's contribution to modernist art without understanding his life and the context within which he worked.

Since the publication in 1981 of Lucy Lippard's impressive monograph, a number of texts on Reinhardt appeared, encouraged perhaps by the 1985 exhibit at the Staatsgalerie in Stuttgart, Germany, and more recently, the exhibition at The Museum of Modern Art in New York (May 30-September 2, 1991), which traveled subsequently to the Museum of Contemporary Art in Los Angeles (October 13, 1991-January 5, 1992). In recent years more attention has begun to be accorded Reinhardt's graphic satires. The handsome Stuttgart catalogue contained all of the PM newspaper examples with a short essay; the MOCA catalogue included four, two from PM, and two from Art News, accompanied by an excellent essay (not specifically on the comics), titled *The Limit of Almost*, by art historian Yves-Alain Bois. Most writers, however, have relegated Reinhardt's graphic satires to a minor position within his total *oeuvre*, maintaining a special place for the so-called 'black' paintings for which his position as a 'father' of Minimal and Conceptual art has been guaranteed. In the scores of essays, reviews and letters on Reinhardt, the cartoons, if mentioned at all, are swept to the margins, noted or footnoted in passing, occasionally denigrated as a creative idiosyncrasy, or something the artist had to do for a time in order to make ends meet. Even Reinhardt's longtime friend, critic and editor Thomas Hess, who is responsible, more than any other single individual for the attention and arguably the importance that the artist's graphic satires now receive in some quarters, was quick to separate the comics and cartoons from the paintings. Hess writes: "The relationship of Reinhardt's comics and satires to his painting is slight—apart from the obvious link to his collages of the 1940s" (Hess, 1975: 47). This response is not unusual, given the sharp distinctions between high art and popular culture current at the time and the "rejective" formalist rhetoric of early modernist criticism. With a different theoretical and historical perspective however, one less tainted by the formalistic constraints and determinations of modernist

---

8. I have no knowledge of a Reinhardt biography being written at this time.

criticism, it may be possible to read the relative importance of the cartoons to the meaning of the artist's work and life as a whole; particularly if we remove them temporarily from their institutional incarceration and begin to re-invest them with their original personal and political meanings. A social contextual reading, one that permits the interpretation of ideology within these works, may provide more assimilable perspectives on the relationship of art and humour, to class politics. Before we begin our re-reading of some of the comics themselves it is important to review the artist's life, for it is within his early beginnings as an artist that Reinhardt's conscious appraisal of some of the issues that were to trouble him for a quarter century or more, are situated.

Much of the critical, art historical and biographical writing on Reinhardt mentions his working-class origin, and alludes to his difference, *outsider* status, and his "separateness" from his contemporaries. Hess suggests that Reinhardt was "in between two groups; in generational terms, he was neither father, brother nor child" (9), even when his birth date of Christmas Eve, 1913, marks him as a near contemporary to Ashille Gorky, Barnett Newman (1905), Clifford Still, and Willem de Kooning (1904), and an almost exact contemporary of Jackson Pollock, William Baziotes (1912), and Franz Kline (1910). Hess offered further evidence, for instance the artist's two year "hitch in the navy" (1944-45), to substantiate Reinhardt's outsider status, claiming that Reinhardt was "thus a man with a difference—an insider without a peer group, without a pigeonhole, regular, but odd" (10). Writing many years later, critic Peter Schjledahl suggested that:

> Reinhardt was (also) of course, one of the major painters of his generation—and had, for that matter, one of the bigger egos. He was an insider whom it pleased to behave like an outsider, ostentatiously swimming against the very historical tide that would publicly legitimize the ambitions of his art. (The legitimation came later to him than to any of his peers) (Schjeldahl, 1976).

For Lucy Lippard, Reinhardt was not so much out of step with his peers, than out of step with his time. She described him in positive terms "as a thirties painter in the forties, and a sixties painter in the fifties" (Lippard 1981), a description that Yves-Alain Bois confirms in his essay. Lippard notes that Reinhardt's immigrant working class Calvinist background was a major influence upon his development. The artist's father was a life-long socialist and union activist (member and organizer for the Amalgamated Clothing Workers in New York), who instilled in his son an early respect for working class politics and a distrust of those in positions of power. From his family he also received an early introduction to the importance of education and with it, a fear of and disgust for poverty. Hess also discusses Reinhardt's poor background and recounts revealing anecdotes regarding Reinhardt's contrary relationship to status and material wealth, emphasizing in passing the artist's strong sense of morality. He tells how Reinhardt once loaned de Kooning the use of his studio and art materials when he was down on his luck, yet simultaneously derided him for living like a pauper, suggesting that it was "undignified" for an artist to be scrabbling about for handouts. But then when de Kooning became successful, Reinhardt was equally critical and somewhat envious of his friend's new found status. "[Willem] de Kooning is living like Elizabeth Taylor. Everybody wants to know who he's sleeping with; about the house he's building and everything. He has no private life," he said in a 1966 interview[9].

Other facts about Reinhardt's life lead one to believe that while he maintained strong contacts with a number of members of his generation, he remained apart, "compartmentalized," according to Lucy Lippard. She gives her interpretation of his separateness, but provides it with a more positive political gloss:

> No one seems to have felt they really knew him well or really were close friends of his, because of this compartmentalization; *perhaps no-one aware of the art world and its issues could be related to entirely as a human being* (emphasis added) (Lippard, 136).

She describes Reinhardt's position within the New York art world of the nineteen forties and fifties "as a devil's advocate and scapegoat" (62), and in conversation with critic Irving Sandler, relates how the artist viewed himself during this time: "I was always the foil at the club" (62). Lippard further emphasizes the artist's position as self-appointed community conscience; underscoring simultaneously his commitment to and detachment from, the New York School, both of which demanded that he adopt a variety of ethical and aesthetic positions. While he looked like a boxer, and at times acted like one, the range of responses that he adapted to his situation were far more complex than any single role, or description of his personality, could accommodate. And certainly, the boxing role was not the most appropriate[10], although some writers, including Hess, were fond of using it.

---

9. An interview with Mary Fuller, April 27, 1966 that was published in Artforum October 1970, reprinted in Rose, B. (ed) *Art as Art, The Selected Writings of Ad Reinhardt*, Berkeley and Los Angeles: University of California Press (1991), original edition (1975:7).

10. Reinhardt's sport was actually wrestling.

> I can see Ad Reinhardt clearly, at the Artist's Club on Eighth Street with his Ivy League air, a touch of Faculty Club sports clothes and crew-cut, his protective coloration, his uniform, among working man's jeans and sweatshirts, with the neck and face of a Roman boxer, bob a bit and swivel his shoulders, ask a mean question, and then shrug and with an uneasy laugh turn aside arguments before they got nasty or personal (Hess, 1975:8).

Other points about his life are noteworthy in this context. During his time in the US Navy, he was hospitalized for some kind of psychiatric disorder but received an honorable discharge. And before it became fashionable in New York's art world to see a therapist, Reinhardt underwent psychoanalysis. He also rejected an important art prize, accepted it formally and then returned it with an accompanying letter explaining that he would be contradicting his criticism of corporate competitions if he was to accept. In 1954 fellow abstract painter Barnett Newman sued Reinhardt for $100.000 for purportedly damaging Newman's reputation and cited the CAA (College Art Association), in the suit for publishing Reinhardt's "The Artist in Search of an Academy. Who are the Artists?"[11] in which Reinhardt satirized twelve artists for being "the latest up-to-date popular image of the early fifties, the artist professor and traveling design salesman, the Art Digest-philosopher-poet and Bauhaus exerciser, the avant-garde-huckster-holy-roller-explainer-in-residence." The suit was dismissed, but Reinhardt and Newman never spoke to one another again (Lippard, 136). Finally, as well, a number of his beautiful Gothic lettered notes seem to indicate some degree of alienation, or what I suggested earlier, was status incongruity.

> Private Life different (sic) than public life Schizophrenic
> Mystery
> Not carefree
> Game, wit, cleverness, removed from the ordinary
> *conventionality*
> leave real personalities at home
> evening clothes
> assume a proper, polite manner
> Mother-pastel, father-darker shades
> concentration on self. (Rose, 1975:101)

Although it is fascinating exercise, it is also somewhat dangerous to read too much into these private notes, except perhaps to recognize in them the develop-

---

11. College Art Journal, Summer, 1954.

ing importance for Reinhardt, from 1940 onward, of his observations regarding the black paintings, particularly his strategies of criticism and negation which I believe are not as one dimensional as Yves-Alain Bois suggests, claiming in his catalogue essay that "Reinhardt was no dialectician" (Bois, 1991:19). One could argue that a comprehension of Reinhardt's position on criticism, especially his complex revealing of the terms and methods of both (self)-criticism, and negation, are central to a reading of his work from 1940 onwards. The positive negations of deconstruction "under erasure" *sous rature*—of Jacques Derrida or Guy Debord's quasi-dialectical "negation of the negation," are actually closer to Reinhardt in spirit perhaps, than the modernist negation—the great modernist refusals—of Nietzsche, Mallarme, Becket and Joyce, with which we are more familiar.

I agree with both Hess and Lippard, that Reinhardt was never more serious than when he was being funny, and never funnier than when he was serious. In essence his criticism, like his humour is simultaneously contrary—negative—and yet striving to be affirmative, resolving and synthetic. Like Derrida, Reinhardt could be said to be beating of the rhythm of both pleasure and repetition according to the cup or cut (coupe). "Dissemination produces itself in the: a cut/cup of pleasure."[12] A further comparison with some of the great satirists and comic artists of our time—Thurber, for instance—who once remarked that those engaged in the comic may well be psychologically deficient'—or even the troubled Lenny Bruce—is not unwarranted. But perhaps this contrariness can be better understood as a transmutation of Freud's famous axiom: "where id goes, there ego shall follow" which in Reinhardt's case could become "where class is, so psychology should follow." This provides access to discussing further the relationships between psychology, class politics and humour, but before I do this, I will interpret a small number of Reinhardt's graphic satires with the object of comprehending and elucidating perhaps, some of the remarks above, and to subsequently arrive at a renewed understanding of the complex relationships between humour and class politics.

The PM newspaper cartoons represent a watershed in Reinhardt's career. The series ran for one year, from January 27, 1946 to January 5th, 1947. Described in its time as a popular anti-fascist, communist or "anti-anti-communist" newspaper, PM was started by multi-millionaire Marshall Field and according to Hess, was an odd paper, "full of bluff and bluster," alternately taking the soft liberal, or the hard left positions as its editors and publisher Field directed. Reinhardt first

---

12. Derrida, Jacques *Dissemination* trans. Barbara Johnson Chicago University of Chicago Press 1981

worked for PM in 1942, but it was not until 1946 that he began to produce one comic strip each issue for a year until the PM editors realized Reinhardt's proselytizing for abstract art did not exactly fit the newspaper's avowedly socialist editorial policy, with its preference for (social) realist modes of representation. To Hess, this was Reinhardt's greatest ironic success—"putting one over the leftists"—but it could be argued also that the social ideology subscribing Reinhardt's extreme abstraction perfectly matched the reconstructive and utopian projects of communism, as it had for a short time in the constructivist/productivist period following the Russian revolution in 1917. At least, if Hess is right, it should not have taken three editors one year to recognize their mistake in hiring him…if that is…it was a mistake. I believe otherwise, for the evidence implies that as shop steward Reinhardt was fired from PM along with 30 other members of the American Newspaper Guild when they attempted to improve their union contract. Obviously, Field's communist sympathies were only skin deep! Reinhardt's openly socialist beliefs must have also seemed a little contrary to others, especially when he was condemning quintessential socialist painting in favour of his own extreme avant-gardist abstraction. This was one aspect of *incongruity* that, from the 1930s through to the late 1940s, he must have had to monitor on a daily basis. How could his commitment to pure non-objective abstraction engage with social reality in an efficacious manner, and how could it lend itself to social change according to the conventional social realist aims of the socialist project? Clement Greenberg, Meyer Shapiro and other writers for The Partisan Review were struggling with similar contradictions.

With their sources in contemporary advertising and mass media the montages of the Dadaists have been cited as the direct formal antecedents to Reinhardt's PM, trans\formation and Art News *comics* (as he liked to call them), but the famous Surrealist montages and collages of Max Ernst are closer prototypes than the political montages of Hausmann, Hoch, Heartfield, and Citroen. This use of Surrealist methodology could also have become a source of anxiety for Reinhardt, particularly as he spent much energy in his first ten PM comics decrying what he termed *low* Surrealism, ironically the very art movement that had provided him with the creative tools—that is collage, the cut/cup erasure (palimpsest)—to critique it.

Thomas Hess has identified how, throughout the comic series, Reinhardt associates illusionistic art—both realist and Surrealist—with big business, right wing capitalist values and "exploitative politics," while non-objective (abstract) art is, by contrast, tied to "progressive, populist, constitutionalist-socialist, characteristically American enlightenment" (Hess 1975:26). Of course the great irony and disappointment for an artist like Reinhardt, one that Hess notes, must have been the fact that during the early 1940s the liberals and socialists identified most strongly with realism, particularly the social realism of the Mexican Muralists, Jack Levine and Ben Shahn, but also the popular illustrative realism of Thomas Hart Benton and Norman Rockwell. Abstract art was not viewed as an entirely appropriate vehicle for the revolutionary desires of the urban proletariat. And what was worse for someone in Reinhardt's position, only the urban intellectual and professional classes seemed to like and understand abstract art.

Interpreting the ways in which the artist represents himself and articulates his aesthetic beliefs in each of the 23 PM comics provides an important entry into the solid relationship between humour and class politics in Reinhardt's satires. His representation of self provides clear insight into the "compartmentalization" and "incongruities" of his character alluded to by his critics. The identity of various figures represented in each of the comics reveal Reinhardt's personal struggles as well as his class sympathies. The identities for most of the PM sheets can be read as an elaborate code for mapping aesthetic and political issues as well as a kind of shorthand for his feelings on a particular issue or set of issues. The artist himself appears in many different disguises in the comics: as a night capped brandy sniffer/drinker; a philosopher/thinker squatting on his haunches; reviewer X; a hobo workman; the no-nonsense crew cut abstract painter; a foppish gent; saluting cavaliers (one fat and one thin); a drummer, and an "intrepid" cyclist artist-reporter. Only two of these—the night capped drinker and the abstract painter—can be properly called *signature* images, but it is my contention that each of these identities carry some personal and political significance for Reinhardt and are used *precisely* for that reason. In the same manner he suggests in his notes however, that one should "leave one's (private) personality at home," and "assume a proper, polite manner" these identities exist as mere ciphers to a complex personality that remains primarily *outside* of the work. The only time Reinhardt's name actually appears, apart from in the standard author's position is in one of his Art News cartoons. Not only do each of these figures represent trace aspects of Reinhardt's persona, but also many of the animals and mythological creatures populating his comics have some allegorical significance to the world of Reinhardt's psyche and class politics. Rats, ants, lizards, snakes, beetles, pigs, crabs, and fish, (low animals, mostly rodents and insects), are often associated inventively with low art, base values and bad, that is reactionary, or dangerous ideas. Other animals, mostly mammals and noble totemic varieties: horses, dogs, monkeys, eagles, tigers, chimpanzees, dolphins, griffins, Llamas, and cows, are referenced in similarly inventive ways to *high* art, good, progressive ideas, 'pure', democratic and quintessentially American cultural values.

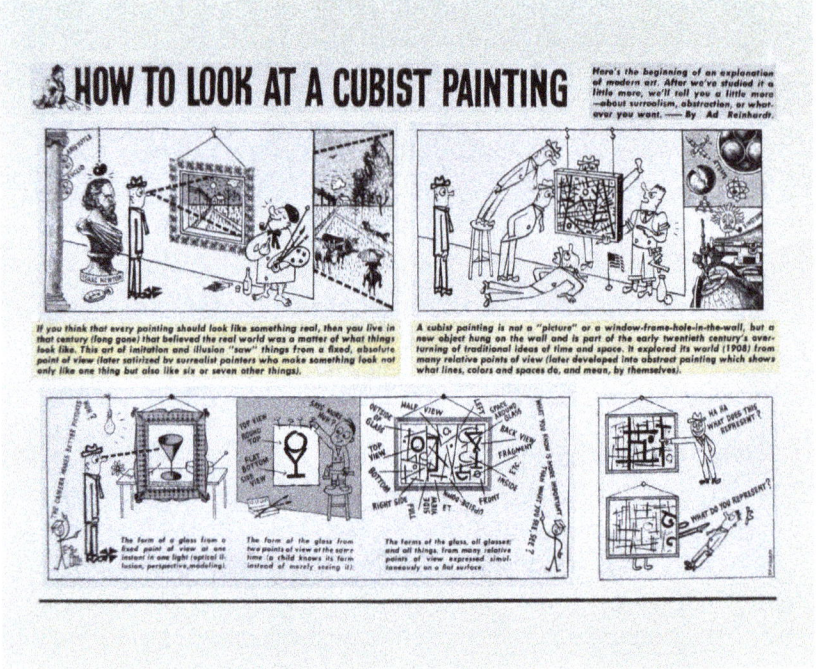

Figure 72: PM #1 *How to Look at a Cubist Painting* Jan. 26, 1946
© Estate of Ad Reinhardt SODRAC (2014)

The first art comic PM #I "How to Look at a Cubist Painting" parodies the then popular 'How To' and self-help books and articles that had entered the postwar mass marketplace. Reinhardt announces in the far top right of the strip:

> Here's the beginning of an explanation of modern art. After we've studied it a little more, we'll tell you a little more—about surrealism, abstraction, or whatever you want.

With extraordinary facility and clarity, in four simple frames, Reinhardt contrasts the predictable old world of Euclidean geometry, Aristotelian philosophy, Newtonian physics, and the new modern world of Einstein's sub-atomic theory, quantum mechanics, relativism (Heisenberg's uncertainty principle), and mass communications. It is easy to see why these comics remained popular aids for teaching students about abstraction for years after they first appeared in print. Note the difference in the comic panel between the stereotype of the old style European (effete therefore unwholesome), naturalist painter with his artist's smock, beret, mahlstick, bottle of wine, pipe and palette, and the all new American (flag waving) modernist (wholesome) abstract painter (Reinhardt caricatured), dressed in no-nonsense worker's overalls, with his bulging muscles, bottle of pure milk, apple, hammer and builder's square. It is noteworthy that this artist figure with his pants hoisted high above his socks and shoes represents a clothing style that Reinhardt himself adopted for his studio attire. Hess suggests that the child tacking up the drawing has a "family resemblance to the hero of *Barnaby*, a popular comic-strip launched in PM by Crockett Johnson, who was a friend of Reinhardt, and for whose wife he illustrated a children's book" (29).

A common element of the PM sheets is the serious intent to the pedagogical framing of the ideas in comic book form and an ironic/satirical 'take'—pretension index—that Reinhardt articulates through his theories of modern art. Hess suggests that "when Reinhardt is being straight and serious, he is usually being funny, and when he makes jokes, he is usually in deadly earnest" (28). The *colophon* or signature image of PM #1 that appears throughout the series, shows the tough muscle-bound abstract painter with the crew cut in the guise of the abstract painting itself, returning the layman's "HA HA What does this represent? with "What do you represent?" This is one of several colophons that appear in nearly all of the PM comics. Many of them are metonymic stand-ins for Reinhardt, as are the stick figure teacher wearing the mortar board in PM #1, and The Thinker, a hatted figure sitting on his haunches with glasses and cane before him in the top left of the frame. this cartoon reinforces Reinhardt's belief that painting should be a serious intellectual pursuit.

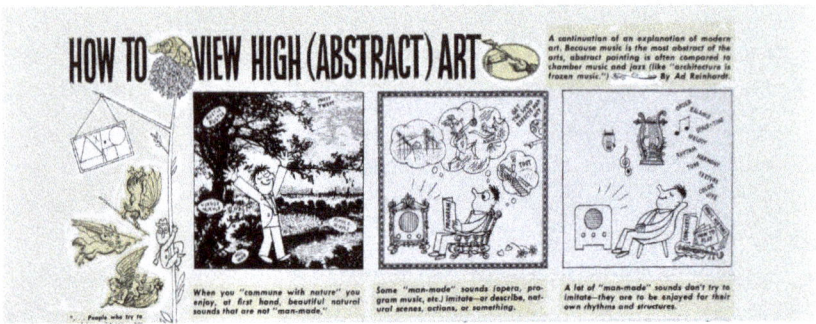

Figure 73: PM #2 *How to View High (Abstract) Art*, February 24, 1946
© Estate of Ad Reinhardt SODRAC (2014)

PM #2 employs some of the familiar elements, devices and arguments that Reinhardt was to use in various ways throughout 1946. The "High" of the title reveals Reinhardt's familiarity with the "high" versus "low" debates occurring in the Partisan Review, The Nation and elsewhere at the time, particularly in the writings of Greenberg, Shapiro, and Dwight MacDonald, and perhaps earlier pieces by the Frankfurt school theorists Adorno and Lowenthal, or literary scholars T.S. Eliot and F.R. Leavis. The six frames are introduced with a short statement in the top right of the page, this time providing a link between music and abstract painting, one of the most resilient of the comparisons between modernist painting and the other arts, its roots in Platonic, and neo-Platonic philosophy, Swedenborgian theology, and Hegelian essentialism[13]. A monk appears on the top of the tree at the far left, another probable stand-in for Reinhardt himself, this time a reflection of the artist's close relationship to Thomas Merton, a former student friend of Reinhardt's, who became a very influential Trappist monk, one of the first and most influential writers in English about Zen Buddhism. The tree is a familiar trope for constructing systems of classification or genealogy, one that Reinhardt was to reproduce in various ways throughout that year, and in subsequent cartoons. Here the appropriated imagery traces the history of western art from the Egyptians, through the Greek, and Roman periods to the Italian Renaissance, and finally to Modernist art, signified at the top by an abstract painting with the Zen Buddhist *gestalts* of the circle, square and triangle. As Hess noted in an Artforum article in 1974 the source materials are:

---

13. See Cheetham, M. *The Rhetoric of Purity: Essentialist Theory and the Advent of Abstract Painting*, Cambridge: Cambridge University Press (1991).

> Easily recognizable for art world readers…photostats and cut-outs from reproductions and 19th century illustrated books he had picked up in secondhand stores. Among the books he used were collections of the prints of Durer (perspective studies), St Sebastian, The Beast of the Apocalypse make multiple appearances, Holbein, Hogarth, Thomas Bewick, (the) Punch illustrator, John Leech, (and) Thomas Nast (Hess 1974:47).

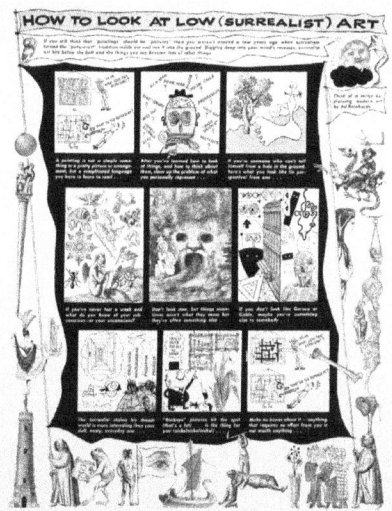

Figure 74: PM #3 *How to Look at Low (Surrealist) Art*. March 24, 1946 © Estate of Ad Reinhardt SODRAC (2014)

PM #3 satirizes Surrealist art and any type of illusionistic painting among the artist's pet peeves that he identifies as "low" culture. And again, with his familiar colophon, Reinhardt enjoins his reader in the second frame to "clear up the problem of what you personally represent." The pennant below the title suggests that Surrealist art "hits below the belt, and the things you see become lots of other things." As interpreted by Hess, the bottom left frame contrasts "the Surrealist erotic dream world," (note the artist figure, and the key holes), to the "troubled PM reader," who again, according to Hess, "holds his head in pain, at the thought of Westbrook Pegler, a vivid right wing columnist who used to attack Eleanor Roosevelt in psychopathic tropes it seemed a form of blasphemy at the time." "Prejudice" Hess suggests, was a synonym for anti-Semitism and the caption ("nickle nickle nickle") paraphrases the radio jingle for Pepsi Cola, a visible sign for big business—another pet hate of Reinhardt's—satirical references to which would appear in many subsequent comics and cartoons. Reinhardt disagreed violently with Pepsi's sponsorship of art prizes, as he did of corporate capitalism in general.

> Pepsi Cola hits the spot, 12 full ounces, that's a lot, twice as much for a nickle too, Pepsi Cola is the drink for you (chorus: nickle nickle nickle).

PM #4 (*How to Look at An Artist* April 7, 1946), reveals again how Reinhardt rails against the low art illusionistic picture maker. The monk with the flag, one of his alter egos, appears at the top left of the panel. This page has a left/right opposition, and a vertical totemic orientation somewhat in opposition to the comic frames of the earlier cartoons. The old reactionary positions are to the left, the good progressive ones to the right. Reinhardt drops in some quotes from Brancusi: "When we are no longer children we are already dead"; Helion, "perspective is a disease of the eyes"; Ben Johnson, "art hath an enemy called ignorance"; Malevich, "We are in a desert where nothing but sensitivity is actuality," and Kandinsky, "Abstract art is concrete." The statements vie for attention against red neck disclaimers from a philistine on the pulpit who announces that "abstract art is foreign, un-American (a reference to the notorious House of Representatives investigation committee under Martin Dies), and the standard popular (dis) missive of modern art: "any child could do better!" Bonfire brushwood (Hess calls this "the dead wood Pepsi Cola edifice"), in preparation for burning, sits atop kindling sticks signifying "profit, greed, prejudice, fear, solipsism, property, money grubbing, ragged individualism, free enterprise"—all according to Reinhardt, "deadwood." And in place of the normal dog eat dog world, we are presented with a rat consuming a beetle and dogs pursuing a mouse, but "Business" we are informed "is still business." Accordingly, defenseless subordinates are pursued and consumed by those in positions of power. The Mannerist *putti* in the foreground convey an ironic sub-text to this extraordinary group of signifiers. One says to the other another classic comment, "I don't know anything about art, But I know what I like…" to which the other replies ironically, "Yeah, isn't it nice that the obligation to be intelligent doesn't extend to the field of art?" The primary text of this image is contained in a box at the top right of the page. "Today every human being who isn't interested in making profits from someone else's work is potentially a special kind of artist. And the right of "art" to be free of "picture making" is part of all the other four freedoms that Reinhardt identifies in an ironic take on the aesthetic philosophies of Schopenhauer, Marx, Dewey, and Huizinger: "Hey! Art is Experience, Art is Useful, Art is Play, Art is Knowledge." Reinhardt identified heavily, some would say self-righteously, with this "special kind of artist who isn't interested in making profits," but he was also painfully aware of the fact that no artists could survive without capitulating in some way to the art market's desire to extract surplus value from their labour. It was a source of acute discomfort to him that many of his contemporaries were by this time in their careers, enjoying considerable success in the marketplace ("behaving like Hollywood stars"), while he was still having problems acquiring a regular dealer for his work, that for ideological reasons, he felt he should do without, but in other ways practically required in order to achieve success. Reinhardt had secured a college teaching position after the war, but his work took at least twelve years longer than his peers to be accepted by the museo-critical establishment. This must have been a source of great anxiety for him, particularly when he saw people he had influenced, taught, or helped in some way, receive the accolades that could, and indeed should have gone to him.

PM #5 (*How to Look at Space* April 28, 1946) demonstrates Reinhardt's understanding of modernist temporal-spatial paradigms. A hairy figure with a bull neck is Man looking forward and back in time, myopically, with one eye closed. The year 1946 is marked with a prominent arrow to the top right of the timeline, and the odd intellectual figure in the woodcut, the night capped drinker (Reinhardt), appears once more. With the artist's remarkable facility, this cartoon examines differing perceptions of space and time, and compares these humorously to modernist notions of history's progress in art. The omni-present subtext is the critique of big business contained in the center panel of the lowest register. The final acknowledgement that "you sir are a space too," provides the ironic reply to the "What do you represent?" question contained in the colophon above.

PM #6 *How To Look* continues his didactic exercise in how to read and appreciate modern art, one that was actually taken very seriously by members of the PM readership, many of whom wrote regularly to the paper's editors to extol the virtues of Reinhardt's straightforward, witty and no-nonsense view of modern art. Hess relates how Sinclair Lewis was among those who wrote fan letters to Reinhardt telling him that his pages had made them understand modern art as never before. But as Reinhardt was to reveal in a candid interview with critic Bruce Glazer some twenty years later, "Actually I was making satires of Bauhaus, Surrealist, and Expressionist pretensions to meaning" (Rose, 1975:15)[14]. In this panel we meet some of the familiar figures of the earlier comics, including the wine sniffer colophon, and the tough abstract painter. Reinhardt again dumps on Surrealism for, as he says, "running the picture art tradition into the ground, and for "out illustrating the illustrators." That is why, "we called it "low" art, see…!" In contrast, the non-illusionistic condition of abstract art paralleled the "condition of pure music," and could thus be accorded the status of "high" art. Finally, industry (Pepsi), and big business get knocked again for their sponsoring of art competitions.

---

14. The interview originally appeared in Art International (Lugano) Winter, 1966-67.

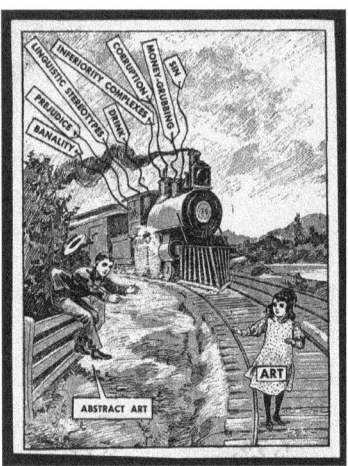

Figure 75: Ad Reinhardt PM #7 *How to Look at Modern Art in America*. June 2nd, 1946 © Estate of Ad Reinhardt SODRAC (2014)

Reinhardt's PM #7 described by Thomas Hess as "a diamond of a satire" (1974: 32), has been widely reproduced, and became an installment on many artists' studio walls for some years after publication. In this sheet Reinhardt replaces his comic frames with a single cartoon image of a tree symbolizing an art historical genealogy. The four canonical roots of modernism—Cezanne, Seurat, Gauguin and van Gogh—are nestled in the rich soil representing the eclectic collection of disparate influences on modernist art: Manet, Poussin, Primitive, Greek Art, Polynesian, children's' art, Daumier, Monet, and Japanese prints. To the lower left of the panel, two fish (Pisces)—allegorical figures representing Business and Art—are locked in mortal combat.

The trunk of the tree is inscribed with the names: Braque, Matisse and Picasso, with at the base of the branches, ranging from left to right (Abstract to Surrealist-Social) other members of the modernist canon: Mondrian, Malevich, Gris, Leger, Arp, Duchamp, Miro, and Klee. Moving from centre to right appear the names: Kandinsky, Bonnard, Ernst, de Chirico, Rouault, Dix and Grosz. It is somewhat odd for the politically astute Reinhardt to place the political artist George Grosz to the extreme right, a move that must have been a source of consternation to many of his PM colleagues and readers. According to Hess, the tree is modeled closely on one produced by Miguel Covarrubias which was published earlier in Vogue. Reinhardt satirizes both this tree, and the modern art genealogy which appears in Alfred H. Barr's famous *Cubism and Abstract Art* MOMA catalogue (1936). The Barr diagram contains a chart of interconnecting modernist movements that was widely used as a teaching aid in the nineteen forties and fifties.

The tree is Reinhardt's guide to the art world "in a nutshell," with pure abstract paintings represented on the far-left branches, to the "low" illustrative work (Rockwell, Wood, Benton et. al.), banished to the "good ole down home" cornfields on the right, articulating again his high/low distinction, this time with a metropolitan/rural (regional), gloss, between non-objective pure abstraction, and illusory (fake), picture making. Weighing one of the main branches of the tree down at certain strategic points, are several weights bearing the labels: subject matter, Mexican art influence, business as art patron (an old boot), studio paraphernalia, nudes, regionalism, illustration, still lives, and landscapes. These reinforce the "low" side of the binary composition by assigning negative characteristics to "low" modernism.

Reinhardt's PM #8 (*How To Look at Art Talk*, June 9 1946), the "Eighth of a series on why modern painting is not a picture" pairs off allegorical animals, figures from various ethnic groups and classes in a simple question/answer type of debating society dialogue, with the exception that Reinhardt's dialogues are laden with visual/textual puns and various ironies Qu: "Is a painting a practical means of propaganda today with all our newspapers and radio?"; "No" replies a llama being attacked by a lion. The top frame of the comic contains another Reinhardt presence, a hobo with arms uplifted bearing the balloon statement "Art is a weapon," a position that Reinhardt believed in implicitly, but one that he uses his working class identity, rather than his aloof academic/intellectual/ philosopher persona to endorse. A middle frame shows two medieval looking ploughmen; the one drawing the plough asks, "Has fine art any relation to prices, profits, private property and prestige? To which the other replies "WELL…" To their right are two buildings, with signs announcing Kootz Gallery, "Paintings for a country estate $100 each" and ACA Gallery "Paintings for a tenement flat $1000 each." Both 57th Street galleries exhibited very different artists; Kootz's abstract modernists: Motherwell, Gottlieb, Byron, Browne, Holty, Baziotes and Romaire Reardon were in a group exhibition titled "Paintings for a Country Estate," hence the ironic reference, playing once again on the regional/ metropolitan split. The ACA gallery showed primarily social realists: Dobkin, Evergood, Groper, and the Soyer brothers. Reinhardt's satire is directed at the galleries prices that he had varied ironically, according to their level of social commitment and symbolic capital.

PM #9, *How to Look Out*, reveals in six hilarious panels, the serious question of why linoleum flooring cannot be considered an abstract painting, as the caption in the 6th frame suggests. Nominally, Reinhardt writes, it could be, but as he says, "you can bring anything you want to it, [but] we cannot guarantee its quality as aesthetic experience." The sheet also contains Reinhardt's famous alteration of a popular narrative of the heroic rescue of a young girl, Little Nell perhaps, who is in mortal danger of being run over by a steam train. In Reinhardt's allegorical picture a young man personifying Abstract Art is about to rescue a young girl (Art) from the oncoming steam engine flying the labels:

banality, prejudice, drink, linguistic stereotypes, inferiority complexes, corruption, money-grubbing, sin." This image was reprinted in Newsweek under the title *The Rescue of Art* August 12, 1946 and has subsequently enjoyed a renewal of life in several other publications (Guilbaut, 1984).

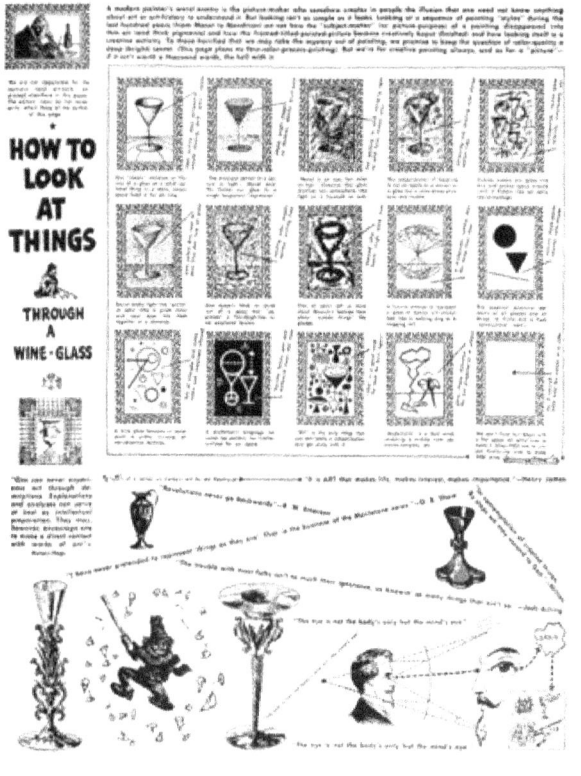

Figure 76: PM #10 *How to Look at Things Through a Wine Glass* July 7, 1946
© Estate of Ad Reinhardt SODRAC (2014)

Figure 80 includes an ironic aside from Reinhardt, posing as the editors: includes an ironic aside from Reinhardt, posing as the editors of this issue:

> We are not responsible for the opinions and artwork expressed elsewhere in this paper. The editor's views do not necessarily reflect those of the author of this page[15].

---

15. Hess suggests the disclaimer is an oblique attack on Abe Chanin whose social realist style and political ideology were "more compatible with the paper's *bien pensant* leftism than Reinhardt's sophisticated dialectic" (Hess, 1975:35).

Hess argues that it must have been clear by this time that the abstract art which Reinhardt was promoting did not concur with the PM editors' views on art, but Reinhardt was not about to change his spots. This page again reflects the artist's dogmatic views on the importance of non-objective (pure) abstraction. Of the 15 images of a wine glass the final one is captioned with "We don't finish but begin with a flat space. An artist tries to make it alive— You are its subject—finally he tries to make you alive." But below the word "alive," a reference to the 'vital inducements' of alcohol, in a typically dead pan ironic fashion, Reinhardt places an image of a prostrate, or *dead* figure, who completes the design of the lower left corner of the frame. Increasingly this becomes Reinhardt's somewhat perverse *modus operandi*; wherever and whenever he posits a position worth holding, he undermines it with a negation, and at times, a negation of a negation. Many of his notes reveal this absolute contrariness; for instance, his 39th Art Plank at the DIAS (Destruction in Art Symposium), London 1966 read:

> 39. The re-negation[16] of the neo-negation of neo-art-as-art[17]

and a few of his undated notes from the sixties reveal further the intensity of his critical attitudes.

> Creeds, codes, cults
> Art is the only valid criticism of art –
> What is not common to works of art and other objects –/
> Art, supreme affirmation of self-sufficiency, separateness
> attributed to objects as distinct from self
> original part-object, breast
> Gothic, female genital, fold within fold, slits, vaults
> Sloping shoulders, chastened animal
> Smooth, rough, nipple texture
> Re-create loved objects, art, images of body, fragments
> Charge the canvas, attack upon the material, defacement
> Drawn in, quartered block that blockage
> reverberation
> Derealization, desubjectification
> No good ideas in art Shit-show, "meaning," misuses in art
> (Rose, 1975:74-75).

---

16. "re-negation" is a pun on renegotiation, a word that is further punned in "neo-negation."

17. MOCA Catalogue p.123, first published in Art Voices Spring, 1963.

PM #11 *How to Look at Looking* (July 21, 1946), continues the promotion of good clean "high" abstraction at the expense of dirty "low" realism, in the company of some ironic quotes from: Schopenhauer, "You must treat a work of art like a great man: stand before it and wait patiently till it deigns to speak"; Herbert Read: "Hitler was a bad artist because he was a bad politician"; William James: "there is nothing in this world so despicable as a bad artist," and J.K. Huysmans: "Art is the only clean thing on earth except holiness." Reinhardt as well as being deconstructive in his approach to subjects, was also fond of making binary lists of statements that often contradicted or undermined one another, or that dialectically resolved antinomies; a thesis and its antithesis, into some transcendental synthesis.

PM #12 *How to look at a Good Idea* (Aug 4th 1946), presents Reinhardt's ironic thesis on labour process, and the important question of value in art. Adjacent to the artist's usual abstract painter colophon appears "the good idea" that consists of "pulling people into painting activity" so that their viewing efforts can have social meaning—higher wages, shorter hours—"instead of merely passively 'looking' at 'pictures', which does not mean that it is not a good idea for anyone to take any artist by the scruff to ask him what his 'pictures' represent." Reinhardt also includes a biting satire (literally), in the person of a rather matronly woman in a bathing suit (Punch cartoon, circa 1920), with bonnet, holding her bare foot above the water to reveal her toe being bitten by a large crab. This cartoon is framed by a caption explaining that this image is from the "Political Good Idea Department," and "All you need is a picture some labels and some paste." Two of Reinhardt's identities, the saluting cavalier and the drummer, also make a cameo appearance.

PM #13 *How to Look at Things Again* (Aug 25, 1946), includes the wine glass abstraction that "frees painting from subject matter, story, skill, fixed and final ideas, from flux, fusion and flicker to a *field* of colour activity." Reinhardt's reference here to colour field painting is some years before Greenberg's pronouncements on the concept became holy writ. His satire of conventional picture making reaches new depths with his "Pig's Eye Department" showing a group of pigs at a trough with paired balloon phrases reading "You can't change human nature," "nope," "The business of art is to copy nature," "yeah that's right," and finally, "What helps business helps you "naturally," a statement that placed in the context of his other scatological wisecracks, reads as an ironic allusion to an advertisement extolling the virtues of some new treatment for constipation.

PM #14, *Hey, Look at the Facts* (Sept 8, 1946), continues Reinhardt's serio/comic art history lectures on modern art in three columns, comparing house building, empirical science, botany, biology, with the works of exemplary (for Reinhardt), modern artists, Kandinsky, Klee and Cezanne, in the company of reproductions of two contemporary abstracts by his mentors Carl Holty and Hans Hofmann. This sheet also includes a somewhat sexist poem by the foppish gent, Reviewer X, satirizing in rhyming couplets the work and person of artist Georgia O'Keefe.

>Georgia O'Keeffe
>Fills me with grief
>Her pelvic bones
>Call forth moans
>
>Never in strait space cubic
>At the Museum of Modern Art
>Have I viewed such extravagant pubic?
>Mistakes of the whole for the part.

PM #15, *How to Look at More than meets the Eye* (Sept 22, 1946), is framed by many quotable quotes on art and nature from: Landor, Catullus, Aurelius, Coleridge, Dryden, Whistler, Dante, and Wilde "It takes a great artist to be thoroughly modern. Nature is always a little behind the age." The sheet contains an extraordinary collection of approximately 150 drawn eyes (pairs and single) from a few "modern old masters" a) Klee, b) Miro, and c) Picasso, with an extensive balloon quote from Philosopher John Dewey comparing art research to intellectual activity and scientific inquiry, issuing from the mouth of a figure whose head is being bandaged by another who replies critically, with a mock/serious Reinhardt line espousing intellectualism, "Yeah, non-modern artists are not so smart." The lower left frame contains a Punch-like comment from a Victorian 'sweet young thing', "Fortune Magazine's survey of the art world in September 1946, says, "Almost the best thing that can happen to almost any good painter, from an art economic point of view, is for him to die" to which her suitor delivers his punning reply, "That's rich huh?"

PM #16, *How to Look at Art and Industry* (Oct 6, 1946), subtitled "a page of jokes and a plea by Ad Reinhardt * 'For the love of money is the root of all evil.'" (New (sic) Testamentis) is framed by a series of pointed quotes about money directed towards the fickle economy of the art world." Reinhardt again attacks the business world sponsorship of art competitions, this time for exploiting art and artists for free advertising. An engraving of the "Death of Socrates" represents the central figure, bearing the label "American Artist," swallowing the hemlock provided by the Nickle drink (Pepsi-Cola) competition, implying, rather heavily—Reinhardt was often this straightforward—that artists participate in their own exploitation.

PM #17, *How to Look at Iconography* (Oct 20, 1946), includes a New Yorker cartoon by Reinhardt's friend painter/ cartoonist Daniel Brustlein (aka Alain). This "Timeless picture of the year" shows a painter vomiting out the window of his studio after painting some of the realistic details of his seascape. The framed cartoon by Alain, a visual pun perfectly illustrating Reinhardt's disavowal of naturalistic painting—for physiological reasons!—is surrounded by an extraordinary series of semi-abstract signs and symbols (icons), representing various objects (coat, tie, coat), stereotypical figures (good Guy, Bad Guy, Fat Guy), plants, creatures, and architecture. The frame to the lower right contains an extraordinary collection of 34 drawn lines, many of them functioning also as visual puns: Straight Line, Dotted Nervous Line, Bee Line, Frau Lein, Alka Line, Sweet Adeline etc., about which twenty years later, Reinhardt suggested sardonically, he was working out his drawing problems "once and for all" (Rose 1975: 16).

PM #18, *How to Look at the Record* (Nov. 3, 1946), permits Reinhardt to do a little self-promotion. He inserts the announcement for his second New York exhibition, a solo show at Betty Parsons Gallery 15, East 57th Street, in company with "Cubism's (sic) climatactic years," and references to Carl Holty and Hans Richter, two of his mentors. The upper and lower registers contain some samples of quasi-heraldic images which Reinhardt has framed with the ironic quote "There is no reason in this great democratic age why everyone should not have a coat of arms." It is interesting that in the text for his Jewish Museum exhibit catalogue, Reinhardt cites that his drawing of heraldic signs that as a youngster, he won a prize for was an early formative influence on his art making activity. One could argue that the inclusion of these signs with the leveling quote about democracy represents another aspect of Reinhardt's status incongruity, specifically his lack of respect for the conventional accoutrements and privileges of power, contrasted with his very real desires for art world success. This ironic disavowal of class-based symbols of hierarchy for evidencing anti-democratic and un-American values, did not in any way, complement his longing for recognition, and respect.

PM #19, *How to Look at It* (The Art of Kartoffel Question (The (sic) Potato Plight), appears as a jaundiced attack on critics and criticism: critics for their "word mongering" and "platitudinous praises," and criticism for its obfuscation and lack of ethics. Reinhardt openly questions whether art could or should be considered a staple commodity equivalent "to potatoes or lumber to be disposed of as one pleases." PM #20, *How to Look at a House* (Dec 1st, 1946), includes a section "How to Look at a gallery" that promotes the Charles Egan gallery which exhibited examples of the high artwork illustrated on this page of De Kooning, Harry Bowden, Joseph Krause and George Cavallon.

PM #21 (December 15, 1946) continues the emphasis on the contemporary New York art scene that Reinhardt had begun to establish in the previous four sheets. This one contains three "How To" sections. The first, "How to Look at Creation" (Precreation, Re-Creation and pure Creation), undertaken by modern artists—who, like ancient gods—create "a NEW world." "How to Look at 3 Current shows" satirically profiles the work of two "somebodies in the art world": Ralston Crawford, the official atom bomb artist (Downtown gallery); Frederick Taubes, "art for art's sake stuff," (AAA gallery); and "one no-body," Ralph Fasanella (44th Street Gallery), a trade union organizer, a non-commercial, non-professional artist" who is praised for representing the "(good) democratic idea that creative painting activity belongs to everyone potentially and not to the few, special hack skilled, 'sound craftsmen' who produce dept. store pictures." This support for the (*faux*) democratization of art is a position that Reinhardt's working class and union background, would have encouraged him to adopt as a political position, but which practically his aesthetic beliefs, and elitist relationships to the academy, teaching and the art world in general forced him to reject. Finally, in the frame at the base of the page "How to Look at a theme," Reinhardt suggests that three good ideas for theme shows are: the Horn, "everybody blow your own horn"; The Horse "Ridiculous of course," and "BeHold the People—Hurray for me, the hell with everybody." PM #22, *How to Look at a Mural* (Jan. 5, 1947), is a richly detailed, masterful analysis of Picasso's *Guernica*. This sheet has the look and feel of a lecture and was probably used subsequently by Reinhardt in his teaching, and by many others since.

PM #23, *How to Look at a Spiral*, was unpublished. The abstract painting colophon for this page design has a spiral painted on it with the byline "Any attempt to make modern painting more intelligible and communicative must involve a serious consideration of the spiral," because it was, as Reinhardt argued, inherently "democratic." The lower night cap drinker colophon is populated with spirals…Our "intrepid artist-reporter" winds up (or unwinds), he writes, an ironic comment on his recent firing from PM. This final unpublished image completed Reinhardt's extraordinary cycle of images that promoted modernist abstraction and simultaneously attacked some of the most entrenched of art world ideologies.

The later satires for TRANS/FORMATION and Art News continue many of the themes explored in the PM pages, but their focus is more specifically on the social reality of the New York artworld, its artists, museums, exhibits, critics, publications and gossip. If Reinhardt's PM were the result of his contract with that newspaper, these later cartoons were specially commissioned by the magazine editors. They differ in other respects. Reinhardt's position within the New York art world was beginning to become more complicated. He had had several successes but his request for a retrospective at the Metropolitan had been turned down and there were also some difficulties in his own life. His marriage in 1945 to Pat Decker had resulted in divorce in 1949. These facts underlie the more pointed features of his criticism and the less didactic and heroic character of these images.

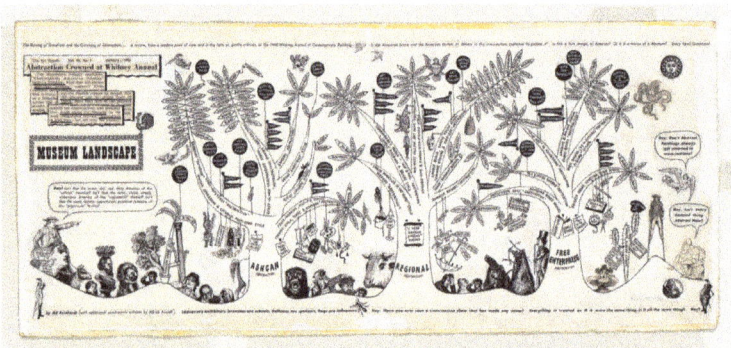

Figure 77: TRANS/FORMATION #1 *Museum Landscape* 1950
© Estate of Ad Reinhardt SODRAC (2014)

The production of TRANS/FORMATION #1, *Museum Landscape* (1950), coincided with the Irascibles group protest of the Metropolitan Museum of Art for its stance against avant-garde art. It contains three trees in the manner of the PM #7 that represents in a quite comprehensive fashion the Whitney Museum annual exhibition of that year (December 16 February 5th). All of the exhibiting artists, with the exception of Reinhardt, are included in this satire, in the company of their sponsors represented by balloons, and their influences, by flags. This is a very complex satire, but its basic elements can be interpreted as a continuation of concerns that the artist had developed previously in the PM series. It is described by Reinhardt as a "review, from a modern point of view and in the form of gentle criticism, of the 1950 Annual of Contemporary Painting. Accordingly, Museum Landscape takes as its theme, the "raising of questions" attending the "crowning of abstraction," a line taken from an Art Digest review (Vol 24 No 7 January 1950). The crowning of abstraction must have been of some concern for Reinhardt, as one of the influential first-generation practitioners whose reputation had yet to rise significantly on the museum/market roster. From his perspective, Reinhardt's career must have appeared to have been eclipsed by the gathering crowd of sycophantic abstractionists who had been caught up in the wave of this or that abstract 'style' without understanding, what was to Reinhardt, the true (pure) meaning of abstraction, an art about art that was aesthetically, morally—and politically—revelatory and revolutionary. One reading of this complex graphic satire would be to interpret it as very personal attack on those whose abstraction did no more than ape the first-generation expressionist work. A subtext of this satire is the sense that abstraction was not fulfilling its promise to provide a symbolic form of freedom and democracy, upon which Reinhardt had placed so much emphasis in his own life and theories of art. It had merely become another successful commodity in the art marketplace. Abstract art had sold out! The figures with balloon statements frame the critical messages Reinhardt wished to communicate to his readers and colleagues. The C18th revolutionary figure (a Reinhardt identity), to the left of the sheet with his hand raised declares,

> "Hey! Isn't that the same, old, sad, dirty America of the 'ashcan' twenties? Isn't that the same, clean, empty, wide-open America of the 'regionalist' thirties? Isn't that the same lonely, opportunist, primitive America of the 'Pepsi cola' forties?"

The miniature artist's articulated wood model answers in mock reply, "Hey. Isn't every damned thing abstract Now?" And above, a praying putti being transported by an angel announces "Hey. Don't abstract paintings always get crowned in cross-sections," a reference to the Whitney curators' avowed aim to produce a "cross section" of contemporary "American Painting," with the exhibition of 161 pictures from 19 States.

The figures below the trees are taken from some of the earlier satires. Many of them have their right or left hands clasped to their heads in gestures of puzzlement or consternation at the situation provided above. Two Napoleonic soldiers, like anthropomorphic inverted comma signs, one fat and one thin, tip their hats to the scene displayed before them. Reinhardt's night-capped drinker is nestled uncharacteristically in an emblematic tondo to the lower right corner with the punning text "Fecit Hic," (Fake it, hic!).

TRANS/FORMATION #2 *Museum Racing Form* 1951 is closer to the multi-framed comics of the earlier PM series. This comic satirizes the artworld penchant for competition by comparing it to a horse race. Reinhardt has assembled the competitors, bespectacled dogs at the very conservative Metropolitan racetrack for the Carnegie Steeplechase, The Whitney Turf Classic, and the National Academy Derby. The prizes are ironically outlined in the next frame: The Guggenheim purse, Rome Prize, Audubon First, Tiffany Award, Biennale, Ten Best, and Winners' circle, followed by The Bookies. The Bets, in which dealers are shown scrabbling to place bets on the contestants of this outrageous race for art world fame. The next frame shows the rear end of a work horse with his master bearing a broom and many rejected critics sheets of hot tips littering the foreground. The race itself is shown as a crazy merry-go-round carousel with the various jockeys wearing the Reinhardt's hated style labels: Ashcanist, Regionalist, Social Expressionist, and Surrealist. The final frames show the racing sheets with the leading jockeys and the season's averages. The last frame titled "Out of the Horse's Mouth" contains a hilarious collection of not so good quotes satirizing, what were to Reinhardt, art world theoretical pretensions, and fake truisms: "Look through outer reality to see inner reality"; Art is too cerebral"; "my painting paints me"; and the psychological kicker, "I'm consciously and collectively unconscious."

TRANS/FORMATION #3 *Art of Life and Life of Art* (1952), once again satirizes the competitive conditions of the art world from the position of a politically enlightened, if disgruntled, insider. This cartoon reproduces many frames from the earlier PM series: the pigs, the beast of the Apocalypse, Durer's *St. Sebastian*, and Callot's hanging tree, with bodies from Goya's *Miseries of War* series, thus producing the most complex allegory of Reinhardt's relationship to the art world. Hess describes this as "Joycean satire" with a "certain "undertone of violence as if Reinhardt were dehumanizing the art world, turning its characters into course food, curses, and sterile abstract verbs" (47). There are many battles and struggles represented in this extended satire that, in many ways, is less a page of jokes than a collection of very hard jabs at artists, the art world, and all its foibles. The "undertone of violence" that Hess detects in this image, is actually quite overt. There are over thirty acts or potential acts of violence and struggle, in this sheet. These include the following: four gladiators fighting, two sumo wrestlers, boxers boxing, five cavaliers shooting, several torture scenes, lions fighting, a cat with a rat in its mouth, Callot's hanging figures, several stabbings, and presiding over all (perhaps), an engraving of David's "*The Oath of the Horatii*," perhaps Reinhardt's salute to his deconstructive self-sacrifice in the name of a higher truth. It is tempting to interpret this aggressive image as an attempt by Reinhardt to sublimate his feelings of powerlessness, and perhaps anger, at perceived abuses from his art world colleagues. For the first time he uses an innovative Derridian (or psychotic) play of language employing the names of the art world to produce punning sentences, such as:

> this panting mio-go round is built on feet of klee! brackman and diller went up the millman to fletcher a quirt or gallatin paalen of walkowitz, jackson fell thon and brook his koener and benton his becker and still kane tomlin avery, and ault tam kingmen cadmus put stuempfig to weber egan!

The *St. Sebastian* martyr is pierced with arrows bearing labels such as: Commercialism, Banality, Careerism, ABSTRACT Pot Boiling, Art Criticism, Gambling, Competitions, Vice, Art Appreciation. Beneath the figure is the Reinhardt Drummer, and Medusa heads.

Art News 1 *Our Favorites* (March 1952), was commissioned by the magazine's managing editor Thomas Hess, on the occasion of the request by Wildenstein Gallery of several art critics to choose their favorite American paintings since 1900. "Art News has requested a well-known painter to make an artist's very personal comment on this critical scene." In order of appearance from left to right, the critics represent their respective papers and magazines: The New York Times, The New York Herald Tribune, LIFE, TIME from the Art Digest, Art News and The Nation.

The early fifties were energetic, exciting, but perhaps also, very difficult years for Reinhardt. In 1953 He married Rita Ziprowski, and a daughter was born in 1954. That same year Barnett Newman sued him for slander. Happily, the suit was thrown out of court, but this event must have shaken him. It is probably no accident that he began to renounce his art principles of asymmetry and irregularity for a monochrome geometric figure (gestalt) that provided greater structure to his work. It is tempting to believe that this obsession with order may have compensated for what otherwise was lacking in his life, critical success, sales, and self-esteem.

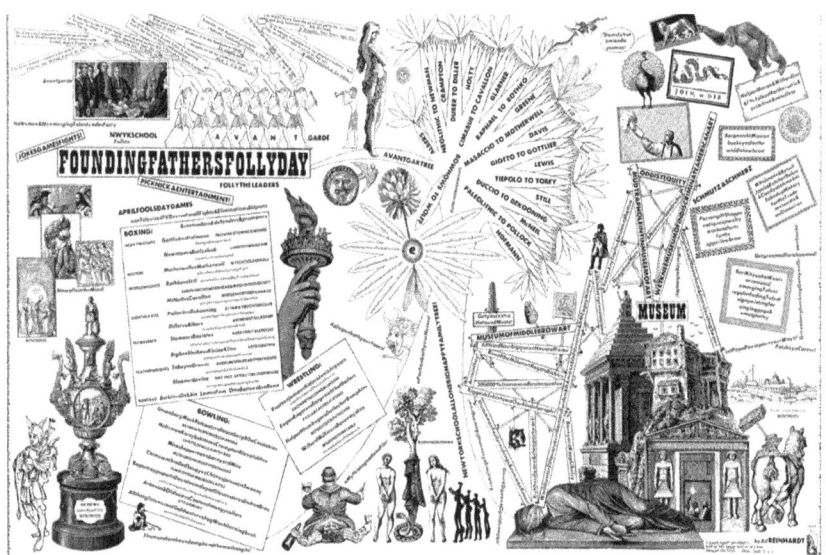

Figure 78: Art News #2 *Founding Fathers Follyday* April 1954
© Estate of Ad Reinhardt SODRAC (2014)

Art News 2 *Founding Fathers Follyday*, "a folly the leaders" follow-up from his PM art world genealogy that was according to Hess part of the magazine's plan to have a special April Fools' Day issue. In this cartoon we witness Reinhardt devising yet another symbolic contest of power (a Mini Olympics no less), between the major agents of the New York art world with pugilists (gallery dealers as wrestlers, the artists as boxers, and the critics, (intellectuals) predictably as bowlers. The cartoon is divided into two halves separated by an avant-garde tree bearing the canon of American abstract art, inserting each of the masters into a humorous, at times, ironic and alliterative relationship to art history: "Neolithic to Newman" "Durer to Diller," "Raphael to Rothko," "Tiepolo to Tobey," "Duccio to Dekooning," and "Paleolithic to Pollock." The prize trophy to the left is the *Art News* New York School Matzohballtitle (Matzo ball title) for a school which has Nowomen (no women) and Noemeerging talentunderforty (no emerging talent under forty). Reinhardt's name appears in the lower left with a revealing quote from Shakespeare's King Lear ii.3.1. "I heard myself proclaim'd; And by the happy hollow of a tree Escaped the hunt'. This is placed in the context of one of the expressive framing sentences that announce the success (and the death), of the New York School of Abstract Expressionism.

> NEWYORK SCHOOL IS ALL OVER AVANTGARDE ARTIS REAL GONE! HAMORICANOB STRUCK A XEPRESSUREISMIS EVER WEAR GREATDAY!
> In plain English: A New York school is all over! Avant-garde art is real gone. Ha Morican Obstruck Axepressure ism is mis ever wear. Greatday!

His own career was slowly on the rise, but Reinhardt's sardonic view of the museum and the relatively popular successes of Abstract Expressionism indicate his defection from his peer group, and the supporting institutions of abstract art. "Allkindsexpressionism" and the (sic) MUDTRAPHOLEINTIN MUSEEM OF ART (Metropolitan Museum had become a WETKNEE MUSEUM OF INDISCRIMINATE AMERICAN ART (a wet knee museum of indisriminate American Art). He also lampoons the Museum of modern art which appears here as the MUSEUM OF MIDDLEBROW ART. With this cartoon Reinhardt has woven his grievances into a veritable carpet of disaffection, casting himself I believe, in the role a tragic King Lear. As Hess suggested "all his friends slowly became convinced that he mean't what he said in his satires, they cooled toward him or became angry with him" (Hess 56). By this time Reinhardt had realized that the art world was so shot through with contradictions and vice, that it was actually unsatirizable and perhaps the one last subject worthy of attention was himself. This is apparent in his 1966 interview with Bruce Glaser.

> Glaser: One can't avoid commenting on the presence of a very sardonic and dry humour in your answers, as well as your writings and cartoons. Is it possible that you have been taken more seriously than you wished?
>
> Reinhardt: This is too serious to be taken seriously. I haven't done any cartoons or satires for a long time because it doesn't seem possible. The art world is no longer satirizable. I suppose there isn't much going on except business, and that's not very funny. Ten years or fifteen years ago (perhaps it was much longer), it was possible for one artist to call another artist an old whore. It's not possible anymore. The whole art world is whorish... (Rose 14).

Reinhardt was one of the few members of his generation who in his life and work, is able to shed some light on Greenberg's enigmatic aside "someday it will have to be told how anti-Stalinism which started out more or less as Trotskyism turned into art for art's sake, and thereby cleared the way, heroically for what was to come"[18]. Although Reinhardt's defense of abstraction as a

---
18. Greenberg, C. "The Late Thirties in New York," *Art and Culture* Boston: Beacon Press (1962:230).

critical practice was based upon somewhat different premises to others of his generation, he did not disavow critical and political practice in order to reach some transcendental aesthetic as a vehicle for self-realization. It is clear from his cartoons and writings that abstract painting, far from capitulating to the closed aesthetic ideology of *l'art pour l'art*, could become a symbolic vehicle for continuous self-interrogation, social and cultural change. His graphic satires must be seen in this light, but perhaps they would not have been produced at all, if not for his philosophical beliefs and hidden injuries of class.

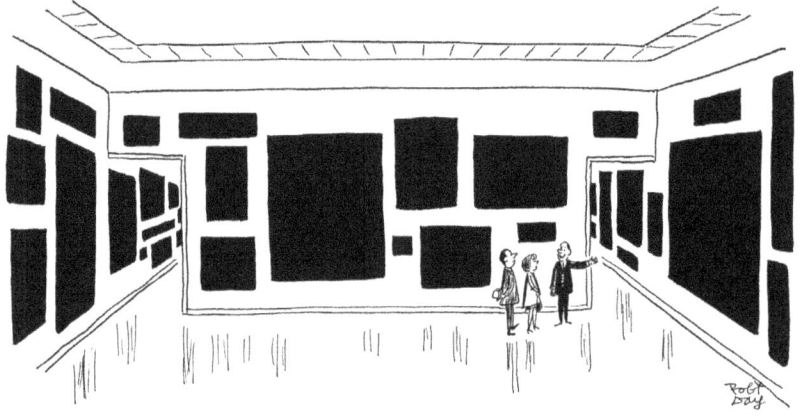

"You will find more on the floor above."

Figure 79: Day, R. New Yorker March 4th 1967 © Conde Nast

CHAPTER 10

Walt Disney's Avant-Garde

> When culture becomes nothing more than a commodity, it must also become the star commodity of the spectacular society. (Guy Debord, Thesis 193:1967)
>
> When you wish upon a star, it makes no difference who you are... (Disneyland Theme Tune)[1]

In chapter nine, I discussed the art comics of Ad Reinhardt, an artist whom I described as an insider who at times, chose to act like an outsider, satirizing the very sectors of the art world that sustained and legitimated his production as an avant-garde painter. I suggested also that Reinhardt's comic satires had a dual didactic purpose that enabled him to both critique illusionistic painting—"low" art—and promote a "high" modernist aesthetic of non-objective abstraction. In this chapter I will engage in a reading of comic satires of contemporary art produced by anonymous artists working for The Disney Corporation who are technically outside the borders of the discursive field of the "high" art world and who therefore have neither the symbolic capital, cultural competency, or the same investment in the system as an artist such as Reinhardt in the context of a wide variety of similar forms of popular culture, a somewhat different critique of high culture's avant-garde. I will argue that mass produced examples of critical insubordination, although structurally similar to those discussed in previous chapters, have a different readership, political intention and therefore perhaps, different affects. My reading of these comics will permit an engagement once again with the distinguishing characteristics of satire and irony, and how they work together to advance a critical position. I will raise questions pertaining to the appropriation and trafficking of cultural products from one

---

1. "When you wish upon a star, it makes no difference who you are....", a song produced by Leigh Harline (music), and Ned Washington (lyrics) for Walt Disney's classic animated film Pinocchio (1940) based on the novel The Adventures of Pinocchio (1883) by the Italian writer Carlo Collodi, subsequently became the Walt Disney Corporation theme tune.

group to another and explore the power relations represented and reproduced through these transactions.

Studies by Schickle (1968), Dorfman and Mattelart (1975), Kunzle (1973), Thomas (1976) among others , indicate that the readership for Disney comics, both in the West and in the so-called Third World countries, has a relatively distinct composition in terms of age and class. There are certain important differences however: for example, the age span of readers in the Third World is less differentiated than those in North America, and the production and consumption of printed Disney comics has been substantially reduced in the West since the late nineteen sixties, a result of the increasing importance of film, television, and digital animation. These studies demonstrate how the comic book appeals to the working and lower middle classes and is a very useful tool for acquiring literacy in countries where large sectors of the urban and rural population have little access to education. Urban working-class youth in both the west and in developing countries probably read comic satires of "high" culture somewhat differently from those within the high culture class fraction, a result simply of their low cultural competency and lack of understanding of high culture projects. Another reason for this is that the readers for various textual and graphic products—for instance, the mid-culture New Yorker magazine and the low culture Walt Disney comics—are very different in age and class composition. The working and middle class readership for Walt Disney comics seek less endorsement and reinforcement for their social position than those within other class fractions. Disney comic readers may use their products to greater educational benefit, to enhance their literacy. In so doing they may reinforce their understanding (and misunderstanding) of art world projects occurring outside of their immediate class boundaries. Paradoxically the comics become instruments for both enlarging and diminishing their readers' understanding of high culture.

The comic strips that I will discuss in this chapter were produced by the studios of Walt Disney in 1978, 1979 [2] respectively. They reveal the appropriation of avant-garde cultural forms from the 1960s and 1970s-kinetic, performance and body art from the dominant cultural level to the popular domain, for the purpose of critical instruction. It is important to recognize that the Disney Corporation usually renovates material from the public domain or from other sources of popular culture that are free of copyright restrictions. Dorfman and Mattelart argue that Walt Disney's *Winnie The Pooh* (after A.A. Milne and E.H. Shephard), *Pinocchio* (after

---

2. These comics are possibly reprints from the mid 1960s or early 1970s although I have been unable to substantiate this. Disney Corporation often recycles comics after a five or ten-year period.

Collidi), and *A Christmas Story* (after Dickens), appeared in various forms with the minimum of acknowledgement and *The Three Little Pigs*, *Snow White and the Seven Dwarfs*, with no acknowledgement at all. The appropriated examples of contemporary art [3] used in the art comics I discuss in this chapter are somewhat unusual with respect to the total output of Disney productions.[4] Perhaps the accelerated market value of Disney collectables has encouraged studio executives to endorse the production of custom-made products of special interest to collectors.[5]

The first comic story appeared in Walt Disney's "Uncle Scrooge" No 170, November 1979 under the title *Gyro Gearloose– The Sculptinker*. The comic title conveniently collapses the status positions of professional and amateur. The contraction of sculptor and tinkerer into Scupltinker, is similar to that provided by Gyro's Gear/Loose surname. In Freudian terms these linguistic games (puns), would represent a form of meaning modification, or substitution, allowing an economy of "psychic energy"—pleasure—to result. The contractions in the title are similar to the modifications used in the classic Freudian example "*tete a tete*" becoming "*tete a bete*," described by Freud as "condensation with slight modification" (Freud 1926:25-6). Beyond the linguistic allusions however, the comic's title also assigns a role identity, and provides an entry to the ideological realm, conflating in one swift and assured gesture, the aristocratic artist/ inventor and creative magus/genius figure, with the proletarian tinkerer, handyman, odd-jobman, or bricoleur. Creativity is coupled with non-creativity, use value with exhibition value, professionalism with amateurism and finally, "extraordinary" science with "normal" science (Kuhn, 1962).[6] The apotheosis of both "high" culture sculptor, and "low" culture tinkerer, is revealed in this absurd fable-like,[7] perhaps Faustian, sketch of Gyro, who manages in typical fashion, to outwit his

---

3. The sources for these examples are somewhat obscured (transformed), by the narrative and the overlaying of the stock characters. Schicke, R., *The Disney Version: The Life, Times, Art and Commerce of Walt Disney* New York: Simon and Schuster (1968), terms this process "Disneyfication."

4. There are other Disney satires of the art world, including a single sheet with the title "Art and Commerce" by Carl Barks, and "Donald Duck at the Modern" (anon) that were unavailable for examination at the time of writing.

5. The international auctioneering company Sotheby Parke Bernet has successfully traded Disney Collectibles and other popular culture products since the mid. 1960s. Original artwork, kitsch objects, mint condition comics, and other objects defined as collectibles have been commanding increasingly high prices during the past twenty years.

6. See Kuhn, Thomas, *The Structure of Scientific Revolutions* (1962), and for a parody of the Kuhnian paradigm see Feyerabend, Paul "Against Method," and "Consolations for the Specialist" in Lakatos and Musgrave "*Criticism and the Growth of Knowledge, Proceedings of the International Colloquium in the Philosophy of Science*" Vol 4 Cambridge: University of Cambridge Press (1965:210.)

7. The fabular/morality aspects of Disney's world have been identified by a number of authors including Dorfman and Mattelart (1975), and Dorfman, A. *The Empire's Old Clothes. What the Lone Ranger, Babar and other Innocent Heroes do to our Minds* New York: Pantheon (1983).

principal competitor, the devilish Emil Eagle. Totemically, the goose and bald eagle are interesting birds to assume an anthropomorphic caste. A structural or symbolic anthropologist would have no difficulty here in approaching the topsy Turvey world of this comic strip armed with Levi Strauss' "iron triangle of the culinary."[8] A postponement of such an analysis, however, enables the comic's satirical critique of high (avant-garde), art to be more readily understood in terms of its vulgar (surface), not necessarily its sub-textual (allegorical), content. Ironic polysemy, particularly where this enriches the potential meaning matrix, thus challenging the interpretive skills of the reader, may actually obscure the primary (ideological), meanings contained within the humorous narrative.

Beyond the hermeneutic challenge, which the literate reader may feel either attracted to, or justified in pursuing, the comic's visual and narrative structure is actually disarmingly simple. Gyro is shown entering his new "invention" into the "art show" of the local art museum. The term art show here, denotes competition which is close to the conditions underlying most post-nineteenth century exhibits. As the able artist-competitor, Gyro is reproducing a central theme of Disney's world, for many of the Disney characters, in good capitalist fashion, are actively engaged in competition with one another. Dorfman and Mattelart (1975), describe this in the most extreme comic examples, as a form of social Darwinism. They also reveal that in a number of the Disney stories many of them produced by the now justly famous Carl Barks, whom it has been suggested was representing his own powerlessness as a form of resistance to the machinations of the Disney machine[9] the negative character types are coupled and contrasted with their opposites. The positive character types are often distinguished by their virtues: honesty, fairness, generosity, wit, intelligence and good looks. They may have luck, are greedy, or have money. The negative (othering) character stereotypes are characterized by their lack of, or rejection, of these same qualities. The pairings are essentially based upon the time honoured binary model of good versus evil. Gyro has Emil as his evil other; Scrooge McDuck, the Beagle Boys; usually unlucky Donald Duck has his unusually lucky Gladstone Gander, and so on.

In the Sculptinker story, inventor Gyro assumes the role of the artist, yet maintains his inventor status, presumably to sustain his identity in the Gear-

---

8. A reference to Sartre's critique of Levi-Strauss, referred to in Scholte, B. (ed) *The Anthropologist as Hero* Boston: Hayes and Hayes, MIT Press (1972); See Diamond, S. *In Search of the Primitive: A Critique of Civilization* New Brunswick, N.J.: Transaction Books (1974).

9. This has been disputed by a number of scholars. In any event Barks has now received his due recognition as an important artist, and his work is now highly sought-after by collectors. A full collection of his work has been produced under the title *Carl Barks Library*.

loose series beyond this episode. This new dual role is actualized in the reader's mind by Emil's curiosity. "Since when has Gyro been an artist?" he says, thus engaging the implicit popular interrogative, "What does art have to do with science?" Gyro's contribution to the exhibition of modern art is his Sculptinker piece, described by Evil Emil Eagle, in his favorite alliterative style, as a "moving mechanical masterpiece." The evidence of special avant-garde activity in this art competition is emphasized through the transposition or indirect representation of the working class. The museum assistants represented here as under-educated laborer's[10]—dogs in the world of birds—are shown moving the Gearloose work into the museum. "Symbolical of symbolism, huh?" one of them ventures casually. "Wow!" the other assistant exclaims in a dead-pan, Stooge-like fashion.

Concerned that his rival Gearloose will attract the judges' attention and win the art prize, Emil is determined to make Gyro's masterpiece work for him as well. True to his evil nature he has projected heavily on to Gyro's ambitions for *The Sculptinker* and responded with his own nefarious intentions. Wearing a beret to disguise himself as an artist, Emil returns to the exhibition with his own art piece, described as a "tube clad arm," sneaks into *The Sculptinker*, thereby transforming it into a type of Trojan Horse and sets about his evil business. Members of the cultured class (culture vultures), enter the exhibition room to view the sculpture. Resembling somewhat their counterparts from mid-nineteenth century British academy or French salon exhibitions, they exclaim in both archaic, and contemporary popular language: "zounds" and "wow, look at that," thus providing Gyro with the appropriate cue to set his "moving mechanical masterpiece" in motion. Top hatted members of the *arte liberale*—the art exhibition judges—then enter and proceed to debate the meaning of the work in symbolic terms, their comments revealing somewhat less intelligence than those voiced previously by the workers.

Gyro enjoins his critics to be "At ease sirs! I haven't pushed the go button yet! Stand back everybody!" But the carefully drawn expression of subterfuge on his face reveals the real motives behind his creation. KABOOM!! Emil, who has been using the cover of the machine to pursue his petty criminal activity of picking pockets, is caught unawares by the blast, and catapulted into the long arm of the law. When asked to explain his "peculiar creation," Gyro lets loose

---

10. Dorfman and Mattelart (1975) argue that when members of the working classes are represented in Disney comics they are usually caricatured, in the company of people from the 'Third World', as animals, or dumb ignorant savages, exhibiting anti-social and/or mob-like tendencies.

a tirade against modern art. "It symbolizes that modern type sculpturing is a big bust! I hate the no talent stuff!" The supremely ironic punchline follows when Gyro's innovative "explosion art" critique of modernism is awarded first prize, literally a trophy. Defeated, the Sculptinker clasps his head in horror and exclaims "Oh, no! My wreckage won!"

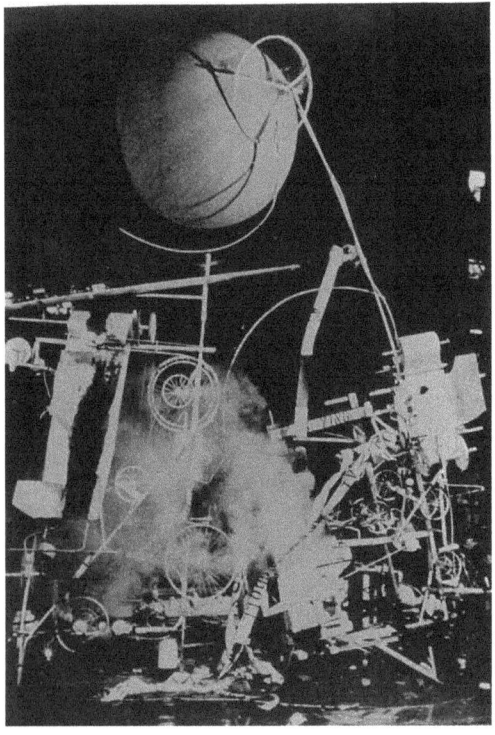

Figure 80: Tinguely, J. *Homage a New York* Museum of Modern Art, New York March 17, 1960. Photographic Archive. The Museum of Modern Art Archives, New York. IN 661.1. Photograph by David Gahr.

The comic strip's narrative and its central image of the exploding modernist "moving mechanical masterpiece" is likely based on a real work by the Swiss/French kinetic sculptor Jean Tinguely, whose famous *Homage 'a New York* (fig. 80) self-destructed in 1960, to the horror and subsequent critical acclaim of the media, outside of New York's Museum of Modern Art. True to its model Gyro's masterpiece capitulates to the institutional demands of advanced art practice. *The Sculptinker* is rewarded with the response—absorption—that all genuinely antagonistic avant-garde art receives, sooner or later, from the institution art. And like Tinguely's own aestheticized anarchism, Gearloose's destructive "creation"—his masterpiece—is cloaked with the progressive, and innovative values of anti-bourgeois modernist ideologies. And yet these are the same ideologies that have secured the stereotypical bourgeois values of individualism, genius, imagination, free will, culture—often packaged in the most extreme, anaesthetic, antagonistic, destructive and negative avant-garde gestures imaginable. Like the hapless Emil Eagle who is caught by the long arm of the law, Gyro receives his unanticipated due, institutional incarceration. The status quo is secured, not however, without first undergoing an attack on its superstructure.

The second comic book example has a more contemporary subject,[11] and is less subtle in its satire of the neo-avant-garde. Its subjects, or better, perhaps, targets, are the Body and Performance Art genres of the late 1960s and 1970s. The Beagle Boys Comic (Walt Disney No 43, August 1978) is probably a reprint from an earlier edition. In *A Bad Day with Buttinski* (Figs. 159-164), the Disney version of the mob—the Beagle Boys—are up to their usual inept plotting of illegal activities. Buttinski Beagle (a substitutive suggestive of a Polish joke), enters the narrative, and in the first two frames the reader is introduced to his major character flaw, his tendency to butt in where he's not wanted. After causing some trouble on the street by interfering with the other Beagles' innocent request of a law officer for directions to the bank they are planning to rob, Buttinski 'toes a ride' on the back of the Beagle's thirties Al Capone, or Keystone Cops-like sedan. Alighting at the 'Crim's country lair', Buttinski pads up to the doorway, only to have the exasperated Beagles slam the door in his face. Buttinski's stupidity is further revealed as this do-gooder intervenes in a cat fight and comes off, as one of his satisfied cousins relates, "much the worse for his buttin' in!" The Beagles celebrate and begin planning their next bank heist, deciding quickly on a novel getaway vehicle—easily identifiable for majority group readers anywhere—the skateboard.

---

11. It can be argued that Disney Corporation was keeping up with trends in contemporary art as much as with current political events. While it is a subject of considerable controversy a few writers (Dorfman, Mattelart and Kunzle), suggest that the Disney corporation was producing anti-North Vietnamese propaganda at the height of the US involvement in Vietnam, anti-student protest comics and strips in the 1960s, as well as comic strips aimed at undermining the Popular Unity Government of Salvador Allende in Chile before the C.I.A. initiated coup of 1973. Critics of this position suggest that it was the translators of Disney material who turned the comics and strips to their own political purposes.

Meanwhile, Buttinski is seen buttin' in on a building painter. And in an attempt to give him a few 'professional' tips on the correct handling of the brush, he fortuitously upsets three paint cans on to the unsuspecting Beagles skateboarding below. The slapstick plot then becomes reminiscent of those immortalized in the films of Buster Keaton, Mack Sennett, the Keystone Cops and Charlie Chaplin, (the origins are beyond Vaudeville to the Punch and Judy, and other post-medieval popular comic prototypes such as the *comedia dell'arte*). The creators of the strip have carefully turned Buttinski's, and the Beagles' disaster (the bank job has been foiled by his good intentions), into a success. In a thoroughly ironic denouement, Buttinski leads the paint splattered Beagles to a contest being held in the Art Centre Square. The stereotypical bohemian looking judge passes them the prize, again a trophy, this time with conventional capital reinforcement, some dollar bills, and proclaims them the "New Body Art Winners!" With a sigh of resignation, one of the Beagles remarks, "It's messy but lots safer than robbin' banks." And like the fool in a Shakespearian tragedy, Buttinski delivers a revealing aside: "Now where would you boys be without me buttin' in?" thus completing the narrative and simultaneously validating his philanthropy.

Whatever psychological motivations encouraged the Disney artists to address the 1970s avant-garde, their political intentions are clear: body art is as illegitimate a pursuit as a life of crime, and both activities are less legitimate, although infinitely more exciting, unless that is, Buttinski is around, than house painting, or perhaps even drawing comic strips as a career. Buttinski becomes the real winner here, always managing fortuitously—Horatio Alger-like—to turn misfortune into fortune. As the typical fool, Stooge figure or Vaudevillian fall guy, Buttinski wins by having his essential character remain intact, while the Beagles accept the 'booby' prize for becoming totally out of character (what self-respecting crim would allow this?), and for being in the wrong place, at the right time.

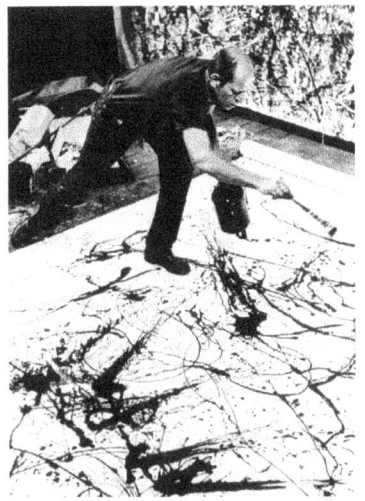

Figure 81: Pollock, J., Painting No 35 LIFE Magazine (1950) © Harry Shunk and Janos Kender J. Paul Getty Trust. Los Angeles

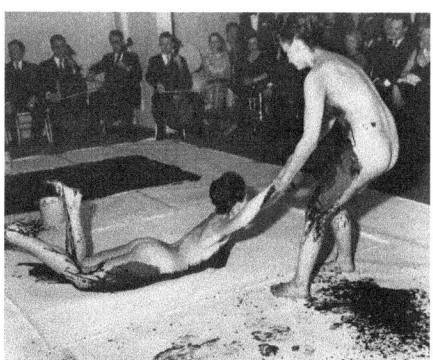
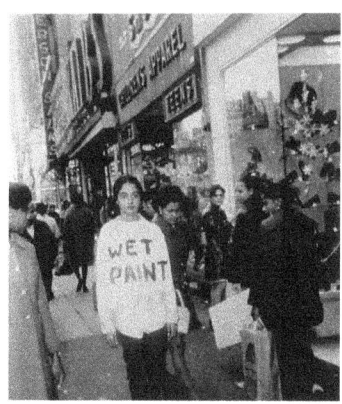

Figure 82: Klein, Y. *Anthropometries* Paris (1960). (2014.R.20) © The Estate of Yves Klein c/o ADAGP, Paris

Figure 83: Piper, A. Street Performance *Catalysis* III (1970)
© Adrian Piper

The Buttinski Beagle comic narrative can be compared to many works of art within the historical and neo-avant-gardes. A useful comparison can be found in French artist Yves Klein's performance of his famous *Monotone Symphony* (1960), and simultaneous demonstration of his *Anthropometry* paintings, (fig. 82), in which nude female models, under the direction of the artist, literally paint with their bodies to the accompaniment of a string quartet playing a single note for the duration of the performance.[12] A work by New York artist Vito Acconci also could have served as a model for the Disney strip. In his filmed performance *Run Off* (1973),[13] Acconci rubs his naked body against a freshly painted blue[14] wall, thus reversing the traditional instrumentality common to modernist painting, of the tool to the surface support, and the brush to the canvas. In this performance, the artist's body becomes the canvas and his movements allow the wall to become the applicator of the paint to his body. Acconci's work is an avant-garde parody of the correct (existential), investure of the self of the Abstract Expressionists, particularly Jackson Pollock. It is also a reversal of the model's roles in the Klein *Anthropometries*. In his performance and body art, Acconci often combines the roles of male performer, actor and demonstrator, with those of director and author. He is simultaneously the performer/subject, and the art object of the work. His body itself becomes the exhibitable work for there is nothing else, save the documentation of the performance, to show.

---

12. *Yves Klein* London: Tate Gallery catalogue (1975).

13. Acconci's *Run-off* was documented on Super 8 film.

14. The blue in the images approximates the colour that Yves Klein called "International Klein Blue."

The commodity status of the work has shifted marginally, from the object (in Klein's case, the paintings are still exhibitable), to the documentation and finally to the artist himself.

In the company of a large number of similar works by artists who have used their own bodies as the subject/object of the artwork: Carolee Schneemann, Adrian Piper (fig. 83), Bruce Nauman, Michel Journiac, Gilbert and George, Paul Cotton, Monty Cantsin et. al.,[15] many of them owing their own existence to these prototypes, the Klein and Acconci performances are slaps in the faces of the bourgeoisie,[16] and calculated attempts to undermine the cultural status quo and continue the innovative traditions of the historical avant-gardes.

The Beagle comic strip reveals the bourgeoisie fighting back, albeit in the disguise of the underclasses. It is truly ironic and yet somewhat predictable, that the unknowing agents of the critique become the Beagles, who in the classical Marxist sense are members of the most marginalized group in capitalist society, the *lumpen proletariat*. With the Beagles as political agents, the anti-social and clearly dangerous activity of robbing banks is channeled paradigmatically into the "messier but lots safer!" critique of avant-garde art.

In the first Disney comic, the eccentric genius Gyro Gearloose, is presented to us as a figure from a bygone age. His "good ole Yankee knowhow" and entrepreneurial skills, are established before us as far more socially legitimate and authentic than this aberrant world of art where, to the outsider, decisions are made at the highest level in a blatantly irrational, fortuitous and irresponsible manner. With the model provided by Freud's representation by opposite, the refuge for individual creative behaviour, skill (Yankee knowhow), in a society dominated by anti-individual corporate and bureaucratic institutions, this comic narrative becomes, ironically, the art world. Taken to its ultimate conclusion, Gyro's revelation endorses the reproduction of the standard range of creative stereotypes, and in particular one of the art institution's key sustaining ideologies—artistic freedom—embodied in the work and alienated behaviour of the artist and sanctified as creative truth.

To different degrees of complexity, both comics, creatively interpreted and placed in wider contexts, may represent a somewhat confusing polysemy. These critiques satirize high culture avant-gardism as meaningless quackery. It

---

15. See Lippard, L. *Get the Message: A Decade of Art for Social Change* New York: E.P Dutton (1984); Goldberg, R. *Performance: Live Art 1909 to the Present* London: Thames and Hudson (1979); Battcock, G. and Nickas, R. *The Art of Performance: A Critical Anthology* New York: E.P. Dutton (1984).

16. In the documentation of the Klein performance, the clothing worn by the audience and the artist, who is both conductor and grand regisseur, is particularly suggestive of haute couture.

would be somewhat simplistic to suggest that these comics represent the sour grapes of the anonymous popular media artists working for the monolithic Disney Corporation[17] whose professional ambitions as high culture artists have been thwarted, or that these comics operate in the same manner as the examples of cultural in\subordination provided by the Punch and The New Yorker cartoons discussed earlier. As forms of graphic propaganda, these examples are crude but intelligent critiques of the dominant high culture. And in the terms of their consumers, the large numbers of youthful readers who enjoy these comics, these satires have the capacity to undermine the ideological authority of the cultural dominant. The claim is stronger than this. The comics have a didactic or propagandistic function that attempts and is probably successful in undermining, for a largely class bound and neophyte audience of non-participants,[18] the significance of the late-modernist neo avant-gardes. We can name this educational process "learning to reject" (Willis, 1977).

---

17. Schickel (1968), Real, Dorfman and Mattelart (1975), have examined the commerce of Disney. They reveal that Disney artists like Carl Barks and Ubbe Iwerks were exploited during their tenure with the corporation. Recently, however, the work of these and other formerly anonymous Disney artists has emerged and allowed them to capitalise upon their creative work in other ways.

18. Bourdieu's category of "non-competency" is applicable here. The implication is that these classes and class fractions have obtained little cultural capital through education.

CHAPTER 11

MAD'S Mad Art World and The Art News of National Lampoon

> I don't think it's going too far to say that for my generation, the generation that protested the Vietnam War, growing up with Harvey's MAD and Harvey's war comics shaped the situation to allow our generation to protest that war…it was the comics about media that made you question how you get your information, and that's a necessary component toward taking any kind of political action. (Gitlin, 1988:184)

Throughout this book, I have argued that cartoon and comic satires of art and artists represent critical positions adopted by subordinate classes and class fractions toward the dominant culture. In the previous chapter I discussed two Walt Disney comic satires of kinetic and body art, suggesting that they subvert the critical significance of the late-modernist art practice. In this final chapter, I will discuss art comics produced in another venue and targeted towards a very different group of readers than those of Walt Disney. My focus will be upon two MAD magazine art satires produced during the 1950s and a late 1970s parody of Art News that appeared in The National Lampoon. I will also explore the complex inter-relationships—the political economy—of satirical intent and parodic form, and cue these once again, to an understanding of the symbolic representation of conflict in the field of cultural production.

In her study of MAD T.V. satires, Siva Ben Porta discusses the close semiotic relationship between parody and satire, arguing that parody can become the strategic vehicle within which satire operates, and that a parodic form may reveal satiric intent. The context and the cultural competency of the reader ultimately determine the difference between the two forms and can provide one measure of the political efficacy of a satire. For instance, a parodist's intention may be to represent a form of ironic mimicry, but the work will be read by its target subjects as destructive and mocking satire, reinforcing alterity and power. The struggle over the political (and economic) meanings of a satire or parody are occasionally determined under the defamation, pornography or copyright codes in courts of law. The outcome of such legal deliberations can provide another form of institutional legitimation for humour genre differentiation. In MAD's case the contestation over the political economy of their parodies has occurred many times, beginning in the 1950s when publisher William Gaines was served a writ for allowing his writers and artists to parody the music of popular song writers (Reidelbach, 1991:61).

To my knowledge, there are no specific studies of the readership of National Lampoon and only a few books within the MAD bibliography (Jacobs, 1973, Benton, 1989, and Estren, 1987), discuss the age and class composition of its readers. The studies reveal that from MAD's inception in the early 1950s, the magazines' producers have been predominantly male, and the readers mostly male, between the ages of 11-21. It is important to recognize that from production runs of tens of thousands of copies in the late 1950s, MAD's circulation grew rapidly and by 1968 it had reached a high of three million copies in several languages. One ungendered, and statistically suspect study revealed that by 1960 MAD's circulation was one million, with the magazine being read by 58% of all college students and 43% of all high school students of those surveyed (188). It is safe to assume that during the 1960s, millions of copies of MAD were circulating at any one time, and this makes it unwise to generalize too broadly about the numbers of readers or the specific classes of readership for the magazine. The same is true incidentally of the readership for The New Yorker, Punch, the Saturday Evening Post, LIFE, TIME, Newsweek and Playboy. Each of these magazines may have subscribers of certain classes and class fractions but they may circulate widely and as a consequence, are read by large numbers of readers from other class fractions, sometimes for many years after publication.

Testimonials for MAD come from a number of astute culture 'temperature takers'. Theodore Roszak for example, asserted in his widely read The Making of a Counter Culture (1968), that the appearance of MAD, and Allen Ginsberg's reading of his poem *Howl* marked the beginning of the generation gap. Pop culture historian Todd Gitlin (1988), suggested that MAD opened "a cultural territory which became available for radical transmutation" (Gitlin 1988: 197-8). In her history of MAD, Maria Reidelbach, reveals the raw beginnings of the magazine as "the personal history of talented editors, writers and artists, many of whom were outsiders of one sort or another, immigrants, or children of immigrants" (1991: 5). Reidelbach also notes that many of these individuals were Jews, or of Jewish origin, among them MAD founders Harvey Kurtzman and Bill Gaines. Kurtzman was born in 1924 of Russian Jewish parents and is described by Reidelbach as "a red diaper baby whose parents subscribed to The Daily Worker and sent their kids to "Camp Kinderland, a left-wing summer camp in upstate New York" (20). EC (Educational Comics) owner William (Bill) Gaines, also with a Jewish background (his father's side, his mother Jessie Postlethaite was a teacher of Pennsylvania Dutch extraction)—and similarly working class, even if his father Max, the founder of EC, had amassed and lost a considerable fortune by the time Gaines had taken over the business in 1947. The younger Gaines' inclinations were very much leftist, anti-bourgeois, and by all accounts, somewhat eccentric to boot.

Art Speigelman, the creator of the Pulitzer prize winning comic novel Maus, the underground magazine RAW now also, a regular, and occasionally controversial, New Yorker cover artist, identified a key element of MAD's politics when he said:

> it was the comics about media that made you question how you get your information, and that's a necessary component toward taking any kind of political action (Gitlin, 184-5).

MAD's early satires of the media, particularly film and television, encouraged them to produce other satires of the most economically and ideologically powerful institutions of the dominant culture including business, education, law and medicine. The worlds of art, theatre and music were also favourite targets for many of the MAD artists and writers, whose class backgrounds often inclined them towards cultural in/subordination from an early age. Throughout the 1950s and 1960s MAD regularly devoted whole issues or special feature sections to satirize an institution from top to bottom. The world of high art was one of their first targets. In April 1955 Bill Gaines and Harvey Kurtzman produced their Special Art Issue of MAD (no. 22). On the opening page they introduced their favorite artist, Bill (Chicken Fat) Elder, who was to be given the "Hollywood treatment," that is, full star billing as an artist celebrity. For the next thirty-five pages of the magazine Elder becomes the subject of art historical study—if not to the usual standards of a full-scale hagiography—at least the tracings of a minor monograph.

The cover of the magazine provides the first entry to the wickedly ironic and satirical intentions of MAD's producers. Parodying an image of a famous

Picasso painting Girl Before a Mirror, Boisgeloup (March 14 1932) the cover is framed by the top border text "TALES CALCULATED TO DRIVE YOU... MAD," with a side caption, a typically MAD pun of the period, "HUMOR IN A JUGULAR VEIN," that over the next few issues was substituted occasionally for "HUMOUR IN A VARICOSE VEIN." The allusions in this cover are more complex than they first appear. Elder parodies the Picasso painting, inserting himself in the image as the screaming reflection in the mirror (after Edvard Munch's famous painting The Scream (1893), of the female model in that painting. The contrast between the photograph of the goggle-eyed male with the toothless mouth in the reflection and the abstracted cubist female (profile and full faced) model, underscores the ironic intent. In the context of both the introduction and the cover title of this Special Art Issue, Elder's self-portrait provides entry to Elder's satire of the artist, modern art and art history. The magazine's introduction also provides an opportunity for a lick at the Hollywood star system, and the forms of valorization associated with it. Institutional award systems, prizes and certification symbolic capital accumulation became a regular MAD target. And from the very beginning of their operation, MAD's use of parody became their principal modus operandi. According to Kurtzman, Will Elder understood parody well. "Of course, what it is, is mimicry," he said. "Willy was so good at it. He understood that you had to have an exact duplicate of what you are parodying" (Reidelbach, 1991:29). If parody was Elder's frame, his intention was to produce satire.

The ensemble of signs represented in this special art issue of MAD reinforce one definition of satire "satire as a critical representation, always comic and often caricatural" (Ben-Porat, in Hutcheon, 1984:49). Caricature becomes a device for stereotyping and "othering" the figures represented in the comic panels, about which I will have more to say later. In Elder's parody, the artist's career is presented to us in five chapters: THE CHILD, THE BOY, THE YOUNG ARTIST, THE COMMERCIAL ARTIST, THE OLD PRO' and SENILITY. Within this typically MAD biographical "schema in the vernacular," to use a MAD'ish phrase, Elder and Kurtzman parody a complex set of relationships with which they are somewhat familiar: art history, criticism, the education and valorization of the artist, high art, popular culture, the work of the sub-cultural avant-garde, and last but not least, the grubby business of art and money. In these early MAD issues, Kurtzman, Elder and the other artists and writers employed by Gaines, introduced and refined an enormous range of innovative techniques including: montage (the mixing of photographic, drawn and text elements), appropriated imagery, extended captions, and advertising detournements that were subsequently to become very influential in the magazine and comic book industry.

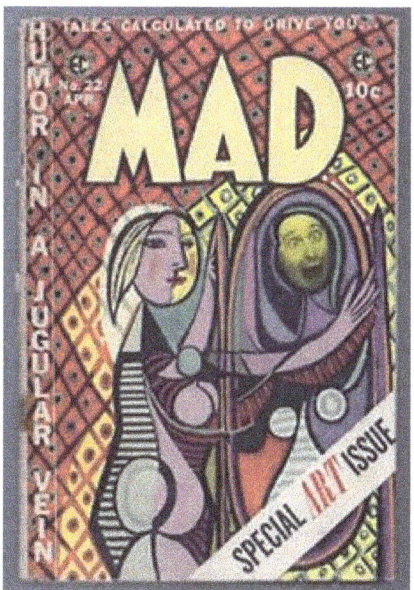

Figure 84: MAD Vol 1 No 22 April 1955 (cover) Public Domain.

Chapter I, THE CHILD, opens with a typically MAD injunction against the purchaser of the magazine: "MAD's first laugh is going to be on you since you thought you were buying a comic book, and you got this sickening mess!" The authors of this narrative proceed to unravel the secret flowering of Elder's artistic genius from his birth as a child prodigy. The opening image, an ad appropriated from the Ladies Home Journal, shows Elder's head montaged on to a baby's body, with an adoring mother, who also happens to sport knuckle dusters on her right hand! This first chapter parodically engages the whole nature/nurture debate with respect to the development of creative talent and the difficulty of coping with a baby who at the age of two months has already asserted himself as a creative magus. Numerous sight gags (a product of Elder's style that earned him the label "chicken fat"), surround the central image of mother and child including: a broken watch, building blocks spelling out the name of Hollywood star Jane Russell (Gentlemen Prefer Blondes, 1953), a worm on the end of a pin, and a poison symbol on the baby bottle with in the lower right frame, child prodigy Elder's 3-D drawing of a horse, a reference to the popular 3D comics of the mid-fifties that MAD had previously parodied in Issue 12, June 1954. On the next page we meet again wunderkind Elder who already at the tender age of two, has emblazoned his home environment, including Uncle Louie's bald head and aunt Brunhilda's best dress, with his trademark materials, chicken fat and H-O Oats. The captions satirize—for MAD producers and readers alike—the numerical titling procedures (i.e. painting #5, painting #50), of the Abstract Expressionists who by this time had already attracted much media attention. The young artist's painting materials and processes become more elaborate in the pages that follow, that in this context can be read as a satire of Jackson Pollock's brew described in the now infamous "Jack the Dripper" LIFE magazine photo essay of 1949, a text that seems now as if it could have been written specially for MAD rather than LIFE! Sometimes he dribbles the paint on with a brush. Sometimes he scrawls it on with a stick, scoops it with a trowel or even pours it on straight out of the can. In with it all he mixes sand, broken glass, nails, screws or other foreign matter lying around. Cigarette ashes and an occasional dead bee sometimes get in the picture inadvertently (LIFE, August 8, 1949).

In the hands of the prodigious Elder, Pollock's media mélange become an over-the-top, fantastically ironic blend of illegitimate art materials and trade names: Duck Fat, H-O Oats, mashed banana pulp, creosote, Bosco, 3-in-1 Oil, Kiwi shoe polish and Halvah! The narrative informs the reader that at the age of four, Elder had "a stroke of genius." Mixing all of the previous ingredients with chlorophyll he proceeded to *sic*, "shmear his painting" over the downtown of the whole city. The lower three frames of this panel show Elder's works signed with various famous artist 'pen' names: Braque, Matisse, Picasso accompanied by the revealing caption: [This] is why very often you can hear observers exclaim, "Why these paintings look like they've been shmeared by a 2 year old." This art historical consecration of the artist's LIFE is interrupted briefly by an in-house advertisement for the MAD reader but continues on the facing page, with genius Elder's creative juvenilia as THE BOY, detailing his early innovative work as a wet window artist, "shmearing" representations of Picassoesque women with "his warm little fatty finger." The following pages declare the young artist's childish interest in "chalk gutter art," "stick ball scores," "kick me hard drawings" and clay sculpture. Appropriated images of coins are accompanied by the caption "Here are some bits of sculpture the little rascal carved just before he left school reform school that is!" The conflation of criminal behaviour and the creative sublime represented here is a conventional popular response to the alienating strategies of the modernist avant-garde. The following frames reveal Elder's "ash tray" that he produced under the pen name of the Florentine mannerist sculptor Benvenuto Cellini, and his "Thinker" (after Auguste Rodin), that we are informed, has used up an entire plasticine set. At the base of the panel is a detourned image of the carved Presidents of Mount Rushmore with a Picasso woman addition to the lower right. The triumphant artist (circled), is shown standing on summit of the mountain with the caption informing the reader that Elder fabricated this entire artwork out of "plasticine, chicken fat and a record number of lollipop sticks!" The following page reveals his talent at art and science, a Renaissance man stereotype whose recent incarnation can be seen in the diabolical artist character of Jack Napier (the Joker), brilliantly acted by Jack Nicholson, in Tim Burton's film *Batman* (1989). The conflation of art and death figure in the next panel frames. Not happy with conventional Valentine's Day drawing ideas "Elder shows his true fibre." No phony heart Valentines for young Elder in this grade school exercise. He produces his creative collage from a real heart!

The next chapter in Elder's artistic career is headed THE YOUNG ARTIST with the captions underscoring the fact that Elder's true role in creative life is the pursuit of "the most importantest thing of all…Money!" A photo appropriation of French modernists appears, with from left to right: Holderer, Manet, Renoir, Astruc, Zola, Le Maitre, Bazille and Monet with the circled addition of MAD's genius Elder, once again inserting himself into the signal events and figures of art history in order to accumulate some symbolic capital. The lower three captioned images identify the artist's introduction to and love of oil paints, with which he produced his very avant-garde paintings: A WALL, THIS CEILING and THIS FENCE! The following page, Elder's creative saga continues with a very ironic parody of arch avant-gardist Marcel Duchamp's famous prescription for a ready-made ("aided"), the moustached reproduction of Leonardo's Mona Lisa LHOOQ (1919). "Realizing that house painting wasn't creative enough…Elder…took to the high road," to paint billboards! In the left frame, we see that he has painted moustaches on kid's faces and in the right—another witty detournement of Duchamp's famous iconoclastic gesture—Elder "paints the moustache off the man from Shleppes." In the lower panel, the phrase "Hot Lips Lipschitz" (a somewhat salacious reference to the American modernist sculptor), is painted in red letters on a drum with a picture of the sun setting on a tropic isle. A reclining nude beach bunny completes this low cult collapsing of the symbolic codes and sacraments of high culture. The lower three frames of the panel show examples of the artist's 'scape' period that includes: "land-scapes…sea scapes…and fire escapes!"

The next page marks an exciting departure in the work of this young avant-garde artist. Elder has advanced to produce his first, very contemporary looking abstract work, an upside-down electrical wiring diagram for a public address amplification system titled, once again in MAD's dead pan fashion, Chicken Fat. His second 'abstract' is a drawing of the human circulatory system that has been summarily executed with a fingernail upon a blackboard and given the appropriate title ECHH! Elder's third artwork, again a vanguard work for the

1950s, is a detail of a weather map over the mid-western U.S. and Canada, titled ironically, Hurricane Carol. For his fourth 'abstract' Elder is introduced to the (sic) "type art where you distort an image to get two views at the same time, as in a playing card King of Hearts called simply Gin. This is followed in the next frame by a 'social realist' abstract #6 called Levittown (after the post WWII planned suburban communities designed by Levit) produced with saws, hammers, nails etc., and a pastiche of a Bufferin analgesic advertisement a favourite Ad for MAD satirists titled Urp! The ultimate irony here, is that none of these paintings are abstracts in the non-objective sense favored by many modernist artists, but they could have passed as ideas for pop art paintings of the kind that Lichtenstein and Warhol were producing in the early 1960s. Is this another instance of the ideas of popular modernists predicting the modernist avant-garde?

Like the artist Fidelman in Bernard Malamud's wonderful art world parody *Pictures of Fidelman: An Exhibition* (1969), who changes his style indiscriminately according to his whim, or his women, young Elder changes his style yet again, this time to work "in the line of Marcel Duchamp's *Nude Descending a Staircase*" to paint his extravagantly titled "I Dreamed I Descended a Staircase in my Playtex Underwear." This image consists of a chrono photographed image—recalling the early C20th images of Edward Muybridge or Jules-Etienne Marey—of six women dancing in their underwear, appropriated from, naturally, a Playtex ad. The following pages of this chapter of Elder's career reveal his growth from "sickening abstraction to nauseating realism." Here, photo realist representations of Ed Sullivan and a 3D Marilyn Monroe vie for attention with family snapshots. The lower frame shows a 'painting' ironically in "full cinemascope" with a typically tongue-in-cheek MAD direction: "Curve to view properly." The facing page contrasts these images with Elder's 'new' work: a representation of Leonardo's Mona Lisa, that the reader is informed is actually one Mona Coznowski; Gainsborough's Blue Boy; George Washington (a detail of the U.S. dollar bill); a reproduction of Vermeer's Young Woman with a Water Jug; Whistler's Mother and finally, to top it all, Michelangelo's Sistine ceiling frescoes, described hilariously as Elder's "most ambitious undertaking."

In the following chapter headlined THE COMMERCIAL ARTIST, we follow Elder's commercial career, somewhat of a continuation of his art career, in which, again following the prescriptions of Situationist *detournement* strategies, he reworks advertisements for a living. The opening image shows Elder painting a gigantic moustache on a billboard image of a model, a favourite MAD gesture in the first intense years of the magazine. The next page includes

Elder's ironic reworking of movie ads, romance magazines, service announcements and the like. The examples on the lower panel of the page show some of MAD's more aggressive humour seeking enterprises—an image of a hampster biting a finger adorned with the caption "It's Fun to Earn Raising Hampster," and a small adjacent image—a hunter sexually mounting a bird accompanied by a juvenile pun: "Learn at Home to MOUNT BIRDS." For northern readers there is also some Canadian content in the lower text of the advertisement that reads Canadian Specific, a pun on the Canadian Pacific Corporation. Included here also is an Elder realist original titled *Playing Croquet on the Front Lawn* (painting number I) in the series, Booze Life in America, a brilliant parody of a Norman Rockwell Saturday Evening Post cover, another very popular MAD target over the years.

The second to last chapter of the Elder biography is titled predictably THE OLD PRO. This section establishes the importance of the artist's mature work as an artist. The captions in the first panel inform us that by the time Elder had reached maturity as an artist, he had worked his way up to "the most important, the noblest, the finest, the bestest, bestest, finest, importantest type of commercial art yes you guessed it comic books!" This then, is the golden chapter of Elder's life as a famous artist and a triumphant example of MAD's cultural in/subordination, the total eclipse or collapse, of high art into low culture. The opening image places Elder in the foreground with his able assistants working behind him, scribbling many popular graffiti slogans: "Go Home Yankee," "Please Applaud," "Round 3," "Fresh Fish," the sophomoric "Free To(i)Let," and in the centre foreground, another trademark parody of a Picasso cubist painting of a woman. The lower panels are drawn in conventional comic book style with the accompanying caption informing the reader of the power of popular culture: "It was when the artist turned to comic books that his genius came to full flower." The next few pages carry a reprint of some of Elder's finest work, "to pad this comic book…," a story that had previously appeared in another MAD issue about one criminal mammal, Melvin Mole whom the editors inform us is a proverbial "man out 'a control." This odd addition to the Elder narrative, described as a "filler" to pad out the magazine to the appropriate length for the printer, can only be described as a MAD parody of itself. MAD, like a good stand-up comic, was never above self-parody, but self-satire was difficult, if not impossible to accomplish without completely undermining their critical raison d'etre.

The Final chapter of the Elder saga performs the perfect closure upon his biography, "SENILITY!" No longer, the ironic caption informs us, "does he measure things by the foolish standards of youth! No longer are his ideals guided by money! Today he enjoys a mellowed, sophisticated, enlightened state of mind, in other words SENILITY!" In keeping with this state, the first three frames of art works produced by the senile Elder are second childhood reversals of the original three art works from the first chapter, produced when Elder was a baby prodigy. The final frame reverses the text from the first, thus cleverly squaring the circle. The reader recalls that the earlier foci of Elder in the appropriated images showed the artist circled. In this famous Civil War image Elder is shown in army uniform with a square box around his head with caption below—MAD's typically over-the-top dedoublement ("Note Elder squared!"). The final pages of the magazine include legitimate ads for EC's short-lived MD comic, stamps, service announcements for employment and the ubiquitous Charles Atlas self-improvement ads that MAD would have included both for the benefit of the magazine's economy and its campy in-house humour.

The second MAD magazine I will consider briefly, as only the brilliant cover and "the story behind the cover" truly engage the rejective categories of modernist art from the primate technical position (even a monkey could do it!) previously discussed in Chapter 8. In this comic MAD's artist is one J. Fred Muggs a chimpanzee pictured dressed in his suit and spats accompanied by a brief caption revealing that he is contemplating the request by MAD to produce a cover painting. The photos on the verso show Muggs bereted and seated, reading a copy of MAD number 30, the famous final issue for 1956 that first introduced Alfred E. Neuman to MAD readers. The headline state-

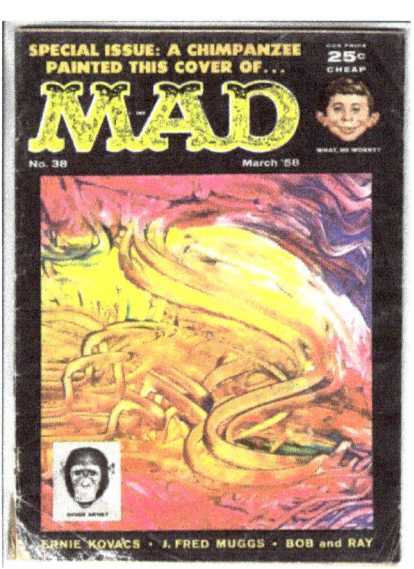

Figure 85: MAD March 1958 (cover)
Public Domain.

ment offers the reader "THE STORY BEHIND THE COVER (Mainly, this story is really behind the cover!)" Once again, MAD Magazine, in its ceaseless campaign to bring culture to America, scores a resounding artistic triumph with the publication of the first magazine cover ever painted by a chimpanzee. By bringing before the discerning public eye the talented work of J. Fred Muggs, MAD hopes that it has earned for him his rightful place among other truly great cover artists like Norman Rockwell, Steven Dohanos and Grandma Moses.

Maria Redelbach, Tod Gitlin and other writers have suggested that "self-denigration has been central to the spirit of MAD" and if "MAD encouraged the questioning of authority, it meant all authority including its own" (Redelbach, 188-89). In terms of MAD's political economy however, their ironic and satirical invectives were always softer when addressing subjects close to home, such as the work and life of the comic artist, a role that most of those associated with MAD—and certainly their readers—held in high esteem. MAD's parodic discourse establishes a complicity with the readers "only because (they) have persuaded them to reject the presuppositions (and power) of the parodied discourse, if indeed they ever accepted those presuppositions" (Bourdieu, 1993:93).

Critics have condemned MAD for being racist, sexist, homophobic and scatological (Reidelbach 188-9), and in a crucial sense, MAD's method symbolically represents the very forms of "othering" associated with these ideological formations and the social behaviors they prescribe. This is the psychological level at which MAD operates and to which their readers respond, both positively and negatively. In a crucial sense MAD's institutional parodies are a strange amalgam of fascination and repulsion of the kind that Homi Bhahba identifies with social stereotypy described in a crucial chapter on the psychoanalytical foundations of subalternity in his book *The Location of Culture* (1994).

Babha's psychoanalytic reworks both Franz Fanon's anti-colonial critiques of race and Edward Said's discussion of orientalism to reveal subalternity as a function of "othering" according to the determinations of stereotypy. Bhahba has this to say about the ambivalence of othering as a locus the prevalence of stereotyping:

> To recognize the stereotype as an ambivalent mode of knowledge and power demands a theoretical and political response that challenges deterministic or functionalist modes of conceiving of the relationship between discourse and politics" (Bhahba 1994: 66-67).

Bhabha argues that one's "otherness" is articulated stereotypically "at once (as) an object of desire and derision, an articulation of fantasy of origin and identity" (67). The othered stereotype is both fear and fetish which he gives a Lacanian twist. suggesting that there is "both a structural and functional suggestion for reading the racial stereotype of colonial discourse in terms of fetishism.

> Fetishism, as the disavowal of difference, is that repetitious scene around the problem of castration. The recognition of difference—as the precondition for the circulation of the chain of absence and presence in the realm of the Symbolic—is disavowed by the fixation on an object that masks the difference and restores an original presence. The functional link between the fixation of the fetish and the stereotype (or the stereotype as fetish) is even more relevant. (p. 67-8)

And subsequently, "fetishism is always a 'play' or vacillation between the archaic affirmation of wholeness/similarity—in Freud's terms" "all men have penises"; in Bhahba's (ours) : "All men have the same skin/race/culture" (and for my purposes—"all artists are neurotic")—and the anxiety associated with lack and difference again, for Freud "some do not have penises"; "some do not have the same skin/race/culture" (and some artists are not neurotic).

Bhabha goes on to assert that within colonial discourse, the fetish represents the simultaneous play between metaphor as substitution (masking absence and difference) and metonymy (which contiguously registers the perceived lack). the fetish or stereotype gives access to an "identity" which is predicated as much on mastery and pleasure as it is on anxiety and defence, for it is a form of multiple and contradictory belief in its recognition of difference and disavowal of it.

> and later "The scene of fetishism is also the scene of reactivation and repetition of the primal fantasy—the subjects desire for a pure origin that is always threatened by its division, for the subject must be gendered to be engendered, to be spoken. For both colonizer and colonized the "stereotype is the "primary point of subjectification" (75).

Many of MAD's send-ups display a commitment to the satirisation of the rich absurdities and injustices of contemporary life under capitalism, and any bureaucratic institutional and/or political orthodoxy. The anarchic spirit represented in MAD's satires may be read as both an index of resistance and accommodation (in/subordinations) to the dominant order. One can recognize the insightful critical intelligence of many of the early MAD issues that respond to the cultural mores and foibles of the day. We should acknowledge therefore the very distinctive and deeply political characteristics—both progressive and regressive—of the MAD humour represented in these two early magazines.

Mikhail Bakhtin has suggested that humour can serve several socio-political functions: it can represent attempts by subordinate groups to contest the power of a more dominant group, usually, in the medieval period, a monarchy. It can also serve to lubricate and ensure the efficient workings of the prevailing status quo, the hegemony of the dominant class(es). In the *Dialogic Imagination*, Bahktin theorized that these two operations can occur simultaneously—dialogically—that is humour can say one thing and mean another. A sign can be doubly coded, or, as he asserts in an important tract regarding the semiotic coding of language, "within a single utterance there may occur two intentions, two voices" (Matejka, 1971:180). Contemporary theorists of irony: Muecke (1969), Enright, (1986), Dane (1991), and Hutcheon (1994), acknowledge the heteroglossic character of irony and warn of the limitations of reductive and formalist definitions. Dane for instance, distinguishes between rhetorical irony, romantic irony and critical irony, arguing that "the history of irony and the novel involves the disparity between the language of the novel and that of the critic" (187). Linda Hutcheon provides a definition of parody that encompasses both literary and visual 'texts'. She argues that parody is a form of imitation, "but imitation characterized by ironic inversion, not always at the expense of the parodied text" (Hutcheon, 1985:55). Hutcheon argues that we must examine parody, satire and irony, in both their literary and visual forms, as processes of reading and interpretation. We must negotiate "the enunciation of the contextualized production and reception of texts, if we are to understand what constitutes [them]" (55). She developed an overlapping Venn diagram consisting of three circles: Satiric Ethos, Ironic Ethos and Parodic Ethos, in order to better explain the interrelationships between each form, arguing that while each ethos can harbour or invoke criticism, the satiric ethos has a slightly stronger proprietary interest in social critique and is therefore (potentially) more politically efficacious. Irony is inscribed in most forms of parody and satire and serves the interests of both humour and criticism. The danger of course, is confusing one for the other.

> **Lampoon**
> n. a personal satire – v.t. to assail with personal satire (From O.F. *lampon*) perhaps from a drinking song with the refrain lampons "let us drink." (Concise Oxford Dictionary)

The final art world comic I will discuss in this chapter is a special form of satire—a lampoon—defined in the dictionary entry above as a "personal satire" akin to the mocking style of the burlesque, defined as "a ludicrous imitation" (Oxford Dictionary). The subject of this National Lampoon satire is the New

York-based art world magazine Art News; the National Lampoon's ARTynews presents quite a different critique of modernist art than either the Disney or the MAD examples discussed earlier.

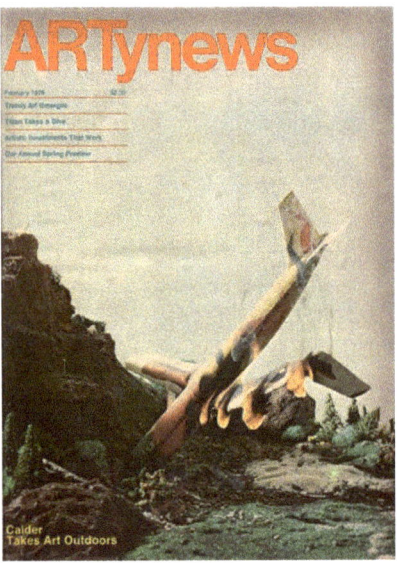

Figure 86: National Lampoon Cover, February 1976 Public Domain.

The publication cataloguing section of the first page provides the context for the Lampoon editors to deliver a straightforward announcement, but they quickly proceed to a high-pitched narcissistic whine, thus setting the sophomoric tone for the whole parody:

> "ARTynews is published monthly c. 1976 by ARTynews Associates. All rights reserved. No part of this magazine or cover may be published in any manner, in whole, or in part while feeling perturbed and upset and like you don't have any respect for us, as though we were the TIME magazine of the goddamn art world, for Chrissake!"

A large photo parody of an artwork by Alexander Calder graces the cover of the magazine. Captioned "Calder Takes Art Outdoors," the photograph shows a crash. of a Braniff airlines plane decorated with Calder's commissioned design. The contents page miniature of the cover, an Art News convention developed in the late 1960s, that the staff of the Lampoon has seen fit to parody, inserts a fake quote from Calder on his method of creation.

> When I complete a work of art, I know that my creations have their own destinies, I am merely their father (the artist in a recent interview).

In this context, Calder's creativity is destined for destruction. The page includes a typical Art News advertisement for an unusual artist material, "Auto-Spred," bearing the ironic endorsement "We take the labour out of art to leave you more time for life." The ad announces that "action drip works," "hard edge" and "colour field" can be produced effortlessly by the patented "Auto-Spred method" that employs the energy of Auto-Ants, each one transporting "a kwantum of colour to a different point on the canvas. Silently. Smoothly. Efficiently."

In sharp contrast to the best of the MAD satires and parodies which exist, typically, as complex heterogeneous ensembles of signs and are therefore richly unstable and unpredictable in their meaning, the typical National Lampoon *modus operandi* conforms to a type of juvenile mimicry (parody), with an ironic edge, a ludicrous sendup—less parody than pastiche: a change of a word there, a punning phrase here, a racy ironic twist, textual inversion or quick punch line, all aimed at the delivery of fast humour the humorist's version of fast food (junkfood)—for instant gratification. This is the somewhat facile working method of the Lampooners. The typical lampoon this is true of the magazine as it is of National Lampoon's television, films, and of the genre as a whole demands little creative effort from either the producers of the satire or its readers. A quick gasp of recognition is all that is required and then one moves on to the next one liner. Less laugh a minute, the conventional regimen of the stand-up comic, than continuous titter. Like Umberto Eco's semiotic analyses of Superman comics and Ian Fleming's James Bond novels, the typical Lampoon text is closed, conforming to its set (iterative) scheme. According to Eco:

> The device of iteration is one on which certain escape mechanisms are founded, particularly the types realized in television commercials: one distractedly watches the playing out of a sketch, then focuses one's attention on the punch line that appears at the end of the episode. It is precisely on this foreseen and awaited reappearance that our modest but irrefutable pleasure is based (Eco 1979, 117).

In Artynews for example, the contents page gives some indication of what is to follow in the iterative manner as described by Eco. Each of the art 'writers' listed here is a famous male crooner, their essay titles, quick and dirty puns: Mel Torme, Photo Realism or Real Photism…page 14; Jerry Vale, Going for Baroque…28 ;

Al Martino on Art and the Law...36; Buddy Greco, Less is more: Abrams opts for the small...74; Perry Como, The Inner Torment of Walter Cronkite...87; Jack Jones, Old Masters for a Perfect Master: the collection of the Guru Maharaj Ji...104; and Vic Damone, From The Fifth of May to a Can of Flan.

The Artynews Departments provide a similar pastiche of The Nation, a familiar exhibition events bulletin for regular Art News subscribers. This section of the lampoon lists exhibitions in Chicago: "Kandinsky at the Pump Room," a famous watering hole; Miami: "Ella at the Copa" (Copacabana); and ditto: "Joey Heatherton at Caesars Palace"; "Allen and Rossie at Lake Tahoe" and so on ad nauseum. The World bulletin announces the wildly unfunny: in "Warsaw: Polish Art is No Joke"; and in "Brussels: Galleries Sprout Wall Murals"; "Belfast: An Exploding Scene"; and "Johannesburg: Malevich's All White Canvases."

The editorial board list replaces the names of the existing 1977 Art News publisher and editors with Frank Sinatra as the new king pin (a mafioso father figure), his daughter Nancy as managing editor, and the rest of the family, Frank Sinatra Junior and Tina Sinatra as associate editors. The inside pages begin with a type of Playboy magazine pastiche of Botticelli's Venus, a la Varga by one Ken Crass (Wayne Mclaughlin) titled *The Tragedy of Marylin Monroe*, 1974 (acrylic on canvas 98 x 60 inches), Collection, Johnny Carson Foundation." The work is reviewed in mock heroic fashion by one "I.M Roode" (a juvenile pun for "I Am Rude.")

The large centrepiece of Ken Crass's *The Tragedy of Marylin Monroe* is a touching frontal portrait of the famous star, capturing the doll-like innocence of her features—the tremendous vulnerability of a child woman in a world that was cruel to her. Both side panels are odalisques in the manner of Botticelli of the Gabor sisters. Zsa Zsa and Eva appear quite serene amidst billowy effusions of pastel flesh, voluptuous and classic. The three panels form a work that would have to be described as a thought-provoking comment on myth making in particular and American society in general.

The facing page carries the "Vasari Diary" department containing a somewhat more arresting parody of the Art News editorial page with its usual inside dopester and groupie news of the day. Those present at the Zad Zed opening at the Museum of Museum Art found thrust into their hands a broadside mimeographed by the Soho Post-Art Peoples Caucus, an activist group exploring the connection between art and politics. I have reproduced the text of that document in its entirety below, my only prefatory comment being that most ARTynews readers know what is to be done should the shoe fit.

MAD'S Mad Art World and The Art News of National Lampoon   267

The Museum in question is of course the Museum of Modern Art, and the fictional "Soho Post-art Peoples caucus," either Artists Working for Cultural Change, or the Art Workers Coalition, both of which were active groups in the Soho art nexus of the late 1970s. The political tract begins, Futurist manifesto style with "Before you read this destroy a piece of art in the gallery…" and concludes after two columns of fulminating idiocy with: "tear up the art books, the coffee table monographs. Send the scraps to Hiroshima, Vietnam, the Jersey Isles." The advertisement in the lower section of this page is a targeted art world lampoon of the new book from the desk of prolific art critic and international cultural power broker, "Barbara Nose" (Rose)—her book, another fake, of course—is titled *The Beginning*. Promotional notes accompany the reproduction of the book, its cover graced with a crushed Campbell's Soup Can cover, itself a satire of one of Andy Warhol's famous Pop parodies.

"The caveman," says Marshall Buckfuller, "was the first cool spectator at a hot event." From this exciting premise springs, a major new work from a widely respected authority on Gothic, Renaissance, Mannerist, Flemish, Abstract Expressionist, Pop, Minimal, Conceptual, and Pre-Historic Art. "No one had time to attend an exhibition," she writes in the introduction, "more immediate problems, like survival predominated. Also, the nonexistence of serial time would have made such scheduling almost impossibly difficult." Insights such as this are generously sprinkled along the path of the reader's tour, a path that begins at the beginning, the infancy of pictorial art." The advertisement ends with a note about the book's "Special Chapters" covering: "Rituals and Magic, Ancestor Worship, Early Wallpaper, Cave Dada, Cave Op," and last but not least, "Cave In."

A 'feature' article titled "Futurism Reconsidered" by Paul M. Pasto is accompanied by an image of Umberto *sic* Braccioli's *Dynamism of a Dog Descending a Staircase*. This image works as a true pastiche in the definitive sense of the term, combining in one extraordinary image Marcel Duchamp's *Nude Descending a Staircase* (1912) and Giacomo Balla's famous painting *Dynamism of a Dog on a Leash* (1912), attributing the final 'work' to the painter Umberto Braccioli, actually Umberto Boccioni, the famous Futurist colleague of Marinetti, Balla, Carra, Severini and their colleagues. This pastiche neatly signals the historical relationships between the painting of the Italians and Duchamp's famous 'Explosion in a Shingle Factory', well documented in the texts by Barr (1954), Soby (1934) and Sweeney (1934), who participated in the canonic construction of MOMA's collection of important modernist art from the early twentieth century avant-gardes. It is tempting to credit the author(s) of the text with an insider's knowledge of the history of Futurism. Only someone with an intimate understanding of the history of futurism, particularly founder Marinetti's political platform for futurist cooking, that would have outlawed the use of pasta because it made the Italian male a poor soldier and sluggish in bed, would understand the subtexts of this parody. But this is probably a happy coincidence, lying in wait for the art history buff. The article begins "Milan— Fill the museum with pasta!" and "The Pope is a Trombone!" and follows with the announcement of a retrospective "Futurism: Lunacy or Insanity," a parodic denunciation that recalls the earlier graphics satires of Futurism and Futurist art discussed in earlier chapters.

This article continues with a pastiche of the titles of paintings in this fake retrospective: Accompanying Braccioli's *Dynamism of a Dog Descending a Staircase*, there is Marinara Spaghetti's *The Noise of the City Rises* up into the Cab and smashes the Anarchist Gaggi in the face, a pastiched reference to two famous paintings that have graced the MOMA gallery walls, Boccioni's *The City Rises* (1910), and Carlo Carra's *Funeral of the Anarchist Galli* (1910-11). Giacomo Belli's dynamic fake study *Steam Turbines Dancing Along a Balcony at the Bal Tabarin* is framed by a pastiche of the Futurist manifesto that is punned effortlessly phrase for phrase, and at times word for word.

> Our utter contempt for all that is moth ridden, worm eaten, dog eared snail paced and backwards leaves us limp with indignation and rage. Hatred boils in our veins for the flatulent, pathetic, fossilized forms of "art" now blessed by the neurasthenic cowards of the so-called academy, effets and charlatans and gasbags whom the somnambulant public is quick to obey with slavish docility. From now on, all that is atavistic, traditional, amend archaic must be banished from our sight. Ours is the age of speed: henceforth the dynamo is our mother, the factory our father, the automobile our uncle, the airplane our aunt, the bridges our cousins, the steamship our grandfather, and the locomotive our grandmother from Turin who sends us melons and cheeses every Christmas. Let every man who fancies himself a painter strip naked and daub himself with factory sludge![1]

Another regular Art News column, New York Reviews, appears in this context. It includes three reviews with illustrations of the work of artists (sic) Klay Raisenbunn at Kissandtelli (Kiss and Telli), Uptown; Visual Arts Gallery; a

---
1. "Futurism Reconsidered" by Paul M. Pasto National Lampoon Artists and Models, August 1976.

pastiche of Klee Reisenborn and Castelli uptown Zad Zed (Imawreck) whose work, a game of Tic Tac Toe, is a no win drawing described as "one of a series of 417 canvases depicting a flat space monochrome abstract pattern of lines, crosses and circles arranged in a primarily totemic design" with commentary by Thomas Hiss, a cheap wordplay on the name of Thomas Hess, former Art News Editor. Philip Godfrey Ear (Midtown), the third artist profiled, bears a remarkable resemblance to Happening's inventor Alan Kaprow, and is presented in accompanying photographs on the facing page. In the top photo he is shown executing a performance piece titled *This Is My Arm* with the caption, "Process is everything" parodying late modernism's self-evident assumptions, and in the lower photograph he is shown "finding" an object (choosing a readymade), for a client in "New York, December 1967." Contradicting himself he is quoted with "I don't believe in process." Ear's reviewer tips his hat in the direction of Robert Russianbucks (Rauschenberg), who attested *a la* Yves Klein to the 'authenticity' of one of this artist's works.

The next two pages contain two more parodies of fake Art News departments, "Collage" and "The World." An advertisement above the Collage essay announces the publication of a work "destined to become a classic in the field of art scholarship," the 32-volume *Encyclopedia of Teeth in Art*. These volumes contain essays with inventive titles by real life art historians: Bernard Berensen, "The Root Canals of Venice"; Dore Ashton, "Concerning Stubb's Horses and Canines," together with punned fake endorsements from other leading art historians (sic) "A bracing accomplishment" (John Canaday, New York Times); and "The most compelling tooth history of art since Vasari's Cupid and Psyche." attributed to John Rewald, New York Review of Books.

Although Artynews is at times complex within in its own iterative scheme when compared to the first MAD satires discussed, the National Lampoon does not function on different registers of meaning. It is not as richly textured, multi-layered, metaphorical, or heteroglossic, as the richest parody or satire. Its strengths, snappy puns, fast delivery, instant appreciation, are also its principal weaknesses. The lampoon is close to the rebus form and unlike the best ironies, satires and parodies rarely transcends its own subject, or indeed, its own genre type. To be successful, the lampoon must closely parody its subject and when the subject itself is a magazine that is predominately language based, containing few images, the modes of address conform to several specific types of linguistic word play. Puns, spoonerisms, reversals, alliteration and assonance, linguistic ellipses and transpositions of various kinds are the staples of the lampoon, and as such rarely match some of the scripto-visual complexity, allegorical narratives and biting criticism of the most successful MAD satires. There is a popular French saying that "he who would pun would pick a pocket." The ArtyNews lampoon is a much less successful assault on the institutions of modernism than the first MAD satire discussed in this chapter—a petty pick pocket in a crowded subway, compared to the architects of the Great Train Robbery.

CHAPTER 12

Thalia Meets Melpomene[1]

> The hostility of the working class and of the middle-class fractions least rich in cultural capital towards every kind of formal experimentation asserts itself both in theatre and in painting, or still more clearly in photography and the cinema. (Bourdieu, P. 1984:32)

The 1990s witnessed a number of extraordinary plays, or performances, involving the plight of the institution art and its public. These performances had bizarre titles, elaborate scenarios and a cast of disreputable players. In downtown Manhattan played Serra's *The Destruction of Tilted Arc*; Washington D.C. premiered *Eros Presumptive*, and back in New York, the curtain opened upon *The Plastic Crucifix in Urine*, these latter two performances dubbed jointly in the popular press as the 'Mapplethorpe, Serrano, Helms Affair.'[2] In Canada there was Vancouver's spectacular *Sniffy the Rat*,[3] a preliminary to Ottawa's controversial *Voice of Fire*, and *Flesh Dress* performances.

It is not my intention here to link these controversial performances, unveiling them as significant acts in a comic-drama of epic proportions, although I must admit the temptation to do so is great. Neither is it my intention, notwithstanding the title and introduction to this chapter, to parody the

---

1. Sections of this Chapter were prepared as a paper under the title "Thalia meets Melpomene: The Higher Meaning of the *Voice of Fire* and *Flesh Dress* Controversies" for a conference organised by Art History faculty from the University of British Columbia which was to take place in Vancouver in 1990. Unfortunately, the conference did not take place for lack of funding. A version of the paper was read subsequently at the annual meeting of the University of Art Association of Canada, held in Kingston's Ontario in 1993 in a session titled *Disciplinarity: Questioning the Borderlines of Art History* chaired by Mark Cheetham (University of Western Ontario). I would like to thank Chris Creighton-Kelly of the Canada Council and Diana Nemiroff, Curator of Canadian Contemporary Art at the National Gallery of Canada for providing me with many of the press clippings for this paper. The paper was subsequently published in Barber, B. Guilbaut, S. and O'Brian, J. *Voices of Power: Art, Rage, Power and the State* Toronto: University of Toronto, Press (1996).

2. For a thorough survey of documents and essays covering the Mapplethorpe and Serrano controversies see Bolton, Richard (ed) *Culture Wars: Documents from the Recent Controversies in the Arts*. New York: The New Press (1992)

3. A young artist announced that he was going to kill a rat as a work of art.

parodied, since the recognition of the tragi-comic circumstances of these performances have already shrunk into the dark crevices of contemporary history. However, I will argue that the fertile conditions for the reproduction of these performances are still very much with us, and for this reason alone, they are worthy of our re-examination, not so much for what they may reveal about the health of art, a subject of continuing concern today, but for what they can tell us about the institutions of art and the plight of their publics.

This case study is an investigation of what I will call the higher meaning of these performances, one that takes as its point of entry, the signatures of those actors at the margins of the production of meaning, who participate nevertheless, in the extended field of cultural reproduction, contaminating the institutional discourses with their chatter, questioning institutional verities with their laughter. I am speaking here of the media and its agents: writers, editors, cartoonists (ironists, satirists, parodists), those interpreters and critics, architects perhaps, of public opinion, who for better and for worse, have a hand on the fevered brow of our culture. In engaging, or better, negotiating the territory at the margins, I will attempt to rescue the *higher* meaning of two of these controversial performances from the clutches of those who would wish them away as isolated and aberrant attempts at state intervention, misguided initiatives of arrogant misanthropes, red necks, miscreants, and philistine.

Our task here then, is to examine the *Voice of Fire* and *Flesh Dress* controversies as these were represented (played out), in the media as examples of what has been described previously in earlier chapters as "the struggle over the meaning of the sign," or signs, for in their separate ways, the *Voice of Fire* and *Flesh Dress* controversies represent struggle(s) over the meaning of an ensemble of intersecting signs, differently oriented, and *accented*: art, architecture, culture, history, capital, education, religion, gender, sexuality, and class. In keeping with the themes established earlier in this book, I will argue that these struggles over the meaning of the signs represent attempts from various constituencies to either accommodate, and sustain, or resist, the hegemony of the dominant culture. This chapter represents a contemporary case study of the process I have described as cultural in/subordination and permits us to examine a range of media and institutional responses to the intrusion of high culture on the consciousness of individuals within different constituencies, social groups and constituencies: from the highest levels of government, the boardrooms of The Nation, the lunchrooms and restaurants, to the proverbial figure on the street. And while the individuals from these various constituencies—perhaps we should call them *classes*—may speak the same language(s), their use of it may be imbued with differently oriented *accents*, reinforcing, underscoring, different types of criticism, privileging in transfigured (symbolic) form separate, identifiable, and often competing ideologies.

We should examine a few of these accents as these were represented in the media. Our method will be this: first we will familiarize ourselves with a few of the facts of the controversies, the purchase of Barnett Newman's *Voice of Fire*, and the exhibition of Jana Sterbak's *Flesh Dress*, then proceed to an overview of the press reports, letters, graphic satires and performance parodies,[4] bearing in mind that we are examining the symbolic representation of the struggle over competing meanings, perhaps better described now, as the *political economy* of the sign(s). In the *Voice of Fire* controversy, the focus will be upon the cartoons, news reports, editorials and letters produced during a four week period (March 8-April 8); and with the *Flesh Dress* one year later, upon several graphic satires printed in various contexts over a one week period (April 4-11, 1991). The chapter will conclude with a review of some of the historical reasons for the contestation over the meaning of the sign, a reductive schema of class based attacks on the avant-garde and some comments concerning the reasons why the most advanced modernist cultural practice has so engaged the public ire.

The nineteenth and early twentieth century had their share of both private and public controversies about art. Unlike many subsequent examples, however, these were related predominantly to the exhibition, and not the sale of works.[5] This change can be attributed to a number of factors, including the decline, some would say, the death of the modernist or historical avant-garde(s), increasing participation by the State in the cultural sphere, represented by increased public funding of artists, museums, art institutions, and finally, the heating up of the international art market at the conclusion of the Second World War.

---

4. The terms irony, satire and parody have quite distinct meanings in this chapter. I have noted these in passing. Graphic satire is used specifically in reference to newspaper cartoons which have a critical and subversive intent. Performed parodies refer to individuals who have (re)produced their own versions of the Voice of Fire as "ironic inversions" and as acts of resistance. Differences lie in the degree of ironic emphasis given to each representation either by the producer or the recipient. For an examination of the specific debates on the differences between parody, irony and satire see chapter 4.

5. Both the exhibition and sale are at the basis of the two examples in this study, with the primary relationship between the two, State funding.

A survey of the recent history of significant public controversies precipitated by the purchase of major works of art by publicly funded institutions would include the mid 1970s purchase by Australia's National Gallery of Jackson Pollock's painting Blue Poles,[6] the Tate Gallery's purchase in 1972 of Carl Andre's famous low sculpture rectangle of fire bricks[7] and the 1990 National Gallery of Canada's purchase of the Barnett Newman painting *Voice of Fire*, each of which commanded an extraordinary amount of press time,[8] one standard measure, at least since the invention of the printing press, of the importance of a public controversy.

An examination of each case would reveal many similarities of a structural or institutional nature to take our theatrical metaphor a little further—the cast of characters, script, *mise en scene*, production schedule, funding, promotion etc., beginning with an institution's decision to purchase the work, and the accompanying infra-institutional wrangling over its cost, its relevance and value to the collection, and available financing. Following this process, the purchase of the work, its delivery and public unveiling, this prefaced by the press release, quiet, if some opposition is anticipated, loud, and triumphant if not. And, given the convention of press releases, this occasions the release, or unleashing of the press. Responses from the fourth estate may vary widely, depending most significantly upon the nature of the public debates attending the purchase, but also upon such difficult to analyze factors as the political (ideological), alliances of those in positions of power within the press hierarchy, the editors, the owner(s) as well as those positions, and values held, by the authors of the reports, essays, and cartoons, the writers and cartoonists themselves. The public and press responses may be acclamatory if the gallery purchase is 'safe', but declamatory, that is, noisy—the object of savage denunciation—if the purchase is deemed questionable. This is the *sine qua non* of the average art controversy. Criticism emanates from and circulates within various discursive communities, often challenged and rechallenged.

---

6. In 1974 the Australian Postal Corporation published a Blue Poles stamp to commemorate the purchase. In another attempt to give State endorsement to the purchase, the Australian Prime Minister of the time, Gough Whitlam, and his wife, distributed the image on their Christmas card.

7. This Andre work (1965), was purchased in 1972 but the furore about the Tate gallery acquisition did not occur until four years later when the purchase was made public. This provides a useful example of the important role of the media in both generating and promoting a public controversy.

8. In all three cases there was generous radio and television coverage as well.

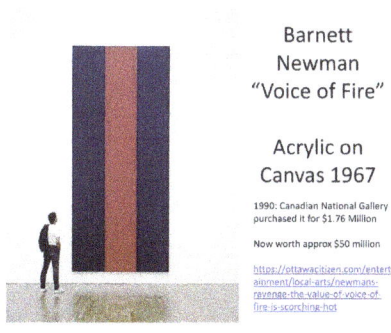
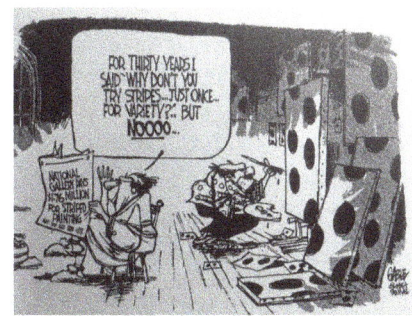

Figure 87: Barnett Newman *Voice of Fire* 1967 © Ottawa Citizen.

Figure 88: Brian Gable Globe & Mail March 17th, 1990.

To review briefly the circumstances surrounding the purchase: In August 1989, Barnett Newman's painting was acquired by the National Gallery of Canada Head of Collections, Brydon Smith, on behalf of the Gallery for the price of $C1.76 million ($US1.6 million), a figure which was subsequently rounded off in many of the media reports to $C1.8 million. On March 7th, 1990, approximately six months after the purchase, *Voice of Fire* was included in a press release announcing the acquisition of some 226 purchases, together with 185 gifts for the year. Within a few days of the announcement, a number of important events transpired. On March 8th the Gallery's press release was commented upon in the Globe and Mail, Canada's national daily newspaper, and then quickly responded to from a number of quarters. On March 9th Felix Holtmann, then Chair of the House of Commons Standing Committee on Culture and Communications, raised the alarm with his very quotable "looks like a couple cans of paint, a roller and ten minutes should do the trick!"[9]

This was not the first time that Newman had his work accused of being painted with a house painter's roller. In an unsympathetic review of the exhibition "American Paintings 1945-47" at the Minneapolis Institute of Arts June 18-September 1 1957, Frank Getlein of the New Republic magazine wrote that at the show's opening someone told organizer Stanton Catlin that "The Institute could have saved a good chunk by getting the plan and having the thing run off by the janitors with rollers" New Republic 137 no's 9-10 August 26, 1957:.21 Newman's reply: The New Republic 137, no 19 October 28, 1957:23, requoted in O'Neill, John P. *Barnett Newman Selected Writings and Interviews* New York: Alfred A. Knopf (1990:210)

---

9. Holtmann's comments were broadcast on an open line radio program in Winnipeg.

Most recently, the repair work undertaken on Newman's slashed painting *Whose Afraid of Red, Yellow and Blue* caused some Dutch historians unhappy with the results to claim that the N.Y. conservator had used a roller. And in the weeks that followed his comment was reproduced *ad nauseam*, in the press, on radio, and television, tempered somewhat by comments from Culture Minister of the time, Marcel Masse, and reinforced by Don Mazankowski, then deputy Prime Minister in the Conservative government of Brian Mulroney.

Unofficially, beginning March 8th, the first performance parodists and satirists began their acts. Bob Beland an Ottawa area silkscreen artist reportedly stated that "for a mere $20.000" he would sell, to anyone interested, a cotton short-sleeved T-shirt with his own pastiche rendition of the *Voice of Fire* screen printed on it. "I think it's a good price," he said, "heck of a deal." Former house painter, turned farmer, John Czupryniak from the Ottawa suburb of Nepean painted his own *Voice of Fire*, and propped it against a fence on his farm. "It took a whole day to do. Everybody loves it," said the artist. The painting "cost him $190.00 in materials," he continued, "and is intended as a statement on behalf of the average taxpayer."[10] The next day, a painting bearing the ironic title *Echo of Fire*, painted by Dave Lesosky and Dave Trendle, was reproduced in the Victoria Times Colonist, with the caption revealing that it had a "fire sale price of 3.2 million." Over the next two weeks cartoons, reports and letters to the editor appeared in many of the French and English dailies across Canada. In the conventional language of journalese many of the reports evidenced a certain objective gloss. However, a closer examination of thirty news reports reveal that opinion was clearly divided over the purchase, with even some of the most positive commentaries clearly demonstrating ambivalence on some aspects of the purchase, particularly the cost of the painting and the timing of the announcement. Unwilling, or without the time to engage in some direct reportage, many of the authors of the reports reproduced sections of the first Canadian Press report that relied heavily upon information provided by the Gallery both in their initial news release, and subsequent public statements, trotting out what became the standard line of defence for the purchase: that Newman's painting is of international significance; other galleries would borrow it for their exhibitions, and the NGC could expect favors in return. The purchase would raise the profile of the contemporary collection, and the international reputation of the new National Gallery designed by Moshe Safdie and finally, the addition of the painting would increase the number of gallery visitors.

---

10. Canadian Press Report Halifax Mail Star March 16, 1990.

A minority of the reports attempted to maintain the expected level of objectivity through a selective contrasting of quotes from individuals on various sides of the controversy, including Government figures, staff from the National Gallery, representatives from the cultural community, including CAR (Canadian Artists Representation), dealers, critics and members of the public. The academic community was conspicuously absent from most of these reports. The objective gloss that many of the authors attempted to sustain, was often undermined severely by the ironic headlines accompanying the report, possibly the result of an intervention from those with editorial power within the newsroom hierarchy. Many of these editors appropriated part, or all of the title of Newman's painting, to provide a proverbial 'hook' for the reader, thus producing a crop of headlines from local and national newspapers directly parodying the purchase, and indirectly adding more fuel to the controversy: "Can this voice put out the fire?"; "National Gallery made a tactical error in not fanning the fire"; "Fire The Curators"; "Painting's elitist message sure to make Canadians burn"; "Cabinet under fire for decision to review 1.8 million art deal"; "Heat's on as *Voice* outrage deepens," and "Masse Sidesteps Firestorm." Even a much later report appearing several months after the controversy had left the editorial pages, appropriated the painting's title for its 'Voices of Fire' trivia point on the history of volcanic eruptions for the Social Studies section of the Globe and Mail.

The news reports and editorials tended to reduce criticism to a number of distinct categories: the timing of the announcement, the cost of the purchase, specifically its percentage of the Gallery's total yearly purchase budget, the quality of the work, and the fact that it was by a dead American artist, not a living (or dead), Canadian one. In their reductive and somewhat repetitive form, these criticisms tended to mask the complex and often contradictory nature of many of the debates. For instance, the performed parodies of the painting, and the critical discussions represented in many of the reports, represented a whole range of stereotypical responses regarding the value of contemporary, specifically abstract art, the issue of state funding for the arts, the role of the artist, and the function of museums within society. The criticisms also invoked a number of political positions with respect to the role of public museums, institutional autonomy, state funding, and even national identity, which ironically, was used by all sides in the debate to reinforce their own ideological positions, whether these be nationalist, pro-Canadian, anti-statist, anti-American, or internationalist in origin.

As far back as May 1988, when the painting first entered the new National Gallery of Canada building, NGC senior curator Brydon Smith had expected, in his words, "tough sailing" on the purchase. However as Globe and Mail staff writer Stephen Godfrey (G&M Sat. April 7), pointed out, the Gallery's March 7 press release acknowledging the purchase, could not have come at a worse time, with the Canadian public reeling from the proposed goods and services tax, acrimonious parliamentary debates on increasing unemployment, and the results of free trade with the U.S., increasing business failures, personal bankruptcies, and deepening problems with the auto, lumber, textiles and fishing industries.

Faced with the opposition played out publicly in various forms in the media, within committees, and other more private venues, the NGC went on the defensive, stereotyped well before Star Trek made it a household phrase, as 'damage control'. The institution positioned its defenses relative to the most important attacks, those from Government and important figures in the media. Additional documents were sent out, selective interviews given to members of the press in an attempt to quell the rising tide of critical responses. The NGC produced a brochure on the purchase that backfired somewhat, indirectly providing a parody of its intended purpose and further evidence for some, of the incompetence of the Gallery staff. The flyer was printed back to front, a classic mistake reminiscent of the stereotypical abstract painting hung upside down, itself the content of an Unger generic striped abstract *Voice of Fire* cartoon (March 5, 1985), published in an April 7th issue of the Globe and Mail. The printing mistake was revealed by Kyle Brown, an observant young viewer from Edmonton, who noticed that the male viewer's jeans label was in reverse. National Gallery spokesperson Helen Murphy affirmed Brown's perception. "The Gallery has a policy of never showing a work flopped (in reverse)," she said, "but in this instance it was a rush job. We wanted to get the information out as quickly as possible, and we didn't look at the brochure proofs. At that point 50,000 had been printed so we distributed them. The next printing will be correct."

Written by curator Brydon Smith, the brochure text attempted to respond to several criticisms of the purchase. The claim that the painting was 'unCanadian' was dismissed with a reference to the reason for its creation "he created it as his contribution to Expo '67 in Montreal," a claim that is disputed in one of the standard reference works on Newman which does not state definitively that the work was produced expressly for Expo. In a parenthetical statement following his description of the painting, Thomas B. Hess wrote:

> This is the only time that Newman used the eighteen-foot dimension for a vertical painting, and he had practically no hope of exhibiting it as there are few ceilings high enough to accommodate it. By a *happy chance* however, he was invited by Alan Solomon to show it in Buckminster Fuller's United States pavilion at Expo '67, Montreal, and the picture was seen there and later in Boston. (Hess 1971:14) [my emphasis][11]

In his defence of the painting, Smith underlined the connections between Newman and those Canadian artists whom he inspired Guido Molinari, Robert Murray and Claude Tousignant. The text extolled the virtues of this "simple painting…complex in form that can convey a range of meanings for those viewers who are willing to slow down and approach it with an open mind." Commenting upon the structure of the painting "while there is twice the quantity of blue the red band is just as important…as the two blue ones. Each part remains separate, and yet all co-exist as a whole"—Smith concluded that this "acts as a reminder of what it is to be independent and free of domination while at the same time part of a larger world." Smith's invocation of the Constitution debates in Canada; a reminder of why Canadians should entrench the Distinct Society Clause for Quebec in the Canadian Constitution, occasioned an ironic response from several writers. The Globe and Mail's Bronwyn Drainie, for instance, wrote: "Hey, a kind of artistic gloss on Meech Lake, Europe in 1991 and perestroika, all in one painting!" (G&M April 21)

If we were to situate the Newman's painting back into its time of production we would have to carefully consider its role as a repository or vehicle for this kind of direct political association, as distinct from its religious or spiritual references, that became the subject of many commentaries and reviews. Even given Newman's lifelong attachment to politics (in 1933 he ran in the mayoralty election in New York), and the fact that some of his later works including *Lace Curtain for Mayor Daley* (1968), produced in protest to the riots and arrests attending the 1968 Democrat Convention in Chicago, exist as a direct commentary on a political situation, the artist, at least after his first solo exhibition in 1950, at Betty Parson's Gallery in New York City, was careful not to suggest in published statements about his work that his paintings could be read politically or be considered politically efficacious. In fact, to be successful in Newman's terms the work of art had to acquire some transcendent condition *over* politics.

---

11. The artist's wife Annalee Newman has reconfirmed that the painting was painted expressly for Expo 67. I have no reason to dispute this claim, but I remain sceptical as to what point in its production it became a painting specifically for Expo.

"Painting, like passion," he wrote, "is a living voice, which when I hear it, I must let speak, unfettered." (O'Neill, 1993:179)

However, in so far as it is true that no artist's work exists within a vacuum, but rather within special social and political contexts which have the capacity to change their meaning over time, it may be argued also, that Newman's works obtained specific meanings in relation to these contexts, both at the time of his paintings' production and subsequently, as they entered different social and political realities, and became subject to the machinations of various discursive communities. Unlike some others of his generation, Newman was supremely aware of the importance of context in the production and one could add, the de(con)struction, of meaning for his work. It is interesting in this respect to compare his comments on the relationship between politics and art from the early years of his career, to those he expressed in the last interview before his death in 1970. In his 1933 mayoralty campaign candidacy paper "On the Need for Political Action by Men of Culture" he opposed the interests of the artist to those of the worker, insisting that the artist's labour should be free, and s/he should not be expected to produce works of use to society:

> It is only the slave psychology of masses in chains, given expression in the Marxian parties that insists that art must be useful. The worker recognizes the true creative artist as his enemy, because the artist is free and *insists* upon freedom. It is therefore a contradiction of his own nature for any artist to hope for anything more from the worker than from the politician. O'Neill, 8)

In the 1970 interview, Newman's position on the freedom of the artist was reiterated from the position of someone who is reviewing the stability of his beliefs over the course of several decades. However, this statement presents a very different emphasis on freedom and conveys quite different political meanings:

> Some twenty-two years ago, in a gathering, I was asked what my painting really means in terms of society, in terms of the world, in terms of the situation. And my answer then was that if my work were properly understood, it would be the end of state capitalism and totalitarianism. Because to the extent that my painting was not an arrangement of graphic elements, was an open painting, in the sense that it represented an open world—to that extent I thought, and I still believe, that my work in terms of its social impact does denote the possibility of an open society, of an open world, not of a closed institutional world. (307-8)

Beyond the tinge of romantic idealism and latent utopianism which marks both statements, the latter one, represents a curious mixing of political ideologies. It is tempting to relate Newman's' position on artistic freedom to that exhibited by his contemporaries, the kind of thinking which Serge Guilbaut and others have recently identified as a kind liberalism, a quixotic transmutation of the Schlesingerian "politics of the vital centre" (Guilbaut 1983:68-9,) or Eliotic Trotskyism (T.J. Clark), that supplanted the anarchism, Marxism and Trotskyism of the 1930s and early 1940s. Newman's remarks can also be compared to those of another foe of fascism, Karl Popper whose famous dissertation on democracy and freedom, *The Open Society and Its Enemies*, engaged a wide, if critical, readership when it was first published in 1945.

Notwithstanding the artist's own ambivalence toward the direct representation of politics in art, the NGC purchase of *Voice of Fire* became as much a symbolic vehicle for political use as it had been in its first Canadian exhibition context at the 1967 World's Fair in Montreal. The painting was not simply a site for a transcendent aesthetic experience, rather it became, in the minds of some, an active signifier in search of some signifieds. Given both the ripe circumstances of its original showing in Montreal, and its subsequent purchase by the National Gallery, these were easily attached. For instance, in defending the purchase, both NGC curator Smith, and NGC spokesperson Helen Murphy, indirectly paraphrased the open society model implicit in Newman's statement by suggesting that Newman's painting illustrates a "borderless, frontier-less society…where there are no frontiers for ideas, visual arts or design" (Ottawa Sun March 18). Many defenders of the purchase supported this view including, for example, John Cruikshank (G&M March 16), who suggested in his positive review of the purchase, that "Canada can best promote its cultural vitality by a policy of openness to the world, including the United States."

We may identify several primary sites of meaning contestation—economic, political, moral and aesthetic—to the purchase of the *Voice of Fire*, each of which bears some relation to the conventional rejective categories for abstract art that were introduced in Chapter 8. These are clearly articulated in the nineteen cartoons, published in various papers that helped to fuel the controversy over the course of the two-month period.

Ottawa cartoonist Dave Beresford's (Ottawa Citizen March 10, 1990) was among the first of these. His image shows a plaid shirted figure gleefully painting a moustache on the central 'zip' of the Newman painting. This graphic satire cliche has a venerable history dating from Marcel Duchamp's famous iconoclastic gesture on a reproduction of the Leonardo *Mona Lisa* that he titled *L.H.O.O.Q*, a linguistic pun based upon the sound of the letters in French meaning "she has a hot bottom." As a sign of rejection, the moustache in Beresford's image relates also to Newman's own moustache which he had a tendency to curl in similar fashion to that expressed in the cartoon. A second cartoon by Zazulak, (Toronto Star Mar 14, 1990) shows two figures, conversing in front of the Newman painting, one a cultured Quebecois in a beret, the other a Anglo Canadian philistine. The Quebecer's statement reads:

> I see it as an abstract expression of our country divided. The blue background symbolic of the potential harmony between English and French isolated by a blazing redneck stripe...a contemporary mirror. What do you see?

To which the Philistine answers dismissively, "1.8 million down the toilet."

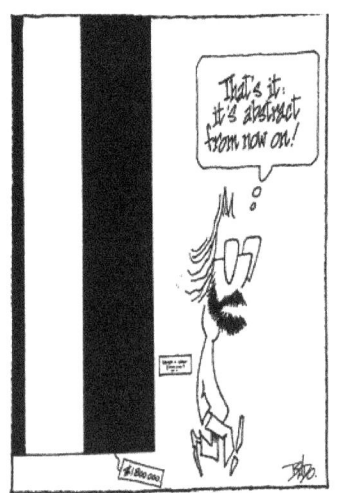

Figure 89: Bado (Guy Badeaux) Le Droit (Montreal) March 15, 1990.

Bado's cartoon example from Le Droit, (Fig 86), illustrates an artist figure, perhaps the cartoonist himself, walking past the base of the painting with its price tag of $1.8 million "C'est decide je me lance dans l'art abstrait!" which translates as "Its decided. I will launch myself into abstract art!" Another cartoon produced by King for the Ottawa Citizen (March 15) titled "Canvas Controversy" has a curator in six frames blandly delivering a formalistic description of the painting "Notice the delicate interplay of verticality and horizontality, the stoic abnegation of unnecessary surface values,...the proclamation of a simple bold uncompromising philosophy." When a distinguished looking middle-aged woman who is passing affirms, "Yes, it is a fabulous painting isn't it?" The male curator replies, "Painting? Who said anything about painting...? I'm talking about the cheque," holding up the $1.8 million.

Gable's hilarious cartoon shows an artist/husband figure painting a canvas with large dots, in his studio full of dot paintings, while his wife engaged in reading the paper containing the announcement of the purchase price of the painting, exclaims: "For thirty years I said, 'why don't you try stripes...just once…for variety?' But Nooooo…" This cartoon humorously brings together the purchase price of the painting with a potential domestic squabble over the value of creative work. The Sudbury Star cartoon from March 17, 1990 contains a stereotypical bearded artist with beret, in his loft space telephoning the National Gallery to offer his own painting of red stripes on a blue background which he states is worth $3.6 million but which he can generously let the gallery have for $3 million." This satirical method is an ironic inversion similar to the parodic performances of the artists mentioned earlier. Cartoonist Sebastian's enigmatic image from the Ottawa Business News (March 24-April 6, 1990) shows a group of what appear to be seeing-eye dogs lining up outside the boardroom door of the National Gallery of Canada, outside of which is a container holding white canes. The satire here relies upon the reader's comprehension of the Board members as replaying the proverbial narrative of the blind leading the blind.

John's cartoon in the Edmonton Bullet (March 28), shows two figures conversing in front of Newman's painting. One says to the other "How could you pay so much for this? It escapes me, I can't see the reason…" to which the gallery curator mockingly replies "Oh, Ha, Ha, Herbie, have you ever heard about thought distillation?…No…Then give me a break!" Unger's cartoon with the caption "What are you blind? You hung it upside down!" was produced four years earlier in 1985 but was republished by the Globe and Mail during the *Voice*…controversy. Cam's cartoon for the Regina Leader Post convicts the reductive Newman painting by contrasting it with an acknowledged master work from the Renaissance, Michelangelo's *David*. As he looks despairingly at the *Voice of Fire* bearing its $1.8 million price tag, Michelangelo exclaims: "Nuts!! I feel like such an amateur." Another Bado cartoon from Le Droit (18 April) shows a puzzled Jean Chretien, head of the Liberal party, and soon to become Prime Minister of Canada, turning the critique of abstraction into a political sign, a clever reworking of the messages contained in the gallery's defensive brochure. The cartoon reads: Je ne comprends pas pourquoi tout le monde insiste 'a appeller ca une toile abstrait J'y vois une percee liberale au milieu d'une mer de bleus! ("I do not know why everyone insists on calling this an abstract painting." I see a Liberal cut [red stripe] through the middle of a sea of blues [Conservatives]"). Hutchings' ironic cartoon, Financial Post (19 April), recalls the horizontality of most of Newman's paintings of this size. Of his striped effort, the cartoon artist says "I realize that it's similar to *Voice of Fire*. The dramatic difference is that mine is horizontal. The National Gallery will love it!"

Roy Peterson's cartoon from the Vancouver Sun (28 March), shows a plaid-coated viewer peering sideways at the *Voice of Fire* while a museum guard says, "At least this one isn't complaining about the price. This one's asking why we hung it upside down…" Mike Graston's cartoon from the Windsor Star (12 April), presents an ironic post-controversy scenario. The gallery officials in this cartoon walk toward the National gallery Acquisitions department containing abstracts of all sizes. The woman, possibly a stand-in for the gallery director Shirley Thomson, declares: "After the government decided to respect our professional judgement and maintain its arm's-length policy, we went out and really blew a wad!"

Finally, four highly symbolic vehicles for rejection: Pritchard's cartoon in the Regina Leader Post (21 April), transposes two paintings, the *Voice of Fire* and *The Silent Majority*. The latter Pop Art-like work presents a thumbs-down sign, which accords ironically with Pop Arts rejection of Abstract Expressionism. Blaine's cartoon in the Hamilton Spectator (29 March), shows three gleeful 'stooges'—Larry, Curley and Moe of the National gallery selection committee—with Newman's painting, price tag and paint roller. Ben Lafontaine's cartoon in Ottawa Magazine, published some months after the controversy had subsided shows a huge foreshortened figure of a museum guard standing next to a father protectively holding his child, as he examines the offending painting. Last but not least, Susan Dewar's enigmatic cartoon published by the Ottawa Sun (4 April 1991) symbolically connects the *Voice of Fire* with the *Flesh Dress* controversy which was to follow a year later. This hard-hitting satire, the only one during the course of the controversy produced by a woman, shows a pork steak-headed Felix Holtmann sporting a ten-gallon hat, cowboy boots, and spurs, and carrying a suitcase full of money. He is leading a pig, either to, or from, the market, encouraging the reader to identify the image with the children's nursery rhyme— "to market to market to buy a fat pig…home again home again jiggity jig!" Dewar's speech balloon caption for Holtmann is a single horizontal stripe, indicating that his resistance to the *Voice of Fire* and the *Flesh Dress* is but a natural product of his red-necked cowboy philistinism, as if, indeed, the word was flesh.

I will have more to say about the conventional categories of rejection represented through these cartoon satires at the conclusion of this chapter. However, before we engage these issues, we should examine the NGC twin controversy, that provoked for a short time, no less a passionate response from the popular press.

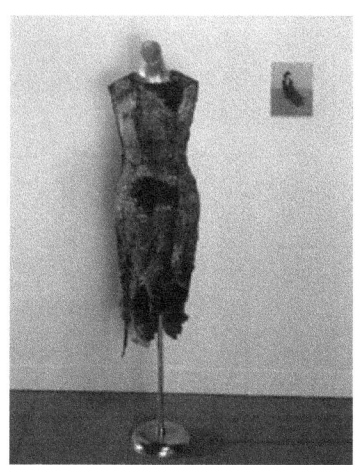

Figure 90: Jana Sterbak *Vanitas: Flesh Dress for an Albino Anorectic* (1987) Collection of Galerie Rene Blouin, Montreal. Photograph, Louis Lussier

The *Flesh Dress* controversy represents a similar set of struggles over the meanings of the sign(s) of modernist art. I will focus upon the graphic satires of the work that appeared in the press over a period of several days. It is important however to first acknowledge a few facts about the *Flesh Dress*. Montreal based artist Jana Sterbak's *Vanitas: Flesh Dress for an Albino Anorexic*, the work's full title, was first shown in an exhibition at Galerie Rene Blouin, Montreal in 1987. In this exhibition, as with the subsequent showing at the National Gallery, the work consisted of two elements: the 'Flesh Dress,' constructed from slabs of prime beef sewn together, mounted on a tailor's dummy, and, on an adjacent wall, a framed photograph of a model posing in the dress.[12]

While scant attention was paid to the first showing of the 'dress', the exhibition at the National Gallery, approximately one year after the *Voice of Fire* controversy, quickly provoked outrage from members of local government, the public, and the media. And like the earlier controversy, this one reveals clearly the contestation over the meaning of various discursive signs, differently oriented and accented. The attacks began shortly after the exhibition opened. Many of the critics directed their attention to the use of expensive meat in the artwork at a time when increasing numbers of people were lining up at food banks. Others attacked the institution for showing work that they argued was inappropriate to the maintenance of decorum in Canada's National Gallery. A few individuals cited the work as a health risk, while others attacked the feminist intent behind the work, arguing that Sterbak had merely reproduced the view of women as consumable object.

Supporters of the work, including Montreal critic Reesa Greenberg,[13] argued for the complex dialectics operating within the work; of how the work stimu-

---

12. See Nemirof, D., *Jana Sterbak States of being Corps a Corps* Ottawa, National Gallery of Canada catalogue 1991: 29-31 and 52-4 (interview).

13. Greenberg, R., "Jana Sterbak" C Magazine (Winter 1987-8: 5-3).

lates discussion to centre around society's expectation of women, their colonization, their self-exploitation and the resulting physiological symptoms, including anorexia nervosa, and bulimia, occasioned by the alienation of the female subject. The work powerfully engages the set of social relationships which, according to anthropologist Mary Douglas (1966), are oscillating between the two poles of purity and danger—the politics of gender and sexuality.

The cartoons that appeared in many papers across the country within a week of the exhibition revealed clearly the extent and foci of the criticism, if not the complexity of arguments either in support of or against the work. For instance, Bado's cartoon (Fig. 91), titled ironically *Vanitas* represents a dress with flies buzzing around it with the caption "Il y en a qui auront toujours Maloney!" ("Some will always have Maloney"), a barbed reference to Ottawa Alderman Mark Maloney who stated that he was "absolutely disgusted and ashamed" of the beef and demanded its removal. He ordered regional health inspectors to examine the work in order to ensure that it did not violate Ontario's public health standards. "People can actually touch the carcass," he said; "that's enough to close it down." (G&M April 2, 1991).

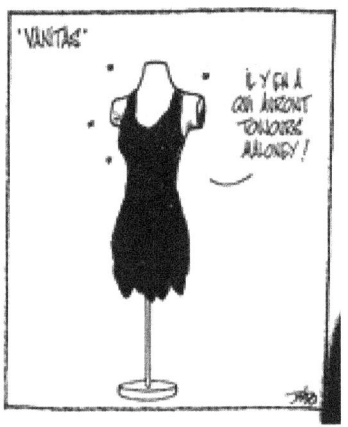

Figure 91: Bado, Le Droit
April 3rd, 1991

The Montreal Gazette's resident cartoonist Aislin (Terry Mosher), drew a be-napkinned, poverty stricken character standing before the steaks of the *Flesh Dress* brandishing a bottle of A1 sauce, a fork and a plate, thus providing an ironic reference to statements by politicians who expressed their rage at the exhibit, including Alderman, Pierre Bourque, who stated that the sculpture shows a "malignant lack of passion" because it wastes food while others in the city are going hungry," and Liberal MP Marlene Catterall, who said that "it doesn't deal with the problem of a system that doesn't distribute food so that people have enough to eat." These and other sentiments relating to the politics of food distribution were endorsed by Ottawa Food Bank manager Dick Hudson and officials from other food relief agencies, who attacked the $300 cost of the meat used in the production of the work (G&M April 2, 1991).

Other cartoons reinforced these basic critiques of the work and added a few others, gender, morality and, as we witnessed previously in the *Voice of Fire* example, state funding of the arts. Cartoonist Mariken Van Nimvegen's uncaptioned twin set meat pants and meat dress in the Vancouver Sun (20 April), both reinforces and deflates the relationship between women and food by providing a pair of genderless pants for a potentially contradictory reading of the original work. One reading of this cartoon could suggest that the pants are female in which case the emphasis on 'woman-as-meat' in the original would be reinforced. However, if the pants are male, then the original meanings may be subordinated in favour of the relationship between the male phallus and the subjugation of women.

A few cartoons depoliticized the Sterbak work to ironize the use of meat in a work of art. Sebastian's *Ottawa Citizen* cartoon (7 April) contains the caption: "Meat Dress—Where's the beef?" which can be translated as "where's the substance?" This merely reduced the issue into a blurted "so what!" while Jim Phillip's Ottawa Sun cartoon "Frankly I prefer my beef barbecued..." subtly domesticates the work, turning it away from the fractious politics of sexuality and power, to suburban respectability. Similarly, although the inversions are a little more ambiguous, the syndicated 'Back Bench' strip distinguishes the ethical high art (existential) reading in the left frame— "This meat dress will make an important statement about man's cultural depravity and bovine nihilistic tendencies"—from the practical, mundane and domestic reading in the caption to the panel on the right—"We'll leave this out here while we're defrosting the fridge." Finally, Nease's cartoon links both the *Voice of Fire* and *Flesh Dress* controversies to invoke once again the debates around state funding for the arts, showing beneath the obligatory sign of the State the *Vanitas Flesh Dress* between a miniaturized version of Newman's *Voice of Fire* and a portrait of the taxpayer as sucker.

In summary, we should now review the arguments used against avant-garde modernist work in general and abstraction in particular, for these represent the underlying ideological positioning to which each class, in essence, gives its name. Both the *Voice of Fire* and *Flesh Dress* controversies conform to the conventional attacks on the behaviour and work of the historical (modernist) avant-gardes discussed in earlier chapters, but they also represent attempts by various discursive communities to accommodate the critiques of the avant-garde. These attacks can be reduced to a number of overlapping categories that underscore the historical and political dimensions of these controversies. To recapitulate: a work of modernist art can be rejected under the following conditions or combination thereof.

Politics: Like its contemporary neo-avant-gardes the historical avant-garde is often condemned for its politics. It is either Bolshevik, communistic, the work of political anarchists; the result of some sort of conspiracy or foreign intervention. The avant-garde work of art is the product of foreigners or members of the underclass, and therefore suspect. "These people don't speak the same language as us," or these people are out to challenge the system, to remove our privileges and destroy our way of life.

Psychology: the work of the avant-garde artist is the product of a deficient mind, the work of the insane, the psychologically aberrant personality, the result of some form of sexual perversion.

Physiology: this is the work of those who have defective vision or loco-motor control, that, as a result, produces a distorted, aberrant perception and thus representation of reality.

Aesthetic: the work of abstract art is ugly, it contravenes the laws of beauty and perfection that are part of nature and ultimately, God.

Philosophy (Ethics/Morality): Avant-garde art offends against standard canons of morality. It is immoral, offensive dehumanizing and decadent, an example of moral degeneracy and decay. The avant-garde artist is an atheist whose work is the work of the devil.

Law: the work of the avant-garde artist is fraudulent, a hoax intended to hoodwink the public into believing it is good, honest, legitimate art. Modernist art is lawless.

Economy: This art is trash, this garbage is not worth the paper, canvas etc. it is drawn, painted on. The labour employed in this work has no redeeming social or economic value whatsoever.

Gender/Race/Sexuality: This work is phallic, unnatural, the result of some kind of perversion, anti-women, racist, misogynistic.

Technical: These criticisms are usually prefaced with remarks like "a child could do this better," or "even a monkey could do it." The avant-garde work is the result of fortuitous forces which have nothing to do with training or God-given talent.

The press reports and cartoons reveal that the criticism of Newman's *Voice of Fire* and Sterbak's *Flesh Dress* work conforms to all the categories noted above. As an example of how these categories may overlap, Felix Holtmann's "couple of cans of paint a roller and ten minutes should do the trick" is a variant of the stereotypical negation often directed at the abstract work of art "my kid could do better than that" or "even a monkey could do it," with the essential difference that Holtmann's technical critique is taken to the highest level of politics.

This selective review of the media coverage of the *Voice of Fire* and *Flesh Dress* controversies articulates the manner in which symbolic representations of ideological positions are used critically against the avant-garde, particularly against those artists practicing abstraction, or otherwise presumed to be challenging the status quo. These examples demonstrate how the media can be employed in ironic, parodic, or satirical fashion to provide critical and interrogative accents to those struggles over the meaning of the signs occurring between various discursive communities. The higher meaning of the *Voice of Fire* and *Flesh Dress* controversies can be summed up succinctly: class politics. I have tried to reveal how the political dimensions of humour—where tragedy meets comedy and *vice versa*—have a crucial part to play in the media's invocation of class conflict. Perhaps there is a simple formula underlying this higher meaning: Persuasion is to Power what Performance is to Politics.

SUMMARY

> In cultural studies academic knowledge ought to formalize what is already popularly known. (During, Simon 1993:22)

Throughout this book, I have attempted to demonstrate a number of points about the relationships between modernist art, popular culture and the politics of humour, as this reflects upon our understanding of class and power relations, both within and between, classes and class fractions. I have insisted throughout that, far from being a benign form of entertainment, graphic humour has a symbolic use that may be understood in socio-political terms. In this, I have followed the example of researchers on humour and sexuality: Dines-Levy and Smith (1988); humour and racism: Barker (1981), Davies (1982), Husband (1988) Klausen (2009), who argue that jokes and cartoons about sex, class and ethnicity provide a symbolic vehicle for expressing boundaries between groups as well as anxieties about physical, social, cultural difference and sexual orientation. I have implicitly endorsed a *conflict* model of humour that suggests that graphic humour can be used, either as an instrument of power, or for resisting and contesting the power of one individual, or group, over another. I have upheld also the notion that humour may act as a mechanism of social *control*, representing the accommodation of individuals and social groups to the dominant socio-cultural order.

Popular Modernisms offers a practical explication to the symbolic contest of cultural power, as this is representative of the struggle between various groups and constituencies over the social meanings and cultural relevance, or lack thereof, of modern(ist) art. I have demonstrated how the "shock of the new" represented in the various activist and antagonist projects of the modernist and post-modernist avant-gardes, have resulted in various socio-cultural responses; that humour in the form of parodies, graphic satires, pastiches, grotesques, lampoons, and burlesques of the products and ideas of high culture—produced by those outside of the production and reception sites of cultural dominance—has served the interests both of tension management and social critique. I have argued that the incidence of graphic parodies and satires of modern art increased with the separation of art from its primitive, sacral and courtly functions into a realm of relative autonomy within the modernist era. I have argued further, that one of the principal ways we can recognize the ideological power(s)—the strength and resilience of modernist (and postmodernist) art—is to examine responses to its various forms that become manifest within specific groups and constituencies outside of their principal domain(s). I have taken care to avoid arguing that this critical process is simply a mechanical 'knee jerk' relationship that introduces more tension into the social matrix. I have attempted to articulate how those working within social contexts at the margins of the dominant culture can display their displeasure with the hegemony of the cultural elite, without necessarily eliciting socially negative consequences.

In the various chapter discussions and case studies, I have revealed how the contest over the meanings of the signs of modern (and postmodern) art is an ongoing process of negotiation, of interpretation and reinterpretation occurring within various discursive communities, with the caveat that these interpretive communities have an ideological purview, and a specific hierarchy of interests and values that can be identified in class terms. In underscoring the dynamic and historical nature of this social process, I suggested that it has the capacity both to lead to changes in the socio-cultural register and/or secure the status quo, or what Fredric Jameson (1989) termed the "cultural dominant."

I have provided evidence to show this socio-cultural process at work at various times, from the birth of modernism in the 1830s and 40s, through to the present, thus revealing this as an ongoing process occurring cross culturally between groups who use the popular media, newspapers, magazines as well as comic books, journals, and now, digital media as their principle vehicle(s) of communication. There is some irony in the fact that the art that has received the most savage denunciation from the culture critics of the subordinate classes—the work

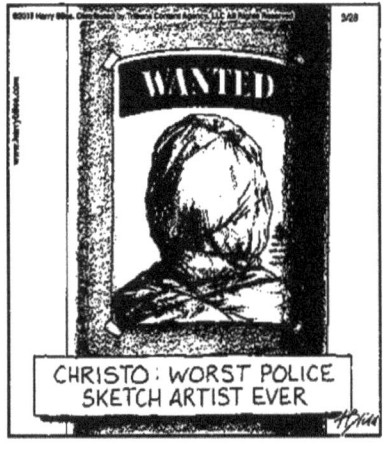

Figure 92: Harry Bliss *Wanted* 2018
© www.harrybliss.com
Pippin Properties NYC

of Marcel Duchamp, Pablo Picasso, Henry Moore, Jackson Pollock, Daniel Buren, Christo, Banksy and Tracy Emin—has also secured the strongest place within the pantheon of high culture.

In passing, I have attempted to underscore the compatibility of various theories of irony, parody, satire and the grotesque, revealing how the privileging of context and reception, as distinct from form, or subject psychology, may allow one to perceive the differences and similarities between humour genre types. Following the work of Bahktin (1965) and Hutcheon (1994), I have argued that irony and parody can provide the vehicles for satirical intent. I have discussed the relationships between an artist's class origins as this may inform his/her/their understanding and appreciation of the forms and institutions of high culture. Finally, I have attempted to provide practical explication, on a micro level, to the political economy of the sign; to show it less denotatively in analytical terms, as the reductive business of encoding and decoding, but the rather more connotative and comfortable process of reading and interpretation. Where some theorists have privileged analysis, I have made a concession to postmodern discourse by emphasizing description and interpretation without, I hope, blurring the image or erasing too many borders.

Enlisting the assistance of the Russian Formalists of the 1920s whose work demonstrates that language can become the site of ideological struggle and further, that the symbolic representation of power differentials in the arenas of culture provide a symbolic representation of the conflict between the classes, I have made some tentative suggestions about the manner in which the social functions of humour can be understood. Implicitly and explicitly, I have employed the political theories of Gramsci, the language theories of Bahktin and Volosinov, and the more recent sociological theories and class research of Bourdieu, to reinforce the notion that the fields of cultural production and reproduction are representations of the struggle between classes and class fractions. I have argued that culture criticism between class fractions is represented symbolically and that different classes are engaged in a symbolic struggle to impose those definitions of the social world which conform most closely to their interests, agreeing with Bourdieu, that "the field of ideological positions reproduces in transfigured form the field of social positions" (Bourdieu, 1977:112).

I have also given credence to the position that class is not an autonomous structural category to which we can ascribe certain discrete values—that it is above, or *below* all, a "lived relationship"—in the sense that E. P. Thompson has described in a quote that I feel summarizes better than most, the contingency of one of our most problematic categories yet still does not evacuate it into the ozone of postmodern discursive relativism or omniscient intersectionality.

> Class is defined by men and women as they live their own history, and, in the end, is its only definition. (E.P. Thompson 1980:10)

I began my study with the aim of exploring art from all sides—*inter alia*—to traverse the borders outside of the institution art and explore it from its margins, even as I recognized that these margins are shifting and undergoing a continual process of redefinition. And yet I have found myself like an expatriate traveler to a former colony he has long since vacated; one who had travelled abroad to live and study in the old imperial centers and returned years later to his country of birth. He is replete with the cultural capital of additional education and overseas experience and finds upon his return that his old school friends of long ago are welcoming yet rather suspicious of his new accent, clothing and his motives for return. And while they enthusiastically provide him with an understanding of the new and independent vitality of the nation, that has recently shed its colonial yoke, he observes that the baggage of the former imperial regime is much in evidence, and moreover, with its structure still intact, both in the rules of the land and the cultures of the people. Using this as kind of metaphor for self-reflection, I can recognize my own expatriate traveler role, as less tourist of my culture, than sentient agent.

If I have a specific desire for the entry of this book into the annals of cultures studied, it would be that it will provide more material evidence for a renegotiation of the terms of discourse for culture, class, ideology and power. Another wish is that it may affirm and assist in the further development of new cultural studies projects including specific ethnographic approaches to the study of graphic humour. And above all, I hope that others might use it as their passport for further contextual study beyond the changing borders of art and art history to the fertile regions of popular culture.

BIBLIOGRAPHY

Adamson, W. *Hegemony and Revolution: A Study of Antonio Gramsci's Political and Cultural Theory*. Berkeley: University of California Press 1980

Adorno, T. *Negative Dialectics*. New York: Seabury Press 1973

———. *Introduction to the Sociology of Music*. New York: Seabury Press 1976

Adrian, A. *Mark Lemon: First Editor of Punch*. London, New York: Oxford 1966

Allen, R. "Critical Theory and the Paradox of Modernist Discourse." Postmodern Issue Screen 28, 2: 69-85, 1987

Allen, C.C. *Are You Fed Up with Modern Art?* Tulsa: Rainbow Press 1952

Althusser, L. *For Marx*. trans. B. Brewster London: N.L. Books 1977

———. *Lenin and Philosophy and Other Essays*. Trans. B. Brewster London: N.L. Books 1971

Anderson, P. *Considerations on Western Marxism*. London: NLR Books 1976

Anderson, A. *The Man Who Was H.M. Bateman*. Exeter: Webb and Bower 1982

Arac, J. *Postmodernism and Politics*. Manchester: Manchester University Press 1986

———. *Genealogies: Historical Situations for Post-Modern Literary Studies*. New York: Columbia University Press 1987

Arato, A. & Gebhardt E. *The Essential Frankfurt School Reader*. Intro. P. Piccone, New York: Urizen Books 1978

Armory Show, the International Exhibition of Modern Art 1913. New York: Arno Press 1972

Bakhtin, M. *Rabelais and His World* trans. Herlene Iswolsky Boston: MIT Press 1965.

———. *The Dialogic Imagination*. trans. Caryl Emerson and Michael Holquist, Austin: U of Texas 1981

Barber, B. Guilbaut, S. and O'Brian, J. *Voices of Power: Art, Rage, Power and the State* Toronto: University of Toronto, Press 1996

Barber, B. *Trans/Actions: Art, Film and Death* New York and Dresden Atropos Press 2013

Barker, M. *Comics: Ideology, Power and the Critics*. Manchester: University Press Manchester and New York Cultural Politics Series 1989

Barr, A. H. *Cubism and Abstract Art*. New York: Museum of Modern Art 1936

Barrier, M. and Williams, M. (eds) *A Smithsonian Book of Comic Book Comics*. New York: Smithsonian Inst. Press and H. N Abrams 1982

Barthes, R. *Writing Degree Zero*. London: Cape 1967

———. *Mythologies*. London: Cape 1972

———. *The Pleasure of the Text*. trans. R. Miller, New York: Hill and Wang 1975

———. *Image Music Text*. trans. Stephen Heath New York: Hill and Wang

Baudelaire, C. *Art in Paris 1845-1862 Reviews of Salons and other Exhibitions*. Trans. and ed. J. Mayne, London, New York: Phaidon 1965

———. *Selected Writings on Art and Artists*. trans. with intro P.E Charvet, Harmondsworth Middlesex: Penguin Books 1972

Baudrillard, J. *Oublier Foucault*. Paris: Editions Galilee 1987

———. *For a Critique of the Political Economy of the Sign*. St Louis: Montana 1986

——— *The Mirror of Production*. trans. M. Poster St. Louis: Telos Press 1975

Bauman, Z. *Legislators and Interpreters: On Modernity, Post-Modernity and Intellectuals* Ithaca N.Y: Cornell University Press 1987

Baxandall, L. *Marxism and History Proceedings of the Marxist Caucus*, College Art Association Meeting 1972

Bell, D. *The Coming of Post-Industrial Society*. New York: Basic 1973

———. *The Cultural Contradictions of Capitalism*. New York: Basic 197

Benjamin, W. *Illuminations* edited with an introduction by Hannah Arendt, H. Zohn Trans. New York: Schocken Books 1969

Benton, M. *The Comic Book in America* Dallas: Taylor Publishing 1989

Ben-Porat, Z "Method in Madness: Notes on the Structure of Parody, Based on MAD TV Satires" Poetics Today 1.

Benamou, M and Caramello (eds) *Performance in Post-Modern Culture*. Wisconsin: Center for 20th century Studies & Coda Press 1977

Bennett, T M, Mercer, C. & Woollacott, J.(eds) *Culture, Ideology and Social Process: A Rea*der. London: Open University Press 1981

Bergson, H., *Laughter: An Essay on the Meaning of the Comic*. trans. Brereton and Rothwell, London: Macmillan 1911

Bernstein, B. *Thurber, A Biography*. New York: Arbor House Pub. Co. 1975,

Bernstein, R. (ed) *Habermas and Modernity*. Cambridge, Mass: MIT Press 1985

Berthoud, R. *Henry Moore: The Authorised Biography*. Boston, London: Faber and Faber 1987

Bhabha, H. *The Location of Culture* London and New York: Routledge 1994

Bhaskar, R. *Scientific Realism and Human Emancipation*. London: Verso 1986

Bocock, R. *Hegemony*. The Open University Key Ideas Series, Chichester, London: Ellis Harwood/Tavistock Publishers 1986

Bois, Y-A *Reinhardt*. San Francisco: MOCA catalogue 1991

Bolton, R. (ed) *Culture Wars: Documents from the Recent Controversies in the Arts*. New York: The New Press 1992

Booth, W. *A Rhetoric of Irony*. Chicago and London: Chicago U Press 1974

Bourdieu, P & Darbel, A. *L'Amour de l'art: Les Musees et leur public*. Paris: Editions de Minuit 1966

Bourdieu, P. and Passeron, J.C. *Reproduction in Education, Society and Culture*. trans. Richard Nice London: Beveley Hills, Sage Publications 1977

———*Outline of a Theory of Practice* Cambridge. trans. R. Nice, London, New York: Cambridge University Press 1977

———*Distinction: A Social Critique of the Judgement of Taste*. trans. R. Nice, Cambridge Mass: Harvard University Press 1984

———*The Logic of Practice*. Stanford: Stanford University Press 1990, original Paris: Les Editions de Miniut 1980

Brantlinger, P. *Crusoe's Footprints: Cultural Studies in Britain and America*. New York: Routledge 1990

Brown, M.W. *The Story of the Armory Show*. Greenwich, New York: Graphic Society 1963

Buchloh, B., Guilbaut, S., and Solkind, D., *Modernism and Modernity: The Proceedings from The Vancouver Conference*. Halifax: NSCAD and NYU Press 1983

Buckley, B. and Conomos, J. (eds) *Erasure: The Spectre of Cultural Memory* U.K. Libri Publishing 2015

Burawoy, M. *The Politics of Production*. London: Verso 1985

Burger, P. *Theory of the Avant-Garde*. Minneapolis: U of Minnesota Theory and History of Literature Vol. 4 1984

Calder, A. *Calder* Intro by J.J Sweeney Museum of Modern Art catalogue, Mew York: MOMA 1943

Calinescu, M. *Faces of Modernity*. Bloomington: Indiana University Press 1977

Calinescu, M. and Fokkema, D (eds) *Exploring Post-Modernism*. Amsterdam and Philadelphia Pa: John Benjamin 1987

Callinicos, A. *Marxism and Philosophy*. London: Oxford University Press 1985

Casswell, L. S. & Gardner J. (eds.), *Drawing the Line: Comics Studies and INKS, 1994–1997* University of Ohio Press (2017)

Castleman, C. *Getting Up: Subway Graffiti in New York*. Cambridge. MIT Press 1982

Champfleury J-F. *Historie de la Caricature*. Paris: 1867-1874.

Cheetham, M. *The Rhetoric of Purity: Essentialist Theory and the Advent of Abstract Painting*. Cambridge: Cambridge U Press 1991

Clark, T.J. *The Absolute Bourgeois: Art & Politics in France 1848-1851*. New York and London: 1973

———*Image of the People: Gustave Courbet and the 1848 Revolution*. New York and London: Thames and Hudson 1973

Cockcroft, E. *Toward a Peoples' Art: The Contemporary Mural Move*ment. New York: Dutton 1977

Crow, T. *Modern Art in The Common Culture* New Haven and London: Yale University Press 1996

Dane, J. *Parody: Critical Concepts Versus Literary Practices, Aristophenes to Ster*ne. Norman and London: University of Oklahoma Press 1988

——— *The Critical Mythology of Irony*. Athens, Georgia and London: The University of Georgia Press 1991

Deitcher, D. "Comic Art Connoisseurs." Art and America, February 1984

Denney, Ruel *The Astonished Muse* Chicago: University of Chicago Press 1957

deCerteau, M. *Ecriture de l'histoire* Paris: Gallimand 1975

de Duve, T. *Att nom de l'art Paris*: Editions Minuit 1989

———*Resonnance du readymade*. Paris: Jaqueline Chambon 1989

de Lauretis, T. *Feminist Studies/Critical Studies* Bloomington Ind: Indiana University Press. 1986

de Man, P. *Resistance to Theory*. Minneapolis: University of Minnesota Press 1986

——— *Allegories of Reading: Figural Language in Rousseau, Neitzsche, Rilke and Proust*. New Haven: Yale University Press 1979

——— *Blindness and Insight: Essays in the Rhetoric of Contemporary Criticism* Minneapolis: University of Minnesota Press 1983

Derrida, J. *Writing and Difference*. trans. A. Bass London: Routledge, Kegan, Paul 1978

——— *The Post-card: From Socrates to Freud and Beyond* trans A. Bass, Chicago: University of Chicago Press 1987

——— *Of Grammatology* trans G. Spivak, Baltimore: John Hopkins University Press 1976

Dewey J. *Art as Experience* New York: G.P Putnum's Sons 1934

Dews, P. *Logics of Disintegration: Post-Structuralist Thought and the Claims of Critical Theory* London: Verso 1987

Diamond, S. *In Search of the Primitive: A Critique of Civilization* New Brunswick, N.J: Transaction Books 1974

Dorfman A. *The Empire's Old Clothes. What the Lone Ranger, Babar and Other Innocent Heroes Do to Our Minds* New York: Pantheon 1983

Dorfman, A and Mattelart, A. *How to Read Donald Duck: Imperialist ideology in the Disney Comic* London: International General 1975

Douglas, M. *Purity and Danger: An Analysis of Concepts of Pollution and Taboo* London: Ark Paperbacks 1966 1984

Douglas, M. "The Social Control of Cognition: Some factors in Joke Perception," MAN 3:3

Dunlap, I. *The Shock of the New*. St. Louis, San Francisco, American Heritage Press 1972

During, S.(ed) *The Cultural Studies Reader* London and New York Routledge 1993

Eagleton, T. "Capitalism, Modernism and Post-Modernism" New Left Review 152:60-73 1984

——— "Awakening from Modernity." Times Literary Supplement, 20 February 1987

——— *The Ideology of the Aesthetic* London Basil Blackwell 1989

Eco, U. *The Role of the Reader: Explorations in the Semiotics of Tex*ts Bloomington: University of Indiana Press 1979

———*Semiotics and the Philosophy of Language* Bloomington: University of Indiana Press 1984

———*Interpretation and OverInterpretation* Cambridge, New York: Cambridge University Press 1992

Estren, M.J. *A History of Underground Comics* Berkeley Straight Arrow Books 1974, 1987

Feinberg, L. *Introduction to Satire* Ames, Iowa: The Iowa State University Press 1967.

Flavell M.K. *George Grosz, A Biography*. New Haven, London: Yale University Press. 1988

Fokkema, D and Bertens, H (eds) *Approaching Postmodernism* Amsterdam; John Benjamins 1986

Forbes, K. *Great Art to The Grotesque* Toronto: Pitt Publishing Co Ltd 1972

Foucault, M. *The History of Sexuality* Volume I: An Introduction Trans R. Hurley, New York: Vintage Books Random House 1978

———*The Archeology of Kno*wledge Trans A.M. Sheridan-Smith New York: Harper and Row 1972

———*Language, Counter-memory, Practice* trans. Bouchard and Simon Ithaca N.Y: Cornell University Press 1977

Frascina, F. *Pollock and After: The Critical Debate* London New York: Harper and Row 1985

Freud, S. *Wit and its Relation to the Unconscious*. trans and introduction A.A. Brill, London: Kegan Paul, Trench, Trubner & Co 1926

Freud, S. *The Standard Edition of the Complete Works of Sigmund Freud* London: Hogarth Press 1960

Frith, S. "Hearing Secret Harmonies." *In High Theory/ Low Culture* ed C. McCabe 53-70

Fry, R. *Vision and Design* London: Chatto and Windus 1921

Gaillie, D. *Social Inequality and Class Radicalism in France and Britain* Cambridge: Cambridge University Press 1983

Gans, H. *Popular Culture and High Culture* New York: Basic Books 1974

Gardner, J. *The Comics of Charles Schulz: The Good Grief of Modern Life* (Critical Approaches to Comics Artists Series) Ohio University Press 2017

Garvin, H.R (ed) *Romanticism, Modernism, Postmodernism* Lewisberg, Pa: Bucknell University Press; London Associated University Press 1980

Giddens A. *The Class Structure of Advanced Societies*, London, Hutchinson 1973

─── "Modernism and Post-modernism" New German Critique 22 15-18 1981

Gitlin, T. *Years of Hope, Days of Rage* New York: Bantam Books 1988

Geldzahler, H. *New York Painting and Sculpture 1940-1970* New York: 1969

Goldstein, J & McGhee P. (eds) *The Psychology of Humour: Theoretical Perspectives and Empirical Issues*, New York and London: Academic Press 1972

Gombrich, E, Hochberg and Black. *Art, Perception and Reality* Baltimore: John Hopkins University Press 1972

Gompertz, W. *What Are You Looking At? 150 Years of Modern Art in the Blink of an Eye* Viking Press (2012)

Gramsci, A. *Selections from the Prison Notebooks of Antonio Gramsci*. Edited and trans. Q. Hoare and G. Nowell Smith, London: Lawrence and Wishart 1971 a selection from the original Italian Edition: *A Gramsci Quaderni del Carere (1928-1935)* (ed)V. Gerratana, Turin, Einaudi 1948-51

─── *Selections from Political Writings Vol I 1910-1920* and *Vol II 1921-1926* ed and translations Hoare, Q. and Mathews London: Lawrence and Wishart 1977, 1978

Greenberg, C. *Art and Culture* Boston: Beacon 1962

Grossberg, L., Nelson, C & Treichler, P. (eds) *Cultural Studies* New York London: Routledge 1992

Guilbaut, S. *How New York Stole the Idea of Modern Art* Chicago: University of Chicago Press 1983

Guilbaut, S.(ed) *Reconstructing Modernism* Cambridge Mass: MIT Press 1990 Dissent: The Issue of Modern Art in Boston Paperback – 1985

Guilbaut, S. Ross, Sussman, Heller, Buchloh et. al. *Dissent: The Issue of Modern Art in Boston* Institute of Contemporary Art : Distributed by Northeastern University Press 1985

Gurevitch, M., Bennett, T. Curran J. and Woollacott, J., (eds) *Culture, Society and the Media* London: Methuen 1982

Habermas, J. *Knowledge and Human Interests* Trans J Shapiro London: Heinnemann 1972

─── *The Philosophical Discourse of Modernity* Oxford: Oxford University Press 1987

Hadjinicoloau, N. *Art History and Class Struggle.* Trans. Louis Asmal, London: Pluto Press 1978

Hall, S., Clarke, J., Jefferson, T., & Roberts, B., (Eds) *Resistance Through Rituals: Youth Subcultures in Postwar Britain* London: Hutchinson 1976

Hall, S. *Cultural Studies: Two Paradigms* in R. Collins et. al. Media Culture and Society a Critical Reader London: Sage 1986

Hammerton, J.A. *Punch Library of Humour Stage and Studio* London: Educational Book Co c.1863

Handwerk, G. *Irony and Ethics in Narrative: From Schlegel to Lacan.* New Haven and London: Yale University Press 1985

Hanninen, S., and Paldan, L.(eds) *Rethinking Ideology* Paris: International General IMMRC 1982

Hassan, I. *The Dismemberment of Orpheus: Toward a Post-Modern Literature* New York: Oxford University Press 1971

Hassan, I. *Paracriticisms: Seven Speculations of the Times* Urbana, Ill. 1975

Hassan, I. "The Culture of Postmodernism." Theory Culture and Society 2 (3), 119-32 1985

Haug, W.F. *Commodity Aesthetics, Ideology and Culture.* New York and Bagnolet: International General 1987

Hebdige, D., *Subculture: The Meaning of Style.* London: Methuen 1979

Heller, M. *Mit Picasso, Macht Man Picasso: Kunst und Kunstwelt im Comic.* Zurich: Museum fur Gestaltung 1990

Hellett, Mark. *The Spectre of Difference: Graphic Satire in the age of Hogarth* (The Paul Mellon Centre for Studies in British Art) Yale University Press

Hess. T. B. "The Art Comics of Ad Reinhardt." Art Forum Vol 12 No 8 April 1974

―――― (ed) *The Art Comics and Satires of Ad Reinh*ardt Kunsthalle, Dusseldorf: Marlborough, Rome 1975

――――*Barnett Newman* New York: Museum of Modern Art 1971

Highet, G. *The Anatomy of Satire* Princeton: New Jersey: Princeton University Press 1962

Hirschkop, K & Sheperd D.(eds) *Bahktin and Cultural Theory* Manchester: Manchester University Press 1989

Hobbes, T. *Leviathan* London: Fontana 1962

Holt, E.G. (ed) *The Triumph of Art for the Public: The Emerging Role of Exhibitions and Critic*s New York: Anchor Press Doubleday 1979

Horn, M. (ed) *The World Encyclopedia of Comics* New York: Chelsea House 1976

―――― *The World Encyclopedia of Cartoons* New York: Chelsea House 1981

Hutcheon, L. *A Theory of Parody: The Teachings of Twentieth Century Art Forms* London and New York: Methuen 1985

―――― *A Poetics of Postmodernism: History Theory Fiction* New York, London: Routledge Kegan Paul 1988

―――― *The Politics of Post-Modernism* London, N.Y: Routledge 1989

―――― *Splitting Images: Contemporary Canadian Ironies* Oxford, Toronto: Oxford University Press 1991

―――― *Irony's Edge: The Theory and Politics of Irony* London, New York Routledge 1994

Huyssen, A. *After the Great Divide: Modernism, Mass Culture, Post-Modernism* Bloomington indiana Indiana University Press 1986

―――― "Mapping the Post-Modern." New German Critique 33, 5-52 1984

Inge, M. T. *Comics as Culture* Jackson and London: University Press of Mississippi, 1990

Jacobs, F. *The Mad World of William M. Gaines* New York: Bantam Books 1973

Jameson, F. *Postmodernism* Durham: Duke University Press 1991

―――― "Post-Modernism or The Cultural Logic of Late Capitalism" New Left Review 146:53-92, 1984

Johnson, E. *A Treasury of Satire* New York: Simon and Schuster 1945

Kaplan, E A. (ed) *Postmodernism and its Discontents: Theories, Practices.* London, New York: Verso 1988

Kellogg W.N. and L.A. *The Ape and the Child* New York: McGraw Hill 1933

Kennedy, E. *A Philosophe in the Age of Revolution: Destutt de Tracy and the Origins of Ideology* Philadelphia: The American Philosophical Society 1978

Kermode, F. *The Sense of an Ending* London and New York: Oxford University Press 1967

Klausen, Jytte. *The Cartoons That Shook the World* Yale University Press. 2009

Klein, M. *Developments in Psychoanalysis* New York: Da Capo Press 1983

Kovarsky, A. *Kovarsky's World* New York: Knopf 1956

Kramer, D. *Ross and the New Yorker* Garden City, New York: Double Day and Co., 1951

Krauss, R. *The Originality of the Avant-Garde and Other Modernist Myths* Cambridge Mass and London: MIT Press 1985

Kris, E. *Psychoanalytic Explorations in Art* New York: International Universities Press 1952

Kristeva, J. *Desire in Language* New York: University of Columbia Press 1980

Kuhn, A. *The Power of the image: Essays on Representation and Sexuality* London: Routledge, Kegan Paul 1985

Kunzle, D. *The Early Comic Strip. History of the Comic Strip Vol 1* Berkeley: University of California Press 1973

Lacan, J. *Ecrits: A Selection* Trans a Sheridan-Smith London: Tavistock 1977

────── *The Four Fundamental Concepts of Psycho-Analysis* edited Miller trans. A. Sheridan, New York: W W Norton 1977

Laclau, E and Mouffe, C. *Hegemony and Socialist Strategy* London: Verso 1985

Lakatos K. and Musgrave, L. *Criticism and the Growth of Knowl*edge, Proceedings of the International Colloquium in the Philosophy of Science" Vol 4, Cambridge: University of Cambridge Press 1965

Langer, S. *Philosophy in a New Key* Cambridge, Mass: Harvard University Press 1942

Langer, S. *Feeling and Form: A Theory of Art* New York: Scribner's Sons 1953

Lasch, C. *The Culture of Narcissism: American Life in the Age of Diminishing Expectations* New York: Norton 1978

Lavin, I. *Bernini and the Unity of the Visual Arts* New York London: 1980

Leavis, F.R and Thompson D *Culture and Environment*, London: Chatto and Windus 1937

Lee, R. "Ut Pictura Poesis, The Humanistic Theory of Painting" Art Bulletin 22:4 1940

Leger, C. *Courbet selon les caricatures et les images*. Paris: 1920

Lehmann, P. *Die Parodie im Mittalter*. 2nd edition Stuttgart: Hiersemann 1963

Lenin, V. I. *What is to be Done* Moscow: Foreign Languages Publishing House 1902

Lippard, L. *Ad Reinhardt* New York: Abrams 1981

Lowenthal, L. "Historical Perspectives of Popular Culture" American Journal of Sociology Vol. 55 1950

Lowenthal, L. *Literature Popular Culture and Society* Englewood Cliffs, New Jersey: Prentice Hall 1961

Lutz, C. A and Collins J. L *Reading National Geographic* Chicago and London: University of Chicago Press 1993

Lyotard, J-F. *The Postmodern Condition: A Report on Knowledge* Minneapolis: The University of Minnesota Press 1984

Lyotard, J-F. *The Inhuman: Reflections on Time* Trans Geoffrey Bennington and Rachel Bowlby Standford, Standford University Press 1991

MacDonald, D. *Masscult and Midcult: An Inquiry into American Popular Culture, and the Role of the Middlebrows in the in the Distortion of Cultural Value*. New York: Partisan Review Press No. 4, 1961

Mahon, D., *Studies in Seicento Art & Theory* London: Greenwood 1947.

Malamud, B. *Pictures of Fidelman: An Exhibition* New York: Farrar, Strauss, Giroux 1969

Marcus, G. *Lipstick Traces: A Secret History of the 20th Century* Cambridge: Mass Harvard University Press 1989

Marschall, R. *America's Great Comic Strip Artists* New York: Abbeville Press 1989

Marx, K., *The German Ideology* (ed) C.J. Arthur, London: Lawrence and Wishart 1968

────── *Preface to a Contribution to a Critique of Political Economy in Karl Marx and Frederick Engels*, Selected Works London: Lawrence and Wishart 1968

Matejka, L. & Pomorska, *Readings in Russian Poetics (Formalist and Structuralist Views)* Cambridge Mass: M.I.T. Press 1971

McCabe, C. *Theory/ Low Culture: Analysing Popular Television and High Film*. Manchester: Manchester University Press 1986

McNall, S., Levine, R., and Fantasia, R. (eds) *Bringing Class Back in Contemporary and Historical Perspectives* Boulder, San Francisco: Oxford Westview 1991

Melley, G. and Glaves-Smith, J.R. *A Child of Six Could Do It* London: Tate Gallery Catalogue 1974

Michelson, A., Krauss, R. Crimp, D.and Copjec J. Eds: *October: The First Decade 1976-1986* Cambridge Mass., London: MIT Press

Mitchell, W.J.T. *Iconology: Image, Text, Ideology* Chicago: Illinois University of Chicago Press 1986

──────*Picture Theory* Chicago & London: University of Chicago Press 1994

Moore, B. Space, Text and Gender Cambridge: Cambridge University Press 1986

Moore, H. "Primitive Art" The Listener Vol. 15:641 April 1941

Moore, H. *Henry Moore Museum of Modern Art* catalogue intro. H. Read, New York: MOMA 1946

Morley, S. (ed) *Punch at the Theatre* London: Robson Books 1980

Morris, D. *The Biology of Art* New York: Knopf 1962

Mulvey, L. *Visual and Other Pleasures* Bloomington: Indiana University Press 1989

Nelson, C. and Grossberg L(eds) *Marxism and the Interpretation of Culture* Urbana Ill: University of Illinois 1988

Nemirof, D. *Jana Sterbak States of Being Corps a Corps* Ottawa: National Gallery of Canada Catalogue 1991

Neumann, E. *The Archetypal World of Henry Moore* trans R.F.C. Hull New York: Bollingen Foundation 1959

Norris, C. *Derrida* London Fontana and Cambridge Mass: Harvard University Press 1987

Norris, C.(ed) *Deconstruction and the Interests of Theory* London: Pinter & Norman; Okl: U of Oklahoma Press 1988

———*Deconstruction, Postmodernism and the Visual Arts* London: Academy Editions 1988

———*What's Wrong with Postmodernism: Critical theory and the Ends of Philosophy* Baltimore: John Hopkins University Press 1990

Ohana, D. *The Intellectual Origins of Modernity* Routledge 2019

O'Neill, J.P. (ed) *Barnett Newman Selected Writings and Interviews*. New York: Alfred A. Knopf 1993

O'Sullivan, J. *The Great American Comic Strip 100 Years of Cartoon Art* College Park Maryland: University of Maryland Dept. of Art 1971

Owens, C. "The Allegorical Impulse: Toward a Theory of Postmodernism" October 12 67-86, 13 59-80, 1980

Owens, C. "Representation, Appropriation and Power" Art in America 70:5 9-21 1982

Pahl, R.E (ed) *On Work: Historical, Comparative and Theoretical Approaches* Oxford: Basil Blackwell 1992

Parker, R & Pollock, G. *Old Mistresses: Women Art and Ideology* New York: Pantheon 1981

Passeron, R. *Daumier* trans. Helga Harrison New York: Poplar 1981; original in French under the title *Daumier: Temoin de son temps* Fribourg: Office du Livre 1979

Pearson, R.M. *The New Art Education* New York: Harper Bros 1950

———— *Experiencing American Pictures* New York: Harper Bros. 1943

———— *The Modern Renaissance in American Art* New York: Harper and Row 1954

Pelles, G. *Art, Artists and Society: Origins of a Modern Dilemma: Painting in France and England 1750-1850* New Jersey, Englewood Cliffs: Prentice Hall 1963

Pinsky, L.E. *Realism of the Renaissance* Moscow: Goslitizdat, 1961. In Russian. London: Routledge & K. Paul, 1962.

Portoghesi, P *Postmodern: The Architecture of the Postindustrial Society* New York: Rizzoli 1983

Poster, M.(ed) *Baudrillard: Selected Writings*. Cambridge: Polity 1988

Powell, C and Paton, G. *Humour in Society: Resistance and Control* Houndmills, Basingstoke, Hampshire: Macmillan Press 1988

Price R.G.G. *A History of Punch* London: Collins 1957.

Radway, J. *Reading the Romance* Chapel Hill: University of North Carolina Press 1984

Read, H. *Henry Moore, a Study of His Life and Work* London: Thames and Hudson 1965

Rees, A.L and Borzello, eds *The New Art History* London: Camden Press 1989

Reeves, K. *Artoons: The Hystery of Art* Toronto: Sound and Vision 1985

Reidelbach, M. *Completely MAD: A History of the Comic Book and Magazine* Boston, Toronto, London: Little Brown and Co., 1991

Reitberger, R. and Fuchs W., *Comics: Anatomy of a Mass Medium* trans. Nadia Fowler. Boston: Little, Brown and Co., 1972

Roberts, J. *Postmodernism, Politics and Art* Manchester: Manchester University Press 1990

Rose, B. (ed) *Readings in American Art 1900-1975* New York: Holt Rinehart Winston 1975

———— *Art as Art the Selected Writings of Ad Reinhardt* Berkeley, Los Angeles: University of California Press 1975

Rosenberg, H., *Art on the Edge: Creators and Situations* New York: MacMillan 1975

Rosenberg, B. and White, D. M. *Mass Culture* New York: The Free Press 1957

———— *Mass Culture Revisited* New York: Van Nostrand Rheinholt, 1971.

Roszak, T. *The Making of a Counterculture: Reflections on the Technocratic Society and Its Youthful Opposition.* New York: Doubleday and Co 1968

Rubin, J.H. *Realism and Social Vision in Courbet and Proudhon* Princeton, New Jersey: Princeton University Press 1980

Ruskin, J. *The Art of England* London: 1883

Ruskin, J. *The True and the Beautiful* New York: John Wiley and Sons 1882

Scharf, A. *Art and Photography* Harmondsworth Middlesex: Penguin Books 1968

Scholte, B.(ed) *The Anthropologist as Hero* Boston: MIT Press 1972

Schickel, R. *The Disney Version: The Life, Times, Art and Commerce of Walt Disney* New York: Simon and Schuster 1968

Schljeldahl, P. *Reinhardt's Needle* New York: Truman Gallery Catalogue 1976

Sennett, R. and Cobb, J. *The Hidden Injuries of Class* New York: Vintage Books 1973

Shikes R. E. and Heller, S. T*he Art of Satire. Painters as Caricaturists and Cartoonists from Delacroix to Picasso.* New York: Pratt Graphics Centre and Horizon Press 1984

Sieberling, J. "Calder: His Gyrating Art Wins International Fame and Prizes" LIFE August 25, 1952

Spahr, J. *Parodies & Pastiches aus dem Sammlung Karikaturen und Cartoons* Basel: Christoph Merian Verlag 1991

——— Sammlung *Karikaturen und Cartoons* Basel: Catalogue 1985

Spielmann, M. *The History of Punch* New York: The Casell Publishing Co. 1895.

Stephenson, R. "Conflict and Control Functions of Humour." American Journal of Sociology 56 1951 569-574

Sylvester, A. *Henry Moore* London: The Arts Council, 1968

Taylor, R. *The Wrong Bag* New York: Simon and Schuster 1961

Thomas, R. *Walt Disney: An American Original* New York: Simon and Schuster 1976

Thompson, E.P. *The Making of the English Working Class* Harmondsworth: Penguin Books 1980

Thompson, J. *Ideology and Modern Culture* Stanford, California: Stanford University Press 1990

Thurber, J. *The Years with Ross an Atlantic Monthly Press* Book, Boston, Toronto: Little, Brown and Co., 1957

Toby, B. *Barney Tobey at the New Yorker* New York: Dodd Mead & Co 1983

Varnadoe, K., and Gopnik, A. *Modern Art and Popular Culture: Readings in High and Low* New York: Abrams and The Museum of Modern Art 1990

Volosinov, V. *Marxism and The Philosophy of Language* trans. L. Matejka and I.R. Titunic, Cambridge Mass: Harvard University Press 1973

Walasek, Helen *The Best of Punch Cartoons: 2,000 Humor Classics*. England Overlook Press (2009)

Wallis, B.(ed) *Art After Modernism: Rethinking Representation* New York and Boston: New Museum & Godine 1984

Walter, B. and Hill, H. *America's Humour: From Poor Richard to Doonesbury* New York: Oxford University Press 1978

Wertham, F. *Seduction of the Innocent* New York: Rinehart and Co 1953

White, D.M and Abel, R. H. *The Funnies: An American Idiom* New York: Free Press 1963

———*The Funnies: An American Idiom* New York: Free Press of Glencoe 1963

Wilde, A *Horizons of Assent: Modernism, Postmodernism and the Ironic Imagination* Baltimore Md: John Hopkins University Press 1981

Wilde, O. *The Artist as Critic: Critical Writings of Oscar Wilde* edited by Richard Ellmann, New York: Vintage books, Random House 1968

Willis, P. *Learning to Labour* London: Gower 1977

Willis, P. with Simon Jones, Joyce Canaan and Geoff Hurd *Common Culture: Symbolic Work at Play the Everyday Cultures of the Young* Boulder and San Francisco: Westview Press 1990

Williams, G. "Gramsci's Concept of Egemonia" Journal of the History of Ideas 21:4

Williams, R. *Culture and Society 1780-1950* London: Chatto and Windus 1958

——— *Keywords: A Vocabulary of Culture and Society* London: Fontana 1976

———*Problems in Materialism and Culture: Selected Essays* London: Verso 1980

———*Towards 2000* London Chatto and Windus, New York: Pantheon 1985

———*Raymond Williams on Television: Selected Writings* London, New York: Routledge 1989

———*The Politics of Modernism* London: Verso 1989

Witek, J. *Comic Books as History: the Narative art of Jack Jackson, Art*

Spiegelman and Harvey Pekar Jackson and London: The University Press of Mississippi 1992

Wittkower, R.& M. *Born Under Saturn, The Character and Conduct of Artists. A Documented History from Antiquity to the French Revolution* New York: Norton Random House 1963

Wittgenstein, L. *Philosophical Investigations* Oxford: Blackwell, 1963

Wolfe, J. *The Social Production of Art* London: Macmillan 1981

Wolfe, T. *The Painted Word* New York: Bantam Books 1976

Woodiwiss, A. *Social Theory after Post-modernism* London: Pluto Press 1990

Wright, T. *A History of Caricature and the Grotesque in Literature and Art* London: Virtue Bros. & Co 1865.

Zizek, S (ed) *Mapping Ideology* London, New York, Verso 1994

Zizek, S. *First as Tragedy, Then as Farce* London, New York, Verso 2009

www.ingramcontent.com/pod-product-compliance
Lightning Source LLC
Chambersburg PA
CBHW041920240526
45473CB00039B/2920